EXPLORATIONS IN ETHNOBIOLOGY: THE LEGACY OF AMADEO REA

CONTRIBUTIONS IN ETHNOBIOLOGY

CONTRIBUTIONS IN ETHNOBIOLOGY

Marsha Quinlan and Dana Lepofsky, Series Editors

Contributions in Ethnobiology is a peer-reviewed monograph series presenting original book-length data-rich, state-of-the-art research in ethnobiology. It is the only monograph series devoted expressly to representing the breadth of ethnobiological topics.

EXPLORATIONS IN ETHNOBIOLOGY: THE LEGACY OF AMADEO REA

Edited by

Marsha Quinlan and Dana Lepofsky

SOCIETY OF ETHNOBIOLOGY

2013

Library of Congress Control Number: 2012956081

ISBN 978-0-9887330-0-8 (paperback)
ISBN 978-0-9887330-1-5 (PDF)

Society of Ethnobiology
Department of Geography, University of North Texas
1155 Union Circle #305279, Denton, TX 76203-5017

Cover photo: Amadeo Rea discussing bird taxonomy with Mountain Pima Griselda
Coronado Galaviz of El Encinal, Sonora, Mexico, July 2001. Photograph by Dr. Robert L.
Nagell, used with permission.

Contents

Preface to Explorations in Ethnobiology:
The Legacy of Amadeo Rea

Dana Lepofsky[†] and Marsha Quinlan[‡]

We are most pleased to present *Explorations in Ethnobiology: The Legacy of Amadeo Rea*, as the inaugural volume of the *Contributions in Ethnobiology* series. The Society of Ethnobiology designed *Contributions in Ethnobiology* as a vehicle for original books on the relationships of diverse human societies with their biological worlds, from the very distant past to the immediate present. The data- and illustration-rich collection of research in the present volume accomplishes the breadth of the series goals, and each chapter springs from the influence of Dr. Amadeo M. Rea, an ethnobiological pioneer and valued colleague. Amadeo Rea was one of the Society of Ethnobiology's original members, published an article in the first issue of the *Journal of Ethnobiology* (Rea 1981), and has continued to inspire ethnobiology with his finely crafted, interdisciplinary, artfully descriptive and scientific work. Here, leading archaeologists, ethnographers, linguists, and prominent Southwestern U.S. biologists, explore much of the range of ethnobiology. They form an instructive overview of the field in homage to the influential role of Amadeo, but also with an eye toward the future of the discipline.

Like any important event, the making of this volume comes with its own story. Some years ago, around the time that Amadeo Rea was considering retirement from his position at the University of San Diego, it struck Alana Cordy-Collins, then Chair of the Department of Anthropology, that Amadeo was such an accomplished colleague that he deserved a Festschrift, a volume in his honor. Too often, she thought, the idea for these volumes does not occur while the honoree is alive to enjoy them. With Amadeo's help, Alana invited several pre-eminent biologists and ethnobiologists to participate in a volume to honor Amadeo and his career. Not surprisingly, given the broad and deep respect both for Amadeo's scholarship and for him as a person, the response to contribute to the volume was swift and positive.

The production of this volume took a circuitous journey. When the Society of Ethnobiology publicized the Contribution Series, however, Dr. Cordy-Collins approached us with this mutually fortunate and fitting opportunity. The *Contributions in Ethnobiology* series, in many ways, is the appropriate home for a volume that honors Amadeo Rea, and even more so because this is the first volume in the series. Amadeo Rea, as the tributes in many of the chapters attest, is a leader in the fields of biology and ethnobiology, both because of his scholarship and his integrity as a person. It is no coincidence that many of the North American ethnobiology leaders, and indeed founders of the discipline, contributed to this volume.

† Department of Archaeology, Simon Fraser University, Burnaby, B.C. Canada [dlepofsk@sfu.ca]

‡ Department of Anthropology, Washington State University, Pullman, WA [mquinlan@wsu.edu]

Of significance, 60% of the chapters in this volume are authored or co-authored by past-Presidents of the Society of Ethnobiology (and this includes Amadeo himself). What's more, the Society of Ethnobiology is the home of ethnobiological scholarship in North America (Wyndham et al. 2011).

The papers in this volume are as diverse as the field of ethnobiology itself. Aside from the chapter summarizing Amadeo's career (Johnson and Kingsley), the papers span geographic areas, temporal frameworks, and methods. But, they are also linked in that they seek to understand and elucidate the complex relationships between humans and their biological world. More specifically, the authors chose ethnobiological topics that Amadeo pursued in his own career, including: linkages between ecological diversity and cultural resilience (Carrothers et al.; Hodgson; McKusik; Nabhan) traditional food systems (Turner et al.), ethnozoology and specifically, ethno-ornithology (Carrothers et al.; Fowler; Timbrook and Johnson), the importance of the "long view" on human-environmental interactions (Brown et al.; Carrothers et al.; Fowler; Hodgson; Johnson and Kingsley; McKusik; Timbrook and Johnson), and folk taxonomy and language systems (Anderson; Brown et al.; Fowler; Hunn; Nabhan).

As this last topic illustrates, and as stated in Principle #5 (Lepofsky and Feeney), ethnobiologists understand the potency of language. We know that words are powerful, and that how we use words reflects our relationship with the world around us. It is for that reason that Amadeo had one request for Alana when he agreed to a book in his honor. His request was, "That we avoid speciesism by treating the proper names of all organisms (not just birds) as proper nouns." On this point, Amadeo feels very strongly. In a note to us, Amadeo said,

"As a writing convention, what we respect we capitalize. That includes our individual names, our cities and countries, our tribes and empires, the lines we draw on maps. But not the species names we give to the plants and animals that we share the Earth with and who (or that) support our continued existence? I have argued (At the Desert's Green Edge:xxvii, col 2; Folk Mammalogy of the Northern Pimans: 125; Wings in the Desert:xvii) *that the proper names of all organisms should be treated as proper nouns, not just to avoid ambiguity (which it does), but to avoid anthropocentric arrogance. Sensitivity to speciesism is not unlike sensitivity to gender issues; once you become aware of it, it's annoying."*

We have tried to honor Amadeo's request here, and we think we were mostly successful. In general, we capitalized only the most specific taxonomic designations (e.g., 'common bean' versus 'Kentucky Blue Bean'; 'cedar' versus 'Western Redcedar'). We disclose that we sometimes regretted our decision to capitalize common names throughout the process. As Gene Hunn's chapter on how we name dog "breeds" demonstrates, it is not always clear what the most specific taxonomic designation is. And, of course, different cultures will assign different levels of specificity to the names of organisms (Berlin 1992), depending on their cultural importance (Hunn 1982) and even the culture's shared appreciation or disdain for that organism (Nolan et al. 2006). Still, we appreciate Amadeo's point and tried to abide by his request. Our grade school teachers would be proud of the amount of time we spent discussing capitalization.

We thank the many people who have contributed to the development and quality of this book. First and foremost, we thank Amadeo Rea, who has made this project a joy as well as an honor. We have much gratitude for Amadeo's University of San Diego colleague, Alana Cordy-Collins, who spearheaded this project, organized the original submissions, and obtained publication funding from the David W. May American Indian Collection at the University of San Diego to support its final publication. Additional funding came from the Society of Ethnobiology. Also at the University of San Diego, we thank Monica Wagner in Sociology/Anthropology and Joyce Antorietto at the Anthropology Museum for correspondence and technology help. The editors are indebted to the volume's anonymous chapter reviewers. We owe special thanks to Eugene Anderson and Catherine Fowler for their considerable consulting on various aspects of the project. Thank you, Margaret Quinlan, for photographic editing and clerical assistance. We are grateful to Kevin Feeney for his conscientious copy editing of the volume, and to James Welch for advice, wisdom, and action along the way. Finally, we thank Cheryl Takahashi for her hard work, skill, and judgment on the book's publishing, design, and layout.

References Cited

Berlin, Brent. 1992   *Ethnobiological Classification*. Princeton University Press, Princeton, New Jersey.

Hunn, Eugene S. 1982   The Utilitarian Factor in Folk Biological Classification. *American Anthropologist* 84(4):830–847.

Nolan, Justin M., Katlin E. Jones, Kenneth Wade McDougal, Matthew J. McFarlin, and Michael K. Ward. 2006   The Lovable, the Loathsome, and the Liminal: Emotionality in Ethnozoological Cognition. *Journal of Ethnobiology* 26(1):126–138.

Rea, Amadeo M. 1981   Resource Utilization and Food Taboos of Sonoran Desert Peoples. *Journal of Ethnobiology* 1(1):69–83.

Rea, Amadeo M. 1997   *At the Desert's Green Edge: An Ethnobotany of the Gila River Pima*. University of Arizona Press, Tucson.

Rea, Amadeo M. 1998   *Folk Mammology of the Northern Pimans*. University of Arizona Press, Tucson.

Rea, Amadeo M. 2007   *Wings in the Desert: A Folk Ornithology of the Northern Pimans*. University of Arizona Press, Tucson.

Wyndham, Felice S., Dana Lepofsky, and Sara Tiffany. 2011   Taking Stock in Ethnobiology: Where Do We Come From? What Are We? Where Are We Going? *Journal of Ethnobiology* 31(1):110–127.

Diversity and its Destruction: Comments on the Chapters

Amadeo M. Rea

Some years ago Gary Paul Nabhan had the idea to measure how biotic diversity in the desert might be affected by human activity. We had been impressed by the abundance and diversity of bird life at the Papago-farmed oasis in northwest Sonora, about 41 km south of the Arizona border. But we were similarly astonished at the paucity of bird life at the U.S. Park Service managed oasis right on the border, only 54 km away. Here the former small O'odham (Papago) settlement of farmers and cattlemen had been relocated to create the national monument and virtually all traces of their former occupation were obliterated (Felger et al. 1992). Now visitors could visit an oasis "untouched" by human hands.

Gary devised a research project consisting of six 5-hectare study plots to be monitored over a period of time throughout the annual cycle. The plots included the two Arizona and Sonora oases as well as a traditionally farmed site, a mechanized farm site, and control plots in the region. The research team consisted of Gary as botanist, Eric Mellink, a Mexican scientist and mammalogist, myself as ornithologist, and Karen L. Reichhardt as plant ecologist and statistician. The subsequent research spawned one book chapter and a number of papers (Nabhan 1982; Nabhan et al. 1982; Rea 1983a; Reichhardt et al. 1994). Our focal interest was Quitovac oasis. About one hectare of our five hectare plot here was a large pond of open water and cattails and bulrush fed by five springs.

The best laid research plans sometimes go awry from circumstances researchers have no control over. Shortly after our formal study began in 1981, Gary Paul Nabhan phoned me to say that our key study plot, the Quitovac oasis, had been seriously damaged. Approximately three hectares of the original research plot had been bulldozed as part of an agricultural improvement project.

Our report (Nabhan et al. 1982) appeared in the second volume of the *Journal of Ethnobiology* entitled "Papago Influences on Habitat and Biotic Diversity: Quitovac Oasis Ethnoecology." What is scarcely mentioned is the destruction. The end of the abstract reads, "Since the initiation of the study, however, a 125 ha area was cleared and levelled for irrigated agriculture. This has dramatically altered life at Quitovac" (124). An aerial photograph included in the article (Fig. 2, p. 129) hints at the environmental destruction.

But pictures can't show the severity of destruction the site suffered. An archaeological record spanning the entire Holocene was no doubt scraped away with the Caterpillar blades. No one is sure how many millennia were encoded here in the tufa and marl sediments. Wiped

Figure 1. Amadeo M. Rea and partner Takashi Ijichi survey a small aspect of the destruction at Quitovac oasis in northwestern Sonora, Mexico, January of 1982. Paleontological and archaeological records were swept away, along with this desert vegetation. Photograph by Gary Paul Nabhan, used with permission.

away to a great extent was a Pleistocene record of Rancholabrean megafauna including mammoth remains that Papago periodically turned up in their daily activities. Was this a kill site for Paleo-Indians? When did agriculture begin at these desert springs? Did the little-known Trincheras culture of Sonora occupy the site? When did O'odham (Pimans) arrive? All we know is that they were there when Lt. Juan Mateo came upon the scene in 1694, beginning recorded history for the site. Only a fraction of this biologically and culturally diverse landscape was left after the bulldozing was finished.

We can point fingers at governmental agencies and ill-conceived projects (The goal was to establish non-native agriculture at the oasis, a plan that collapsed.). As at Quitovac, much of what we study as ethnobiologists and ecologists is really a microcosm for the rest of the Earth around us. In my opening address for the 11th Annual Ethnobiology Conference in Mexico City in 1988 (subsequently published as the "President's Page" in the Society's Journal [Rea 1988]), I pointed out the modern continuing loss of language diversity, cultural diversity, and biological diversity. As a consequence "… the world in our era has been undergoing a period of *pervasive homogenization*" (Rea 1988:iii).

I think deep inside every ethnobiologist there is an appreciation for the diversity of the world and an abhorrence for destruction in its various forms. Many of the papers gathered in this volume reflect, at least indirectly, this on-going tension between diversity and destruction. The destruction may be linguistic, cultural, or archaeological. We can add ecological destruction to the list, somewhat more in the public awareness than the other three. What is lost ultimately is a way of perceiving reality, as Gene Anderson explores in detail in his philosophical paper.

Catherine Fowler offers us a window into the Northern Paiute perception of bird life based on the knowledge of just two women—probably the last holders of this information. Similarly Jan Timbrook and John Johnson salvage similar kinds of avifaunal information from the notes of John Peabody Harrington. In both cases, *in situ* oral transmission has been broken: a return of the information and world view to the original community, if that is desired, will of necessity come from the written record rather than from elders.

It is fortunate that the archeological sites Charmion McKusick reports on were preserved long enough for scientific study. Most of the sites in the fertile Gila River floodplain to the southeast of these were destroyed by the Anglo-American settlers in the Safford Valley, attracted to the same environments that brought their prehistoric predecessors to the location. Much of the archaeology of the Phoenix area, the Hohokam heartland, was ravaged in the same way (see Wilcox 1987). This is an archaeological problem the world over.

Terminal occupation of a site, as Charmion McKusick reports here, should interest us intensely, for selfish reasons if nothing more: such sites may hold the clues to causes of cultural demise, causes we avoid facing squarely today. Did prehistoric people over-extend themselves in a xeric environment? Do we? The problem of cultural collapse brings to my mind two relevant works. Charles L. Redman's *Human Impact on Ancient Environments* (1999) is a short, textbook approach to the problem worldwide, seen through the lens of archaeology. A more detailed analysis of the same problem, but carried into our own cultural back yard, is Craig Dilworth's *Too Smart for Our Own Good: The Ecological Predicament of Humankind* (2010).

Where Charmion draws conclusions about differential plant and animal uses revealed in the archaeological record, Wendy C. Hodgson analyzes living pre-Columbian remains still found in the Southwest—clones of agaves growing near archaeological sites, persisting by means of vegetative (rather than sexual) reproduction. Five anthropogenic cultivated species are now known, four of them discovered by Wendy and her colleagues. They survive in remote areas not impacted by modern development. Agave cultivation provided an additional agricultural resource for prehistoric peoples living in xeric areas only marginally suited for agriculture.

The chapter by Steve Carothers, Dorothy House, and R. Roy Johnson illustrates the connection between ecological and cultural diversity and destruction. They note that it was only in the late 1960s that the United States Congress began to enact a series of federal legislative acts in an effort to curb the destructive impulses of a very young nation: the National Environmental Policy Act (1969), the Clean Air Act (1970), the Endangered Species Act (1973), and the Archaeological and Historic Preservation Act (1974). This was possible, they note, because of a change in general public awareness. A temporary victory for Earth? At every moment forces are at work to weaken or entirely eliminate even these safeguards. The environment that sustains us is a political football.

Did Gila River Pima modifications of the riparian community in Southern Arizona enhance the population of the Ferruginous Pygmy-Owl? Breninger (1898:128) noted that in the Phoenix region with the planting of trees, "this Owl has gradually worked its way from the natural growth of timber bordering the rivers to that bordering the banks of irrigation canals, until now it can be found in places ten miles from the rivers." On the Gila River Reservation, ornithologist M. French Gilman (1915) noted that cottonwoods and willows along Pima canals were well patronized by woodpeckers (The owl nested in woodpecker holes.). Pima esteemed their shady cottonwoods and willows and maintained living fence rows along ditch banks, creating a paradise for birds. By the time of my arrival on the reservation in 1963 the riparian woodland was entirely gone, but mature cottonwoods with their fence rows still lined canal banks on the middle and upper parts of the reservation (see Fig. 3.5 in Rea 1983b:176–180). This little owl was apparently gone.

Nancy Turner and associates relate a delightful account of one particular Native woman who was central to the maintenance of native foods traditions through which the Gitga'at interact with local species. Perhaps we need to introduce the idea of a *keystone person* in cultural continuity—as important as the keystone species that Gary Paul Nabhan mentions in his contribution.

Ethnobiologists involved with the ethnographic aspect of our hybrid science know that language is the key to understanding the world view of a people. Just as taxonomy is the beginning of biological studies, folk taxonomy is the indispensable door to understanding the *perception* of the natural world by a culture different from our own. Essential to that process is understanding the domains and ranks of terms. That linguistic exploration is our work. While many ethnobiologists and linguists have contributed to the development of this tool, a major synthesizer has been Brent Berlin, especially his 1992 work.

Eugene Hunn takes this Berlinian framework and shows, with an example from our own culture and language, that the framework is not rigid. His chapter is a delightful exploration of the English word 'dog', Hunn shows that the entire set of ranks, from life-form to folk varietal, can be encompassed within English 'dog' nomenclature. He calls this extension of the framework *taxonomic elevation*. Will it prove to be characteristic of other domesticates of very high cultural salience? We now have the concept to play with.

While Eugene Hunn treats us to a linguistic fractal, Cecil Brown and associates offer us a particle-dense parallel study of archaeobotanical data and linguistic data. Figures 1–3 of their chapter are gems, distilling truly massive amounts of information into three maps. What I find most interesting is that the paleobiolinguistic data average three thousand years younger than the archeobotanical evidence of domestication. Several ideas for this are postulated.

Something to think about next time you're enjoying a pipian mole (probably of great culinary time depth also). For historic desert Pimans, any source of oil was esteemed, from Saguaro seed to pumpkin seed. Here, as in so many of his contributions to ethnobiology, Cecil harvests linguistic diversity.

The Upper Pimans (that is, Tohono and Akimel O'odham, long known as the Papago and River Pima) have two moieties: the Coyotes and the Buzzards (Turkey Vultures). I've always thought of this as the height of psychological insight: a summation of humanity into two opposing Jungian archetypes. Coyote (who is also one of the creator gods in Piman mythology) is always running around, getting himself and others into trouble, an innovator. Buzzard, another of the four Original Beings, is the opposite, cautious to a fault, contributing nothing to the original creation of the cosmos except for the hydrologic system of watersheds, streams, and rivers in the desert environment. Coyote is in your face, Buzzard the shadow (Eugene Anderson might see here a reflection of Chinese yin and yang.).

Throughout our careers, Gary Paul Nabhan and I have had various occasions to work together on (mostly) Piman projects, with a mutually enhancing cross-pollinization. As we've worked, I've often thought that we embodied the two Piman archetypes of Buzzard and Coyote. In his contribution here, Gary looks at Coyote's organisms—plant and animal—through the lens of two unrelated cultures in the Sonoran Desert: the hunting-gathering-agricultural Pimans and the hunting-gathering-seafaring (non-agricultural) Seri. The metaphors of Coyote's biota play out quite differently between them. Some interesting ideas are suggested. Meanwhile, Coyote has gone off sniffing at another carcass somewhere.

While it may not be initially obvious, Eugene Anderson's philosophical digression was stimulated by a seeming fault line in the Upper Piman scientific world view. Pimans are the repository of a body of really esoteric biological knowledge encoded in sung poetry, folk tales, mythology, and tradition. This body of knowledge was based on acute observations of natural history and transmitted orally. On the other hand, Tohono and Akimel O'odham (Papago and River Pima) have a theory of illness that is at odds with empiricism. "Staying sickness," afflicting only O'odham, is caused by a violation of certain specific animals and a few plants. It must be diagnosed by a shaman and cured by someone who has received "power" and songs from that organism or has been given the healing songs by someone who has. In an elaborate investigation of epistemology among several cultures, including Western, Gene looks at kinds of knowledge. At the conclusion of this survey, he offers two insights that I think should be highlighted. First, people living a purely subsistence life style "live in a world about which they know—and must know—a very large amount of factual information, and toward which they have an intensely ethical stance." His second claim is "Native American systems of environmental thought are based on an experiential or phenomenological substrate that is very different from 'religion' or 'science' as the modern Western world knows them, and that cuts across the western philosophical distinction between 'is' and 'ought.'"

This essay deserves serious reading by ethnobiologists. Lest we be left with the notion that empiricism is the bottom line for evaluation of another's culture and world view, I would like here to throw out several thoughts. First, we westerners are saturated from birth to death with the values of consumerism and (evolutionary) progress through advanced technology, so much so that it is almost impossible for us to conceive of anyone thinking differently. It takes a heroic effort to set aside our cultural blinders when working with others for whom these are not values. For starters I recommend Jeremy Rifkin's *Declaration of a Heretic* (1985). His final chapters are as relevant today as they were almost 30 years ago. After that, the essays of (the unrelated) Wendell Berry and Thomas Berry may have more to tell us than any urban philosopher.

Second (and Dr. Anderson's contribution reminded me of this), the Western mind is intensely imbued with dualism, either directly or indirectly, from our Judeo-Christian-Islamic traditions. I think the tribal people I work with, at least the traditionalists, are much better understood within a non-dualistic mindset more akin to Buddhist thought. I think Thich Nhat Hanh's writings on "interbeing" come closer to Piman thought than many of our Western values, although Piman ethics is not as sharply articulated as his.

Third (and this relates to dualism as well), there are many windows to reality. Religion is one. Science is another. It is the same reality out there. Fundamentalists see a conflict. So do dogmatic scientific empiricists. Both are metaphorically challenged. Scientist-theologians such as Francisco J. Ayala, John F. Haught, Kenneth M. Miller, and Brian Swimme are refreshing antidotes to such dualism. Ethnobiologists should be no stranger to the need for cross-disciplinary studies. Nor to the need to grasp metaphor.

Extinction comes in various forms: it can be biotic, linguistic, or cultural. In his slim collection of reflections, *Cross-pollinations: The Marriage of Science and Poetry*, Gary Paul Nabhan (2004:12) writes:

> Extinction seldom comes in one fell swoop, with a bulldozer's scoop or the shot of a single gun barrel. Instead, it occurs when a web of supporting relationships unravels. It occurs whenever we or any other species are unable to sustain mutually beneficial interactions with those around us, those with whom we have been historically associated.

It seems to me that is where we stand as ethnobiologists: scientists trying to grasp the web of supporting relationships between language, culture, and the biotic environment, keenly aware of the beauty of diversity (Figure 2) and equally aware of the processes of destruction and homogenization. And somehow what we do may lead to appreciation of the first and perhaps concomitantly a slowing or even halting the second. We hope!

Figure 2. Artist Takashi Ijichi in the Sierra Estrella, south-central Arizona, making preliminary sketches of desert plants that will be used for sumi-e paintings in Amadeo's ethnobotany of the Gila River Pima. Native artists had long used the area for animal petroglyphs. Photograph by Amadeo M. Rea, used with permission.

References Cited

Berlin, Brent. 1992   *Ethnobiological Classification: Principles of Categorization of Plants and Animals in Traditional Societies.* Princeton University Press, Princeton.

Breninger, George F. 1898   The Ferruginous Pygmy Owl. *The Osprey* 2:128.

Dilworth, Craig. 2010   *Too Smart for Our Own Good: The Ecological Predicament of Humankind.* Cambridge University Press, Cambridge.

Felger, Richard S., Peter L. Warren, L. Susan Anderson, and Gary P. Nabhan. 1992   Vascular Plants of a Desert Oasis: Flora and Ethnobotany of Quitobaquito, Organ Pipe Cactus National Monument, Arizona. Proceedings of the San Diego Society of Natural History, No. 8, San Diego.

Gilman, M. French. 1915   Woodpeckers of the Arizona Lowlands. *The Condor* 17:151–163.

Nabhan, Gary Paul. 1982   *The Desert Smells Like Rain: A Naturalist in Papago Indian Country.* North Point Press, San Francisco.

Nabhan, Gary Paul. 2004   *Cross-pollinations: The Marriage of Science and Poetry.* Milkweed Editions (Credo), Minneapolis, MN.

Nabhan, Gary P., Amadeo M. Rea, Karen L. Reichhardt, Eric Mellink, and Charles F. Hutchinson. 1982   Papago Influences on Habitat and Biotic Diversity: Quitovac Oasis Ethnoecology. *Journal of Ethnobiology* 2:124–143.

Rea, Amadeo M. 1983a   Sonoran Desert Oases: Plants, Birds and Native People. *Environment Southwest* 503:5–9.

Rea, Amadeo M. 1983b   *Once a River: Bird Life and Habitat Changes on the Middle Gila.* University of Arizona Press, Tucson.

Rea, Amadeo M. 1988   President's Page. *Journal of Ethnobiology* 8(2):iii–iv.

Redman, Charles L. 1999   *Human Impact on Ancient Environments.* University of Arizona Press, Tucson.

Reichhardt, Karen L., Eric Mellink, Gary P. Nabhan, and Amadeo Rea. 1994   Habitat Heterogeneity and Biodiversity Associated [sic] with Indigenous Agriculture in the Sonoran Desert. *Etnoecológica* 2(3):21–34.

Rifkin, Jeremy. 1985   *Declaration of a Heretic.* Routledge & Kegan Paul, Boston.

Wilcox, David R. 1987   Frank Midvale's Investigation of the Site of La Ciudad, Vol. 4. Arizona Department of Transportation, Phoenix.

Amadeo M. Rea and Ethnobiology in Arizona: Biography of Influences and Early Contributions of a Pioneering Ethnobiologist

R. Roy Johnson[†] and Kenneth J. Kingsley[‡]

Abstract

As a scientist, Amadeo M. Rea is exceptional for the diversity of interrelated fields to which he has made major contributions. This chapter traces some of the roots and contributions of Amadeo's career. As soon as he began studies in the mid-1960s, other professionals recognized his exceptional insight and breadth. Working with leading authorities, he has reached a level of competence in several fields of study that a single individual in any one field rarely attains. Amadeo's breadth hence exemplifies the best of the field of ethnobiology. His strengths and contributions embrace ornithology, botany, archaeo-ornithology, paleo-ornithology, and conservation biology. His studies centered on Arizona, but also ranged geographically from temperate rainforests of the northwestern U.S. to tropical rainforests of the Peruvian Amazon and arid southwestern deserts of the U.S. and Mexico. He has inspired colleagues and students to think more broadly in making the mental connections between the biology of the past with that of the present to help ensure the biological integrity of the future.

> *"August of '63, I went off to the desert. Since I was a kid I wanted to go to the desert. The desert was my thing I had every issue of* Desert Magazine *and* Arizona Highways *since I was able to buy them. Probably since the 5th grade. The 5th grade is when I joined the* Cactus and Succulent Society of America. *Scraped together 3 dollars and 50 cents. I don't know where I got it. I just wanted to go to Arizona and teach and I wanted to work with Indians. That was my dream come true."*
>
> (Amadeo Rea, April 12, 2012)[1]

Introduction

Amadeo Michael Rea's career, in many ways, exemplifies the goals of the discipline of ethnobiology. Amadeo is a keen observer of the natural and cultural world and the links between them. He has benefited from the expertise and knowledge of a wide range of academic and

---

† Johnson & Haight Environmental Consultants, 3755 S. Hunters Run, Tucson, AZ 85730.
   Ph: 520-298-8418 [rroylois@aol.com]
‡ 1015 N. Via Terrado, Tucson, AZ 85710. Ph: 520-870-8766 [ken.kingsley7@gmail.com]

non-academic colleagues, and has in turn used this knowledge to promote the preservation of cultural and biological diversity. Indeed, this integration of applied and pure research, and traditional and western scientific knowledge systems, are the hallmarks of the discipline of ethnobiology and of Amadeo's career.

Amadeo's understanding of biological processes and organisms, past and present, far exceeds that of most present-day biologists. He is especially well versed in studies of systematics, distribution, and other factors in relation to present-day faunas and floras. In addition, Amadeo is fluent in a number of disciplines in which most biologists have little or no expertise or understanding. These include sub-disciplines of and disciplines related to ethnobiology, including paleo-ornithology, archaeo-ornithology, ethnobotany, and conservation biology. Attaining this degree of expertise in so many fields is not just a result of intellectual brilliance and energy, but is also largely due to Amadeo's strong characters of humility, patience, and perseverance. These characters have allowed him to learn from a wide array of outstanding professionals as well as non-professional Pima consultants. He continued to build upon a wide range of inputs and observations to become one of the leaders in the advancement of understanding of the interrelationships of people and their environments, especially among the Pima.

Amadeo's interdisciplinary approach to biology and related sciences is one of his greater contributions, as he has continued research in these ecological life sciences and added the human elements to the mix to yield ethnobiology. His interest in, and contributions to many fields is particularly evident in his expertise in avian osteology. This expertise has in turn led to contributions to avian systematics, zooarchaeology, and paleo-ornithology (See Appendix 1 for a list of Amadeo's publications). His work in the more elusive field of ethology (behavior), gives him a broad understanding not only of the bird anatomy but also of interrelationships amongst birds as expressed through the study of avian behavior. In addition, the importance of some of these avian traits were related to Amadeo by Native American consultants, as discussed in his two books on birds of the Gila River Indian Reservation (Rea 1983a, 2007).

This paper traces some of the origins and milestones of Amadeo's career and follows threads that led to his preeminence as an ethnobiologist.

Rea's Early Years

Amadeo's interest in natural history and his work with Native Americans began early in his life. Amadeo was born 15 October 1939 and grew up on a small ranch in El Dorado County, north-central California, in the heart of the Mother Lode country. His mother had much to do with an early interest in birds and natural history in general. Amadeo converted to Catholicism during his senior year in high school, and after graduating from high school in El Dorado County he attended San Luis Rey College in San Diego County, California. Amadeo entered the Franciscan Order in 1960, while still in college (Figure 1). After graduation in 1963, he became a teacher at St. John's Indian School in Komatke (or Komadk; see Rea 2007) village on the Gila River Indian Reservation southwest of Phoenix, Arizona. In the reservation's mission high school, he taught a wide variety of subjects, including biology and general science (Figure 2).

This section of the Gila River provided Amadeo with an ideal location for his studies of birds and plants. No one had studied the avifauna of the middle Gila River in Arizona since M. French Gilman (1914), a government employed educator, who explored the reservation between 1907 and 1915 and published 11 important ornithological papers (Rea 1983a; see also paper by Caroth-

Figure 1. Fr. Amadeo M. Rea with female Kestrel at Mission San Miguel, California, August 1961. Photograph by William F. Bowman, used with permission.

ers et al. in this volume). In 1963, Amadeo found an environment that was very different from what Gilman had found 55 years earlier. The Gila, formerly the largest river in central Arizona, now had ceased to flow through the Reservation. This was due to multiple factors—upstream dams, and other desertifying processes (e.g., inappropriate irrigation techniques and overgrazing; Johnson and Simpson 1988; Rea 1988). The lush riparian gallery forests of cottonwood-willow (*Populus-Salix*) that formerly lined the river were gone. Several species of birds that Gilman had found common had been extirpated or were rare along the Gila River (see paper by Carothers et al. in this volume). Few ornithological papers had been published on the general area around Phoenix (Anderson 1972), and the only book written about birds of the area was a small, incomplete, popular book published much earlier (Robinson 1930). Thus, much of Amadeo's ornithological findings were new to Arizona ornithology.

Gila River Birds and Allan R. Phillips.

In 1963, Amadeo's ornithological work led him to contact Allan R. Phillips. Phillips, Arizona's leading ornithologist and avian taxonomist, was just finishing the definitive work, *The Birds of Arizona* (Phillips et al. 1964). Phillips' encouragement from that point forward had much to do with launching Amadeo on a life-long career as a scientist. The two formed not only a strong professional relationship but also a life-long friendship that lasted until Allan's

Figure 2. Amadeo's high school biology students with bird and mammal study skins they have made: *Front row:* Chester Hernandez, Norma Beatty; *Back row:* Benedict Lupe, Michael Dazen, Amadeo Rea, Regina Saraficio, and Christine Stevens. St. John's Indian School students, Komadk, Arizona, 1967. Photograph by Thomas W. Fennell, used with permission.

death in 1996 (Figure 3). That bond was so great that Amadeo is considered to be "Allan's ornithological progeny" (Dickerman 1997:4). In later years, the two often collaborated, and Amadeo was the author of 14 sections in Phillips' most important books, *The Known Birds of North and Middle America: Part I* (Phillips 1986) and *The Known Birds of North and Middle America: Part II* (Phillips 1991).

Even though only a year elapsed between Amadeo's contacting Allan and the release of *The Birds of Arizona*, Allan was pleased to add several of Amadeo's important records to avian distribution in Arizona. More of Amadeo's records were later included in an annotated checklist of the state's birds (Monson and Phillips 1981). Examples of some of Amadeo's important records for Arizona in these two books include: (1) the only spring record of a Least Flycatcher (*Empidonax minimus* Baird & Baird) for Arizona, which was also the only specimen for central Arizona; (2) the only specimen of Philadelphia Vireo (*Vireo philadelphicus* Cassin) for central Arizona and one of four for the state; (3) two of only three specimens of Tennessee Warbler (*Vermivora peregrina* Wilson) for the entire state; and (4) the only specimen of Prothonotary Warbler (*Protonotaria citrea* Boddaert) for central Arizona and one of four specimens for the state. These and additional important records for birds constituted an impressive list, especially for a person who had been in Arizona for such a short time. Since the beginning of his career Amadeo has gone on to identify fifteen new taxa of bird (Table 1).

Gila River Plants

As with birds, earlier published botanical records allowed Amadeo to assess the degree of change in the plants of the Gila River Reservation. In addition to plants being good evidence of environmental change, numerous plants are important ethnobotanically to the Pima to use as food and for other uses, such as medicines and basketry (Rea 1983a, 1997). Thomas H. Kearney and Robert H. Peebles, botanists at the Sacaton U.S. Field Station, had collected extensively on the Reservation during the 1920s and 1930s (Rea 1997). These government botanists prepared the definitive book on Arizona plants, *Arizona Flora* (Kearney and Peebles 1951). Early historic biological inventories for any location in Arizona are scarce due to a general lack of early scientific

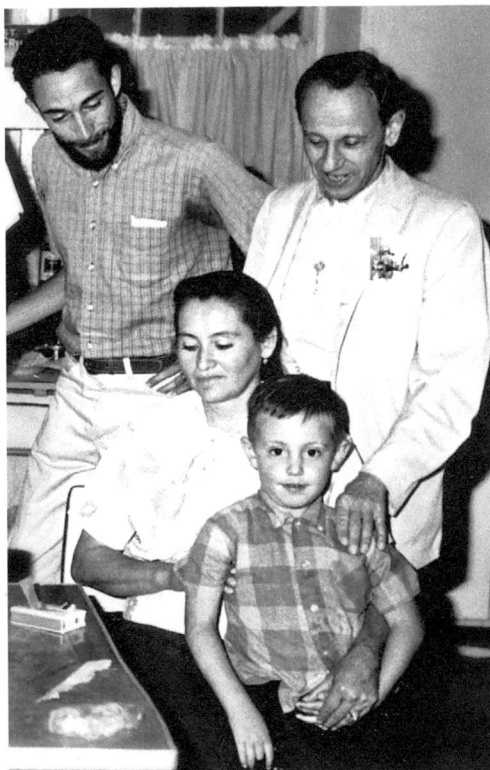

Figure 3. Amadeo with Allan Phillips, and his wife and son, Juanita and Eddy Phillips, on the day of their first face to face meeting, September, 1968. Photograph by R. Roy Johnson, in Dickerman 1997, used with permission.

Table 1. New bird taxa described by Amadeo Rea.

Callipepla squamata hargravei Rea 1973
Polioptila californica atwoodi Mellink and Rea 1974
Parus wollweberi vandevenderi Rea 1986
Cistothorus palustris browningi Rea 1986
Cistothorus palustris deserticola Rea 1986
Campylorhynchus brunneicapillum sandiegense Rea 1986
Troglodytes troglodytes ochroleucus Rea 1986
Troglodytes troglodytes obscurior Rea 1986
Troglodytes troglodytes muiri Rea 1986
Troglodytes bewickii anthonyi Rea 1986, nom. nov.
Vireo huttoni sierrae Rea 1991
Vireo huttoni unitti Rea 1991
Vireo huttoni parkesi Rea 1991
Rhynchopsitta phillipsi Rea 1997
Certhia americana phillipsi Unitt and Rea 1997

work in this largely unsettled region. It was fortunate that Amadeo came to an area where ornithological and botanical surveys had documented earlier conditions. By the early 1960s non-Indian biologists were generally not allowed to conduct biological studies on reservation lands. It was also, then, fortunate that a person of Amadeo's great scientific interest and dedication arrived on the reservation under the auspices of a sponsoring group approved by the Pimas.

Amadeo's Graduate Career

In the fall of 1968, with strong encouragement from Phillips, Amadeo began graduate studies at Arizona State University in Tempe. He finished in spring 1969 with a Master of Science degree in zoology. This degree was granted after Amadeo wrote the largest Master's thesis in the history of the Zoology Department (Rea 1969; Amadeo Rea, pers. comm.). From Arizona State University, Amadeo moved to Tucson where he started work on a Ph.D. program in the Department of Ecology and Evolutionary Biology at the University of Arizona (UA), in the fall of 1969. He continued work at the University through the next year and then took a leave of absence in 1971 to explore another phase of his career.

Ornithology and Archaeo-ornithology at Prescott College

During his leave of absence, Amadeo joined Prescott College in central Arizona as Biology Instructor, a position he would hold until 1973. Although this move did not directly further his formal education, it expanded his experiences as he worked with several well-known faculty members with interests that intersected his own. At Prescott, Amadeo became an integral part of a rapidly growing interdisciplinary movement and network of scientists working to advance science in general, and especially ecology, anthropology, and related disciplines in the southwestern U.S. and northwestern Mexico. Prescott faculty members of various disciplines (e.g., biologists, cultural anthropologists, and archaeologists) worked closely with one another. They also worked closely with scientists at other research and educational institutions, such as the Museum of Northern Arizona (MNA) and the Arizona State Museum at the UA. In addition to this interdisciplinary, inter-institutional faculty, Amadeo also encountered and inspired a highly motivated group of students, schooled in the developing tradition of experiential education.

Prescott College Colleagues and Mentors

Amadeo became part of an intricate web of academic and scientific endeavor. A large number of Prescott faculty had ties to the UA. This bound the two institutions together in advancing science in the Southwest and Arizona in particular. Amadeo benefited from this institutional bond.

Among Amadeo's mentors on the Prescott faculty, perhaps the most influential was the archaeologist/biologist, Lyndon Lane Hargrave, a noted Arizona pioneer in Southwest archaeology, archaeo-ornithology, and ornithology, who came to Prescott in retirement. Hargrave learned the "shotgun method" of studying birds, and developed a large and important collection of bird specimens, including skeletons and feathers for use in identification of avian remains from archaeological sites. Hargrave contributed lists of birds found in prehistoric sites for several anthropological publications. His early work might be considered some of the first North American ethnoornithological work since it emphasized the importance of birds to humans.

Hargrave was also the first archaeologist to apply principles of biological nomenclature to the classification and naming of Indian pottery (Colton and Hargrave 1935; Hargrave 1937). In 1933, Hargave's publications and reputation attracted 19-year-old Allan Phillips who traveled from Tucson to Flagstaff to join him in working with birds at MNA. Phillips' first published paper was work done in conjunction with MNA (Phillips 1933) and during the 1930s and 1940s Hargrave and Phillips coauthored several ornithological papers (e.g., Hargrave and Phillips 1936). Hargrave now joined Phillips as one of Amadeo's most important mentors. Established in 1966, by 1971 Prescott College already had a reputation for excellence in the field of anthropology, including archaeology, as well as in ecology, especially ornithology. This small private college, with approximately 250–300 students, emphasized hands-on experience through field and lab work. It encouraged independent, interdisciplinary studies. When he moved to Prescott, Hargrave brought his private collection of bird bones, feathers, and skins, which was probably the largest private comparative collection of bird bones in North America. Amadeo had discovered the importance of studying bird bones early in his career and now took full advantage of his time at Prescott, working with Hargrave, increasing his proficiency at identification of avian bones, and developing his knowledge of comparative osteology.

Amadeo also had the opportunity to work with several other important anthropologists on the Prescott faculty. Among them was Robert C. Euler, head of the anthropology program and the leading expert on Grand Canyon archaeology. Euler had a distinguished anthropological publication record (e.g., Euler and Tikalsky 1992) and Euler and Henry F. Dobyns, a widely published social anthropologist, were experts on Indians of the Southwest. The two cooperated on several books (e.g., Dobyns and Euler 1971) and in 1970, Euler and Dobyns, were elected President and Secretary, respectively, of The American Society of Ethnohistory. Also, the Treasurer of this society in 1970, Bernard (Bunny) Fontana, served on Amadeo's Ph.D. Committee as a University of Arizona faculty member. Association with these outstanding anthropologists helped to enlarge Amadeo's interests beyond biological fields and increased his ability to integrate ethnological, biological, anthropological, and historical information. Dobyns later wrote one of the finest books on the historic abuse and destruction of Sonoran Desert riparian oases (Dobyns 1981), similar in many ways to Amadeo's *Once a River* (Rea 1983a). George J. Gumerman, junior member of the Prescott anthropology program, and a graduate of the UA, would become an eminent Southwest archaeologist, publishing numerous scientific papers (e.g., Gumerman and Haury 1979). After 35 years as a leading expert on Southwest archaeology, Gumerman spent five more years as Director of the Arizona State Museum. This position, probably the most prestigious in Southwestern anthropology, was earlier held by Emil Haury who was a mentor to both Gumerman and Amadeo at the UA and about whom more will be said in the next section of this paper.

Amadeo's biologist colleagues at Prescott included R. Roy Johnson, who conducted research on the ecology of riparian birds, one of Amadeo's major interests. Amadeo and Roy's working together was fortuitous. Johnson would later help to establish the scientific field of riparian ecology by organizing and chairing three important national riparian conferences (Johnson and Jones 1977; Johnson and McCormick 1979; Johnson et al. 1985) and publishing dozens of papers in the field of ornithology and riparian ecology.[2] Amadeo also used information from avian work being done by Johnson at Blue Point Cottonwoods (BPC, Johnson and Simpson 1971) on the Salt River (major tributary of the Gila River) in his first book on the Gila River Indian Reservation (Rea 1983a).

At Prescott, Rea, Hargrave, Phillips, and Johnson soon formed an important riparian connection. In 1969, Johnson began an avian study with James M. Simpson on the Salt River upstream from Phoenix (Johnson and Simpson 1971). Prescott students assisted with the study by conducting ornithology class field trips to the area. Hargrave had first visited BPC in the 1930s. Later, at Hargrave's suggestion, Phillips made several collecting trips from Tucson to BPC during the 1950s and recorded several important birds (Phillips 1951; Phillips et al. 1964). Phillips, in turn, told Johnson and Simpson about the area. From the late 1950s into the 1990s, Johnson and Simpson made more than 100 trips to BPC, collecting and recording additional important birds (Johnson and Simpson 1971; Johnson et al. 2000). Due to the efforts of all of these scientists, BPC has the longest documented history of avian records from central Arizona. Also, of particular importance is the fact that BPC is located along the only remaining relatively free-flowing lowland portion of the Salt River. The remainder of the Salt has been dammed and is dry downstream. Amadeo thus used BPC as an important comparative area for understanding conditions that had existed along the Gila River on the Reservation before the Gila had been dammed in the early 1900s and greatly changed through desertification (Rea 1983a).

Amadeo and Prescott College Students

Amadeo came into the Prescott College milieu as both a junior faculty member and while still a Ph.D. student at UA. Since nearly all students lived on campus, and Amadeo spent most of his waking hours in the ornithology lab there, he associated freely with the students. The ornithology lab became an important meeting ground, where Amadeo and Prescott students spent many evenings putting up specimens and discussing birds and other life forms and experiences. The close association with Amadeo was of inestimable importance in the personal and professional development of his students, many of whom went on to graduate work and became professionals in ecology, biology, and anthropology.

One of the highlights of the Prescott experience for several Prescott students was a research and collecting trip to the Peruvian Amazon (Figure 4), which Amadeo organized and led. Students lived for three weeks in a rainforest village, associated with the villagers, ate their foods (including large rodents, e.g., Capybara and agouti), and collected specimens of animals ranging in size from ants to anacondas. Specimens were returned to Prescott to greatly expand the educational and research resources available to students. For all of the students, this was a first-class introduction to tropical ecology, an experiential education in ethnobiology, and an opportunity to stretch well beyond the typical college education in zoology.

Two biology students at Prescott College with which Amadeo had contact, Gary Paul Nabhan and Jonathan Jantzen, deserve special mention because of their outstanding professional accomplishments after leaving Prescott. As a teacher at Prescott, Amadeo became a mentor and colleague to Gary. Amadeo first introduced Gary to some of the Southwestern Native Americans about whom Nabhan has written so profusely and eloquently (see Chapter 7, this volume). Gary's dissertation work at the University of Arizona was directed by Emil W. Haury, who was also one of Amadeo's mentors. Dr. Nabhan went on to become one of

the best known and most prolific writers on Southwestern ethnobiology and conservation, publishing a wide variety of popular and scientific works (Nabhan 1982, 1985). The two have also coauthored several joint papers (Nabhan and Rea 1982). Gary also continued to work with some of his Prescott professors (Nabhan et al. 1981) and fellow Prescott alumni (Nabhan and Sheridan 1977). Thus, a line of extraordinary science and conservation philosophy passed from Lyn Hargrave to Allan Phillips, then to Amadeo Rea, and Gary Nabhan. This lineage of biologists has inspired many students who have authored a large number of important scientific papers, often ethnobiological oriented.

Another of Amadeo's interesting and exceptional Prescott students of note was Jonathan Jantzen. Jonathan had studied ornithol-

Figure 4. Amado Rea and Prescott College student Leslie White skinning birds, Yagua village below Iquitos, Amazon River, Peru, December 1971. Photograph by Roger F. Pearson, used with permission.

ogy before coming to Prescott (under Robert Fleming, Jr., leading authority and author of the definitive work on birds of Nepal). So, at Prescott College he worked with Amadeo in the bird collection. After leaving Prescott, Jonathan obtained a law degree and eventually ended up in his current position as Attorney General of the Tohono O'odham Nation (formerly Papago Indian Reservation). Thus, Jonathan works with a group of Native Americans whose culture Amadeo has long studied. With degrees in both biology and law, Jonathan is in a unique position to encourage the Tohono O'odham to protect their natural resources as well as their culture.

Prescott College and Museum of Northern Arizona

At Prescott College, Amadeo became an important part of an interrelated group of professionals from various fields related to his interests. Much of his professional growth during this time occurred because of a special relationship between members of Prescott College and those of the Museum of Northern Arizona. Several of the faculty at Prescott had been affiliated professionally with the Museum of Northern Arizona (MNA). Hargrave had been employed there as a biologist and archeologist during the 1930s. R. Roy Johnson worked with MNA as a Research Associate while Amadeo was teaching at Prescott and several joint field projects were conducted with Johnson and Rea's Prescott students and MNA biologists working together. This gave students valuable experience and MNA diligent, inexpensive labor. An ornithologist who worked with Rea and Johnson was Steven W. Carothers, who was Curator of Biology at MNA (see Chapter 12, this volume). A few years later Carothers received his Ph.D. in ornithology and published several important papers that were based on research involving the Prescott team (e.g., Carothers et al. 1974; Carothers and Johnson 1975). Carothers went on to establish SWCA Environmental Consultants, one of the largest environmental consulting firms in the U.S., with over 700 employees. Numerous professionals working in the field of environmental consulting can trace their roots back to Prescott and/or MNA at the time Amadeo was there. Wherever Amadeo worked, Gila River Indian Reservation and now Prescott College, he had a profound and long-lasting influence on students (Table 2).

The Prescott-MNA team collaborated in excavation and analysis of Stanton's Cave, a large site along the Colorado River in Grand Canyon National Park. The field team was headed by Euler, and provided a challenging educational experience for archaeology students, who excavated over 100,000 bones and hundreds of artifacts, much of which were buried in dried ground sloth dung. The bones came to the ornithology lab, where students sorted them into vertebrate classes (bird, mammal, reptile, fish). Rea and Hargrave identified the bird bones and co-authored a section of the final report. Artifacts went to the Prescott College Archaeology Lab, where students pieced them together and photographed them. Euler edited the final report (1984), a classic on Southwestern archaeology, geology, and paleobiology. Thus, Amadeo's work not only continued to help train and influence students, but also contributed to science.

This period of study and work was one of pivotal importance for Amadeo. It was with these activities that Amadeo began his progress toward the diversity of disciplines that would eventually formulate his great scientific strength. At Prescott he found the perfect combination of tools that would allow him to take a fresh new look at birds through time and space. It was during this time that he named his first new bird, a subspecies of Scaled Quail (*Callipepla squamata hargravei* Rea; Table 1) (Rea 1973). After continuing to work with Hargrave for years and naming the aforementioned scaled quail after him, Amadeo finished a coauthored paper after Hargrave's death (Rea and Hargrave 1984).

Doctoral Research on Piman Ethnobiology

Doctoral Mentors at the University of Arizona

Amadeo returned to UA from Prescott in 1973 to finish his graduate studies in the Department of Ecology and Evolutionary Biology. His major professor, Steven M. Russell, is best known for his definitive work on the birds of British Honduras, now Belize (Russell 1964), and a book on the avifauna of Sonora, Mexico (Russell and Monson 1998). Since Allan Phillips was now living in Mexico, Amadeo had the advantage of being able to learn from both Phillips' and Russell's knowledge of birds of the American tropics. Bernard (Bunny) Fontana, also on Amadeo's Ph.D. committee, is an expert on the Northern Pima (Fontana 1983; Fon-

Table 2. List of students influenced by Amadeo's teachings as well as other faculty members at Prescott College who are known to have continued into professional lives. While a sample of key publications are listed, it is important to note that this group has published at least five times as many scientific papers as referenced here.

Students and Colleagues of Amadeo Rea	Publications
John G. Blake, Biology Professor, University of Missouri, St. Louis.	Blake and Loiselle 2001, 2002.
Christopher Estes, Instream Flow Director (Retired), Alaska Department of Fish and Game.	Estes and Orsborn 1986; Reiser, et al. 1989.
Kenneth J. Kingsley, consulting ecologist and conservation biologist.	Kingsley 1996, 2002.
David M. Leslie, Jr., Adjunct Professor & Unit Leader, Oklahoma Cooperative Fish and Wildlife Research Unit.	Douglas and Leslie 1986; Leslie and Douglas 1980.
Gary P. Nabhan, Researcher at the University of Arizona Southwest Center and former Director of the Center for Sustainable Environments, Northern Arizona University.	Nabhan 1982, 1985.
Christopher J. Norment, Associate Professor, Department of Environmental Science and Biology, State University of New York, Brockport.	Norment 2002, 2003; Norment and Douglas 1977.
Margaret A. O'Connell, Co-director of the Turnbull Laboratory of Ecological Studies, and Professor of Biology, Eastern Washington University.	Campbell et al. 1996; O'Connell et al. 1989.
Thomas E. Sheridan, Curator of Ethnohistory at the Arizona State Museum.	Sheridan 1995a, 1995b.
Lawrence E. Stevens, Curator of Ecology and Conservation, Museum of Northern Arizona.	Stevens et al. 2001; Stevens and Huber 2003.

tana and Schaefer 1989). Amadeo gives Bunny much credit for his interest and work with Native Americans.

Amadeo made a wise decision at UA that would stand him in good stead in his scientific endeavors. He added Emil (Doc) Haury to his Ph.D. Committee.[3] Haury was the leading expert on the Hohokam culture (Haury 1976), who some believe are ancestors of the Pima, and was considered "the Dean of Southwestern archaeologists." Now, Amadeo had the advantage of having worked with two Southwest archaeologists, Hargrave and Haury, both of whom had worked together over a period of decades but had gone in separate but interrelated directions. These two leading Southwestern archaeologists are known as the joint discoverers of a famous log that was called "the Rosetta Stone" of American archaeology (Douglass 1929:770). This log, HH-39[4], was discovered near Showlow, Arizona, on an archaeological expedition led by Hargrave, with Haury as his assistant, in 1929 (Cordell 1997; Lyndon L. Hargrave, pers. comm.). Tree rings from this log bridged a gap in tree-ring dates for archaeological sites from the Southwestern U.S. This, in turn, allowed dates to be established for a large number of important prehistoric ruins throughout the Southwest that had previously eluded dating (Douglass 1929; Haury 1962). This dating was done by A.E. Douglass, the originator of the University of Arizona Dendrochronology [tree ring] Laboratory. Thus, with Haury on his Ph.D. committee, Amadeo had accomplished what few people have done—studied under two of the most famous names in Southwestern archaeology, Lyndon L. Hargrave and Emil W. Haury, and also continued under the tutelage of two of the best known names in Southwestern ornithology, Allan R. Phillips and Steven M. Russell.

Native American Mentors as Consultants

While living on the Gila River Indian Reservation, Amadeo developed a unique friendship with many Pima. As a graduate student and researcher, he continued to work with these native consultants in learning as much as he could about their culture, their language, and their plants and animals. Most important to him were several Pima elders, who shared knowledge with him that might have been lost had he not approached them with humility and patience (Figure 5). This information has served as the basis for his ethnobiological studies by providing great amounts of both folklore and scientific information that was not available to other scientists. Amadeo has shared this knowledge with the scientific and lay communities through several books and other writings (see especially Rea 1983a, 1997, 2007). In addition to the indigenous classification system and uses of native plants and animals, Amadeo recorded the elders' observations of natural history and also of behavior and changes in populations over time as a result of human impacts.

Ethnobiological Synthesis of the Piman Peoples

The Pimans include the Pima and a large number of related native peoples throughout southern Arizona, northern, central, and eastern Sonora, and western Chihuahua, Mexico. Amadeo's comprehensive works on the Piman ethnobiology represent the combination of knowledge gleaned from all of his mentors and his own experiences. They serve as an inspiration to current and future researchers. He synthesized information gleaned from both professional and non-professional consultants with his own studies, since 1963, to formulate a scientific databank unexcelled for Piman peoples.

Although Amadeo has published a large number of scientific papers on the Pima and Pimans, his major work is found in four books, *Once a River* (1983a), *At the Desert's Green Edge* (1997), *Folk Mammalogy of Northern Pimans* (1998d), and *Wings in the Desert* (2007) (See Appendix I for a complete list of publications). In these works, Amadeo has accomplished several things. First, he dispelled and corrected misconceptions present in older writings by

Figure 5. Amadeo M. Rea with lowland Pima Bajo, don Pedro Estrella T., collecting ethnobotanical voucher specimens from a cliff along the Río Yaqui north of Ónavas, Sonora, México. Photograph by Dr. Wade Sherbrooke, used with permission.

earlier anthropologists working with the Pima that contained errors in recording ethnology, archaeology, and/or natural history,. Second, he presented new scientific information, often known only to Native Americans, specifically the Pima. Third, he demonstrated the formerly undocumented Piman sophistication regarding classification of plants and animals. And fourth, through searching old records and working with the oldest Pima consultants, Amadeo presented previously unknown information regarding changes in the environment of the Gila River from pre to post-dam times.

As is typical of good ethnobiological research, Amadeo's close relation with Piman knowledge-holders produced several "scientific facts" that had been previously unobserved by Western scientists. Two examples illustrate this. First, the knowledge of hibernation in the Common Poorwill (*Phalaenoptilus nuttallii* Audubon) was not reported by Euro-American scientists until the mid-1900s (Jaeger 1948, 1949). However, Pima legends and stories, as well as recounting of this fact, had been handed down for innumerable generations. Second, the definitive work on Arizona birds considered the Belted Kingfisher (*Megaceryle alcyon* Linnaeus) as a winter resident and migrant in Arizona, and further stated that "the past status in Arizona [for this species] is much clouded in doubt" (Phillips et al. 1964:67). However, Amadeo found that some of the oldest living Pima actually found them nesting along the banks of the Gila River early in the 1900s.

Amadeo and New World Vultures

We end our review with one last example of Amadeo's scientific inquisitiveness and attention to ecological details—his work with New World vultures. These attributes are a fundamental part of what makes Amadeo an exemplary ethnobiologist. Vultures serve an important function in many societies in disposing of unwanted carcasses and preventing the spreading of some diseases (Ogado 2010). "Coyote and buzzard [vulture] … are two of the most important beings in the Piman culture" (Rea 2007:95). While at Prescott, Amadeo kept Black Vultures (*Coragyps atratus* Bechstein; Rea 1998b) and Turkey Vultures (*Cathartes aura* Linnaeus; Rea 1998c) in a large cage and studied their behavior. He treated them as pets, entering the cage to feed them and spend time observing them (Rea 1973). As late as 1983, the AOU Check-list (the "bible" for North American avian classification) still placed vultures in the Falconiformes with hawks, eagles, etc. (AOU 1957, 1983). However, based on morphological and anatomical evidence, and on behavior, Amadeo concluded that they were more closely related to the Ciconiiformes (ibises, spoonbills, storks and allies). He published several scientific papers proposing this (Rea 1980a, 1980b, 1983a, 1983b, 1985, 1998a, 1998b, 1998c) that were ignored by most of the North American ornithological community. Finally, after DNA and other evidence suggested that the earlier classification was incorrect and Amadeo had been correct for three decades, the AOU recognized Amadeo's insights and moved vultures from Falconiformes into Ciconiiformes (AOU 1998). (AOU 1998:51). Unfortunately, New World vultures have once again been returned to the Falconiformes (AOU 2011) and the philosophical battle continues.

Summary

Although Amadeo gave up his life as a Franciscan friar, he has never abandoned his pursuit of the truth nor his humility and frugality. He has retained his passion and generosity. On the face of it, the lack of material wealth would seem to have limited his ability to accomplish some things that are important to a researcher interested in field ecology, such as obtaining funds for supplies and travel. The positive side of Amadeo's lack of concern for "the almighty dollar" was that it freed him, physically and mentally, to live, eat, and sleep science, particularly ethnobiology. In addition, Amadeo's congenial nature, wide interests, and humble, non-threatening personality made him a welcome traveling companion and visitor. This has allowed him to gain access to a large variety of Native American consultants as well as some of the best scientific minds in ethnobiology and related fields. Others with greater material means for conducting field research were, therefore, happy, even anxious, to have Amadeo accompany them, whether on a field trip into "Indian Country" in the Southwest or an expedition to the American tropics. It was widely known that in addition to his pleasant and interesting companionship, he could be counted on to do more than his share of menial chores in camp, as well as scientific work.

One of Amadeo's most endearing and scientifically valuable characteristics is humility, possibly learned early as a Franciscan friar and retained throughout his life. In this respect, he is unique. He is neither threatening to, nor threatened by others, whether scientists or lay persons. He is willing to listen to other's analyses and then discuss them in a rational manner. Nonetheless, Amadeo can be very persistent about his findings and conclusions after carefully considering the scientific evidence for something in his area of expertise.

Amadeo put all of this to work in establishing a life devoted to integration of both biological and anthropological sciences. His great strength is as a synthesizer and amalgamator of data for the central Gila River-Salt River region of Arizona, especially for the Pima. Thus, he joins a long line of scientists of the Southwest, starting with Hargrave and Haury and continuing through Phillips, Dobyns, Euler, Johnson, Gumerman, and Nabhan.

Unquestionably, Amadeo has excelled as a scientist and a human being. Amadeo has held several important positions in museums and on scientific boards, published a large number of scientific papers, and presented numerous papers at professional meetings, often as a featured speaker. His broad experiences and perceptive analyses have put him in demand for conducting peer review of other's scientific manuscripts and publications.

Notes

1. Interview with Amadeo Rea at the Denver Botanic Gardens on April 12, 2012. See Chapter 4, this volume, and also:
   http://ethnobiology.org/education-and-outreach/our-mentors-speak
2. Later, Johnson also became head of the National Park Service Cooperative Resources Studies Unit at the University of Arizona.
3. Later, Haury was also Gary Nabhan's major professor during Nabhan's doctoral studies.
4. HH-39 is Hargrave and Haury-39 or Haury and Hargrave-39, depending on who is telling the story.

References Cited

American Ornithologists' Union (AOU). 1957 *Check-list of North American Birds*, 5th ed. American Ornithologists' Union, Baltimore, MD.

American Ornithologists' Union (AOU). 1983 *Check-list of North American Birds,* 6th ed. American Ornithologists' Union, Washington, D.C.

American Ornithologists' Union (AOU). 1998 *Check-list of North American Birds*, 7th ed. American Ornithologists' Union, Washington, D.C.

American Ornithologists Union (AOU). 2011   Check-list of North American Birds. Available at: http://www.aou.org/checklist/north/ (verified 16 September 2011).

Anderson, Anders H. 1972   *A Bibliography of Arizona Ornithology: Annotated.* University of Arizona Press, Tucson.

Blake, John G., and Bette A. Loiselle. 2001   Bird Assemblages in Second-growth and Old-growth Forests, Costa Rica: Perspectives from Mist Nets and Point Counts. *Auk* 118:304–326.

Blake, John G., and Bette A. Loiselle. 2002   Habitat Use, Movements, and Survival of Manakins (Pipridae) in Second-growth and Old-growth Forests. *Auk* 119:132–148.

Campbell, Lori A., James G. Hallett, and Margaret A. O'Connell. 1996   Conservation of Bats in Managed Forests: Use of Roosts by *Lasionycteris noctivagans. Journal of Mammalogy* 77(4):976–984.

Carothers, Steven W., and R. Roy Johnson. 1975   Recent Observations on the Status and Distribution of Some Birds of the Grand Canyon Region. *Plateau* 47:140–153.

Carothers, Steven W., R. Roy Johnson, and Stuart W. Aitchison. 1974   Population Structures and Social Organization of Southwestern Riparian Birds. *American Zoologist* 14:97–108.

Colton, Harold S., and Lyndon L. Hargrave. 1935   Naming Pottery Types, and the Rules of Priorities. *Science* 82(2133):462–463.

Cordell, Linda. 1997   *Archaeology of the Southwest*, 2nd ed. Academic Press, Inc., New York.

Dickerman, Robert W. 1997   Biography of Allan R. Phillips 1914–1996. In *The Era of Alan R. Phillips: A Festschrift*, compiler Robert W. Dickerman, pp. 1–8. Horizon Communications, Albuquerque, NM.

Dobyns, Henry F. 1981   *From Fire to Flood: Historic Human Destruction of Sonoran Desert Riverine Oases.* Ballena Press Anthropology Paper No. 20, San Jose, CA.

Dobyns, Henry F., and Robert C. Euler. 1971   *Havasupai People.* Indian Tribal Series, Phoenix, AZ.

Douglas, Charles L., and David M. Leslie, Jr. 1986   Influence of Weather and Density on Lamb Survival of Desert Mountain Sheep. *Journal of Wildlife Management* 50:153–156.

Douglass, Andrew E. 1929   The Secret of the Southwest Solved by Talkative Tree-rings. *National Geographic Magazine* 56(6):736–770.

Estes, Christopher, and John F. Orsborn. 1986   Review and Analysis of Methods for Quantifying Instream Flow Requirements. *Journal of the American Water Resources Association* 22(3):389–398.

Euler, Robert C., and Frank Tikalsky, eds. 1992   *The Grand Canyon: Intimate Views.* University of Arizona Press, Tucson.

Fontana, Bernard L. 1983   Pima and Papago: Introduction. In *Handbook of North American Indians: Southwest*, ed. Alfonso A. Ortiz., Vol. 10, pp. 125–136. Smithsonian Institution, Washington, DC.

Fontana, Bernard L., and John P. Schaefer. 1989 *Of Earth and Little Rain: The Papago Indians*. University of Arizona Press, Tucson.

Gilman, M. French. 1914 Notes from Sacaton, Arizona. *Condor* 16:255–259.

Gumerman, George J., and Emil W. Haury. 1979 Prehistory: Hohokam. In *Handbook of North American Indians: Southwest*, ed. Alfonso A. Ortiz, Vol. 9, pp. 75–90. Smithsonian Institution, Washington, D.C.

Hargrave, Lyndon L. 1937 Handbook of Northern Arizona Pottery Wares. *Museum of Northern Arizona Bulletin* No.11.

Hargrave, Lyndon L., and Allan R. Phillips. 1936 Bird Life of the San Francisco Mountains, Arizona. No. 3: Land Birds Known to Nest in the Pine Belt. *Museum Notes* 8(9):47–50.

Haury, Emil W. 1962 Recollections of a Dramatic Moment in Southwestern Archaeology. *Tree-Ring Bulletin* 24(3–4):11–14.

Haury, Emil W. 1976 *The Hohokam: Desert Farmers & Craftsmen, Excavations at Snaketown, 1964–1965*. University of Arizona Press, Tucson.

Jaeger, Edmund C. 1948 Does the Poor-will "Hibernate"? *Condor* 50:45–46.

Jaeger, Edmund C. 1949 Further Observations on the Hibernation of the Poor-will. *Condor* 51:105–109.

Johnson, R. Roy, and James M. Simpson. 1971 Important Birds from Blue Point Cottonwoods, Maricopa County, Arizona. *Condor* 73:379–380.

Johnson, R. Roy, and Dale A. Jones, eds. 1977 *Proceedings of the Symposium on Importance, Preservation and Management of Riparian Habitat*. USDA Forest Service General Technical Report RM-43, Forest and Range Experimental Station, Ft. Collins, CO.

Johnson, R. Roy, and J. Frank McCormick, eds. 1979 *Proceedings of the 1978 National Symposium on Strategies for Protection and Management of Floodplain Wetlands and other Riparian Ecosystems*. USDA Forest Service General Technical Report WO-12, Washington, D.C.

Johnson, R. Roy, and James M. Simpson. 1988 Desertification of Wet Riparian Ecosystems in Arid Regions of the North American Southwest. In *Arid lands: Today and Tomorrow*, eds. Emily E. Whitehead, Charles F. Hutchinson, Barbara N. Timmermann, and Robert G. Varady, pp. 1383–1393. Westview Press, Boulder, CO.

Johnson, R. Roy, Jean-Luc E. Cartron, Lois T. Haight, Russell B. Duncan, and Kenneth J. Kingsley. 2000 A Historical Perspective on the Population Decline of the Cactus Ferruginous Pygmy-Owl in Arizona. In *Ecology and Conservation of the Cactus Ferruginous Pygmy-Owl in Arizona*, eds. Jean-Luc E. Cartron and Deborah M. Finch, pp. 17–26. Forest Service General Technical Report RMRS-GTR-43, Rocky Mountain Research Station, Ogden, UT.

Johnson, R. Roy, Charles D. Ziebell, David R. Patton, Peter F. Folliott, and Robert H. Hamre, tech. coords. 1985 *Riparian Ecosystems and Their Management: Reconciling Conflicting Uses. First North American Riparian Conference; 1985*. USDA Forest Service General Technical Report RM-120, Forest and Range Experimental Station, Ft. Collins, CO.

Kearney, Thomas H., and Robert H. Peebles. 1951   *Arizona Flora.* University of California Press, Berkeley.

Kingsley, Kenneth J. 1996   Behavior of the Delhi Sands Flower-loving Fly (Diptera: Mydidae), a Little-known Endangered Species. *Annals of the Entomological Society of America* 89:883–891.

Kingsley, Kenneth J. 2002   Population Dynamics, Resource Use, and Conservation Needs of the Delhi Sands Flower-loving Fly (*Rhaphiomidas terminatus abdominalis* Cazier) (Diptera: Mydidae), an Endangered Species. *Journal of Insect Conservation* 6:93–101.

Leslie, David M., Jr., and Charles L. Douglas. 1980   Human Disturbance at Water Sources of Desert Bighorn Sheep. *Wildlife Society Bulletin* 8(4):284–290.

Monson, Gale, and Allan R. Phillips. 1981   *Annotated Checklist of the Birds of Arizona,* 2nd ed. University of Arizona Press, Tucson.

Nabhan, Gary P. 1982   *The Desert Smells like Rain: a Naturalist in Papago Indian Country.* North Point Press, San Francisco, CA.

Nabhan, Gary P. 1985   *Gathering the Desert.* University of Arizona Press, Tucson.

Nabhan, Gary P., and Amadeo Rea. 1987   Plant Domestication and Folk Biological Change: The Upper Piman/Devil's Claw Example. *American Anthropologist* 89:57–73.

Nabhan, Gary P., and Thomas E. Sheridan. 1977   Living Fencerows of the Rio San Miguel, Sonora Mexico: Traditional Technology for Floodplain Management. *Human Ecology* 5:97–111.

Nabhan, Gary P., Alfred Whiting, Henry Dobyns, Richard Hevly, and Robert Euler. 1981   Devil's Claw Domestication: Evidence from Southwestern Indian Fields. *Journal of Ethnobiology* 1:135–164.

Norment, Christopher J., and Charles A. Douglas. 1977   *Ecological Studies of Feral Burros in Death Valley.* University of Nevada National Park Service Cooperative Resources Studies Unit Contribution 17.

Norment, Christopher J. 2002   On Grassland Bird Conservation in the Northeast. *Auk* 119:271–279.

Norment, Christopher J. 2003   Patterns of Nestling Feeding in Harris's Sparrows and White-crowned Sparrows in the Northwest Territories, Canada. *Canadian Field-Naturalist* 117:203-208.

O'Connell, Margaret A. 1989   Population Dynamics of Neotropical Small Mammals in Seasonal Habitats. *Journal of Mammalogy* 70:532–548.

Ogada, Darcy. 2010   Notes from the Field: Why We Need Vultures. East Africa Project, The Peregrine Fund, 16 December 2010. Available at: http://blogs.peregrinefund.org/article/683 (verified 14 September 2012).

Phillips, Allan R. 1933   Summer Birds of a Northern Arizona Marsh. *Condor* 35:124–125.

Phillips, Allan R. 1951   [Fifty–first Christmas bird count at] Salt River, (Maricopa Co.), Arizona, December 26, 1950. *Audubon Field Notes* 5:170-171.

Phillips, Allan R. 1986   *The Known Birds of North and Middle America: Part I.* Allan R. Phillips, Denver, CO.

Phillips, Allan R. 1991   *The Known Birds of North and Middle America: Part II.* Allan R. Phillips, Denver, CO.

Phillips, Allan, Joe Marshall, Jr., and Gale Monson. 1964   *The Birds of Arizona.* University of Arizona Press, Tucson, AZ.

Reiser, Dudley W., Thomas A. Wesche, and Christopher Estes. 1989   Status of Instream Flow Legislation and Practices in North America. *Fisheries* 14(2):22–29

Rea, Amadeo M. 1969   The Interbreeding of the Boat-tailed Grackle in Secondary Contact in Central Arizona. M.S. Thesis, (Department of Zoology), Arizona State University, Tempe.

Rea, Amadeo M. 1973   Turkey Vultures Casting Pellets. *Auk* 90:209–210.

Rea, Amadeo M. 1980a   New World Vultures: Diminishing and Misunderstood, Part 1. *Environment Southwest* 489:3–7.

Rea, Amadeo M. 1980b   New World Vultures: The Scavenging Niche, Part 2. *Environment Southwest* 490:12–13.

Rea, Amadeo M. 1983a   *Once a River: Bird Life and Habitat Changes on the Middle Gila.* University of Arizona Press, Tucson.

Rea, Amadeo M. 1983b   Cathartid Affinities: A Brief Overview. In *The Biology and Management of Vultures of the World,* eds. Sanford R. Wilbur and Jerome A. Jackson, pp. 26–54. University of California Press, Berkeley.

Rea, Amadeo M. 1985   Cathartid Affinities: A Brief Overview. In *Vulture Biology and Management,* eds. Sanford R. Wilbur and Jerome A. Jackson, pp. 26–54. University of California Press, Berkeley.

Rea, Amadeo M. 1988   Habitat Restoration and Avian Recolonization from Wastewater on the Middle Gila River, Arizona. In *Arid lands: Today and Tomorrow,* eds. Emily E. Whitehead, Charles F. Hutchinson, Barbara N. Timmermann, and Robert G. Varady, pp. 1395–1405. Westview Press, Boulder, CO.

Rea, Amadeo M. 1997   *At the Desert's Green Edge: an Ethnobotany of the Gila River Pima.* University of Arizona Press, Tucson.

Rea, Amadeo M. 1998a   Introduction to New World vultures. In *The Raptors of Arizona,* ed. Richard L. Glinski, p. 23. University of Arizona Press, Tucson.

Rea, Amadeo M. 1998b   Black Vulture. In *The Raptors of Arizona,* ed. Richard L. Glinski, pp. 24–26. University of Arizona Press, Tucson.

Rea, Amadeo M. 1998c   Turkey Vulture. In *The Raptors of Arizona,* ed. Richard L. Glinski, pp. 27–31. University of Arizona Press, Tucson.

Rea, Amadeo M. 1998d *Folk Mammalogy of the Northern Pimans.* University of Arizona Press, Tucson.

Rea, Amadeo M. 2007 *Wings in the Desert: A Folk Ornithology of the Northern Pimans.* University of Arizona Press, Tucson.

Rea, Amadeo M., and Lyndon L. Hargrave. 1984 The Paleoavifauna of Stanton's Cave, Grand Canyon. In *The Archaeology, Geology and Paleobiology of Stanton's Cave, Grand Canyon National Park, Arizona,* ed. Robert C. Euler, pp. 77–91. Grand Canyon Natural History Association Monograph #6.

Reiser, Dudley W., Thomas A. Wesche, and Christopher Estes. 1989 Status of Instream Flow Legislation and Practices in North America. *Fisheries* 14(2):22–29.

Robinson, William H. 1930 *Our Friendly Birds.* Chandler Arizonan, Chandler, AZ.

Russell, Stephen M. 1964 A Distributional Study of the Birds of British Honduras. *Ornithological. Monograph* No. 1.

Russell, Stephen M., and Gale Monson. 1998 *The Birds of Sonora.* University of Arizona Press, Tucson.

Sheridan, Thomas E. 1995a *Arizona: a History.* University of Arizona Press. Tucson.

Sheridan, Thomas E. 1995b Arizona: the Political Ecology of a Desert State. *Journal of Political Ecology* 2:41–57.

Stevens, Lawrence E., Tina J. Ayers, Jeffery B. Bennett, Kerry Christensen, Michael J.C. Kearsley, Vicky J. Meretsky, Arthur M. Phillips III, Roderic A. Parnell, John Spence, Mark K. Sogge, Abraham E. Springer, and David L. Wegner. 2001 Planned Flooding and Colorado River Riparian Trade-offs Downstream from Glen Canyon Dam, Arizona. *Ecological Applications* 11:701–710.

Stevens, Lawrence E., and Ronald. L. Huber. 2003 Biogeography of Tiger Beetles (Cincindelidae) in the Grand Canyon Ecoregion, Arizona and Utah. *Cincindela* 35:41–76.

Appendix 1:
Publications of Amadeo Rea

1963 The Nesting of White-tailed Kites. *Western Bird Bander* 38:36–39.

1964 Chestnut-sided Warbler in Southern California. *Condor* 66:303.

1967 Age Determination of Corvidae, Part I. Common Crow. *Western Bird Bander* 42:44–47.

1967 Some Bird Records from San Diego County, California. *Condor* 69:316–318.

1968 (with D. Kanteena) Age Determination of Corvidae, Part II: Common and White-necked Ravens. *Western Bird Bander* 43:6–9.

1968 Age, Sex, and Race Determination of Yellow-bellied Sapsuckers. *Western Bird Bander* 43:46–47.

1969 Species, Age, and Sex Determination in the Genus *Tyrannus*. *Western Bird Bander* 44:32–35.

1969 The Interbreeding of the Boat-tailed Grackle in Secondary Contact in Central Arizona. (M.S. Thesis, unpublished; Arizona State University).

1970 Winter Territoriality in a Ruby-crowned Kinglet. *Western Bird Bander* 45:4–7.

1970 The Status of the Summer Tanager on the Pacific Slope. *Condor* 72:230–233.

1970 [A review] *Vertebrates of the United States*, Blair et al., Second Edition. *Western Bird Bander* 45:44.

1970 Age Determination in the Red-shafted Flicker. *Western Bird Bander* 46:36–37.

1971 A Proposed Age-sex Manual for Western Birds. *Western Bird Bander* 46:36–37.

1971 (with G. T. Austin) Key to the Age and Sex Determination of Verdins. *Western Bird Bander* 46:41.

1972 Notes on the Summer Tanager. *Western Bird Bander* 47:52–53.

1973 Turkey Vultures Casting Pellets. *Auk* 90:209–210.

1973 The Scaled Quail, *Callipepla squamata* Vigors, in the Southwest: Systematic and Historical Considerations. *Condor* 75:322–329.

1973 (with L. Kostritsky) Obituary: Maria Koepcke. *Auk* 90:735–736.

1973 A Case of Interordinal Copulation. *Wilson Bulletin* 85:337–338.

1976 (with G. T. Austin) Recent Southern Nevada Bird Records. *Condor* 78:405–408.

1977 Historic Changes in the Avifauna of the Gila River Indian Reservation, Central Arizona. (Ph.D. Dissertation; University of Arizona).

1977 (with M. Wilson) Late Pleistocene Williamson's Sapsucker from Wyoming. *Wilson Bulletin* 89:622.

1978 [A review] *The Audubon Society Field Guide to North American Birds: Western Region* by Miklos D. F. Udvardy. *Wilson Bulletin* 90:472–473.

1978   The Ecology of Pima Fields. *Environment Southwest* 484:8–13.

1978   Identification of [a] Bird Bone. In *Las Vegas Ranch Ruin-East and Las Vegas Ranch Ruin-West: Two Small Prehistoric Prescott Indian Culture Ruins in West Central Arizona*, ed. F. Barnett, p. 76. *Museum of Northern Arizona Bulletin.* 51.

1979   Velvet Mesquite: [Tree of Life for Desert Indians]. *Environment Southwest* 486:3–7.

1979   (with N. Hamblin) La Avifauna Arqueológica de Cozumel. *Boletín de la Escuela de Ciencias Antropológicas de la Universidad de Yucatán* 37:21–49.

1979   Hunting Lexemic Categories of the Pima Indians. *Kiva* 44:113–119.

1980   New World Vultures: Diminishing and Misunderstood, Part 1. *Environment Southwest* 489:3–7.

1980   New World Vultures: the Scavenging Niche, Part 2. *Environment Southwest* 490:12–13.

1980   Late Pleistocene and Holocene Turkeys in the Southwest. *Los Angeles County Museum Contributions in Science.* 330:209–224.

1981   Resource Utilization and Food Taboos of Sonoran Desert Peoples. *Journal of Ethnobiology* 1:69–83.

1981   California Condor Captive Breeding: A Recovery Proposal. *Environment Southwest* 492:8–12.

1981   Avian Remains from Las Colinas, a Classic Hohokam Site of Phoenix. In *The 1968 Excavations at Mount 8, Las Colinas Ruins Group, Phoenix, Arizona*, eds. L. C. Hammack and A. P. Sullivan, pp. 297–302. *Arizona State Museum Archaeological Series* no. 154.

1981   (with G. T. Austin, E. R. Blake, P. Brodkorb, M. R. Browning, W. E. Godfrey, J. P. Hubbard, G. McCaskie, J. T. Marshall, G. Monson, S. L. Olson, H. Ouellet, R. S. Palmer, A. R. Phillips, W. M. Pulich, M. A. Ramos, and D. A. Zimmerman) Ornithology as Science. *Auk* 98:636–637.

1982   (with G. P. Nabhan, K. L. Reichhard, E. Mellink, C. F. Hutchinson) Papago Influences on Habitat and Biotic Diversity: Quitovac Oasis Ethnoecology. *Journal of Ethnobiology* 2:124–143.

1983   Sonoran Desert Oases: Plants, Birds and Native People. *Environment Southwest* 503:5–9.

1983   Cathartid Affinities: a Brief Overview. In *The Biology and Management of Vultures of the World*, eds. S. R. Wilbur and J. A. Jackson, pp. 26–54. University of California Press, Berkeley.

1983   *Once a River: Bird Life and Habitat Changes on the Middle Gila.* University of Arizona Press, Tucson.

1983   (with A. Ferg) Prehistoric Bird Bone from the Big Ditch [Hohokam] Site, Arizona. *Journal of Ethnobiology* 3:99–108.

1983   Reply to Bahr [on *Once a River*]. *Journal of Ethnobiology* 3:187–189.

1984   Raymond Maurice Gilmore, 1 January 1907 – 31 December 1983. *Environment Southwest* 505:3–10.

1984   Obituary: Raymond Maurice Gilmore. *Journal of Ethnobiology* 4:97–99.

1984   (with L. L. Hargrave, deceased) The Paleoavifauna of Stanton's Cave, Grand Canyon. In *The Archaeology, Geology and Paleobiology of Stanton's Cave, Grand Canyon National Park, Arizona*, ed. R. C. Euler, pp. 77–91. Grand Canyon Natural History Association Monograph No. 6.

1985   (with T. R. Van Devender and M. L. Smith) The Sangamon Interglacial Vertebrate Fauna from Rancho la Brisca, Sonora, Mexico. *Transactions of the San Diego Society of Natural History* 21(2):23–55.

1985   (with N. L. Hamblin) Isla Cozumel Archaeological Avifauna. In *Prehistoric Lowland Maya Environment and Subsistence Economy*, ed. M. Pohl, pp. 175–192. Peabody Museum Papers Vol. 77. Harvard University Press, Mass.

1986   So What Good's a Dead Bird? *Environment Southwest* 513:12–17.

1986   (with S. L. Olson and P. Brodkorb) Comments on the Application to give 'Precedence' to Threskiornithidae Richmond, 1917, over Plataleinae Bonaparte, 1838. Z. N. (S.) 2136. *Bulletin of Zoological Nomenclature* 43:12–13.

1986   Black Vultures and Human Victims: Archaeological Evidence from Pacatnamu. In The Pacatnamu Papers, vol. 1, eds. Christopher B. Donnan and Guillermo A. Cock, pp. 139–144. Museum of Cultural History, University of California, Los Angeles.

1986   Verification and Reverification: Problems in Archaeofaunal Studies. *Journal of Ethnobiology* 6(1):9–18.

1986   The Following Contributions: In *The Known Birds of North and Middle America*, Part I, ed. Allan R. Phillips. [Privately published Dec. 1986], Denver, Colorado:

    Geographic Variation [of *Corvus corax* L]. pp. 65–66 + map.

    [Geographic Variation of] *Corvus brachyrhynchos* Brehm. pp. 68–70.

    (?) *Corvus caurinus* Baird. p. 70.

    [Geographic Variation of] SW (Pacific) Races [of *Lanius ludovicianus* L]. pp. 78–79.

    Geographic Variation: (1) NW Races [of *Parus wollweberi* (Bonapart)]. pp. 89–90.

    Geographic Variation: (1) "Brown-crowned" Pacific Races [of *Aegithalos minimus* (Townsend)]. pp. 95–96.

    [Geographic Variation of] (2) Pacific Lowland and SW Races [of *Cistothorus palustris* (Wilson)]. pp. 114–116.

    Geographic Variation: (1) NW, Peninsular, and Insular Races [of *Campylorhynchus brunneicapillum* (Lafresnaye)]. pp. 118–119.

[Geographic Variation of] (2) W Races [of *Troglodytes troglodytes* (L)]. pp. 138–140.

Geographic Variation: (1) Pacific Coast Races [of *Troglodytes bewickii* Audubon]. pp. 148–151.

Appendix B. Species Limits in some N. American *Corvus*. p. 213.

Appendix C. Measurements of N. American *Corvus corax*. p. 214.

Appendix D. Specific characters of American *Lanius*. p. 215.

1987   (with G. P. Nabhan) Plant Domestication and Folk Biological Change: the Northern Piman/Devil's Claw example. *American Anthropologist* 89:57–73.

1987   Introducing Ethnobiology [editorial]. *Environment Southwest* 519:3–4.

1987   [A review] *Gathering the Desert*, by Gary Paul Nabhan. *Environment Southwest* 519:15.

1987   [A review] *People of the Desert and Sea: Ethnobotany of the Seri Indians*, by Richard Stephen Felger and Mary Beck Moser. *Environment Southwest* 519:14.

1988   Habitat Restoration and Avian Recolonization from Wastewater on the Middle Gila River, Arizona. In *Arid Lands: Today and Tomorrow*, eds. E. E. Whitehead, C. F. Hutchinson, B. N. Timmermann, and R. G. Varady, pp. 1395–1405. Westbutte Press, Boulder, Colorado.

1988   The President's Page. *Journal of Ethnobiology* 8(1):iii–iv.

1989   The President's Page. *Journal of Ethnobiology* 8(2):iii–iv.

1989   Past President's Page. *Journal of Ethnobiology* 9(1):iii–iv.

1990   (with K. L. Weaver) The Taxonomy, Distribution, and Status of Coastal California Cactus Wrens. *Western Birds* 21:81–126.

1990   Naming as Process: Taxonomic Adjustments in a Changing Biotic Environment. In Proceedings First International Congress of Ethnobiology, Vol. 1, eds. Darrell A. Posey and associates, pp. 61–79. Bélem, Brazil.

1990   The Riverine Pima Ecosystem: a Sustainable Desert Lifeway. In Proceedings First International Congress of Ethnobiology, Vol. 2, eds. Darrell A. Posey and associates, pp. 51–56. Belém, Brazil.

1991   (with T. R. Van Devender and W. E. Hall) Faunal Analysis of Late Quaternary Vertebrates from Organ Pipe Cactus National Monument Packrat Middens, Southwestern Arizona. *Southwestern Naturalist* 94–106.

1991   Geographic Variation [of Vireo huttoni] (1) Small Pacific Coast Races. In *The Known Birds of North and Middle America, Part II*, ed. Allan R. Phillips, pp. 183–186. [Privately published May 1991], Denver, Colorado.

1991   (with T. R. Van Devender and J. I. Mead) Late Quaternary Plants and Vertebrates from Picacho Peak, Arizona. *Southwestern Naturalist* 36:302–314.

1991   Gila River Pima Dietary Reconstruction. *Arid Lands Newsletter* (Fall/Winter) 31:3–10.

1994   (with Eric Mellink) Taxonomic Status of the California Gnatcatchers of Northwestern Baja California, Mexico. *Western Birds* 25:50–62.

1994   (with K. L. Reichhardt, E. Mellink, and G. P. Nabhan) Habitat Heterogeneity and Biodiversity Associated with Indigenous Agriculture in the Sonoran Desert. *Etnoecológica* 2(3):21–34.

1995   (with P. Unitt, E. Palacios, E. Mellink, L. Alfaro, and S. Gonzáles) Noteworthy Records of Birds in Northwestern Baja California, Mexico. *Western Birds* 26:144–154.

1997   The Indeterminate Parrot of Nuevo León. In *The Era of Allan R. Phillips: A Festschrift*, comp. Robert W. Dickerman, pp. 167–176. Horizon Communications, Albuquerque.

1997   (with P. Unitt) Taxonomy of the Brown Creeper in California. *The Era of Allan R. Phillips: A Festschrift*, comp. Robert W. Dickerman, pp. 177–185. Horizon Communications, Albuquerque.

1997   *At the Desert's Green Edge: An Ethnobotany of the Gila River Pima.* University of Arizona Press, Tucson.

1997   (with Robert W. Dickerman) In Memoriam: Allan R. Phillips, 1914–1996. *incl.* A. M. Rea, "A Man Bigger than Life: Some Reflections." *The Auk* 114:496–499.

1998   "New World Vultures," "The California Condor" (with Noel Snyder), "The Turkey Vulture," "The Black Vulture." In *The Raptors of Arizona*, ed. Rich Glinski, pp. 23–36. University of Arizona Press, Tucson.

1998   *Folk Mammalogy of Northern Pimans.* University of Arizona Press.

1998   Corn Man and Tobacco Woman: A Story of Pima Cosmology. In *Stars Above, Earth Below: Native Americans and Nature*, ed. Louise Craft, pp. 207–221. (Alcoa Foundation, Carnegie Museum of Natural History, Pittsburgh.) Roberts Rinehart Publishers, Niwot, CO.

2000   Condór Californiano. In *Las Aves de Mexico en Peligro de Extinción*, eds. Gerardo Ceballos and Laura Márquez Valdelamar, pp. 199–205. Sección de Obras de Ciencia y Technología, Instituto de Ecología, Universidad Nacional Autónoma de México, D.F.

2004   (with David H. Ellis and a host of others) Summer Diet of the Peregrine Falcon in Faunistically Rich and Poor Zones of Arizona Analyzed with Capture-release Modeling. *Condor* 106:873–886.

2007   Ethnobotany: Whose Perspective? *The Plant Press* 31:17.

2007   The Poorwill in Pima Oral Tradition. *Archaeology Southwest* 21:7.

2007   *Wings in the Desert: A Folk Ornithology of Northern Pimans.* University of Arizona Press, Tucson.

2008   Historic and Prehistoric Ethnobiology of Desert Springs. In *Aridland Springs in North America: Ecology and Conservation*, eds. Lawrence E. Stevens and Vicky Meretsky, pp. 268–278. University of Arizona Press, Tucson.

Ten Principles of Ethnobiology:
An Interview with Amadeo Rea

Dana Lepofsky[†] and Kevin Feeney[‡]

On April 12, 2012, Dana Lepofsky interviewed Amadeo Rea at the 35th Society of Ethnobiology (SoE) meetings held at the Denver Botanic Gardens. Kevin Feeney filmed that interview[1] then did follow up interviews with Amadeo on the phone on 21 and 25 July 2012. Throughout the interviews, Amadeo Rea guided us on an exploration of his rich and diverse ethnobiological career and shared insights gained through his work with Pima, Papago, and other Native American communities. Amadeo's experiences and insights are broadly relevant to the field of ethnobiology and exemplify many of the fundamental components of ethnobiological work in the 21st century. In this chapter, we use excerpts from these interviews with Amadeo to highlight what we feel are the foundational principles guiding the field of ethnobiology today, principles which are aptly illustrated by Amadeo Rea's words and experiences.

Principle 1. Ethnobiology is Inherently Interdisciplinary

The very term *ethnobiology* evokes the inherent connections between "nature" and "culture," connections that more narrow disciplinary approaches often overlook. What makes the field of ethnobiology unique is the combination of tools from neo- and paleoecology, biology, medicine, anthropology, archaeology, and linguistics with the cultural knowledge and wisdom of indigenous communities. Ethnobiologists ask questions and seek answers that provide the linkages between these different kinds of knowledge. Without these connections, our understanding of people's lives and how they interact with their environment would be incomplete.

Amadeo illustrates the importance of this connection:

> *If you're finding bones in an archaeological site, [you should ask], what does this mean to people who really lived and who really told stories? And [who] still sing songs about these organisms, these birds that we're finding? So what does this* really *mean? For instance, why do we get so many Prairie Falcon bones...[in archaeological sites]... Well of course, it was never a puzzle to the*

† Department of Archaeology, Simon Fraser University, 8888 University Drive, Burnaby, B.C. Canada [dlepofsk@sfu.ca]
‡ Department of Anthropology, Washington State University, Pullman, WA [kevin.feeney@wsu.edu]

Indians why those [bones] would be there. It's a puzzle for the archae-
ologist or the outsider who doesn't know the culture.

However, to acquire the broad set of skills and knowledge needed to become an accomplished ethnobiologist requires holistic training and being surrounded with mentors and advisors who recognize the value of building bridges between disciplines and
communities.

As Amadeo observes, however, clear academic paths for acquiring the requisite
combination of skill-sets required for superior ethnobiological work are sometimes
lacking, and thus it may be up to aspiring ethnobiologists to build their own unique
academic paths.

One of the problems I see with ethnobiology is…people who are well-
trained in biology but poorly trained in anthropology, or the opposite
of that, and that's what the academic world produces. You don't study
metaphor or linguistics, or conceptual kinds of things, if you're going
through a biology program. It's pretty cellular. Being able to get whole
organism biology is difficult.

The thing that I hope will happen is that students going through can…
get sympathetic committee members who will say "you have to be a
good anthropologist to understand these things, you have to be a good
biologist to understand this." So, [there is] no use in being an ethnobi-
ologist if you really don't understand your ethnography.

Principle 2. Ethnobiology is Inherently Cross-cultural

Ethnobiologists believe in sharing knowledge cross-culturally and have a deep respect
for cross-cultural knowledge. They understand that ways of learning and knowing vary
and are culturally dependent. As a result, ethnobiologists are often good teachers and
good students.

Amadeo had the following to share about his teaching and learning experience with
his Navajo, Mescalero Apache, White Mountain Apache, Pima, and Papago students,
whom he taught in the 1960s:

[Teaching] was a great learning curve. You know, the kids liked me and
I liked the kids. And we just sort of hit it off. And it was a lot of fun. You
know, [there had] to be a different way of teaching. [The Native Ameri-

can kids] just don't take to the books so much, but they loved to skin birds. I taught them all how to skin birds, and make specimens.

… And, I also found out, and this was a big breakthrough on teaching sciences, I found out that they were all good artists. The boys especially were good artists. The girls were good artists too.

…. But, my approach to teaching worked better by getting these kids to draw something – taking them out in the field to draw these plants, draw these birds, to draw these diagrams. It was something to do with the language barrier that drawing worked.

Well, you know, you go to a group of people and you think you're bringing them something. And, after 3 years, I said, "I'm the one that is learning. You're the ones that are teaching."

Principle 3. Ethnobiological Research is Founded on Mutually Respectful, Trusting Relationships between the Ethnobiologist and the Descendent Communities

Ethnobiologists are keenly aware that conducting ethnobiological research is a great privilege. They acknowledge that community consultants take considerable time to share their knowledge, and recognize fully the value of this knowledge. They also know that these learning opportunities are rare and special; in many cases, the knowledge that is being shared is held by only a few individuals in the community. Researcher-consultant rapport is essential in ethnobiology, and key relationships may be established in the very first meeting with people, as reflected in Amadeo's account of meeting his students' families:

I started meeting people. It was interesting because for some reason, some people would come to the school and the Indians wouldn't, they really wouldn't talk to them, and for some reason they would talk to me. I don't know what it was… And my Principal said, "Amadeo, this is weird. Indians never talk to strangers, but they talk to you."

So, it just sort of opened. I became the… what would you say… the blank notebook that they could write on… to tell their stories.

A key part of building and maintaining trusting and successful relationships with descendant communities is respectful and accurate dissemination of research results. Indeed, the choice to pass on ethnobiological knowledge to an outside researcher is dependent on trusting the ethnobiologist to treat their teachings respectfully. Amadeo has made it a priority in his career to make sure that people's voices and knowledge are well represented in his texts:

> ... I like to quote people, to say what THEY say, not what I think they said. What they said, not what I filtered through what I think they said, or what I think they meant, or summarizing things. Let them talk. Put it in there. And so, this is their English. I didn't edit it... It's their speech...

> I've always asked people that I'm working with if I tape record a song or I tape record a conversation, "Is it OK for me to use it?" And also, I am always trying to bring it back and say "Here's the transcription, do you want to make any changes?" And usually they say, "No, that's ok" or they see something that's unclear and they say, "Well, let's clarify that point." But I always, I try to be always open.

Principle 4. Ethnobiological Knowledge must be Situated within Culturally-specific Worldviews

For most indigenous people and others in long-situated societies, their ethnobiological knowledge is much more than lists of useful plants or animals. Many cultures specify appropriate ways of interacting with their biological worlds that are, in turn, embedded in more general rules about the right way to live. Understanding the complexity of peoples' relationships with their biological worlds, and how these relationships are expressed within specific cultures, are fundamental goals of ethnobiological research.

As Amadeo illustrates, ethnobiological knowledge cannot be isolated from its cultural context:

> When the press was doing [my ethno-ornithology book] Wings in the Desert... they sent me the cover, and they have this big drawing of roadrunner on it. And, so that was going to be the cover. You know, roadrunner is a cliché first of all, and I said, "You know I don't think this is acceptable to Pimans." I said, "Did you read my roadrunner account?"

> When the series of roadrunner songs was initially transcribed in 1903 by Frank Russell, with monolingual Pimans, he translated some of the songs, but

he didn't translate all of the songs. I worked with a translator, and I had all the songs translated. And the roadrunner is associated with venereal disease. And the songs are really interesting; they're sort of brazen.

One of the songs that didn't get translated, the roadrunner songs—and these were songs to be used in curing of venereal disease, so they're curing songs—so, one of the songs is about the vagina singing [about the] joy at what she's going to get.

And the other song that didn't get translated, but it's translated in [Wings in the Desert]—the Piman is there and the English is there—the other [roadrunner] song is about the penis, and he's, he's got his red head, and he's going to shoot water out of his head.

I won't get into the whole genitalia that's involved in the roadrunner metaphor, but I [didn't] think this is the best ... the best bird to put on the cover for the Pima ... I said, "How about the Turkey Vulture?" because every Piman can relate to Turkey Vulture, because they are Coyotes or Turkey Vultures [i.e., they are a member of one of these moieties]. So they changed it.

Principle 5. Language and Metaphor are Essential Avenues for Understanding Worldview and Cultural Systems

Ethnobiologists know that language and culture are inextricably intertwined. Through language, researchers can access the tangible and non-tangible aspects of ethnobiological knowledge systems. For instance, in the following conversation, Amadeo explains how a single Piman term—**Ba'ivchul**—led to his understanding not only of kingfisher ecology on the Gila River, but also the symbolic role of the kingfisher in the Piman worldview:

*You know the key to this whole thing is finding out what people call things. Once you have that key, like **Ba'ivchul** ...*

[I asked], "What can you tell us about the river?"

*[They responded], "The river was running, there were birds nesting in the river ... oh yeah, there was **Ba'ivchul**"*

Ba'ivchul. OK, I have a key, now I have a handle… [I asked], "What are these [Ba'ivchul]?"

[They answered], "They nest in the holes in the banks of the [Gila] river, and they fished."

Well, this isn't how you would imagine… a dry river with nothing but Salt-cedars.

"Well, what did he look like?"

"He was so big, about the size of a flicker…."

They're kingfishers! Kingfishers were nesting in the river! Ornithologists don't even know about kingfishers [in the desert]. However, then I had a handle and I could talk to anybody about Ba'ivchul. When you go to the village a few miles up the River, there are songs by a few singers. There are a whole series of songs about kingfishers. [They] no longer existed [there] of course, and… ornithologists didn't even know [kingfishers had] bred in southern Arizona.

But, the thing [is] getting a handle on something—you've got a handle that you can use for this system.

[Then, you can ask], "What did you do, what do you know about that kind of thing", and then a person always interested in metaphor will ask, "What does this mean for them, what is Ba'ivchul?"

Ba'ivchul has a really important place in the Creation Story[2]… it's been misinterpreted and people have not known about what Ba'ivchul was—[scholars knew] what it meant ornithologically, what it meant behaviorally, but [not] what does it mean symbolically and metaphorically for Pima.

Its [metaphorical meaning is] really esoteric, it… it's just as complex as anything you can imagine out of Greek mythology…

But getting into that thing and finding out what that is… [That] opens the door of ethnobiology through taxonomy and [allows us to] find out… find out what the Ba'ivchul are.

Principle 6. Ethnobiology Recognizes the Inextricable Connection between Indigenous People and their Landscapes

Ethnobiologists recognize that you cannot begin to understand people's culture, or people's lives, without understanding the landscape in which those lives are embedded. Furthermore, seeking to understand that physical landscape is often the start of and foundation for establishing relationships between the ethnobiologist and the community members. This process is poignantly illustrated in Amadeo's early experiences working with the Pima to understand the ecology of the Gila River before it was transformed by watershed deterioration, irrigation, dams, and municipal developments. For the Pima and Papago, much of their world revolved around the intricate ecology of the Gila River.

> … I was coming as a scientist and a teacher and one of the authors of Birds of Arizona [Alan Phillips] wrote to me and said to me, "Amadeo, why don't you find out what those old Indians know about the Gila River before it went dry." Because it was a major river in Southern Arizona. It was a destroyed river. It is no longer a river. Well, that was in '64, '65 and I started asking people.

> I started asking the gardener, the local gardener [of the school where Amadeo was teaching], and through the years he was one of my main consultants. But, it spread to other people in that generation—his generation. So, I was dealing with people who were born in the early 1900s. And they knew a lot about the river. They knew about swimming in the river, they knew about fishing in the river. Well, [today] there [is] a puddle in the river[bed] after a rain, but no river. And, there hadn't been a river for 30 years or so. [But], they still knew about these things.

Indeed, these elders were raised as members of a riverine culture. Although ecocide had desiccated the Gila River, the river culture, or remnants of it, lived on.

> People loved to talk about what things were like. And, I think the people appreciated, old people really appreciated, that somebody had the interest to find out about these things.

Principle 7. Ethnobiology Recognizes the Importance of Cultural Time

Western Scientists have not often appreciated the value of local and traditional knowledge and some have short-term views on culture and ecology. This abbreviated view often results in shifted ecological and cultural baselines (thinking what you see has always been so). In contrast, ethnobiologists understand that local and traditional knowledge is grounded in long-term experiences and knowledge of specific places. Indeed, they know that native residents of an ecosystem, who often have little or no formal education, can be cultural vessels of multi-generational *in situ* environmental observation and interaction. Consequently, ethnobiologists recognize the importance of inter-generational knowledge and traditions. While people who call themselves archaeologists or historical linguists make up only a small portion of the larger ethnobiological community, most ethnobiologists recognize the importance of deep time in traditional knowledge systems.

What I was trying to do in that book [Once a River: Bird Life and Habitat Changes on the Middle Gila] *was use ethnographic data, and even folk taxonomy, to reconstruct what the conditions of the Gila River were. You know the Gila River is now dry for most of its extent, but I was trying to use that Pima information to reconstruct what was there, what the river was like.*

When I began my work, there were people old enough... who still remembered the river when it was running. And I did have Hispanic documents from Jesuits, and then a little bit [from] Franciscans, but mostly Jesuits, which means that it's pre—when were the Jesuits expelled?—1767, I guess. So, I had documents from the 1690s to 1767 that also covered what Europeans saw when they came up into Pima Country. So, taking that information, taking the ethnographic perspective, the folk taxonomy, and all of this, I was able to reconstruct what a marvelous desert oasis this whole central arid portion of Arizona was.

I've been going through as many of those Jesuit vocabularies as I can find, and that have survived to modern times, and looking at plant and animal names in there, and this has been very revealing. Also, because the whole southwest—well desert—is sensitive environment, it is easily changed environment. So, it's interesting to see all over Pima Country—both in Sonora, Mexico, and Southern Arizona, and Central Arizona—what kinds of things Pimans were naming, and describing, and using, not just on the Gila River but in other places, about their local environment. And the Jesuits, of course, didn't have an idea... well, they were just recording words. They were just, it was an intellectual pursuit for them, but the information they recorded was so [vital]—"Oh yeah, well here's the name for this, and this word is cognate with words that I have gotten from modern people, and so that organism was there. Huh, how about that."

But again, it's looking at three and a half or so centuries, but in three centuries, even one century in the desert, you can have drastic, drastic changes in environmental conditions.

In our interview, Amadeo also lamented a lost opportunity to learn from elder generations:

I regret when I look back—there were people who were really, really old at the time. In their 80's and 90's. They didn't work with me. I didn't know the questions to ask. I didn't know what riches that I had just fallen into—this gold-mine of information. There were people there who had seen the covered wagons going across to California. They were alive in the 1880s and 1890s ... and they were old. But, none of these people did I break the ice and talk to. Every once in a while the people who were born in 1910, would say, when I asked a question, they would say, "Oh, I'll have to ask the old people." And they would. And then they'd come back and say, "No, we didn't do that or this is how we did it."

Principle 8. Ethnobiological Research Requires Good Listening

In our fast-paced culture, many people feel a need to fill all the spaces in a conversation. As a result, discussions can move so quickly that people don't really hear what is said. As exemplified by Amadeo's experiences shared below, ethnobiologists recognize the importance of allowing people to tell their stories at their own pace:

You just said something really important: Being a good listener, [not] just being able to ask the question ... Well, I'll just tell a story ...

Takashi my partner came to Arizona, around Christmas, and I had asked [Joe Giff], an older man who is now dead, I asked him a question, and Takashi said, "I'm going to town [Phoenix—he was gone at least a couple hours] ... to get a jacket." So, he went to town to get a jacket and came back, and Joe Giff was still talking. Takashi said, "You shouldn't tire him out." I said, "Shssh. He's still answering the question I asked him before you left" ... But, you know, you ask a question, and you better be ready for a 2 hour, or 2-½ hour or a 3 hour answer.

Amadeo related another story that demonstrates not only the importance, but also the patience required of listening:

One time, I went into this village on the Gila River Reservation. The fellow was—I taught his daughter and his son in high school—a real cattleman. And, I went and I asked him, "Can I interview you today?" He had just fried eggs on the stove. Two fried eggs and they were sitting there. He said, "Yeah we'll talk. Get the tape recorder and we'll talk." We talked and we talked. ... This is about at least 7:30 or 8 in the morning. It came to 10 o'clock and I said, "Leonard, your eggs." He said, "that's OK, this is more important." It got to be lunchtime and I was getting hungry and the eggs were still sitting in the frying pan. I said, "Well, maybe you should eat your eggs." He said, "No, we need to get through this." I tape recorded for hours. All I did was keep changing the tapes and he kept talking. Wonderful stuff.

Principle 9. Ethnobiology is often Applied Research

Ethnobiological research is valued for its tangible and non-tangible applications. Tangible applications include restoration and conservation of culturally significant biota and related ecosystems. Non-tangible applications can include community education, assistance with legal issues, preservation of cultural knowledge and tradition, and promoting cultural pride.

Amadeo's ethnobiological research provides examples of the ways in which ethnobiological research is being applied today—in education, litigation, and restoration.

I'm finding that educators on the Reservation are taking my works and developing talks and Powerpoints from my books (I don't do this. I'm a real Luddite). But, there are Powerpoints and pictures, and Pima things, and developing workbooks... This bird says this, and what is this bird called? and what color is this bird? You know, the cardinal, this is how you say it in Pima.

Regarding restoration, Amadeo describes how:

... the Pima want[ed] to [restore] a section, a mile or so of the [Gila] river... [When asked] what do the old people want? They said, "We want to see a river."

So they put in about a mile of new river, but the company that's putting it in, that whole design, they got a hold of me and asked what plants, what birds were there, what trees should go in, what do they mean to people, and what are the ethnographically significant plants that grow there?

So my research has had a lot of practical application to restoration.

[I told them] "if you're going to have these things the Pima knew and sang songs about, you need to have this little marshy area."

It happened! A few years after that was done, there was … some Green Heron in some cottonwoods. [The cottonwoods] were [almost] big enough—not yet, pretty soon, and the Herons will nest in there.

Amadeo's ethnobiological work has also had legal applications. Amadeo served as an expert witness in two different legal disputes involving the Gila River Indians, one of which was ultimately settled out of court.

Well … when the Gila River Indian Community was doing their water claims case, I forgot when it was closed, but I was one of the chief witnesses for that … There were three of us mainly who worked on that, and I did the ethno-biological, dietary, diabetes impact from the loss of river, and how it impacted people psychologically and … physically.

[That case] was the largest water claims case settlement that was ever set-tled … in U.S. court. And the tribe won. It never went to court, so that was interesting. I worked on it for several years and produced one of the three main documents for that …

I ended up doing work on reviewing all of the diabetes literature on the tribe, and of course that's the tribe with the highest diabetes rate in the world. The next tribes are in Australia who … are competing with Pima as far as high diabetes rates. So, I had to go through all the literature and we sat down and I said, "Well, I'm not, I'm not a physician. I do the ecological, environmental, folk taxonomic, and all of that …" and so the rest of the team—one's an histo-rian and the other one was engineering and water hydrology—said, "it looks like you come the closest to doing the diabetes stuff, so … you better be the one to do it." So they collected all the boxes of material for me to review.

So, it was interesting because I spent months going through all of the studies … that had been made over … decades of research on Pima diabetes… and then did produce the document on it. My earlier work … for the case for the tribe, the claims case, had been "how did the loss of river affect the diet, and the diet then affect the diabetes?" But here, I had to look at the actual diabetes part of it.

... that was [a] very practical application of all those years of work... at that time I had just the mammal book and Desert's Green Edge, *but primarily the* Desert's Green Edge *material was what... was really the crux of our argument in court on how the loss of the river impacted the tribe.*

In the case that did proceed to trial, Amadeo shared the following about his court testimony:

It was really interesting because the opposing tribe [San Carlos Apache]... had a really sharp and very nasty attorney on their side. And this was my first opportunity to ever be in court and testify... [it was] pretty frightening. I didn't know what, really what to expect.

[During a court recess] the opposing attorney comes over to me, and... "Oh crap!" They had already warned me that this guy is... he can just absolutely demolish somebody in court. So he comes over to me and says, "I want you to know that my wife and I (and his wife was an attorney also), my wife and I have read all of your books, and all of your publications," and he said, "we have deep appreciation for your scholarship and all that you have done." And I thought, "Wow!" So, somebody was reading all of these things.

So, when it came time to cross-examine me, he didn't have anything to say. It was... it was really nice. And I asked our attorney afterwards, our trial attorney, I said, "Well, you know, how did that go? That's my first experience in court." "Well," he said—Joe Sparks [the opposing attorney] was his name—he said, "Sparks either will, if he doesn't ask anything it's because your testimony is so awful that he doesn't even have to bother... or, your testimony was so good that it just stands on its own and there's nothing for him to say." I said, "I hope it's the latter."

Principle 10. Always Try to "Give Back" to the Communities with which you Work

A desire to "give back" to communities is a natural outgrowth of mutually trusting and respectful relationships, and the recognition of how truly valuable the sharing of knowledge is.

We end our interview with these final thoughts from Amadeo, reminding us about both the privileges and responsibilities of being an ethnobiologist.

You know … [if] you take from the community … you bring it back to the community … I think that's a very important thing. And I think it's mostly happening, but I still hear people say, "Oh yeah these nutritionists, or these people studying diabetes, and so forth. They just get their degrees and you never hear from them again. What do they do to help us?"

Sometimes [there's an] underlying assumption that [community members] aren't interested [in the ethnobiological research], but people are interested. It's just that … scientists haven't built their bridges to Native communities.

Notes

1. Visit the Society of Ethnobiology website http://ethnobiology.org/education-and-out-reach/our-mentors-speak to view the complete audio interview with Amadeo, and Johnson & Kingsley's chapter (this Volume) for a bibliography of Amadeo's work.
2. See *Wings in the Desert* (2007) pages 196–198 and 237 for more information about the role of kingfisher in the Piman Creation Story.

Amadeo Rea with Berta Alicia Durate Rodríguez and family examining her mother's weaving outside of a huki (woman's weaving hut) in Los Pilares village, Sonora, México, 2003. Photograph by Alexander W. Stevens, used with permission.

What Shapes Cognition?
Traditional Sciences and Modern International Science

E.N. Anderson[†]

Abstract

Amadeo Rea's pioneering excursions into ethnobiology were among the first to foreground emotional and aesthetic concerns as well as material that seemed "factual." His work raises the question of why people who have great factual knowledge of their environment also believe much that seems magical or imaginary to outsiders. I argue that we need to take the verifiability of traditional beliefs into account, and explain those aspects of their science that seem unrealistic in view of wider evidence. I further suggest that accounting for such ideas requires considering how humans process information, including confirmation biases, emotional distortions, and political issues. Traditional environmental knowledge is scientific and makes sense; ethnobiologists need to see *why* it makes sense to particular people at particular times.

Introduction: Amadeo Rea and an Oodham Cognitive Paradox

Everyone seems to agree that we do not see the world "as it is." It would overload our minds to attend equally to everything that impinges on our senses. The human brain processes information more or less as people process foods: discarding, chopping, grinding and reassembling, cooking everything down, and eventually emerging with a "made dish" that may have no resemblance to the ingredients that went into it. Indeed, food processing may create a pheasant made of soy protein, or a fish made of wheat gluten.

Despite our commonsense understanding that human thought processes are selective, there are still scholars that have suggested, and argued, that seeing the world through a modern scientific lens will produce something closer to "the truth".[1] These scholars would also argue that everybody else's traditions of discovery and knowledge are mere nonsense and superstition without even a resemblance to science (e.g., Wolpert 1993). By "scientific" I refer to cultural knowledge systems that purport to be true and to summarize useful working knowledge about the natural world. This is a wide definition, but necessary for present purposes (Gonzalez 2001).

† Department of Anthropology, University of California, Riverside, CA 92521-0418 [gene@ucr.edu]

In contrast, I argue that traditional and local science—ethnoscience—contains a wealth of knowledge that is both correct (by international bioscientific standards) and valuable. In pragmatic matters related to everyday living, traditional cultures hold their own, often proving far ahead of contemporary international science in knowledge of local ecology, local edible and medicinal plants, and other locally grounded and practical fields (Rea 1997, 1998, 2007; also Anderson 2003; Anderson and Medina Tzuc 2005; Hunn 1990, 2008; Rose 2000, 2005; and other standard ethnobiological sources).

Part of the reason why western scientists do not readily recognize the value of traditional knowledge is that, traditional communities often package knowledge along with poetry, metaphor, art, religion, and all the wonders of the imagination. What is often less recognized by western scholars is that contemporary international science can likewise be artful. Scientific illustration is an art form (Blunt and Raphael 1979; De Bray 1989). "Elegance" is a well-recognized benefit in a theory, and I have heard laboratory scientists praise the elegance of particular experiments. Thus, we should not be surprised when Australian aborigines teach hardheaded ecological knowledge through art and story (Gould 1969; Morphy 1998; Myers 2002) or when Tibetan teachers (as they say) "mount the rider of thought on the horse of song."

Amadeo Rea's research exemplifies the complex and intertwined knowledge systems of traditional communities. His works record not only the pragmatic knowledge of the Oodham, but also folklore, religion, and local tales. As such, they document a fascinating mix. Most of the data are empirically verifiable under any paradigm of science. Sometimes the lore is more poetic and less "factual" in bioscientific terms, but clearly understandable by anyone familiar with southwestern natural history. For instance, I can never look at Say's Phoebes, which nest commonly around my house, without thinking of Rea's story of their Oodham name. To the Oodham, the Say's Phoebe is the "wind's grandchild," and is literally a grandchild of the wind goddess. Anyone familiar with the bird knows how perfectly this fits. It is a small flycatcher, with the most light and buoyant flight of any bird I know, and with long, soft, descending calls that merge into the whistling desert wind. It hovers, swoops, and rides the powerful downslope winds of my mountain-foot home as if indeed nestling on its grandmother's breast.

Oodham culture illustrates what may be considered, at least in modern bioscientific eyes, a cognitive paradox. The Oodham knew their environment extremely well—every bird, every track, every grass blade. Yet the Oodham's religious and magical lore about the environment seems unique to their culture, or at least to Southwestern Native communities. It is not shared (at least not in any detail) by other communities. It is also hard to verify in bioscience. The Say's Phoebe exemplifies the point: seeing it as the wind's grandchild clearly rests on a profound knowledge of the bird and its flight, but, if taken literally rather than as a poetic image, it is not a part of modern bioscientific knowledge of the phoebe. This, and Oodham beliefs about birds and plants in general, pose a larger question that could be asked of people more broadly: *Why do we find this mix of detailed and perceptive factual knowledge together with beliefs that are hard to explain in empirical terms?* This is a paradox that needs unpacking.

In this paper, I begin to examine this question, to shed some light on the discussion of how indigenous people interact with their environment. To do this, I first present a general overview of cognitive bias, to provide context for the later discussions. I then present an overview of how scientists have tried to explain error in human thought and perception, including a discussion of hot and cold cognition. This is followed by a discussion of ideas about why such errors are perpetuated, and in particular the role that culture plays in perpetuating beliefs. I follow this with a more detailed examination of "truth" and science in two traditions with which I am familiar. First, I examine how scholars have described Chinese medicine vis-a-vis western medical science, with a view to defending the position that Chinese medicine counts as a science. I then summarize the Maya cognitive system and add notes on scientific systems in general. The Maya example illustrates the empirical and, to some extent, theoretical nature of a scientific tradition in a small-scale society. I conclude that traditional systems are different from western systems and from each other, but all can be considered science. All, however, contain ideas—usually inferences about "black box" variables—that do not meet modern scientific standards of truth. These ideas provide insights of their own, into how humans culturally construct the world, and how they add spiritual and aesthetic dimensions that may not be recognized as relevant to modern international bioscience.

Cognitive Bias: The Natural and the Supernatural

All students of cognition and of epistemology agree that knowledge is, to some extent, socially constructed (Hacking 1999; Kitcher 1993). This being the case, error can creep in at every stage of the construction process. But beyond that basic agreement, schools of thought explain truth and error in different ways. Some think we carve nature at the joints; others doubt that nature *has* joints.

Many social scientists see humans as creatures of culture, learning almost everything they know or believe. Conversely, some radical sociobiologists and evolutionary psychologists stress the inborn, genetically determined side of human thinking (see Kitcher 2001). Still others (e.g., Barkow et al. 1992) admit the importance of learning and environment, but hold that people are particularly good at learning some things (such as language) and have predispositions in certain directions. Examples of the latter are liking landscapes like those of our putative ancestral home in East Africa, or preferring fatty foods, which were healthy for humans when they were harder to come by (Eaton et al. 1988).

A longstanding stream of theory that ties cognitive errors to learning goes back at least to John Locke (1975, orig. 1697). Locke held that people depend on learning and reasoning, not on instinct, and that errors occur when people remain in ignorance and do not think or test their views. He was also aware of emotion. He introduced the term *tabula rasa*, "blank slate," for the learning brain, but he explicitly did *not* mean that the brain was literally blank; in spite of living long before genetics and mathematical models, he had a thoroughly modern awareness of cognitive processing biases, innate emotions, personality differences, and other such factors. Indeed, his book, now rarely read even by those that cite it, remains an excellent introduction to cognitive studies.

Another set of theories of cognitive biasing goes back to the work of Immanuel Kant (Kant 1978, orig. 1798). Kant argued that we distort the world in several ways for the sake of cognitive convenience. Kant also, importantly, held that our knowledge of the world is based on interaction with it. We form continually better or more useful approximations, on the basis of interacting with whatever is out there. But we never know everything, so our mental representations of the world are always different from the world itself. The study of the resulting mess he labeled *phenomenology*, and it lies behind modern cognitive social science.

Kant emphasized two opposing principles. The first was the principle of *aggregation*: we group like with like, according to whatever dimension we think proves "likeness." The other was the principle of *differentiation*: we over-differentiate things that we want or need to see as different, turning shades of gray into black and white. In spite of the intervening centuries, Kant's thought still casts a very long shadow over modern social science; the fields simply cannot escape him. This particular Kantian theory rose again most recently in the structural theory of Levi-Strauss (1962, 1963). Levi-Strauss identified dyadic oppositions, such as male and female; he pointed out—I believe correctly—that all cultures over-aggregate "males" and over-aggregate "females," while over-differentiating "males" and "females." All males are alike according to some essence, and are totally different in some essential way from all females. Some cultures recognize more genders (I have heard rumors of a New Guinea culture with six genders), but they still essentialize them.

Related is Arthur Kleinman's (1980) concept of the "explanatory model", which people use in times of illness. Worldwide, people integrate idiosyncratic thoughts and circumstances with popular ideologies about illness, to come up with a speculative account, or explanatory model, of how they got sick, how it will affect them, and what they can do to make it better. Writing about Chinese medicine, Kleinman notes that people feel the need to develop explanatory models that go well beyond available evidence. These are necessary for explaining, predicting, and making sense out of observations. They may be necessary to provide a simple, structured way to learn and remember data.

Simplest and most straightforward of inborn biases in cognition are errors due to apparently innate heuristics and biases in processing information. According to this theory, we are fairly good approximators, but are afflicted with difficulties in processing probabilistic data. We have trouble with base rates, overall probabilities, sampling, randomness, complex causation, and the like (Anderson 1996; Kahneman 2011; Kahneman et al. 1982; Nisbett and Ross 1980; Piatelli 1994). Tversky's work (e.g., Tversky 1977) especially revealed a human tendency to process in error, especially to underpredict the amount of variability in a sample. His work showed that humans instead perceived clusters, types, patterns, and winning or losing streaks when statistically there were none. No wonder we need statistics departments.

Some conclude from these cognitive inaccuracies that humans are inevitably irrational (e.g., Nisbett and Ross 1980). Others argue that these heuristics are simply a function of our evolution as excellent approximators, processing information to give maximal useful knowledge for minimal outlay of cognitive effort. Gerd Gigerenzer (2002; Gigerenzer et al. 1999) is probably the person who has staked the most on this claim; Boyd and Richerson (2005) follow him. Gigerenzer points out that our biasing heuristics are, under normal circumstances, more useful than they are distorting. Herbert Simon (1957) expressed an earlier, similar opinion, noting that people "satisfice" on information to save information-seeking costs and thus produce "bounded rationality."

Moreover, there are errors of perception that are very hard to escape unless one has a fairly sophisticated scientific tradition. It is easy to believe that the earth is flat and the sun goes around it. It is easy to believe that the heart, not the brain, is the center of emotion; the heart "beats faster" or "skips a beat" under emotional stress, while the brain does nothing one can really feel.

To a great extent, the scholars ask questions about the nature of cognitive errors that lead them to particular answers. Tversky and his various associates were interested in documenting cognitive limitations, sometimes with the goal of helping people do better (Kahneman 2011; Nisbett and Ross 1980). Gigerenzer is trying to figure out how people cope, using whatever information-processing methods work best, fastest.

Another source of error is the universal human tendency to see intention in everything. The "default option" in interpreting the world is to assume willful, intentional action (Atran 2002). This is probably the root of religious belief (cf. Atran 2002). Trees, rocks, and winds must have spirits making them fall, roll, or blow. Even the modern scientist cusses out her computer when it malfunctions.

Cold Cognition, Hot Cognition, and Wishful Thinking

Cognitive psychologists (e.g., Nisbett and Ross 1980) distinguish between the theories of "cold cognition" and "hot cognition" to understand cognitive bias. The above are theories of "cold cognition"; that is, they refer to simple errors or biases in reasoning, rather than to emotion-driven errors. Contrasting with these are theories of "hot cognition," which see emotion as causing the real problems in accurate judgment. The ancient Greeks were great believers in the problematic side of hot cognition, and advised people to damp down their emotions and be rational. A fear and distrust of emotion in decision-making has lasted to this day, but has recently been challenged by psychologists (e.g., Damasio 1994), economists (Frank 1988), sociologists (Stets and Turner 2006) and philosophers (Nussbaum 2001), who see emotion as helping decision-making as often as, or more often than, hindering it. The relationship of emotion to cognition continues to defy analysis (see Elster 1999 for a very comprehensive view of the problem). Probably the best summary of the whole matter is still David Hume's: "Reason is, and ought only to be the slave of the passions, and can never pretend to any other office than to serve and obey them" (Hume 1984, orig. 1740:462).

Many explain error from particular kinds of self-interest. Factually wrong claims by particular interested parties are often so obviously motivated by selfish concerns that no one thinks twice about the matter; we know why tobacco companies and their scientists still say smoking is safe, and why coal-burning utility corporations deny global warming (Oreskes and Conway 2010). We know why individual scientists defend their own concepts long after others have abandoned them.

Some of the biases arising from self-interest involve wishful thinking, which is, in the end, emotion-driven. Wishful thinking has risen to formal theory status in the important work of Shelley Taylor, whose book *Positive Illusions* (1989) remains basic. She and many others have pointed out adaptive reasons for optimism, but it has its costs. Wishful thinking enters into matters such as losing body fat. People often adopt the theory of fat that gives them the most hope for the least effort expended. They seek a pill or a magic diet—anything to avoid the need to change their whole regimen. Others decide that they have "fat genes," thus providing themselves with an excuse for not even trying to lose weight.

Contrasting with wishful thinking in a Levi-Straussian sort of binary opposite could be a cognitive distortion; this might be called counter-wishful thinking: believing in scary things as a projection of one's guilt and fear. This is a commonly heard and quite reasonable folk explanation for belief in ghosts.

Why Errors are Perpetuated: The Role of Culture

Usually less clear than how errors arise in the first place are the reasons why whole scientific traditions, or whole cultures, perpetuate certain errors. Science is supposed to be self-correcting. Moreover, because they are untrue, distortions stemming from self-interest, wishful thinking, and other errors should cancel out through discovery or be limited to a few people.

However, there are situations where error persists indefinitely in a whole tradition or culture. In these cases, social theories become necessary in order to explain the persistence of error. The fields of history of science and science studies often operate to explain why errors persist.

Not surprisingly, scientists, like most other people, are often the prisoners of their culture's thoughtways. As early as 1620, Francis Bacon argued that conformity to received wisdom damages science and rational thought (Bacon 1901, orig. 1620). For instance, modern-day positivist science has self-correction built in, but not necessarily perfectly (Kitcher 1993). Karl Popper's famous rule that scientific theories should be "falsifiable" (Popper 1959) has one limit: the only way you can really show a belief is falsifiable is to falsify it. That takes it out of the knowledge pool. For actual working knowledge, we have to make do with independent verification—ideally, verification by several independent people working from different perspectives or in different places (Kitcher 1993). This means that all knowledge is somewhat tentative. A fiendishly clever Popperian is always around the corner, trying to disprove it. Very often, the Popperian succeeds. In the words of H.L. Mencken: "Explanations exist; they have existed for all time; there is always a well-known solution to every human problem— neat, plausible and wrong" (Mencken 1920:158). We humans tend to observe in the natural world what makes sense to us in the internal logic of our culture. Cultures, while usually accurate about their environment, are inherently ethnocentric and contain other objectively wrong (falsifiable) biases. The cold cognitive theory of Thomas Kuhn (1962), argued that paradigms last (changing slowly if at all) until something clearly better comes along.

Hot-cognitive theories attribute paradigms and their changes to class struggle and power-knowledge. Marxian theory, from Marx to Bourdieu, teaches that error will happen and will be perpetuated when the self-interest of a whole social class is involved. In some societies, most scientists may be in a particular class. In that case, Marxian theory, and many other theories as well, would predict that the scientists would share an obvious bias. A more narrowly historical explanation explains the situation that holds when the scientific community is dominated by a few individuals at a few elite schools; their ideas triumph, for better or worse. Anthropologists and psychologists are familiar with the "era of the schools" in the early 20th century, when Franz Boas dominated much of American cultural anthropology while A.R. Radcliffe-Brown and Bronislaw Malinowski dominated much of English social anthropology. Boas was theoretically quite open, but Radcliffe-Brown in particular taught a rather specific form of structural functionalism that had very wide influence on British anthropology and sociology.

Michel Foucault (e.g., 1965, 1970) and his many followers have held that scientific knowledge is constructed and maintained largely to keep people in their place; its goal is *control*—not truth, and not necessarily wealth either. A great deal of what we once "knew" as "truth" now seems transparently faked up to keep certain people in their place. Racism and sexism with "scientific" rationales are only the most obvious cases. Foucault studied especially the fields of crime, gender, and mental illness. He often went beyond his factual evidence, but he still demonstrated to most people's satisfaction that political explanations are abundantly obvious and clear in those areas. However, in the periods he studied, science really knew little about these areas, and offered few facts to deploy; meanwhile, the social pressures on doctors and leaders were great. In the absence of valid information and in a situation where policy was demanded, "science" had no way to avoid or transcend politics, and thus came to reinforce structures of power—it served to keep the powerful in place and keep the rest pacified.

Psychology, for one field, has become more scientific since the periods of which Foucault wrote, and in the process has become less subject to political pressures (as any reading of the American Psychological Association's journals over the years will demonstrate; for one thing, there is enough political controversy within the field to keep dogmas at a minimum).

Political discourse is all too often the deployment of deliberate falsehoods for the purpose of stirring emotions and preventing rational thinking (Marcus 2002; Westen 2007). Science is not supposed to function that way, but it certainly does in the case of "scientific racism," as well as much of old-fashioned sexology and mental illness theory. Not only Foucault and his many followers, but also quite independent critics of racism (e.g., Gould 1981), have demonstrated this. For example, Gould discusses, and deconstructs, the IQ concept (Gould 1981).

Relativism and Truth

All this leads some extreme relativists to think we create our images of reality such that science is purely a social construct, like religion and magic, and has no privileged truth-value. To relativists, science stands with religious and cosmological beliefs as "collective representations" (Durkheim 1995, orig. 1912) of the community. Under this theory, beliefs are projections of people's concepts of their social systems. Foucault's theory may be a special case of this relativistic constructionist theory, in which beliefs are specifically the projections of people's concepts of power and control within society. In contrast, Marx held that people act on the basis of correct information about their world and their class position. They distort belief to serve class interest, but they are in touch with reality. Marx had very little patience with the pure-constructionist idea, which he attacked as Hegelian idealism.

The extreme-constructionist or relativist position has been generally criticized. However, critics admit varying degrees of value to the approach, since we must not only explain error but also the profound differences in representing the "true" (empirically, cross-culturally verifiable data) in traditional sciences as opposed to modern international science. Ian Hacking (1999), for one example, takes a nuanced relativist view, while Philip Kitcher (1993), Bruno Latour (2005), and Larry Laudan (1996) argue for varying forms of nuanced realist positions. These philosophers of science point out that one must explain why particular *questions* were asked in the first place, and why *particular* truths were sought, attended to, noticed, and believed. This can be even more interesting than trying to explain errors.

Anthropologists, of course, have long adopted various forms and levels of relativism. There is a longstanding rationalist tradition in anthropology, going back to Edward Tylor (1871) and other Victorian sages, that tries to supply "reasonable" explanations for "bizarre" beliefs, whether abroad or at home, but there is also a tradition of seeing "truth" as heavily conditioned by culture (Rosaldo 1980).

Interest in, and debate over, these matters goes back to the dawn of the field, and was developed by Franz Boas and his students, notably Paul Radin (1927, 1957). A. Irving Hallowell made particularly important contributions to understanding how traditional Indigenous people think about reality—often inferring supernatural beings or powers from ordinary events that seemed to Hallowell to be mundane and practical. A whole line of research stemmed from Hallowell's work on northern North American Indigenous peoples (see e.g., A.F.C. Wallace 1970; see also Anderson 1996). In his excellent book *Loon* (2001), Henry Sharp deals with Canadian Athapaskan beliefs in giant otters, dinosaur-like monsters, and mile-long fish that produce earthquakes by twitching their tails. Explaining such beliefs (as opposed to merely recording them) remains challenging, not least because the beliefs not only persist, but often "sell" to Euro-Canadian settlers. In my own research in British Columbia, I found that many non-Indigenous people in Haida Gwaii (the Queen Charlotte Islands) often believe in the "gogeet" (***gagitx***), the demon were-otter of Haida legend. Anglo-Canadians in south-central British Columbia often believe in the sasquatches and (in the interior) the lake monsters of local Salishan tradition. In fact, the lake monster of Lake Okanogan has become a major tourist attraction—some cross-cultural influence from Loch Ness is evident. It is not surprising that at least some anthropologists, after working with Northwest Coast First Nations, take a radically relativist stance toward knowledge (e.g., Goulet 1998).

In the wider world of anthropological theory, a full Kantian phenomenological agenda has been developed and applied to traditional worldviews, notably by David Abram (1996) and Tim Ingold (2000). Ingold has been particularly preceptive and persuasive in dealing with total experience of environment—physical, cognitive, emotional, and aesthetic. His work is not without challenge (Istomin and Dwyer 2009) but has produced new and more fully nuanced views of traditional worldviews.

Historians of European science must deal with the strikingly slow accumulation of corrections to early errors. ("Error" here refers to ideas that we now generally agree are counter-factual or counter-evidential, however credible they may have been in earlier times.) It is a truism among historians of science that alchemy and chemistry were not separated in Europe until a couple of centuries ago; we now see the one as nonsense and the other as truth, but it did not look like that to anyone until 1700 or later.

Errors sometimes persist a long time even in modern laboratory science. It is one thing to deal with the beliefs of a people who really had no way of testing the mile-long fish theory until recently; it is another to deal with the persistence among modern laboratory scientists of beliefs that seem even more obviously counterfactual. American geologists long resisted the overwhelming evidence for continental drift (Oreskes 1993). Another example is the extreme *tabula rasa* view of learning. Steven Pinker (2002) has demolished this view, and rightly wonders why it lasted so long. (Pinker incorrectly fathers this belief on John Locke [1975, orig. 1697], but Locke was no such fool, and had very modern ideas about innate and learned cognition). Pinker raised the question: how could virtually all psychologists and most anthropologists in the early 20th century believe that all animals learned in the same way and could learn pretty much the same stuff, without their learning processes being structured by evolutionary histories (e.g., Skinner 1960)? The *tabula rasa* view was supported by a huge mass of "objective" data, but we can now see that the data were very selectively attended, while a far larger mass of disconfirming data was simply ignored. Today, the pendulum may have swung toward an equally extreme belief in genetic determinism (Pinker's book exemplifies this overenthusiasm). Why has American mainstream culture changed—in only two generations!—from attending to one set of facts to attending to another opposite set, without ever coming to an impartial judgment? This kind of dramatic shift suggests that a drive for truth and accuracy is not a sufficient explanation for accurate material in a tradition.

Chinese Medicine and Cognition

In Chinese medicine, the relativist position has been beautifully articulated by Nathan Sivin (2000), introducing a book of essays on Chinese medicine by the great student of Chinese science, Joseph Needham. Sivin is arguing against Needham's forthright view of Chinese traditional science as just a way-station on the golden road to modern international science. Needham, who was writing in the 1950s and 1960s, judged Chinese science according to that standard, and saw too much modern medicine in Chinese traditional medical approaches. Sivin takes the opposite view, the view that Chinese medicine has little (if anything) in common with modern medicine and therefore little (if anything) to offer it:

> Like most people who explore the history of science today, I do not see knowledge, no matter where, as converging toward a predestined state. I see today's knowledge, not as an endpoint, but as a fleeting moment in a long sweep of creation. My experience in research has led me to view science as something that people invent and reinvent bit by bit, never completely constrained by what is already there, never pulled by some immutable goal, often mistaken, always on the edge of obsolescence. That view makes its history not a procession of destined triumphs but a meandering journey … [Sivin 2000:1].

Evidently Sivin does have a standard of truth; he speaks of "mistakes" and the like. But, in dealing with Chinese medicine he is exquisitely careful to make no judgments about whether particular cures work or not, and about whether particular theories have any relation to reality or not. He is also meticulously careful not to relate Chinese science to modern international science. He does not test claims against each other, trace influences, or seek ancestries.

There is an obvious benefit to this relativism—especially obvious if one compares Sivin's work with Needham's. Using the cultural-relativist approach, one can understand people in their own terms, and describe their system in its own terms, instead of seeing it as just a patchwork of hits and misses. By contrast, Needham's work seems to Sivin (and to many other readers) embarrassingly and naively judgmental. Needham was interested in, and aware of, the wider system of Chinese medicine. However, all modern historians of Chinese science now seem to agree that he spent too little effort understanding that tradition in its own terms. They feel he made unsupported claims about Chinese scientific advance and about the truth of Chinese science in Western terms. These now seem ethnocentric, and fail to stand up to better scholarship (Sivin 2000 discusses this very gently, but cites others who are more forthright).

Also, the Sivin approach avoids the situation of judging some Chinese ideas as nonsense because it doesn't fit modern science, only to discover a few years later that the traditional Chinese were right and the modern scientists were wrong. (This position can be embarrassing to those who judged it all nonsense.) A recent case of world importance is the use of sagebrush (*qinghaosu*, *Artemisia annua*) as a malaria cure; dismissed for years, it was finally tested by contemporary Chinese scientists, giving us our best current anti-malaria drug, artemisinin. There are also cases where Chinese medicine seems to have been right but we do not know, and are not doing enough research to find out whether this is the case, in fact, with most of the herbal remedies.

There is, however, one problem with the Sivin approach, a problem that is avoided by the Needham approach. This problem is the fact that the people studied—in this case Chinese doctors, but it could be Maya farmers, Athapaskan hunters, or any knowledge holders—actually care a great deal about whether their knowledge is practical and useful. They want to cure the sick, and make a living in the process. Thus, however indifferent historians of science can be to the truth-value of an assertion or a theory, their subjects of study *are not indifferent*. The problem of why the Chinese believed that sagebrush cured malaria is thus easily resolved. The problem of explaining their belief in dragons is obviously more challenging (Brook 2010). It is not to be dismissed by saying "people will believe any old thing" or by seeing the belief as power-knowledge for social control. Dragons appeared not only to imaginative scholar-artists, but to my very hard-headed and pragmatic fishermen friends on the Hong Kong waterfront. The problem is one of explaining why superb scholars and expert fishermen, who know countless details about every tiny insignificant fish in their environment (Anderson 1972), believe in dragons. The specific answer probably lies in fear-driven mental projections. Even I could easily imagine monsters in the roiling, swirling clouds and waves of typhoons.

Similarly, the problem with explaining Chinese medical beliefs that we now know to be genuinely wrong (such as correspondence and hot/cold theories) is not a problem of explaining why closet scholars came up with an arbitrary and ridiculous scheme; it is a problem of explaining how millions of excellent, committed, caring doctors, who actually tracked their treatment histories and recorded the results, could continue to believe. I discuss part of the answer in a previous publication (Anderson 1996) and suggest the actual experiential cues that led to the basic generalizations in Chinese folk medicine. An anonymous reviewer of this publication pointed out that western medicine has a similar past, using bloodletting to treat conditions. Bloodletting was originally intended to reduce the sanguine humor, and in fact does work (in a rather blunt-instrument fashion) to relieve high blood pressure and the like. In fact, bloodletting was part of a Galenic tradition in western medicine that also influenced Chinese medicine.

The story of Chinese medicine leads me to a preliminary conclusion, to be suitably qualified below. It would seem that a proper history of science, or ethnography of knowledge, has three steps. First, one must understand the system in its own terms, with a fully relativist "willing suspension of disbelief" (to quote Samuel Taylor Coleridge's famous phrase about reading fiction). Second, one must then do one's best to understand the system in terms of whether it does its job or not. Inevitably, this means judging it in terms of whether it actually works, in terms of some system based on objective cross-verification. Then, third, one must work to understand why people believe, suppose, or conjecture the actual things they think—both the accurate knowledge and the not-so-accurate. Explaining the accurate knowledge is often easy: people believe it because they know it works, and they need knowledge that is actually correct. Explaining the misses requires more thought. Explaining the *pattern* of hits and misses requires *much* more thought.[2]

Cognition in Yucatec Maya Science

With the help of Maya friends, I recently published a trilogy on Maya ethnoscience in Quintana Roo (Anderson 2003; Anderson 2005; Anderson and Medina Tzuc 2005). By and large, my findings confirm and extend other findings on Maya ethnoscience, going back many decades (e.g., Redfield and Villa Rojas 1934), and even centuries if one counts some 18th century Colonial Spanish herbal compilations that are surprisingly sophisticated ethnobotanies (Andrews 1980; Barrera and Barrera Vásquez 1983; Gubler 2005). Most of the medical claims in this literature are still untested with Western science. When tested, the plants usually turn out to have some medical value (Anderson 2003; Ankli 2000).

I turn initially here to the basic Maya folk biology: classification, natural history, and biological aspects of worldview. This will reveal the simplest and most direct form of cultural construction: the basic classification system as a cultural artifact, but one shaped by perceptions of biological and environmental reality. Similarities between Maya and modern international bioscientific terminology are many, and are explained at least in part by the fact that biological relationships are both evident and important to both Maya folk scientists and international biologists. I hope to show, also, that naming is based on Kantian principles of aggregation and differentiation. Natural categories are always and fully recognized, often with sophistication that has impressed formal biologists. But the number of recognizably different forms lumped under one term is based on a sliding scale: the smaller and less salient the animal or plant, the more it is likely to be lumped with other similar ones.

The Yucatec Maya folk classification system is typical of Native American ethnobotanical systems in general, and is particularly similar to the systems found in other Maya languages (Atran 1993, 1999; Berlin 1992; Berlin et al. 1974). Taxonomies are very shallow, with a lack of higher-order terms. There is no word for "plant," for instance, but the plant kingdom is recognized by the counting particle—**kul**. (Maya, like Chinese, appends particles to numbers to indicate what sort of entity one is counting.) A minimum of life-form taxa exists: **che'** "tree," **aak'** "vine," **su'uk** "grass" (now, and perhaps originally, referring only to small grasses) and **xiiw** "herb," a recent borrowing from Nahuatl (**xiuitl**) that replaced the native Mayan word **teek** for herbs. Related is **kuxuun** "fungus," but the Maya seem to see fungi as a separate category from true plants. Spanish has provided a number of broad terms so useful that they have been borrowed into Maya. Notable among them are *planta* "plant," *arbusto* "shrub," *helecho* "fern," and *zacate* "large grass" (a Nahuatl word, but borrowed via Spanish). *Ixi'im*, "maize," is a unique term; as the staff of life, it is not classified under any higher category (Figure 1).

Figure 1. Maize, the sacred plant, staple food, focus of agriculture, and source of 75% of calories in traditional Maya homes.

Below this level, no general terms exist until one gets to the folk-generic level. Few generics are broken down into folk specifics, and these are often post-Spanish creations, as in the case of **chujuk pak'al** and **suuts' pak'al** for sweet orange and bitter orange respectively, or the extension of **jaas**, originally "mamey (*Pouteria mammosa*)," to the banana, the mamey becoming **chakal jaas** "reddish **jaas**." However, classifying plants by broad color categories (dark or light, etc.) seems pre-Columbian. An interesting cut is by gender: many plants have male and female forms. The male often has more pointed leaves, the female the rounded ones; or sometimes the male is more saturated in color. Some Mayan healers make much of these distinctions (Faust 1998) but most people regard them lightly. Some plants have two names; achiote (*Bixa orellana*) is either **kiwi'** or **k'uxub**, some speakers using one and some the other; some use the latter for the tree and the former for the prepared paste used in spicing food (Figure 2).

Similarly, no cover term for "animals" seems to exist. Wild animals are **ba'alche'** "things of the trees." Animal life-form taxa are **ch'ich'** "bird," **kaan** "snake," **yik'** "insect" (but usually restricted to bees and similar large flying insects), and **kaay** "fish." Once again, Spanish brought useful terms like *bicho* "bug, small pestiferous creature" and *insecto*. Neither Maya nor folk Spanish has a term for mammals (*mamíferos* in book Spanish).

Several folk generics could also be considered life-form taxa, depending on how one feels about such terms. I consider them generics, however, because they are usually used as the

Figure 2. Achiote, **kiwi'** or **k'uxub**.

second word in a combined name (e.g., *saak ak* "white turtle"). These include terms like *ak* "turtle," *much* "frog/toad," and *lukum* "worm." *Siinik* "ant" can contrast at two levels: focally, it means any very small ant (each identifiable kind of big ant has its own name), but *siinik* can extend to mean "ants in general." Once again, all the life-form taxa immediately break out to folk generics, with no intermediate categories. (Covert categories may exist, explaining the readiness with which the Maya borrow Spanish intermediate taxa like *loro* for "parrot" and *palma* for palms in general; the Maya language names each species of parrot and palm separately.) Few folk generics have subdivisions. *Ch'om* "vulture" does, being divided into *chak pool ch'om* "red-headed vulture," (i.e., Turkey Vulture, *box pool ch'om*, "black-headed vulture," the Black Vulture, *batab ch'om* "ruling vulture," the King Vulture, and *sak ch'om* "white vulture," the Wood Stork). But there is evidence in early dictionaries (specifically the *Calepino de Motul;* Arzápalo 1995) that originally the vultures all had their own names, and rise of a folk generic with folk specifics under it is due to influence by Spanish and/or Nahuatl.

All large, conspicuous plants and animals, and all useful plants and animals, have distinctive names. In spite of the implication of the term "folk generic," these always correspond to species in Linnaean taxonomy. This applies even to wasps and bees, small but economically important for their honey or, at least, as stinging creatures to avoid carefully.

The small, more obscure, and more useless the plant or animal, the more likely it is to be classified under a truly generic term. These terms correspond structurally to the "folk generics" above, but cover wider groups. Fairly prominent but not very useful creatures have names that do indeed correspond loosely to Linnaean genera. Small insignificant items have names that cover whole Linnaean families or even orders: *kisay* "true bug" (order Hemiptera), *tulix* "dragonfly" (order Odonata).

It is reasonable that there are no mid-range terms comparable structurally (in taxonomic position) to the orders and families of Linnaean taxonomy. Maya taxonomies go directly from kingdom to life-form to generic (see e.g., Berlin et al.1974; Hunn 1977). This is found also in Rea's Oodham terminologies, and many (if not all) Native American systems of folk biology. Apparently the Maya had a latent need (or covert categories) for intermediate terms, because Spanish terms like *helecho* "fern" and *lagartijo* "lizard" have become loanwords in Maya.

It naturally happens that some animals are important to some Maya individuals but not to others. The more one is out and about in the milpas, the more one needs to know about flycatchers, which are common and highly diverse but are very difficult to distinguish. Villagers who rarely stray from town know them all as *takay* (from the noisy cries of the most obvious species, the Couch's Kingbird, *Tyrannus couchi*). More environmentally sophisticated villagers restrict this term to big noisy flycatchers, and call smaller ones *yaj*. This word means "pain" and refers to the calls of the smaller *Myiarchus* flycatchers, whose mournful whistles sound absurdly like the whining of a child with a bit of an ache. Truly knowledgeable farmers add a third flycatcher catgory, *juiiro*, with reference to the loud, ringing call—*hweero, hweero,*

hweero... —of the Bright-rumped Attila (*Attila spadiceus*)—a call which comes in late winter, announcing the season for clearing weeds and preparing a second-year milpa. Because of the timing of the bird's call, the same bird has the alternative name of **pak'sak'aj**, "plant-your-fallow-field." ***Juiiro*** is extended to cover other middle-sized flycatchers. Thus the **takay** category can be split into three. Everyone recognizes that all three terms are general categories that cover a range of clearly different birds. My coworker Felix Medina Tzuc lumped the Piratic Flycatcher (*Legatus leucophaius*)—a very rare bird in the area—as a **takay**, but knew that it was distinctive in that it bullied other birds out of their nests and took over the nests for its own use.

Another example of local biological expertise concerns **yuyum**, "orioles." Focally this term means the Alta Mira Oriole (*Icterus gularis*), which nests at the ends of branches. The term is extended to other orioles. Veteran woodspersons recognize a subcategory, **jonxa'anij**, "palm-nesters," for orioles that nest deep in the crowns of palms. Only recently did genetics prove that branch-tip orioles and palm orioles are in fact separate subclades within the oriole clade (Hoekstra and Price 2004). The two common orioles of Yucatan—the Alta Mira (*Icterus galbula*) and Hooded (*I. cucullatus*)—look almost exactly alike, but are in these different clades. They are each more closely related to quite dissimilar orioles. Maya classification recognizes this. Apparently the Maya were a few thousand years ahead of western biologists in this as in many other insights.

Spanish introduction of new animals has led to some new folk specifics and other extensions. The White-lipped Peccary (*Tayassu pecari*) was **k'eeken**. This name came to be used for the domestic pig, leaving the Peccary as **k'aaxijk'eeken** "forest pig." The tapir was **tsiimin**, but that name transferred to the domestic horse by 1600 (see the *Calepino de Motul*). There must have been a time when the tapir was something like ***k'aaxijtsiimin**, but now it is simply *tapir*. The domestic fowl is **kaax**, from "Castilian"; the bird was **kastelan ch'ich'** "Castilian bird" or **kastelan uulum** "Castilian turkey" in the early dictionaries and sources (cf. Restall 2004, who notes the turkey became "*Maya ulum*," i.e., **maayaj uulum**). Later, the chicken became **kaxlan ch'ich'** or **kaxlan**, and eventually just **kaax**. The Brocket Deer, **yuuk** (*Mazama americana*), existed in two varieties, red and gray (**chak yuuk** and **ya'ax yuuk**). The goat was assimilated to it and took over the name **yuuk**. These "marking reversals" are common in Native American and other taxonomies, in situations of this sort, where newly introduced animals and plants become commoner than local similar items. (see Brown 1994; for similar evolutions in the closely related Tzeltal language, see Hunn 1977.)

New plants continue to arrive in Quintana Roo, and they have names. Often the names come with the plant. This is the case with a much earlier borrowing, the Old World rose, is naturally known as *rosa*. An interesting example of the Maya ability to borrow new plants and then conserve them carefully is provided by the Bourbon Roses that flourish in Maya gardens all over the Yucatan peninsula. They appear to be of the variety La Reine Victoria, developed in France in 1872 (see Beales 1985:337); they have been propagated by cuttings

(Figure 3). A more recent acquisition is **noni** (*Morinda citrifolia*), a Hawaiian medicinal plant used for diabetes and many other conditions. It was introduced to Quintana Roo around 2004, and has spread rapidly, becoming a widely grown plant in dooryard gardens and commercial plantings (Figure 4).

Plants also come of their own and acquire Maya names. The sow thistle (*Sonchus oleraceus*), a weed, has invaded my study area since I began work there, and is called by newly generated names such as **repollo k'aax** (a Spanish/Maya hybrid meaning "forest cabbage"). This is only one example of a common phenomenon.

This knowledge of plants and animals is applied, and extended, in the practices of daily living. It is pragmatic and useful. It is supplemented by other kinds of experiential knowledge. For instance, the older rural Maya know every sizable animal's tracks and can identify traces quite imperceptible to me.[3] The Maya also know animal foods, and preserve or protect trees and bushes that bear fruit and leaves important to game animals. They know the nesting habits of wasps, bees, and ants, and know when and how to get honey as well as how to avoid stinging forms. They know how to call and hunt every useful animal, and hunt very successfully indeed. A sad result is that the game is shot out, in spite of quite careful and serious attempts to conserve it; there are too many good hunters with hungry families.

However, the Maya also have a separate realm of lore far outside the realm of laboratory biologists. Plant knowledge that does not stand scientific testing is largely confined to medicinal beliefs based on the "doctrine of signatures," probably learned from the Spanish

Figure 3. My field assistant Aurora Dzib (left) with her aunt and Bourbon Rose var. Reine Victoria.

Figure 4. **Noni** in the dooryard garden of my field assistant Felix Medina Tzuc.

(perhaps with some pre-Columbian parallels). The only one of real significance is the idea that yellow-flowering plants treat jaundice and yellow bile. Otherwise, non-empirical plant lore consists mainly of the assumption that if one plant looks like another, it very possibly treats the same condition; this causes minimal confusion, since no one trusts it very far.

A few plants are used in witchcraft and magic. Spanish Rue (*Ruta chalepensis*) and Maya **siipche'** ("tree of the god of deer," *Bunchosia* spp.) both have magic cleansing effects. In fact, both are antiseptic and the Rue (at least) is a stomachic, so the religious or magical belief is based on some empirical reality. Their use in cleansing and apotropaic ceremonies runs far beyond their antiseptic value, however. Less empirical is the belief that the **xtabay**, the demon woman of folklore, lives near Ceiba trees (*Ceiba pentandra*) and combs her hair with cactus or thorny vine fruits; these plants cause some disquiet among the fearful.

Animals are a different matter, in that they are more subject to folktale and legend. The usual minor folktales found in every rural community have their variants here: snakes that whistle, snakes that fly, snakes that jump, spirit creatures that guard magic treasure, animals (such as cats) used by witches, and so on. (No local snakes whistle or fly, but one species of fer-de-lance can strike hard enough to appear to jump.) Hummingbirds and flycatchers are used in love magic. More strictly Maya is the concept of **way** or **waay**, spirit animals. These have a pre-Columbian identity—the word occurs in Classic texts—but now the term applies largely to a Spanish belief in witches that transform themselves into goats, dogs, donkeys, and other domestic livestock. Earlier Maya beliefs in **way** associated with native animals have now almost died out among the Yucatec, though the **way kot** (eagle witch) still occurs occasionally, and were-jaguars once incurred fear. Apparently the original **way** were animal companions or counterparts to the human soul, like the **ch'ulel** of highland Maya. (The Yucatec cognate, **k'ulel**, is tantalizingly attested in early Colonial period sources, without our knowing much about what was meant.)

More serious is the belief, fast weakening but still quite strong among more traditional families, in the Lords of the Forest (**yumilk'aax**) and Lords of the Field (**yumilkool**; with other deities, these constitute the **yuntsilo'ob**, the supernatural Lords. They are sometimes called the **noojoch p'ok**, "big hats," a term originally applying to the spectacular headdresses of the ancient Maya gods). Notable among the Lords of the Forest is Siip, the god of deer, who protects deer as humans protect livestock. Other common animals have their protectors. Ceremonies called **loj** (*actas de gracia* in Spanish) provide offerings to these beings, to get their good will and thank them for benefits received. This must be done or the Lords will withhold good things and cause misfortunes. For instance, a **loj ts'oon** "ceremony of the gun" must be held when a gun has killed several—not many—animals. (The number varies with the hunter and his sense of his luck, but it is never large.) This ceremony involves considerable effort and expense, and serves as a disincentive to kill too many. The Lords can often be heard whistling or rustling; the voice of the wind in the trees is often theirs, and they are, themselves, winds (**ik'**), in some ultimate sense.

"Winds" can be a term used for any and all supernatural forces. Some animals are **k'ak'as ik'**, "evil winds," such as the **bok'ol ooch** or **chok'ol ooch** "demon opossum," which appears to be an opossum but is actually an evil spirit, known by its grumbling noise. ("It's just an old opossum. They grumble like that," says Felix Medina Tzuc.) Possibly an evil spirit, but held by some to be a real animal, is the **jijits'bej** "faints in the road," an animal so feckless that it dies when it crosses an open road. (A similar term applies to shrews in Tzeltal [Hunn 1977]. There are no shrews in Quintana Roo, and the creature has become folkloric.)

The above discussion adds to our temporary conclusions by filling out a picture of how a very complicated system, highly realistic by international bioscientific standards, can still accommodate some information that does not pass international tests. I turn to a consideration of how these types of information are maintained in the culture.

Some Determinants of Maya Views

In bioscientific terms, Maya natural history is a mix of material that is clearly true, material that is still under judgment, and supernatural material that can only be considered, by the outsider, as false, or not provable, or unscientific.

All the material on everyday use, natural history, relationships, and practical matters such as hunting is verifiable in terms of international bioscience, with the exception of some minor magical practices. Nature has joints, and both the Maya and the biologists know enough to carve nature there.

Yet, humans may be programmed with the ability to classify (Atran 1990; Berlin 1992), but biological knowledge and domains are not innate. Biological knowledge varies too much, not only from one culture to another, but from one Maya woodsperson to another. It is clearly learned, and learned with difficulty over years. Consider the case of beekeeping, important and very well cognized in the Maya case. Humans certainly did not keep bees throughout our evolutionary history. Evolution must have given us learning ability, perhaps especially keen in the realm of managing resources for food-getting, rather than particular hardwired plans (Boyd and Richerson 2005); this learning ability was, much later, applied to domesticating and keeping certain species of insects. The Maya domesticated at least two species of bees, quite independently from the European domestication of the honeybee.

Among the Maya, plant and animal lore may give one some power and prestige. Milpa skill, indeed, is a mark of true Maya status. Knowing uses for the edible but not very tasty nuts of the Ramon (*Brosimum alicastrum*, Maya **oox**) is a valued skill (Figure 5).

Such a highly respected skill as beekeeping does not help in holding power over the neighbors, but it does yield respect. Beekeeping knowledge among the Maya is explained by actual pragmatic and empirical experience in keeping bees for honey production, but it also involves religious knowledge: bees too have a god, for whom **loj** ceremonies are held. This god was formerly so important that temples in the Postclassic city of Tulum still feature his image. Other areas of Maya traditional knowledge seem also to be a mix of pragmatic knowledge and religious wisdom. Maya traditional medicine is still largely untested, but some of it, at least, is well demonstrated as useful, by laboratory work. Much of the rest would very likely pass the same tests; it works in the field. Other Maya plant knowledge is religiously constructed, such as continuing reverence for the Ceiba tree, sacred to pre-Columbian Maya religion.

In some cases, wishful thinking is part of the explanation for the magico-religious cognition. A belief that deer bezoars and eyeteeth give good luck in hunting (a Spanish-derived belief—probably with pre-Columbian equivalents) clearly makes sense in this regard. People want luck, and want it in a form that they can carry while hunting! The fact that the items in question are the most odd and striking easily portable features of the most coveted game animal probably explains why they are the items selected.

We have no way of knowing whether Mayan **loj** ceremonies (for the bee god, for hunting, for fields, for orchards) work to keep the spirits happy. On the other hand, the **loj** very clearly have the classic Durkheimian function (Durkheim 1995, orig. 1912) of getting people involved in

Figure 5. Group preparing foods from Ramon nuts. Photograph by Aurora Dzib, used with permission.

their social system and its moral code; the Maya are quite aware of this, and mention the value of getting the community together. Perhaps more important in this case, the *loj* reaffirm the values of society. This makes *loj* ceremonies potentially extremely important in animal husbandry and hunting, in agriculture, and forestry. Relevant is the fact that *loj* ceremonies have gone on as Maya changed from pagan to Catholic to Protestant, the *loj* being reinterpreted along the way. The spirit addressed is clearly less important than the real people involved.

Darwinian theory would predict good sense in activities like farming and hunting, because they are related to food; rational maximizing or "optimal foraging" is expected. This is approximately what we find among the Maya, with the ceremonies enforcing social rules and processes that are valuable to making a living. (Darwinian theory predicts less instrumentally rational behavior in other realms, such as sexual selection, but my research does not address that issue.)

The errors (in bioscientific terms) in Maya science are strictly in the realm of "hot cognition"—overreacting to values, emotions, and perceived spirit beings, and over-hoping that some form of divine intervention might help. These are partly an understandable emotional overshoot of a basically pragmatic, rational science practiced by human beings who care about their work. Such beliefs are partly a function of the universal, desperate human need to gain control over uncertainty by seeking help, justice, and caring from supernaturals. They are partly a function of the emotional involvement that always expresses itself in story, song, art, and metaphor. As anthropologists expect (following Malinowski 1948), "magical" beliefs often occur particularly in realms of high danger (hunting big game …) or high uncertainty.

Discussion

From the Chinese and Maya examples, and building on previous theories about cognition, I offer some tentative generalizations about perceptions, folk science, and science more broadly. First, culture is, among other things, a corrector. It supplies a gyroscope or cybernetic device to keep individual errors from getting out of hand. Culture must very often be a corrector instead of a distorter. However, culture can also amplify error and make everything worse. It does so in racism, even in our "scientific" society. In Chinese medicine, it does so in the basic principles abstracted from practice. In Maya animal lore, culture amplifies errors in regard to the spirits and magical beings that guard the forest and control realms over which humans have inadequate control. Ideas about power and ideas about agency (including the kind westerners call "supernatural") are critically related to this.

Second, science is real. People need to interact with the world in such a way that they may eat. This involves knowing some actual, verifiable lore. In the case of a group that is as close to the subsistence margin as the Maya of Quintana Roo, the knowledge must be very extensive and very accurate—otherwise everybody dies. I have now seen the results of three hurricanes passing through the area, and have been made very forcibly aware of just how much a Maya farmer has to know and do in order to live.

Third, science occurs everywhere and is about practice. It is not a collection of ideas generated in academic halls without reference to daily, ongoing interaction with the environment (as Sivin seems to imply). Science cannot be understood without reference to practice, whether the practice in question is beekeeping in the remote rainforest or laboratory work in the aseptic halls of a research university. However, practice includes the practice of power and authority as well as the practice of knowledge-seeking, and science often reflects the influence or outright imposition of elite or hierarchic views on a cultural group.

Fourth, science structures this practice and knowledge, by the process that Anthony Giddens calls "structuration" (Giddens 1984). Structures are dynamic, and change rapidly at need, but they are there, and important. They make the knowledge easier to remember and transmit. They make it more sensible. They link it to other knowledge.

Fifth, error is not an inevitable trap. People are not fools, and are not slaves to instinct or heuristics or the delusions of power. They can actually get pragmatic knowledge right, if they work at it long enough and have no other more appealing options. People may react from thoughtless emotion, but eventually they sometimes act in their rational self-interest. (One is sometimes tempted to say they do this only when they have exhausted all other alternatives, but that is probably too cynical.) The more extreme sociobiologists and evolutionary psychologists, who insist that humans are incapable of thinking outside the Darwinian box, are simply wrong. This applies *inter alia* to those scholars who follow the current fad of claiming that "savages" are necessarily ecologically wasteful and destructive, and also to those who hold that traditional Indigenous people live "in harmony with nature." The Maya, for one example, are far from the cartoon "savages" of the films *Avatar* and *Apocalypto*. They do not live in some sort of New Age paradise, and indeed they overhunt game animals seriously, but they do have an attitude toward animals that is very different from—and much more conserving than—that of many human groups. Humans, traditional or not, are sometimes good managers, sometimes not.

Sixth, the one major domain of dubious lore in Maya ethnoscience—the religious and ceremonial aspect—raises another key point: rational self-interest does not work without emotional and social involvement (Hume 1984; Milton 2002). Humans need some positive affect—some real "affection"—to make rationality work. They also need ongoing social construction and re-construction of such emotion (as well as of the rest of the knowledge). People may be expected to have basically accurate knowledge of matters like getting food and making a living. At the other extreme, knowledge of supernatural beings is, by definition, a matter of guesswork and inference, and is maximally available for wishful thinking and collective representation. In between are challenging systems like medicine. The medical beliefs of a given culture (even of modern international biomedical culture) are always a crazy-quilt of empirically proven material and wildly offbeat material that must be analyzed on its own terms.

Marvin Harris (1968) advocated a "research strategy" of starting with the most down-to-earth, practical, biologically grounded explanations, and working toward more interpretive or spiritual or psychological explanations as necessity directs. A Marvin Harris-type "research strategy" (Harris 1968) can be appropriate in studying traditional knowledge. One would first (following Harris) see if a particular item or body of knowledge could be explained by its being accurate and directly useful. If it were shown to be inaccurate in bioscientific terms, or otherwise difficult to explain by immediate utility, one would next seek out cold-cognitive explanations. If these were inadequate, one would go to hot cognition: self-interest, wishful thinking, collective representation of the social system, and last of all, naked politics. I put Foucauldian explanations last *not* because they are least important, least influential, or least salient, but only because they seem tactically easiest to look at as a final step. The Foucauldian explanation tells us why socially constructed knowledge takes the exact final shape it has on the ground.

Other things being equal, the clearer and more direct the feedback from reality, the more accurate will be the knowledge (in modern as in traditional systems). Distortion will be progressively greater as the possibility of accurate knowledge lessens. But even the clearest and most direct feedback is often insufficient to dislodge entrenched ideas that serve the self-interest of some powerful group, be it the ruling class or only the senior geologists who resisted continental drift long after it was proved to occur.

A tendency to move from supernatural to natural explanations for illness seems widespread in history. This follows Weber's idea of "disenchantment" (Weber 1948): the spirituality of traditional worldviews becomes progressively reduced by modernization. Religious or spiritual views on medicine appear when science has nothing dramatically successful to offer. As science develops, the role of religion can be expected to shrink (Weber 1948). Either way, views on illness show a human need to systematize the world, and, more specifically, a desperate need to make "sense" of illness (Kleinman 1980). When faced with crisis, people feel they have to do *something*, or at least that they understand what is happening to them. Failing that, people will try anything that looks as if it fits with other knowledge (nature as model, body as microcosm). Again, we come back to the classic anthropological notion that supernaturals are invoked when naturals fail.

Traditional belief systems do not necessarily make the same distinctions between science and religion that characterize contemporary European discourse. (The conflict between "religion" and "science," for instance, is a 19th-century invention; earlier scientists tended to think they were doing God's work finding out his will for the universe—this was true, for instance, of Boyle and Newton. [See Bowler and Morus 2005; Gould 1999].) For one well-treated example, Zapotec science is based partly on principles that bioscientists would call "supernatural," but that the Zapotecs accept as natural. Partly because of this "supernatural" grounding, Zapotec knowledge enjoins certain ways of dealing with the world. By outsider standards, some of these would be considered "factual," others "moral" and "ethical" (Gonzalez 2001). The Zapotec do not see these as separate. Similarly, Yucatec Maya worldviews are derived from a set of assumptions about the world that include emotional involvement and strong ethical teachings. The world is based on non-neutral assumptions; its reality demands that people maintain the forest, keep trails clean, kill nothing unnecessarily, and waste nothing. Amadeo Rea's Oodham friends would recognize all of this, and I have recently studied similar worldviews in Madagascar and Australia.

What seems shared and basic in these cases is a very long cultural record of involvement with the landscape and *all* its natural parts—rocks, soils, biota, winds, waters (see, again, Ingold 2000). When one depends on virtually every plant and animal, or at least on hundreds of species, one gets a comprehensive, totalizing knowledge of the landscape. Every rock, soil, plant, and animal is taken *seriously*. None is cognitively rejected. All are seen as part of a total picture—not a static one, but a dynamic one, with both cyclic and irreversible processes always going on. When one takes something seriously, one cannot help feeling emotional concern for it. Normally, this must be expressed through taking some responsibility for the thing in question. One must be interested in it. One must help, protect, or support it if it is a positive contributor to one's material or psychological welfare. Conversely, one cannot avoid fearing and loathing it if it is a threat. This functional cultural focus on natural things makes those natural things (or correlates of them) likely focus for supernatural attention as well.

Nothing could be more different from the modern American view of nature, at least as exemplified by my students and neighbors. Class questionnaires done in the early 2000's by Kimberly Kirner and myself in introductory anthropology classes revealed that students (at least at the University of California, Riverside) rarely know the names of even five native plants or animals. Similar to Gail Wagner's (2008) finding that South Carolina college students could only name 1.9 native vines, 1.7 native wildflowers or weeds, and 1.4 grasses correctly, Hendrick's and my work with Californians finds that our locals simply do not see our native plants or animals. They do not notice bird song, admittedly hard to hear over the roar of traffic. Some even actively reject having attention drawn to such phenomena. They live in a world of machines—internal combustion engines and electronic devices. They are exquisitely attuned to these and are emotionally highly involved with them.

The difference in awareness, openness, and emotional involvement makes religious representation of the landscape natural—even inevitable—for traditional rural people. Modern southern Californians are not quite religious about their machines, but sometimes their passion verges on supernatural representation. People name, talk to, and humanize their cars and computers. They see these as individuals with something like life and will. At the very least, they are protective and emotionally involved with these machines in a way similar to the psychological involvement that the Maya have with their crops and animals. Clearly, economic involvement (Marx and Engels would say involvement through labor) drives wider phenomenological involvement.

In short, people who are required to know about all aspects of their environment, and who must be open to learning more, and who must also develop moral codes for managing their environment, will develop intense emotional components to their knowledge. This is all a part of taking the world seriously. All this will, in turn, be collectively represented (Durkheim 1995) in supernatural terms.

There is thus some truth to the old cliché that "the Indians" live in a religious or spiritual world, but that cliché misses the point, which is that "the Indians" live in a world about which they know—and must know—a very large amount of factual information, and toward which they have an intensely ethical stance. The detailed factual knowledge and the moral philosophy are not separable from each other, or from the supernatural beliefs. Moral rules are given by the gods, or spirits, or nature personified in some way; the problem of deducing an "is" from an "ought" is resolved by seeing the "oughts" as natural laws, part of the "ises."

This does not mean that Native Americans always live by their highest ethical principles, any more than anyone else does. The Maya I know are deeply committed to the morality of not overhunting—not killing more than they need—but they have shot out the game in the Yucatan Peninsula. The gap between morality and performance may be left for another venue (Anderson and Medina Tzuc 2005). What matters in the present context is an epistomological claim: Native American systems of environmental thought are based on an experiential or phenomenological substrate that is very different from "religion" or "science" as the modern Western world knows them, and that cuts across the western philosophical distinction between "is" and "ought."

Like science, folk environmental aesthetics can only be understood as the product of constant interaction with the environment, and the cultural construction of individual and community experiences derived from this.

Until recently, most social scientists seemed to believe that people were rational (in at least some sense), and that error was functional on the rare occasions when it occurred. Today, the pendulum has swung far to the other extreme, and one is more apt to encounter the belief that there is no truth and that all "knowledge" is arbitrary social construction. Both these views are inadequate. People seek truth, but they fall into "inevitable illusions" (Piatelli 1994). The wonder is that science, including folk science, survives and flourishes. But, somehow, it does.

Notes

1. The truth is that modern science has a long history of persistent errors that lasted far longer than they rationally should have done. A large percentage of the science I learned as an undergraduate is now not only disproved, but is mentioned only to get a cheap laugh in a beginning class! Surely, much of what we solemnly teach as fact today will be up the same creek in 40 more years.

2. The same sort of heuristic, *mutatis mutandis*, applies to studies of other mental realms, such as aesthetics. Taste in art has been regarded in Foucauldian terms as merely a social construction to assert power—snobbism, in short (Bourdieu 1979). This view was subjected to a blistering critique by Elster (1981), who argued not only that there was much more to art than that, but that the naïve functionalism of Bourdieu was not only inadequate for the purpose but inadequate for social science, because it left out critical questions of intention, consciousness, and human judgment in general. It is clear that an adequate account of human taste would have to include, at the very least: inborn human preferences for certain general types of patterns and scenes (Barkow, Cosmides and Tooby 1992), cultural history with all its contingencies and borrowings, ethnic relations, resistance (Scott 1998), and, yes, snobbism and its uses in asserting power and control. It would, however, also need to include serious inquiry into human emotional experience in all its richness, and why humans find, for example, so much in Shakespeare and Mozart, so much in forests and mountains, and so much in bird song and flowers. We cannot understand traditional cultures without some attention to the universality of such concerns. More recently, a steady rise in attention to aesthetics in ecological anthropology can be observed, for instance in the Australian literature (e.g., Myers 2002, Rose 2000) as well as in research on Southwestern peoples (e.g., Evers and Molina 1987). It is clear that aesthetic experience is closely linked with other attitudes toward landscape and environment, including conservation.

3. The Maya would appreciate and agree with the Elizabethan English view of hunting: "There is a saying...that he cannot be a gentleman which loveth not...hunting, which I have heard old woodmen...well allow...[and] that he cannot be a gentleman which loveth not a dog."—Anon., *The Institucion of a Gentleman*, 1568, quoted in Almond (2003:33). Indeed, not only do Mayans hold similar hunting views to English gentlemen, but Maya heads of households are always addressed as Don and Doña, as proper gentlefolk.

Acknowledgements

Amadeo Rea was a pioneer in studying how people relate to their environments, not only economically and religiously, but also artistically and poetically. His sensitive descriptions of Oodham myth, ritual, poetry, and folklore take us into a realm of full experience of nature, in which emotional reactions and interactions are culturally constructed in art and song. Few ethnobiologists or students of traditional knowledge had ventured into this area before (though Boas, among others, indicated the way long ago). Amadeo Rea's works on Oodham natural knowledge are among the very few studies of knowledge that comprehensively present all the above considerations, and that give accounts of knowledge that are adequate for the sort of analysis I am advocating in this paper. In fact, much of my approach was developed through learning from Dr.

Rea and his books. His works deserve to become classics, and his wise and humane approach to knowledge needs to be shared.

Thanks, first of all, to the Maya of west central Quintana Roo, especially Felix Medina Tzuc, Jacinto Cauich, Pastor Valdez, and Aurora Dzib Xihum de Cen; also to my long-suffering family; to the University of California, Riverside, and the Sostenibilidad Maya project, for funding and other support; to Betty Faust for all manner of cooperation; and to many others who made this work possible; and to Dana Lepofsky and Marsha Quinlan for enormous editorial effort. Thanks also to Peter Gardner, Kimberly Hedrick, and David Kronenfeld for long and animated discussion of this paper.

References Cited

Abram, David. 1996   *The Spell of the Sensuous.* Pantheon, New York.

Almond, Richard. 2003   *Medieval Hunting.* Sutton Publishing, Thrupp, UK.

Anderson, E.N. 1972   *Studies on Hong Kong's Boat People.* Orient Cultural Service, Taipei.

Anderson, E.N. 1996   *Ecologies of the Heart.* Oxford University Press, New York.

Anderson, E.N. 2003   *Those Who Bring the Flowers.* ECOSUR, Chetumal, QR.

Anderson, E.N. 2005   *Political Ecology in a Yuctec Maya Community.* University of Arizona Press, Tucson.

Anderson, E.N., and Felix Medina Tzuc. 2005   *Animals and the Maya in Southeast Mexico.* University of Arizona Press, Tucson.

Andrews Heath de Zapata, Dorothy. 1979   *El libro del Judio: Medicina domestica.* Dorothy Andrews Heath de Zapata, Mérida, Mexico.

Ankli, Anita. 2000   Yucatec Mayan Medicinal Plants: Ethnobotany, Biological Evalutation, and Phytochemical Study of *Crossopetalum gaumeri.* Thesis, Doctor of Natural Sciences, Swiss Federal Institute of Technology, Zurich, Switzerland.

Arzápalo Marín, Ramón. 1995   *Calepino de Motul.* Universidad Autónoma de México, Mexico City.

Atran, Scott. 1990   *Cognitive Foundations of Natural History.* Cambridge University Press, Cambridge.

Atran, Scott. 1993   Itza Maya Tropical Agro-Forestry. *Current Anthropology* 34:633–700.

Atran, Scott. 1999   Itzaj Maya Folkbiological Taxonomy: Cognitive Universals and Cultural Particulars. In *Folkbiology*, eds. Douglas L. Medin and Scott Atran, pp. 119–204. MIT, Cambridge, MA.

Atran, Scott. 2002   *In Gods We Trust: The Evolutionary Landscape of Religion.* Oxford University Press, New York.

Bacon, Francis. 1901 (orig. ca. 1600)   *Novum Organum.* Ed. by Joseph Devey. P.F. Collier, New York.

Barkow, Jerome H., Leda Cosmides, and John Tooby. 1992 *The Adapted Mind.* Oxford University Press, New York.

Barrera, Alfredo, and Alfredo Barrera Vásquez. 1983 *El Libro del Judío.* Instituto Nacional de Investigaciones sobre Recursos Bioticos, Xalapa, Veracruz.

Beales, Peter. 1985 *Classic Roses.* Holt, Rinehart and Winston, New York.

Berlin, Brent. 1992 *Ethnobiological Classification: Principles of Categorization of Plants and Animals in Traditional Societies.* Princeton University Press, Princeton.

Berlin, Brent, Dennis Breedlove, and Peter Raven. 1974 *Principles of Tzeltal Plant Classification.* Academic Press, New York.

Blunt, Wilfred, and Sandra Raphael. 1979 *The Illustrated Herbal.* Thames and Hudson, New York.

Bourdieu, Pierre. 1979 *La distinction.* Editions de Minuit, Paris.

Bowler, Peter J., and Iwan Rhys Morus. 2005 *Making Modern Science: A Historical Survey.* University of Chicago Press, Chicago.

Boyd, Robert, and Peter J. Richerson. 2005 *The Origin and Evolution of Cultures.* Oxford University Press, New York.

Brook, Timothy. 2010 *The Trouble Empire: China in the Yuan and Ming Dynasties.* Harvard University Press, Cambridge, MA.

Brown, Cecil H. 1994 Lexical Acculturation in Native American Languages. *Current Anthropology* 35:95–117.

Daly, Martin, and Margo Wilson. 1996 Violence Against Stepchildren. *Current Directions in Psychological Science* 5:77–81.

Damasio, Antonio. 1994 *Descartes' Error.* G. P. Putnam's Sons, New York.

De Bray, Lys. 1989 *The Art of Botanical Illustration.* Wellfleet Press, Secaucus, NJ.

Durkheim, Emile. 1995 *The Elementary Forms of the Religious Life.* Translated by Karen Fields. Free Press, New York.

Eaton, S. Boyd, Melvin Konner, and Marjorie Shostak. 1988 Stone Agers in the Fast Lane: Chronic Degenerative Diseases in Evolutionary Perspective. *The American Journal of Medicine* 84:739–749.

Elster, Jon. 1981 Snobs. *London Review of Books,* 3(20):10–12.

Elster, Jon. 1999 *Alchemies of the Mind: Rationality and the Emotions.* University of Chicago Press, Chicago.

Evers, Larry, and Felipe S. Molina. 1987 *Yaqui Deer Songs: Maso Bwikam. A Native American Poetry.* University of Arizona Press, Tucson.

Foucault, Michel. 1965 *Madness and Civilization.* Random House, New York.

Foucault, Michel. 1970 *The Order of Things.* Random House, New York.

Frank, Robert. 1988 *Passions within Reason.* Harvard University Press, Cambridge, MA.

Giddens, Anthony. 1984 *The Constitution of Society.* University of California Press, Berkeley.

Gigerenzer, Gerd. 2002 *Adaptive Thinking: Rationality in the Real World.* Oxford University Press, New York.

Gigerenzer, Gerd, Peter Todd, and the ABC Working Group. 1999 *Simple Heuristics That Make Us Smart.* Oxford University Press, New York.

Gonzalez, Roberto. 2001 *Zapotec Science.* University of Texas Press, Austin, TX.

Gould, Richard A. 1969 *Yiwara: Foragers of the Australian Desert.* Scribners, New York.

Gould, Stephen Jay. 1981 *The Mismeasure of Man.* W. W. Norton, New York.

Gould, Stephen Jay. 1999 *Rocks of Ages: Science and Religion in the Fullness of Life.* Ballantine, New York.

Goulet, Jean-Guy. 1998 *Ways of Knowing.* University of Nebraska Press, Lincoln.

Gubler, Ruth. 2005 *An Eighteenth-Century Herbal: Book of Very Reliable Remedies for Curing Various Ailments with Well-Proven and Beneficial Plants from This Province of Yucatan.* Labyrinthos, Lancaster, CA.

Hacking, Ian. 1999 *The Social Construction of What?* Harvard University Press, Cambridge, MA.

Harris, Marvin. 1968 *The Rise of Anthropological Theory.* Thomas Crowell, New York.

Hoekstra, Hopi E., and Trevor Price. 2004 Parallel Evolution Is in the Genes. *Science* 303:1779–1781.

Hume, David. 1984 *A Treatiste on Human Nature.* (Orig. 1739–1740.) Ed. Ernest Mossner. Penguin, London.

Hunn, Eugene. 1977 *Tzeltal Folk Zoology.* Academic Press, New York.

Hunn, Eugene. 1990 *N'Chi-Wana, the Big River.* University of Washington Press, Seattle.

Hunn, Eugene. 2008 *A Zapotec Natural History: Trees, Herbs, and Flowers, Birds, Beasts and Bugs in the Life of San Juan Gbëë.* University of Arizona Press, Tucson.

Ingold, Tim. 2000 *The Perception of the Environment: Essays in Livelihood, Dwelling and Skill.* Routledge, London.

Istomin, Kirill V., and Mark J. Dwyer. 2009 Finding the Way: A Critical Discussion of Anthropological Theories of Human Spatial Orientation with Reference to Reindeer Herders of Northeastern Europe and Western Siberia. *Current Anthropology* 50:29–50.

Kahneman, Daniel. 2011 *Thinking, Fast and Slow.* Farrar, Straus and Giroux, New York.

Kahneman, Daniel, Paul Slovic, and Amos Tversky. 1982 *Judgment Under Uncertainty: Heuristics and Biases.* Cambridge University Press, Cambridge, UK.

Kant, Immanuel. 1978 *Anthropology from a Pragmatic Point of View.* (Ger. Orig. 1798.) Translated by Victor Lyle Dowdell. Southern Illinois University Press, Carbondale, IL.

Kitcher, Philip. 1993 *The Advancement of Science.* Oxford University Press, New York.

Kitcher, Philip. 2001 Battling the Undead: How (and How Not) to Avoid Genetic Determinism. In *Thinking about Evolution: Historical, Philosophical, and Political Perspectives,* eds. Rama S. Singh, Costas B. Krimbas, Diane B. Paul, and John Beatty, pp. 396–415. Cambridge University Press, Cambridge, UK.

Kleinman, Arthur. 1980   *Patients and Healers in the Context of Culture*. University of California Press, Berkeley.

Kuhn, Thomas. 1962   *The Structure of Scientific Revolutions*. University of Chicago Press, Chicago.

Latour, Bruno. 2005   *The Politics of Nature*. Harvard University Press, Cambridge, MA.

Laudan, Larry. 1996   *Beyond Positivism and Relativism*. Westview, Boulder, CO.

Levi-Strauss, Claude. 1962   *La Pensee sauvage*. Plon, Paris.

Levi-Strauss, Claude. 1963   *Structural Anthropology*. Basic Books, New York.

Locke, John. 1975   *An Essay Concerning Human Understanding*. (Orig. 1697.) Ed. Peter Niddich. Oxford University Press, Oxford.

Malinowski, Bronislaw. 1926   *Myth in Primitive Psychology*. W. W. Norton, New York.

Malinowski, Bronislaw. 1948   *Magic, Science and Religion*. Free Press, Glencoe, IL.

Marcus, George E. 2002   *The Sentimental Citizen: Emotion in Democratic Politics*. Pennsylvania State University Press, University Park, PA.

Mencken, H.L. 1920   The Divine Afflatus. In *Prejudices*, second series, pp. 155–179. Alfred A. Knopf, New York.

Milton, Kay. 2002   *Loving Nature*. Routledge, London.

Morphy, Howard. 1998   *Aboriginal Art*. Phaedon, New York.

Myers, Fred. 2002   *Painting Culture: The Making of an Aboriginal High Art*. Duke University Press, Durham, NC.

Nisbett, Richard, and Lee Ross. 1980   *Human Inference*. Prentice-Hall, Engelwood Cliffs, NJ.

Nussbaum, Martha. 2001   *Upheavals of Thought*. Cambridge University Press, Cambridge.

Oreskes, Naomi. 1993   *The Rejection of Continental Drift*. Oxford University Press, New York.

Oreskes, Naomi, and Erik Conway. 2010   *Merchants of Doubt*. Bloomsbury Press, New York.

Piatelli, Massimo. 1994   *Inevitable Illusions*. Viking, New York.

Pinker, Stephen. 2002   *The Blank Slate: The Modern Denial of Human Nature*. Penguin, New York.

Popper, Karl. 1959   *The Logic of Scientific Discovery*. Hutchinson, London.

Radin, Paul. 1927   *Primitive Man as Philosopher*. Appleton, New York.

Radin, Paul. 1957   *Primitive Religion*. 2nd ed. Dover, New York.

Rea, Amadeo M. 1997   *At the Desert's Green Edge: An Ethnobotany of the Gila River Pima*. University of Arizona Press, Tucson.

Rea, Amadeo M. 1998   *Folk Mammalogy of the Northern Pimans*. University of Arizona Press, Tucson.

Rea, Amadeo M. 2007 *Wings in the Desert: A Folk Ornithology of the Northern Pimans.* University of Arizona Press, Tucson.

Redfield, Robert, and Alfonso Villa Rojas. 1934 *Chan Kom, a Maya Village.* University of Chicago Press, Chicago.

Restall, Matthew. 2004 Maya Ethnogenesis. *Journal of Latin American Anthropology* 9:64–89.

Rose, Deborah. 2000 *Dingo Makes Us Human: Life and Land in an Australian Aboriginal Culture.* Cambridge University Press, New York.

Rose, Deborah. 2005 An Indigenous Philosophical Ecology. *Australian Journal of Anthropology* 16:294–305.

Scott, James. 1990 *Domination and the Arts of Resistance.* Yale University Press, New Haven.

Sharp, Henry. 2001 *Loon.* University of Nebraska Press, Lincoln.

Simon, Herbert. 1957 *Models of Man.* Wiley, New York.

Sivin, Nathan. 2000 Editor's Introduction. In Joseph Needham and Lu Gwei-Djen, *Science and Civilisation in China, Vol. 6, Biology and Bioloigcal Technology, Part IV: Medicine,* ed. Nathan Sivin, pp. 1–37. Cambridge University Press, Cambridge.

Skinner, B.F. 1960 *Science and Human Nature.* MacMillan, New York.

Smith, Euclid O. 2002 *When Culture and Biology Collide.* Rutgers University Press, New Brunswick, NJ.

Stets, Jan, and Jon Turner, eds. 2006 *Handbook of the Sociology of Emotions.* Springer, New York.

Taylor, Shelley. 1989 *Positive Illusions.* Basic Books, New York.

Tversky, Amos. 1977 Features of Similarity. *Psychological Review* 84:327–352.

Tylor, Edward. 1871 *Primitive Culture, Researches into the Development of Mythology, Philosophy, Religion, Language, Art and Custom.* John Murray, London.

Wagner, Gail E. 2008 Botanical Knowledge of a Group of College Students in South Carolina, U.S.A. *Ethnobotany Research & Applications* 6:443–458.

Wallace, Anthony F. C. 1970 *Culture and Personality.* Random House, New York.

Westen, Drew. 2007 *The Political Brain: The Role of Emotion in Deciding the Fate of the Nation.* PublicAffairs, New York.

Wolpert, Lewis. 1993 *The Unnatural Nature of Science.* Harvard University Press, Cambridge, MA.

Pre-Columbian Agaves: Living Plants Linking an Ancient Past in Arizona

Wendy C. Hodgson[†]

Abstract

Mesoamerican cultures have long used members of the genus *Agave* for food, fiber, beverage and numerous other purposes. Several agaves were pre-Columbian cultivars and their distributions reflected their movement by humans. As with other New World cultigens, cultivation of agaves is correlated with clonal reproduction and sterility. *Agave murpheyi, A. delamateri, A. phillipsiana, A. verdensis,* and *A. yavapaiensis* are pre-Columbian agave domesticates that occur in Arizona. These plants are a direct link to plants once farmed by Hohokam and other groups, possessing attributes that would be beneficial to farmers. The plants and their favored characters have persisted for centuries via vegetative reproduction. Their origins are unknown, but plants may have originated in northern Mexico, having been dispersed northward via trade or migration. In addition, evidence suggests that preColumbian farmers grew more than one type of agave at a site. Morphological, cytological, ecological, ethnobotanical, archaeological and molecular studies are instrumental in answering a number of questions.

Introduction

The genus *Agave* (Agavaceae) is composed of over 200 species native to arid and semiarid regions of the Americas with a center of diversity in central Mexico (García-Mendoza 2002). Agaves have been of great economic and social importance for the people of Mesoamerica and arid America (Colunga-GarcíaMarín and May-Pat 1993), providing important sources of food, fiber and beverage. In Yucatan, Mexico, people use every part of wild and cultivated variants of agaves for 40 different purposes, and it is suspected that many more uses were lost or not recorded (Colunga-GarcíaMarín and May-Pat 1993). Agaves have a rich history with humans as these plants have been cultivated in Mexico from at least the Late Preclassic through the Postclassic Period (400 B.C.–A.D. 1500) (Zizumbo-Villarreal et al. 2009). Howard Scott Gentry, prominent botanist and world authority on the genus *Agave*, stated that agaves were seminal to early agricultural developments in Mexico, calling the human-agave relationship a "symbiosis" (Gentry 1982) because people benefitted from the various

† Desert Botanical Garden, 1201 N. Galvin Parkway, Phoenix, AZ 85008 USA [whodgson@dbg.org]

Agave products and in return tended and dispersed *Agave* propagules (Hodgson and Saly-won 2012). Within the Southwest, plants were also used for making paper, soap, shampoos, medicines, armed fences, and fermented beverages, as well as for use in construction and ceremonial activities, and as ornamentals (Bruman 2000; Callen 1965; Castetter et al. 1938; Gentry 1982; Hodgson 2001a). However, their close symbiotic relationship in the Southwest was never fully recognized or appreciated until recently.

This chapter provides a brief overview of the genus *Agave*, its importance to cultures, and of research identifying the possibility of agave cultivation in the American Southwest highlighting exciting recent research that focuses on five agave pre-Columbian domesticates in Arizona. These five agave species are still found in the modern landscape, having persisted for centuries via vegetative reproduction. As a result of these findings, Arizona is identified as an area of intense agave pre-Columbian cultivation.

The Genus Agave

The genus *Agave* is the largest of nine genera in a strictly American family Agavaceae, which occurs from southern Canada south to South America. *Agave* is a young genus, believed to have originated approximately 10 million years ago (Good-Avila et al. 2006). Its geographic center of origin is in Mexico from which populations spread into the American Southwest and Florida south into the Caribbean Islands, and to Central America and tropical South America. Although the vast majority of species are found in Mexico, the genus has been very successful in colonizing arid and semi-arid regions, including Arizona. Agaves occur from sea level to 2450 meters (8000 ft) in elevation and thrive on well-drained, non-alkaline soils, particularly those that are limestone or igneous in origin (Gentry 1972). The tolerance for freezing and drought is varied amongst species, with some enduring as little rainfall as thirteen to zero centimeters (5 to 0 in) in a year, to over 76 centimeters (30 in) in the mountains where they may also experience snowfall.

Agaves have short, thick stems that are usually shorter than the terminal bud, or apical meristem (Figure 1). They can be as small as 10 cm (4 in) tall or as large as 2-½ meters (8 ft) or more, their size generally decreasing the more northerly the latitude. Agave leaves are arranged in a rosette, are succulent, fibrous, variously shaped, and have margins armed with teeth or fibers or have neither. Agaves are usually monocarpic perennials that spend years to mature, producing a flowering stalk from the apical meristem after which the plant dies. Few species are polycarpic, that is, plants produce stalks from leaf axils more than once and do not die. Many species are able to reproduce by vegetative and/or sexual means, or solely vegetatively or sexually. Sexual reproduction results in the formation of seeds with enhanced genetic variability and the resulting offspring are genetically different to some degree from parent plants. Vegetative reproduction in agaves can result in the formation of small plants

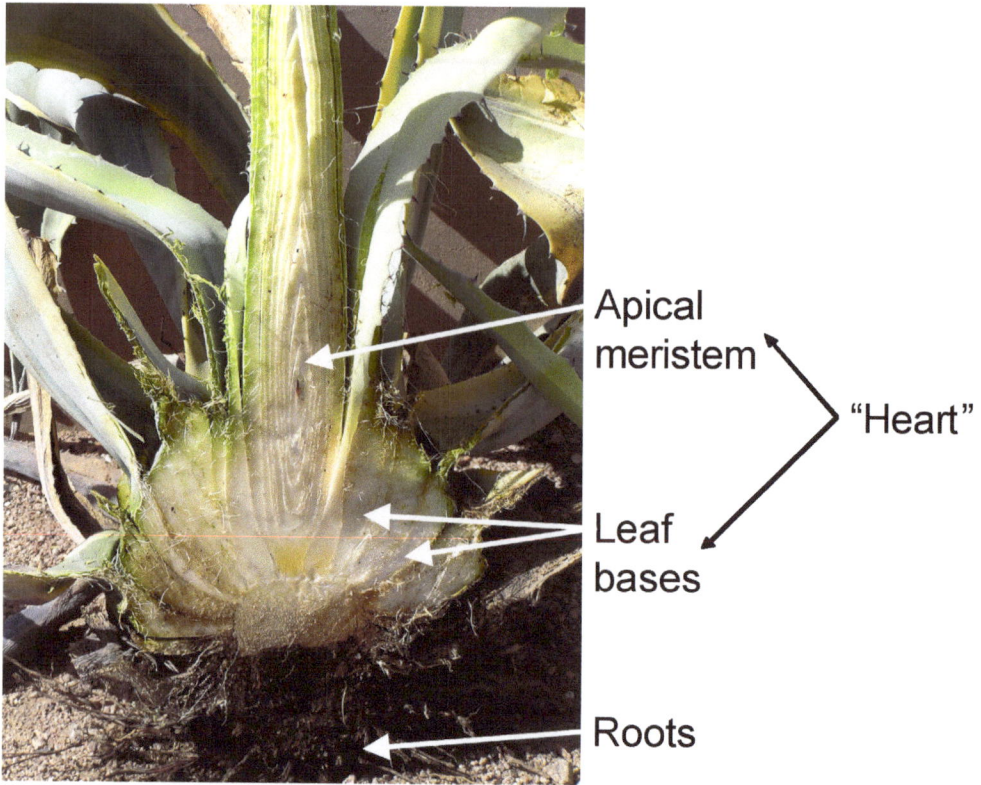

Figure 1. Cross section of stem and leaves showing apical meristem, leaf bases, "heart" and roots.

from rhizomes ("pups, offsets"), or from the inflorescence ("bulbils, hijos"). Plants resulting from vegetative reproduction are usually genetically identical or nearly identical to the parent plant and are described as being clonal, with the plants existing in clones.

Once agaves reach maturity, their carbohydrate-rich stem develops the flowering stalk from its apical meristem, a process that spans a relatively short amount of time. Carbohydrates that are synthesized in the leaves accumulate in the stem during the maturation process, and with water and other nutrients, provide resources necessary for the production of the flower stalk (Nobel 1977). It has been shown that as the flower stalk of *A. angustifolia* Haw. elongates, the stem and stalk become more fibrous and less carbohydrate-rich (Colunga-GarcíaMarín et al. 1993). The main carbohydrates stored are different types of fructans, including the recently discovered agavin (López et al. 2003). Fructans are beneficial to plants as they can help protect against dehydration imposed by drought or freezing (Wiemken et al. 1996) and are beneficial to human health (Kaur and Gupta 2002; López et al. 2003; Schneeman 1999). Agave stems and leaves may also have bitter-tasting soapy molecules called sapogenins, whose presence is an excellent defense mechanism against herbivory. The higher the amount of sapogenins, the more bitter the taste.

The flower stalks can be small and only a meter tall (3 ft) or massive, reaching heights of 10 or more meters (30 ft). Flowers are usually yellow but can range from white to maroon-red. Most species are believed to be out-crossers, that is, they require pollen from other plants of the same species for successful fertilization although many may accept their own pollen towards the end of their flowering period. Hybridization between different species is not uncommon if their distribution overlaps. Fruits, when present, are capsules that house many flat, black seeds that are dispersed by wind.

Agaves are extremely important economically, providing food, fiber, and nutritious beverages to indigenous people as well as distilled liquors to modern agave consumers. Tequila comes mainly from *A. tequilana* Weber "var. azul" while *A. angustifolia* provides much of the mescal throughout Mexico (Reveal and Hodgson 2001). Some are important fiber producing agaves, including *A. sisalana* Perrine and forms of *A. angustifolia,* in a world wide industry and/or are used as ornamentals in such distant places as Nepal and various countries in Africa. Many agaves were pre-Columbian cultivars, their distributions and morphology the result of selection and distribution by humans. A number of agaves, including *Agave americana* L. (with exception of ssp. *protoamericana* Gentry), *A. desmettiana* Jacobi, *A. sialana, A. neglecta* Small, *A. weberi* Cels ex Poisson, *A. murpheyi* Gibson, *A. delamateri* Hodgson & Slauson, *A. phillipsiana* Hodgson, *A. applanata* Koch ex Jacobi, *A. karatto* Mill., *A. decipiens* Baker, *A. verdensis* Hodgson & Salywon, and *A. yavapaiensis* Hodgson & Salywon may all be ancient cultivars that have their origins in Latin America or the Caribbean. Cultivation of ancient New World cultigens is correlated with clonal reproduction and sexual sterility, in that no seed is produced from sexual reproduction. As importantly, vegetative reproduction perpetuated favorable characteristics selected by farmers and allowed agaves to persist for over seven hundred years.

Despite agaves' importance for multiple uses, there are only limited data denoting the kinds of agaves pre-and post-Columbian farmers grew at any one time (Colunga-García-Marín and May-Pat 1993); such was the case for the southwestern U.S. and northern Mexico until recent studies.

Agaves as Food

Those who had access to agaves, whether it was through harvesting from the field or through trade, utilized these multipurpose plants. Pre-Columbian, historic and even present-day peoples highly valued agaves for their source of sweet, flavorful food. Harvesting and processing agaves was a complex process requiring time and energy. Not all agaves are edible, their edibility depending on their sapogenin content and other toxic compounds (Gentry 1982). In addition, only those agaves that showed signs of flowering were generally harvested because of the plant's ability to store carbohydrates in the stem and leaf bases for the production of its flowering stalk. In comparison, non-flowering agaves are not sweet, due to a far less amount of stored carbohydrates. Thus, harvesters needed to know not only what kinds of agave were edible, but when to harvest the plants. Mature agaves that show signs of flowering will have larger, more bulbous stems and innermost leaves that splay outward, becoming more bract-like, rather than forming the tight conical bud characteristic of the innermost leaves of immature agaves.

Agaves were traditionally pit-baked by many cultures, allowing the breakdown and digestion of their complex fructans. The tender young flower stalk or base of the stalk was eaten raw, roasted or baked (Hodgson 2001a). However, it was the stem (also called the "heart" or "head" in the U.S., and *cabeza* by Mexico inhabitants) of a soon-to-flower agave that was the preferred food once roasted or baked (Figure 1).

Preparing agave progressed from roasting the stalks or hearts atop a fire to baking many hearts in rock-lined pits (Colunga-GarcíaMarín and Zizumbo-Villarreal 2006; Figure 2). Baking the hearts in pits enabled processing en masse and the generation of surplus, as well as facilitating social interactions and exchange. The sweeter and less fibrous baked agave heart and the attached sweet but more fibrous leaf bases (Figure 3) were eaten on the spot or stored indefinitely after the cooked material was cut and pounded into thin sheets, cakes or loaves and quickly dried to minimize spoilage (Hodgson 2001a).

Long term, moist heating, such as boiling in water or pit-baking, will hydrolyze the more complex carbohydrate fructan into oligofructose and the even more easily digested and exceedingly sweet fructose (Schneeman 1999). In arid regions, where water availability is limited, pit baking using rock-lined pits was a superb method to make edible the stored carbohydrates (mostly fructans) within the agave stem and leaf bases.

Development of Agave for Subsistence

Before the development of agriculture, agave represented a basic food source for gathering in arid and semi-arid areas from central Mexico north to central Arizona (Colunga-García-Marín and Zizumbo-Villarreal 2006). Agaves have been used for food since at least 11,000 years ago (Callen 1965; Smith 1965), the peduncles and heads pit-baked and used in the same way since 9000 B.C. (Callen 1965; Smith 1986). Agaves formed the main part of the diet in cultures at least from 5200 B.C. to A.D. 1540 in arid and semiarid regions of Mexico (Callen 1965) and were the basic food source to which other plants, such as maize, beans and squash were eventually added (Colunga-GarcíaMarín and Zizumbo-Villarreal 2006).

Agaves are excellent candidates for cultivation in arid areas and many do well in soils too thin or mineral-deficient for other more water or nutrient-loving crops such as maize, beans or squash. Many agave species can reproduce via vegetative means through the production of pups and bulbils from the rhizomes and inflorescence shoots, re-

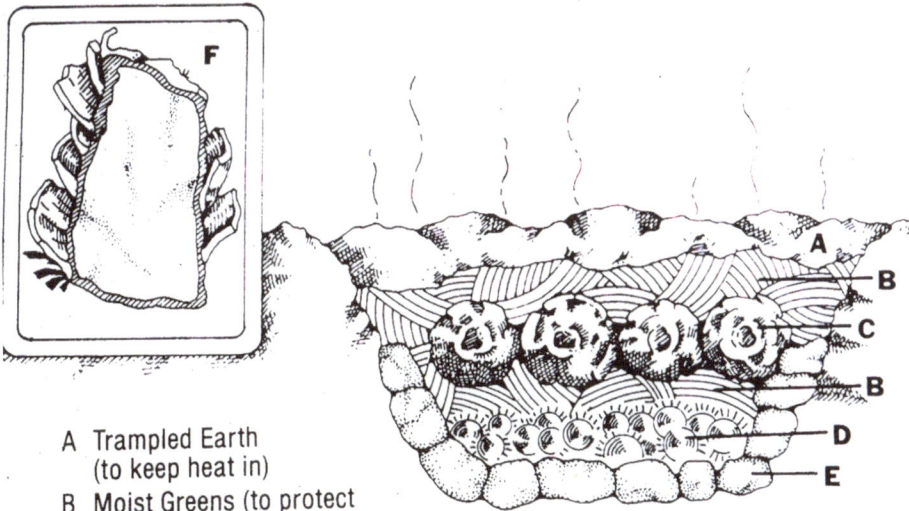

A Trampled Earth
   (to keep heat in)
B Moist Greens (to protect
   and steam hearts)
C Agave Hearts
D Coals
E Rocks (for retaining heat)
F Section of Cooked Heart

B.

Figure 2. A. Agave hearts in coals before being covered. B. Cross-section of an agave roasting pit. Line drawing courtesy of Desert Botanical Garden.

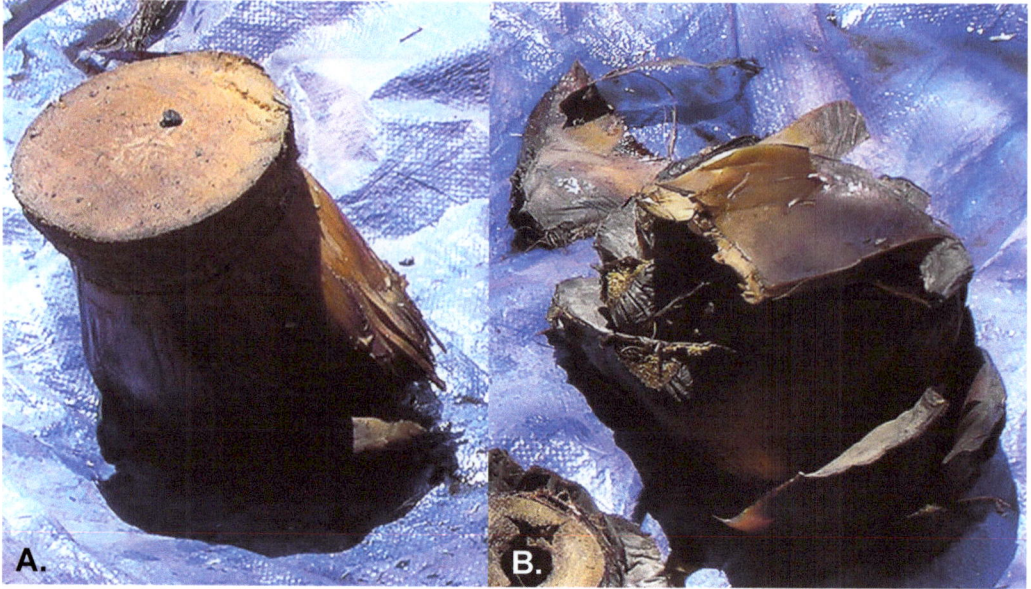

Figure 3. A. Less fibrous baked agave core. B. Fibrous baked leaf bases.

spectively. Vegetative reproduction of agave allows for the selection and "fixing" of its favorable attributes, with successive generations often expressing these same characteristics. Although advantageous for harvesters and processors, these phenomena are the cause of considerable confusion about the taxonomy of different agave taxa whose origins may be complexly interrelated. Certain characteristics that would be advantageous for selection by harvesters and farmers could be taste, fiber strength and rot-resistance, cloning (by rhizomes or stalk shoots), size of plants at maturity, reduced maturation time, ease of leaf cutting, smaller, less offensive or complete absence of spines, time of flower stalk initiation, pest resistance and drought (and cold?) resistance.

Plants that provide a multitude of uses with limited germplasm is not a favorable situation for the farmer. Colunga-GarcíaMarín and Zizumbo-Villarreal (2006) showed that through somatoclonal mutations or hybridization/introgression events, Mesoamerican farmers created new entities, selected for yield and quality of fiber, food, beverage, and other special products, while also maintaining existing favored phenotypes through vegetative reproduction. New entities, whether selected for and grown in Mesoamerica, the Caribbean or the arid Southwest, provided a number of favorable attributes that benefitted people's needs. Growing several of these entities at any one time and place, whether they be forms, races, varieties or distinct species, could meet many needs of farmers. In Arizona, evidence suggests that pre-Columbian farmers grew more than one kind of agave in a particular site. One possible explanation is that such plantings of different species with different flowering times provided the farmers an extended time for harvesting the hearts for food and beverage. Individual wild agaves (including those that may or may not offset) flower within a specific time period but are not closely synchronous, allowing the harvester to collect plants over a period of time, despite his/her having to expend considerable energy and time to locate the appropriate plants. Flowering stalks in cultivated species are produced in close synchrony within and among populations, a characteristic that would seem disadvantageous, as the window of opportunity to gather this food source was narrow. A way to circumvent this was to dry and store agave for a considerable amount of time. Farmers could also grow different kinds of agave that initiate stalk production at different times, thereby extending the agaves' harvest period (Tables 1, 2).

Little is known about the kinds of agaves pre-and post-Columbian farmers grew at any one time; only recently have great strides been made in identifying specific species in Arizona. Evidence suggests, however, that over all, the diversity of agaves has greatly declined over the centuries. For example, on the Yucatan peninsula there is no direct archaeological evidence that can shed light on the diversity of agaves in the Pre-Columbian era (Colunga-García-Marín and May-Pat 1993). However, by comparing historic and present day use of agaves and studying their molecular and morphological characteristics, it was determined that the diversity of agaves has gradually been lost as a consequence of agricultural intensification of one type of the fiber-producing henequen, *Agave fourcroydes* Lem. (Colunga-GarcíaMarín and May-Pat 1993). In the past, selection for different characteristics, in this case those relating to fiber that were better adapted to local climate and edaphic conditions, resulted in variants with different morphological characteristics and life cycles. In pre-contact Mayan cultivation of *Agave fourcroydes,* selection and maintenance of diverse properties were probably closely linked to a multipurpose use of this resource, as well as with its cultivation within a wider range than at present (Colunga-GarcíaMarín and May-Pat 1993). A similar loss of genetic diversity in the production of tequila is due to the exclusive cultivation of the blue agave (*Agave tequilana* Weber var. *azul).* Selection of different phenotypes produced by somatoclonal mutations and hybridization or introgression events as initiated in the past by indigenous peoples no longer occurs (Colunga-GarcíaMarín and Zizumbo-Villarreal, 2006; Valenzuela-Zapata and Nabhan 2003; Vega, et al. 2001).

Agave Cultivation in Arizona

Arizona has more species of agave than any other state in the U.S., providing numerous resources to many people who had access to the plants through harvesting or trade (Castetter et al. 1938; Gentry 1982; Hodgson 2001a). It would only make sense that as important as agave was to people in Arizona, it would also be cultivated, as its use was too extensive to be sustained by gathering alone (Bohrer 1991). However, only recently has evidence begun to emerge that suggests cultivation of agaves in Arizona. Paul Minnis and Stephen Plog (1976) hypothesized certain populations of *Agave parryi* Engelm (Figure 4) that were found north of their natural range, away from the Mogollon Rim of north-central Arizona and near archaeological sites and features, represent a range extension by human activity. Archaeologi-

Table 1. Characteristics of cultivated agaves and native, untended agaves.

Species	A. delam	A. murph	A. phillip	A. verden	A. yavap	A. chrys	A. utah	A. parryi
Rosette Size (height)	0.6–1 m	0.6–1.2 m	0.75–1 m	50–60 cm	50–60 cm	0.5–1.2 m	15–70 cm	15–75 cm
Head Size*	Medium	Medium	Medium	Medium	Large	Vary	Vary	Vary
Leaves								
Easily cut*	Yes	Yes	Yes	Yes	Yes	No	No	No
Teeth size*	Small	Small	Vary	Small	Small	Vary	Vary	Vary
Teeth deflexed or straight*	Yes	Yes	Vary	Yes	Yes	Vary	Vary	Yes
Reproduction								
Sexual	No	Rarely	No	Rarely	Rarely	Yes	Yes	Yes
Asexual	Yes	Yes	Yes	Yes	Yes	Rarely	Vary	Yes
Bulbils[1]*	No	Yes	No	No	No	No	No	No
Pups*	Yes	Yes	Yes	Yes	Yes	Rarely	Vary	Yes
Flowering time*	July–Aug	Mar–June Aug–Sept	June–July	June–July	May–Aug	May–Aug	May–July	July–Aug
Synchronous*	Yes	Yes	Yes	Yes	Yes	No	No	Vary
Fruit	No	Rarely	No	Few	Few	Yes	Yes	Yes
Seed	No	Rarely	No	Few	Few	Yes	Yes	Yes
Place where Native	NW Mex?	NW Mex?	NE Mex?	AZ	AZ/CA/UT/NV	AZ?/NW Mex?	AZ?/NW Mex?	AZ/NM/TX/N Mex
Chromosome number	4n	2n	4n	2n	2n	2n	2n	2n
Taste[2] (1-5, with 5 being very sweet)	5	3–4	5	5	5	3–4	3–4	4

[1] Bulbil production on undamaged stalk.

[2] Based on summary of unscientific survey of public at three agave roasts, V-V Archaeological Fair, Verde Valley, 2007, 2008, 2009.

* Characters possibly selected for by agriculturists.

Table 2. Approximate harvesting and flowering times for cultivated and native agaves.

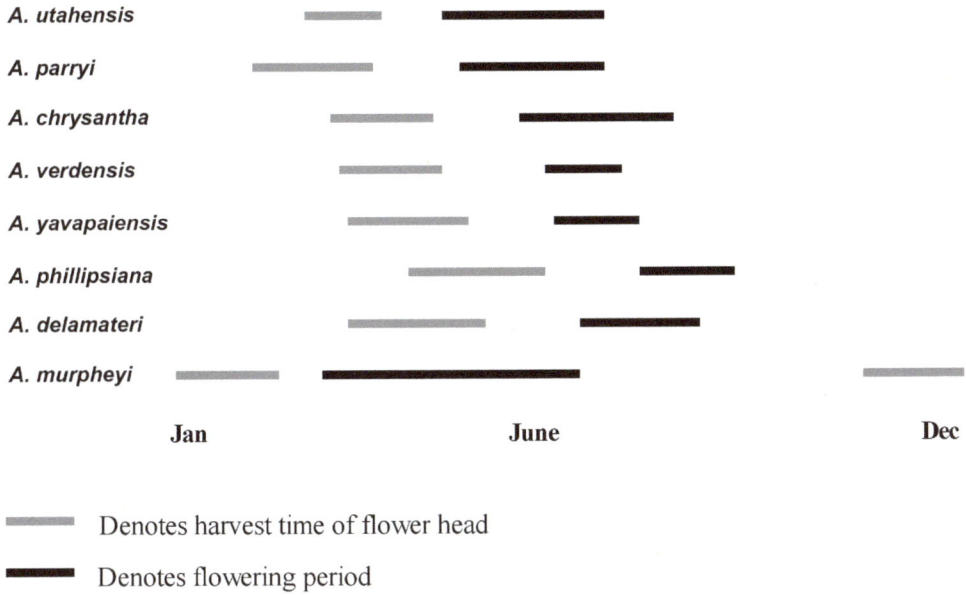

	Jan	June	Dec
A. utahensis			
A. parryi			
A. chrysantha			
A. verdensis			
A. yavapaiensis			
A. phillipsiana			
A. delamateri			
A. murpheyi			

▬▬▬▬ Denotes harvest time of flower head

▬▬▬▬ Denotes flowering period

Figure 4. *Agave parryi*, showing the often extensive clones produced.

cal features associated with agave cultivation were found in southern Arizona in the Phoenix (Bohrer 1987; Gasser and Kwiatkowski 1991), Tucson (Fish et al. 1985, 1992; Miksicek 1987) and Safford areas (Fish et al. 2004). Such features include agave fragments, roasting pits, core scrapers/pulping planes, agave tabular knives, numerous rock piles and rock-bordered grids (Bohrer 1987; Fish et al. 1985, 1992, 2004). Because these archaeological sites lacked preserved taxonomically informative characters such as leaves or flowers, it was presumed that *Agave murpheyi* Gibson (Figure 5) and perhaps another cultivar of ultimate Mexican origin were grown (Fish et al. 1992). While archaeological studies left little doubt about extensive *Agave* cultivation in southern Arizona, little attention was given to the natural history and evolutionary affinities of *Agave murpheyi* and how humans may have manipulated it (Hodgson and Salywon 2012). Additionally, prior to the 1990s, the presence and significance of specific agaves were often overlooked despite their occurrence in areas for which archaeological and botanical studies were conducted.

Methods

Literature reviews (including ethnographic, archaeological, and taxonomic/systematic) and extensive field surveys with regards to potential cultivated or domesticated agave species in Arizona were begun in the mid-1980s and have continued since. Familiarity with the taxonomy and systematics of the genus *Agave*, particularly on a more regional level (Southwest and northern Mexico), is required to understand the role of agaves in cultures. To understand differences amongst agaves necessitates understanding similarities on a broad scale. This includes a multidisciplinary approach involving morphology, biogeography, phenological, cytological and recently, molecular studies. Thousands of hours surveying and documenting agave sites and plants (herbarium specimens, photos, information) ensued. Such surveys were based on previous accrued knowledge and recognition of patterns involving both agave and human settlement. Herbarium specimens with leaves, flowers, fruits, detailed notes (location, plant attributes and measurements) and photos were made, vouchering an individual plant's existence. Additionally, visits to regional and non-regional (Harvard) herbaria were necessary to study specimens from earlier collectors. Cytological (pollen viability, chromosome number and behavior) and molecular studies were and continue to be conducted by Desert Botanical Garden researchers and scientists associated with University of Georgia. Discussion or collaboration amongst other researchers involving different disciplines including systematics, ethnobotany, biogeography and archaeology was necessary and proved fruitful. Clearly, to better understand the role of agaves in human subsistence patterns, a botanist's perspective together with that of archaeologists and others was and continues to be needed.

Figure 5. *Agave murpheyi*. A. Habit, note spathulate leaves and cloning nature. B. Close-up of leaf, note small, porrect marginal spines. C. Close-up of bulbils on flower stalk.

Results: Agaves in Arizona

Since the mid-1980s continuing studies have resulted in the identification of no less than five agave domesticates—distinct species and lineages—farmed by Arizona pre-Columbian peoples (Hodgson and Salywon 2012). Most, if not all, are believed to be not native to Arizona; rather, they may have originated in northern Mexico and were traded north, one as far as the Grand Canyon. All of these rare agaves have been able to persist unattended and minimally altered through vegetative reproduction following cultural abandonment (around 1450 A.D.) and subsequent absence of agrarian cultures until after European contact (Parker et al. 2007). Thus, these plants—living archaeological artifacts shaped by past human selection and domestication—provide a rare opportunity to trace the genetic lineage of extant populations back to their pre-Columbian farmed ancestors. Plants observed today are basically genetically the same as those plants farmed centuries ago. Such is not the case for most domesticated crops, whose lineages have long been altered or lost over time as a result of sexual reproduction.

Arizona Pre-Columbian Agave Domesticates

Agave murpheyi *Gibson, "Hohokam Agave"*
Agave murpheyi Gibson (Figure 5) is a moderately large agave that freely offsets from rhizomatous buds. Its cream flowers are produced from January through March. Following flowering, the flower stalk produces plantlets, or "bulbils" (Figure 5c) that can remain on the stalk for many months where they either dry or fall onto disturbed ground where they may take root. Plants occasionally produce fruit and fertile seed. Nearly all of the 60 or so known clones of this species are in pre-Columbian, historic and contemporary Indian fields and gardens in Arizona and Sonora, with the majority near archaeological features (Hodgson 2001a). Approximately 45 "wild" clones (clones not associated with historic or contemporary gardens) grow along major watersheds in central Arizona at elevations between 400 and 1000 m (1300–3300 ft). Clones do not exist in natural vegetation *per se,* but often grow within pre-Columbian linear basalt cobble alignments, rock piles, and terraces on naturally occurring terraces, low ridges or bajadas, often in association with agave processing tools (Green and Effland 1986; Hodgson 2001a; Rankin and Katzer 1989). At several sites plants grow with another pre-Columbian cultivated agave, *A. delamateri* Hodgson and Slauson.

    Agave murpheyi has characteristics that were selected by pre-Columbian farmers for food, fiber and beverage. These characteristics include 1) cloning nature, 2) thin, easily cut leaves with small, straight, marginal teeth, 3) fine, rot-resistant leaf fibers (Hodgson 2001a) and 4) short maturation time of eight to 10 years with supplemental water. Unlike other agaves, development of the flower stalk begins in late fall and early winter when other fresh foods were not plentiful (Tables 1, 2). As with all of the pre-Columbian cultivars, flowering is nearly synchronous within and often amongst populations, making the plants easier to harvest. Because cooked agave pulp stores well, large quantities could be harvested at once. The hundreds of bulbils and numerous offsets could be easily transported via trade or migration, or planted. The species may have originated in the arid region of northwestern Sonora State, Mexico (which borders Arizona), possibly involving *A. angustifolia* L., another species used extensively for numerous purposes whose genetic makeup and distribution has been greatly influenced by humans (Colunga-GarcíaMarín and Zizumbo-Villarreal 2006; Gentry 1982).

Agave delamateri *Hodgson and Slauson, "Tonto Basin Agave"*
Agave delamateri (Figure 6) is a relatively large, freely cloning plant with gray-green leaves flushed with maroon. Its flowering is synchronous with the initiation of flower stalk production in early May; its broad panicle with long lateral branches perpendicular to the thick produces large cream-maroon flowers that mature from late June to July. The Tonto Basin Agave has never been seen to produce fruit or seed; thus, reproduction is purely by vegetative reproduction via offsets.

All of the more than 90 clones of this rare species have been documented within the Arizona Uplands or pinon-juniper woodlands in central Arizona, often on alluvial terraces or ridges overlooking major drainages at elevations between 700 and 1550 meters (2300–4900 ft). Its cloning nature, easily cut leaves, very fine, strong fibers, excellent taste, and summer flowering behavior (thus, late spring-early summer harvesting for food) are all attributes for which pre-Columbian farmers could have selected (Hodgson 2001a; Table 1). *Agave delamateri* may have its origins in northwestern Mexico, in northwestern Chihuahua State or northeastern Sonora because it probably originated in a more mesic environment and shows affinities with other northern Mexico agave species (Hodgson and Salywon 2012).

Agave phillipsiana *Hodgson "Grand Canyon Agave"*
Agave phillipsiana Hodgson (Figure 7) is a recently described new species first found in Grand Canyon National Park (Hodgson 2001b). Later surveys for this plant resulted finding it from several locations south of the Grand Canyon, although it is still only known from fewer than 30 sites, all restricted to north-central Arizona at elevations between 730 and 1430 meters (2400–4700 ft). Plants occur near archaeological features (habilitation and agricultural), including cliff dwellings (that date back to Kayenta ancestral Hopi), linear alignments and roasting pits (Hodgson 2001a, 2001b). Mature plants are a relatively large and produce offsets. Its numerous lanceshaped dark green leaves are easily cut. Development of flower stalks is synchronous, but occurs later than most Arizona agave species, beginning in June with flowers maturing from late August to September (Tables 1, 2). Reproduction is solely by vegetative means via offsets as no capsule or seed has ever been observed. The plant's cloning nature, easily cut leaves and relatively late flower stalk development are likely a few of the attributes selected for by pre-Columbian farmers.

Figure 6. *A. delamateri*. A. Habit, note long, widely spaced lateral branches perpendicular to main stalk. B. Close-up of leaves, note gray-maroon color. C. Close-up of flowers, note large, thick flowers with maroon tinge.

Like the other agave domesticates in Arizona, *Agave phillipsiana* is not native to Arizona. Plants are easily differentiated from the indigenous and rarely cloning Kaibab agave (*A. utahensis* Engelm. ssp. *kaibabensis* (McKelvey) Gentry; Figure 8), which also has been used for food and fiber. The Kaibab agave has shorter, more compact and fibrous leaves, characteristic of agaves that have evolved in a more arid and sometimes colder environment (Burgess 1985). *Agave phillipsiana* is a larger, more open plant with longer and fewer leaves, characteristic of agaves that have evolved in a moister and warmer environment such as that found in the mountains of northwestern Mexico, where this domesticate may have its origins (Hodgson 2001b).

Agave yavapaiensis *Hodgson & Salywon* "Page Springs Agave"

The rare "Page Springs agave" (Figure 9) was recently discovered and named as a new species (Hodgson and Salywon 2012). It is only known from less than 10 sites in north-central Arizona within a localized area, usually in agriculturally-favorable basalt soils with or near the many archaeological features located between 900 and 1200 meters in elevation. Plants are mid-size, freely offset, produce leaves that have mostly downturned teeth, are linear in shape, dark gray-green and are easily cut. Development of the narrow panicle is synchronous, the flowers produced from June to early July (Tables 1, 2). Such synchrony in flowering, cloning nature, easily cut leaves and excellent taste may have been characters selected for by pre-Columbian farmers. Reproduction is mainly vegetative via its offsets although a few fruits, with even fewer seed, are occasionally produced. Unlike the aforementioned agave domesticates, its extent of farming appears to have been limited to a very localized area, suggesting that it may have been a regionally significant, signature plant (*sensu* Gasser and Kwiatkowsky 1991) not traded elsewhere.

Agave verdensis *Hodgson & Salywon* "Sacred Mountain Agave"

The Sacred Mountain agave (Figure 10) is another recently discovered, rare agave believed to be a pre-Columbian domesticate. It is only known from less than 40 sites in a localized area of north-central Arizona. Plants occur near major settlements from 1130–1400 A.D., and important farming and trade activities from 1300–1400 A.D. (Pilles 1981). Plants are moderately large, freely cloning and have light gray-green, easily cut leaves. Development of the narrow panicle is synchronous, with the flowers maturing mainly in June (Tables 1, 2). These characteristics as well as excellent taste (and other characteristics not yet known) were probably selected for by pre-Columbian farmers. Like the Page Springs agave, its extent of farming appears to have been limited to a localized area, suggesting that it may have been a regionally significant, signature plant not traded elsewhere. Both Sacred Mountain and Page Springs agaves resemble the native *A. chrysantha*, or golden flowered agave (Figure 11) that grows at higher elevations but they are different in leaf, flower and fruit characters.

Figure 7. *A. phillipsiana*. A. Habit, note long, gray-green leaves. B. Close-up of rosette. C. Close-up of flowers, note light cream flowers.

Figure 8. *A. utahensis*. A. Habit, note spike-like flower stalk (ssp. *kaibabensis*). B. Rosette, note rigid, heavily armed leaves (ssp. *kaibabensis*). C. Close-up of flowers (ssp. *utahensis*).

Figure 9. *A. yavapaiensis*. A. Habit, note cloning nature and synchrony in flowering. B. Rosettes, note linear leaves with numerous but small, mostly deflexed marginal teeth. C. Close-up of flowers, note light yellow color.

Figure 10. *A. verdensis*. A. Habit, note cloning nature and synchrony in flowering. B. Close-up of rosette, note wide, spoon-shaped leaves. C. Close-up of flowers, note pale cream-yellow color.

Figure 11. *A. chrysantha*. A. Rosette of flowering individual. B. Flowering stalk, note golden yellow color of flowers. C. Close-up of flowers, note golden yellow color.

The Sacred Mountain agave and other Arizona agave domesticates do not grow in isolation of each other. Recent surveys discovered sites where the Sacred Mountain agave, Tonto Basin agave and Grand Canyon agave grow together. Such a practice would provide different attributes of multi-purpose plants to meet the multiple needs of people.

Discussion: The Next Steps

The evidence supporting domestication of these agaves is that they 1) are always found associated with archaeological sites and/or features; 2) produce very little or no fertile seed; 3) reproduce readily by vegetative means, mostly by offsets (*A. murpheyi* also produces bulbils on the flower stalk), making them easier to propagate; 4) have leaves that are more easily cut than wild species, hence they are somewhat easier to harvest; 5) have relatively uniform intra- and inter-population morphology; 6) have synchronous flowering within each taxon; and 7) have roasted "heads" that taste sweeter and are less fibrous than other wild species (Hodgson and Salywon 2012; Table 1).

Without question is that recent findings, in conjunction with the increasing amount of archaeological and botanical evidence supporting agave cultivation, are painting a picture of agave cultivation at an extraordinary level in Arizona, putting the multi purpose agaves in their proper place amongst different groups as an extremely valuable resource at one time or another. Of the 21 *Agave* taxa in Arizona 12 are endemic to Arizona, and of these, five are pre-Columbian domesticates (Hodgson and Salywon 2012) believed to have originated in northern Mexico and traded and/or transported as far north as Grand Canyon in northern Arizona (Hodgson 2001b). Additionally, the Arizona native *A. parryi* was also traded and cultivated by pre-Columbian people in north-central Arizona (Parker et al. 2010). Further research among agaves in northern Mexico, particularly those in Sonora and Chihuahua, is necessary to seek their wild progenitors and other potential undiscovered ancient cultivars.

Despite the recent advances in understanding the role of agaves in Arizona, there remain many taxonomic and cultural questions. To answer these, it is necessary to involve other disciplines including molecular genetics, cytology, archaeology, nutrition, ecology, ethnobotany and population biology. It is also critical that contemporary people (Yavapai, Apache, Paiute, O'odham), whose history includes agaves as an important resource, be involved in this research.

With the help of molecular analysis by Drs. Al and Kathy Parker, University of Georgia, Dr. Andrew Salywon and the author hope to answer several questions. Preliminary molecular analysis indicates that although there are low levels of genetic diversity within *A. murpheyi* and *A. delamateri,* relative to other clonal, wild species, there is variation both within and among populations. This suggests that the evolutionary history of these agaves is far more complex than a single introduction followed by minimal artificial selection as was once previously suggested (Parker et al. 2007).

Molecular analysis of Hohokam and Tonto Basin agave genetic analyses also supported the hypothesis that these plants were traded amongst groups inhabiting different areas of Arizona (Parker et al. 2007). Understanding agaves in their cultural context may help us better understand migration and trading patterns and intergroup relations in the pre-Columbian Southwest and northern Mexico. How agave research situates within the context of recent migration studies (e.g., Clark 2001; Lyons 2003) is an important area of research.

Other questions for which a multidisciplinary approach may help answer questions regarding these agave domesticates are 1) their progenitor and place of origin, 2) their levels of genetic diversity, 3) frequency of mutations since the initiation of cultivated populations in Arizona (and northern Mexico), 4) whether each species' was introduced into the region once or multiple times, and 5) whether genetic (and morphological?) differentiation within these agaves relate to differences in habitat and/or cultural context, including agricultural practices and preferences (Parker et al. 2007). How have they influenced wild populations and what other species are being overlooked, especially in Mexico?

There are many other outstanding questions to be addressed in future agave research. Some of these involve a more nuanced understanding of the history of cultivated agaves. For instance, we could ask 1) how many plants were cultivated in any given area and time, and how extensively, or 2) why are only certain kinds of agaves cultivated in one area and not in another, seemingly appropriate area, 3) what were their uses and why were they important, 4) were they a famine food or staple or both, and 5) how extensively were they traded and with whom. However, some research questions are directly relevant to the future of cultivated agaves. For instance, it is unclear how these rare cultural and natural resources will be protected given that possible hybrids or plants whose existence depended on people are not protected by the Endangered Species Act.

Whatever the question to be answered, an amazing story continues to develop, centering on the fact that remnants of agave populations that presumably were once grown on a large scale by pre-Columbian farmers are seen in the landscape today. It is assumed that many other types were probably developed but have since disappeared. Given the extent of pre-Columbian agave cultivation, attempts to identify "species" should proceed with caution. This is especially true in and around areas with known extensive agave cultivation, but is likely true in other areas because many cultivated varieties are now extirpated. Thus, the delineation between what are indigenous and what are direct or indirect descendents of ancient cultivars can become blurred. Scientists must look at landscapes from a cultural perspective and evaluate "normal" wild species more critically within their cultural and "natural" landscape (Hodgson 2004).

Acknowledgments

The author is indebted to many, particularly Amadeo Rea, who has inspired, encouraged, and taught her so much more than for what he takes credit. Several trips to Sonora and many hours discussing everything from relationships to linguistics will be remembered with gratitude and respect to Amadeo, a dear friend.

References Cited

Bohrer, Vorsila. 1987 The Plant Remains from La Ciudad, a Hohokam Site in Phoenix. In *Specialized Studies in the Economy, Environment, and Culture of La Ciudad*, eds. JoAnn Kisselburg, Glen Rice, and Brenda Shears. *ASU Anthropological Field Studies No. 20*. Office of Cultural Resource Management, Department of Anthropology, Arizona State University, Tempe.

Bohrer, Vorsila. 1991   Recently Recognized Cultivated and Encouraged Plants Among the Hohokam. *Kiva* 56:227–235.

Bruman, Henry. 2000   *Alcohol in Ancient Mexico*. University of Utah Press, Salt Lake City.

Burgess, Tony L. 1985   Agave Adaptation to Aridity. *Desert Plants* 7:39–50.

Callen, Eric O. 1965   Food Habits of Some Pre-Columbian Indians. *Economic Botany* 19:335–343.

Castetter, Edward F., Willis H. Bell, and Alvin R. Grove. 1938   The Early Utilization and the Distribution of *Agave* in the American Southwest. *University of New Mexico Bulletin: Ethnobiological Studies in the American Southwest* Vol. VI.

Clark, Jeffrey J. 2001   Tracking Prehistoric Migrations: Pueblo Settlers Among the Tonto Basin Hohokam. *Anthropological Papers of the University of Arizona, No. 65*. University of Arizona Press, Tucson.

Colunga-GarcíaMarín, Patricia, and Filogonio May-Pat. 1993   Agave Studies in Yucatan, Mexico. I. Past and Present Germplasm Diversity and Uses. *Economic Botany* 47:312–327.

Colunga-GarcíaMarín, Patricia, Julian Coello-Coello, Lida Espejo-Peníche, and Lilia Fuente-Moreno. 1993   Agave Studies in Yucatan, Mexico. II. Nutritional Value of the Inflorescence Peduncle and Incipient Domestication. *Economic Botany* 47:328–334.

Colunga-GarcíaMarín, Patricia, E. Estrada-Loera, and Filogonio May-Pat. 1996   Patterns of Morphological Variation, Diversity, and Domestication of Wild and Cultivated Populations of *Agave* in Yucatan, Mexico. *American Journal of Botany* 83:126–140.

Colunga-GarcíaMarín, Patricia, and Filongio May-Pat. 1997   Morphological Variation of Henequen *(Agave fourcroydes, Agavaceae)* Germplasm and its Wild Ancestor *(A. angustifolia)* under Uniform Growth Conditions: Diversity and Domestication. *American Journal of Botany* 84:1449–1465.

Colunga-GarcíaMarín, Patricia, Julian Coello-Coello, Luis E. Eguiarte, and Daniel Pinero. 1999   Isozymatic Variation and Phylogenetic Relationships between Henequen *(Agave fourcroydes)* and its Wild Ancestor *A. angustifolia* (Agavaceae). *American Journal of Botany* 86:115–123.

Colunga-GarcíaMarín, Patricia, and Daniel Zizumbo-Villarreal. 2006   Tequila and Other *Agave* Spirits from West-central Mexico: Current Germplasm Diversity, Conservation and Origin. *Biodiversity and Conservation* 16:1653–1667.

Fish, Suzanne K., Paul Fish, Charles Miksicek, and John Madsen. 1985   Prehistoric Agave Cultivation in Southern Arizona. *Desert Plants* 7:100, 107–112.

Fish, Suzanne K., Paul Fish, and John Madsen. 1992   Evidence for Large-scale Agave Cultivation in the Marana Community. In *The Marana Community in the Hohokam World*, eds., Suzanne K. Fish, Paul Fish, and John Madsen, pp. 73–117. *Anthropological Papers of the University of Arizona* No. 56, University of Arizona Press, Tucson.

Fish, Suzanne K., Paul Fish, Arthur MacWilliams, Guadelupe Sanchez de Carpenter, and Karen R. Adams. 2004   Growing Conditions and Crops: the Field Evidence. In *The Safford Valley Grids: Prehistoric Cultivation in the Southern Arizona Desert,* eds. William E. Doolittle and James A. Neely, pp. 79–94. *Anthropological Papers of the University of Arizona, No. 70,* University of Arizona Press, Tucson.

García-Mendoza, Abisaí. 2002   Distribution of *Agave* (Agavaceae) in Mexico. *Cactus and Succulent Journal* 4(74):177–188.

Gasser, Robert E., and Scott M. Kwiatkowski. 1991   Regional Signatures of Hohokam Plant Use. *Kiva* 56(3):207–226.

Gentry, Howard S. 1972   *The Agave Family in Sonora.* Agriculture Handbook No. 399. Agricultural Research Service. USDA.

Gentry, Howard S. 1982   *Agaves of Continental North America.* University of Arizona Press, Tucson.

Good-Avila, Sara V., Valeria Souza, Brandon S. Gaut, and Luis E. Eguiarte. 2006   Timing and Rate of Speciation in *Agave* (Agavaceae). *Proceedings of the National Academy of Science* 103:9124–9129.

Green, Margerie, and Richard W. Effland. 1986   Settlement, Subsistence and Specialization in the Northern Periphery: Research Design for Mitigative Recovery at Sites in the New Waddell Dam Borrow Areas. *Archaeological Consulting Services Report* 40:1–54.

Hodgson, Wendy. 2001a   *Food Plants of the Sonoran Desert.* University of Arizona Press, Tucson.

Hodgson, Wendy. 2001b   Taxonomic Novelties in American *Agave* (Agavaceae). *Novon* 11(4):410–416.

Hodgson, Wendy. 2004   Ancient Agave Cultivars and Ancient Peoples: A Synthesis of our Research. *Sonoran Quarterly* 58(3):6–10.

Hodgson, Wendy, and Andrew Salywon. 2012   Two New *Agave* Species (Agavaceae) from Central Arizona and their Putative Domesticate Status. *Brittonia* 64(3).

Hodgson, Wendy, and Liz Slauson. 1995   *Agave delamateri* (Agavaceae) and its Role in the Subsistence Patterns of Pre-Columbian Cultures in Arizona. *Haseltonia* 3:130–140.

Kaur, Narinder, and Anil K. Gupta. 2002   Application of Inulin and Oligofructose in Health and Nutrition. *Journal of Biosciences* 27(7):703–714.

López, Mercedes G., Norma A. Mancilla-Margalli, and Guillermo Mendosa-Diaz. 2003   Molecular Structures of Fructans from *Agave tequilana* Weber var. *azul. Journal of Agricultural Food Chemistry* 51(27):7835–7840.

Lyons, Patrick D. 2003   Ancestral Hopi Migrations. *Anthropological Papers of the University of Arizona No. 68.* University of Arizona Press, Tucson.

Miksicek, Charles. 1987   Late Sedentary-Early Classic Period Hohokam Agriculture: Plant Remains from the Marana Community Complex. In *Studies in the Hohokam Com-*

munity of Marana, ed. G. Rice, pp. 187–216. *Anthropological Field Studies No. 15*. Arizona State University, Tempe.

Minnis, Paul E., and Stephen E. Plogg. 1976   A Study of the Site-specific Distribution of *Agave parryi* in East Central Arizona. *Kiva* 41:299–308.

Nobel, Park S. 1977   Water Relations of Flowering *Agave deserti*. *Botanical Gazette* 45:480–486.

Parker, Kathleen C., James L. Hamrick, Wendy Hodgson, Dorset W. Trapnell, Albert J. Parker, and Robert K. Kuzoff. 2007   Genetic Consequences of Pre-Columbian Cultivation for *Agave murpheyi* and *A. delamateri* (Agavaceae). *American Journal of Botany* 94:1479–1490.

Parker, Kathleen C., Dorset W. Trapnell, James L. Hamrick, Wendy Hodgson, and Albert J. Parker. 2010   Inferring Ancient Agave Cultivation Practices from Contemporary Genetic Patterns. *Molecular Ecology* 19:1622–1637.

Pilles, Peter J. Jr. 1981   The Southern Sinagua. *Plateau* 53(1):6–17.

Rankin, Adrianne G., and Keith Katzer. 1989   Agricultural Systems in the ACS Waddell Project Area. In *Settlement, Subsistence and Specialization in the Northern Periphery: The Waddell Project*, ed. Margerie Green, pp. 981–1020. *Archaeological Consulting Services, Ltd., Cultural Resources Report no. 65*. Tempe, Arizona.

Reveal, James L., and Wendy Hodgson. 2002   Agave. Agavaceae. In *Flora of North America North of Mexico*, Vol. 26, ed. Flora of North America Editorial Committee, pp. 442–461. Oxford University Press.

Schneeman, Barbara O. 1999   Fiber, Inulin and Oligofructose: Similarities and Differences. *Journal of Nutrition* 129:1424S–1427S.

Smith, C. Earle, Jr. 1965   The Archeological Record of Cultivated Crops of New World Origins. *Economic Botany* 19:323–334.

Smith, C. Earle, Jr. 1986   Preceramic Plant Remains from Guila Naquitz. In *Guila Naquitz. Archaic Foraging and Early Agriculture in Oaxaca*, ed. Kent V. Flannery, pp. 265–301. Academic Press, New York.

Valenzuela-Zapata, Ana G., and Gary Nabhan. 2003   *Tequila! A Natural and Cultural History*. University of Arizona Press, Tucson.

Vega, Katia Gil, Mario G. Chavira, Octavio M. de la Vega, June Simpson, and George Vandemark. 2001   Analysis of Genetic Diversity in *Agave tequilana* var. *Azul* using RAPD Markers. *Euphytica* 119(3):335–341.

Wiemken Andres, Norbert Sprenger, and Thomas Boller. 1996   Fructan—An Extension of Sucrose by Sucrose. In *Sucrose Metabolism, Biochemistry, Physiology and Molecular Biology*, eds. Horacio G. Pontis, Graciela L. Salerno, and Ed Echeverria, pp. 179–189. American Society of Plant Physiologists, Rockville, MD.

Zizumbo-Villarreal, Daniel, Fernando González-Zozaya, Angeles Olay-Barrientos, Rafael Platas-Ruíz, Mariza Cuevas-Sagardí, Laura Almendros-López, and Patricia Colunga-García-Marín. 2009   Archaeological Evidence of the Cultural Importance of *Agave* spp. in Pre-Hispanic Colima, Mexico. *Economic Botany* 63(3):288–302.

The Paleobiolinguistics of Domesticated Squash (*Cucurbita* spp.)

Cecil H. Brown[†], Eike Luedeling[‡], Søren Wichmann[§],
and Patience Epps[¶]

The English use of common names of cultivated cucurbits is almost hope-lessly muddled. One man's winter squash is another man's pumpkin … Summer squash in U.S. markets are *C. pepo*, although not all *C. pepo* are summer squash. In northwestern Mexico and the southwestern United States, *C. argyrosperma* is also used as a summer squash. A few of the English names are more specific, though: most cushaws are *C. argyrosperma*, the "regular" *haal* of Pima, and cheese pumpkins are *C. moschata*. We live in an imperfect world.

Amadeo M. Rea's *At the Desert's Green Edge*, p. 304

Abstract

Historical-comparative linguistics is used to explore the domestication and spread of squash (*Cucurbita* spp.) in the Americas. Information relating to the reconstruction of words for squash for major New World ancestral languages, such as Proto-Catawba-Siouan, Proto-Otomanguean, and Proto-Arawakan, are assembled. This information is compared chronologically and geographically with crop-origin findings from archaeology and botany. Dates for the earliest archaeologically retrieved remains of domesticated squash tend to be on the average 3000 years older than the earliest linguistic dates, suggesting that squash typically developed considerable significance for precontact people only well after first being domesticated. Linguistic evidence also indicates that squash acquired considerable salience and broad distribution in Mesoamerica much earlier than elsewhere in the New World.

† Northern Illinois University and University of West Florida; 1700 Scenic Highway #601, Pensacola, FL 32503 USA [brown.cecil@yahoo.com]
‡ World Agroforestry Centre, Nairobi, Kenya.
§ Max Planck Institute for Evolutionary Anthropology, Leipzig, Germany.
¶ University of Texas at Austin, Austin, TX, USA.

Introduction

Paleobiolinguistics employs the comparative method of historical linguistics to reconstruct the biodiversity known to human groups of the remote, unrecorded past (e.g., Blench 2007; Brown 2006a, 2006b, 2010; Diebold 1985; Fowler 1972, 1983; Friedrich 1970; Hill 2001; Shepard and Ramirez 2011; Siebert 1967; Whistler 1977). Comparison of words for biological species from modern genetically related languages facilitates reconstruction of biological vocabularies of ancient proto-languages (e.g., Brown 2006a, 2006b). This study uses paleobiolinguistics to establish where and when domesticated squash became significant to precontact Native American groups. For proto-languages of the New World, we determine whether or not terms for squash pertained to respective vocabularies. Automated approaches developed within the ASJP Consortium (Holman et al. 2011; Wichmann et al. 2010) facilitate determination of where a proto-language was spoken and when it was spoken at the latest. Consequently, if a word for squash reconstructs for a proto-language, it is possible to determine where and when precontact people were familiar with the crop. This information can be combined with data from archaeology and botany to expand knowledge of the precontact history of domesticated squash.

Crop-Origin Studies of Squash

At European contact, native agriculturalists in North America and Central America relied primarily on a group of three crops: maize, squash, and beans. The widespread geographical occurrence of this agrarian triad in historical times suggests its considerable antiquity in the Americas. As a result, each of these "three sisters" has received substantial attention in crop-origin studies. These studies focus on where and when plants were domesticated and how they spread. Such research typically involves identification of wild progenitor populations and archaeological retrieval of ancient macro-remains. Modern investigations of crop-origins research expand to include plant micro-remains (phytoliths, pollen, and starch grains) and genetic and molecular approaches.

Table 1 lists some of the contemporary crop-origin and related studies treating squash. These studies provide information on where and when squash domestication occurred in the New World (Table 2). Five species of squash have been domesticated. These are *Cucurbita argyrosperma* Huber (Figure 1), *C. ficifolia* Bouché (Figures 2, 3, 4), *C. moschata* (Duchesne ex Lam.) Duchesne ex Poiret (Figures 5, 6, 7), *C. maxima* Duchesne ex Poiret (Figure 8), and *C. pepo* L. (Figures 9, 10). Three of these, *C. ficifolia*, *C. moschata*, and *C. maxima*, were domesticated in South America and two, *C. argyrosperma* and *C. pepo*, in Mexico (Sanjur et al. 2002). *C. pepo* was also independently domesticated in eastern North America (Decker-Walters 1993, Sanjur et al. 2002) (Table 2). Macro-remains of *C. pepo* from Guilá Naquitz cave in Oaxaca, Mexico attest to the oldest date, 10,000 BP, for any domesticated squash in the Americas (Table 2).

Table 1. Some contemporary crop-origin and related studies treating squash.

Study	Approach	Region
Decker-Walters et al. 1993	Wild Progenitor and Genetics	Eastern North America
Dillehay et al. 2007	Macro-Remains	Peru
Duncan et al. 2009	Micro-Remains (Starch Grain)	Peru
Hart and Sidell 1997	Macro-Remains	Eastern North America
Hart et al. 2007	Micro-Remains (Phytoliths)	Eastern North America
Lema 2011	Macro-Remains	Argentina
Lira 1995	Taxonomy and Ecogeography	Latin America
Lovis and Monaghan 2008	Macro-Remains	Eastern North America
Piperno and Dillehay 2008	Micro-Remains (Starch Grain)	Peru
Piperno and Stothert 2003	Micro-Remains (Phytoliths)	South America
Piperno et al. 2000	Micro-Remains (Phytoliths)	Lowland American Tropics
Piperno et al. 2002	Micro-Remains (Phytoliths) and Genetics	New World in General
Piperno et al. 2009	Micro-Remains (Phytoliths) and Wild Progenitor	Mexico
Ranere et al. 2009	Micro-Remains (Phytoliths) and Wild Progenitor	Mexico
Sanjur et al. 2002	Genetics	New World in General
Smith 1997	Macro-Remains	Mexico
Smith 2006	Macro-Remains and Wild Progenitor	Eastern North America
Zizumbo 1986	Wild Progenitor	Mexico

Table 2. Crop-origin information for the five domesticated species of squash.

Domesticated Squash Species	Domestication Location	Approximate Date In Years BP of Earliest Known Fossil Evidence (NI = No Information)			
		Eastern North America	Western North America and Northern Mexico	Southern Mexico and Northern Central America (Mesoamerica)	Southern Central America and South America
C. pepo	1. Mexico,[1] 2. Eastern North America[2]	5000[2]	4000[3]	10,000[5]	1000–550[6]
C. argyrosperma	Mexico[7]	500[8]	1150[8]	7000[9]	NI
C. moschata	Lowland Northern South America[10]	NI	NI	6500[9]	9300–8000[11]
C. ficifolia	Bolivian Andes[12]	NI	NI	NI	5100[13]
C. maxima	Andes[7]	NI	NI	NI	4400–3200[6]

[1] Smith (2001)
[2] Smith (2006)
[3] Fritz (2011)
[5] Smith (2001)
[6] Pearsall (1992)
[7] Piperno and Pearsall (1998); Sanjur et al. (2002)
[8] Fritz (1990)
[9] McClung de Tapia (1992)
[10] Dillehay et al. (2007); Sanjur et al. (2002)
[11] Dillehay et al. (2007)
[12] Pearsall (1992); Piperno and Pearsall (1998)
[13] Piperno (2011)

Figure 1. *Cucurbita argyrosperma* subsp. *argyrosperma* in Oaxaca, Mexico. Photograph by Rafael Lira Saade, used with permission.

Figure 2. *Cucurbita ficifolia,* **mayil** (Tzeltal), Chiapas, Mexico, 1966. Photograph by Brent Berlin, used with permission.

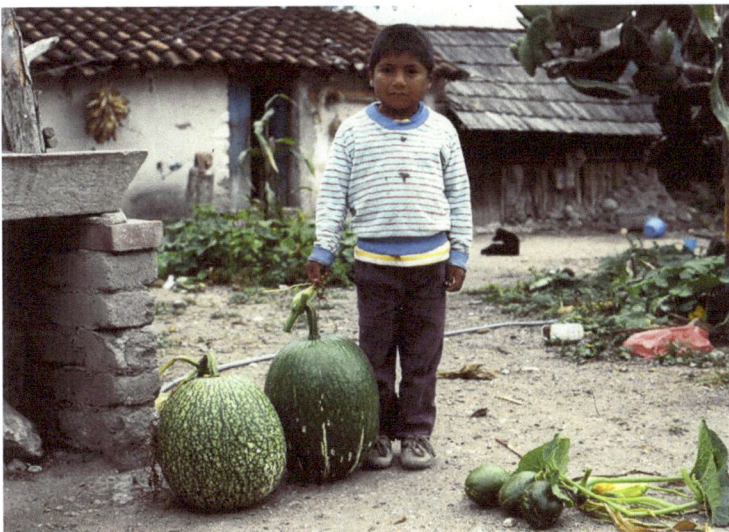

Figure 3. *Cucurbita ficifolia,* Oaxaca, Mexico. Photograph by Rafael Lira Saade, used with permission.

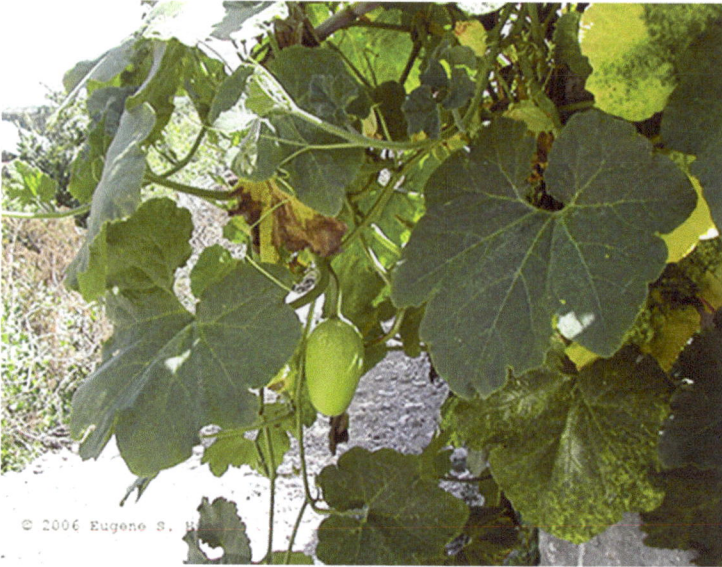

Figure 4. *Cucurbita ficifolia*, Oaxaca, Mexico. Photograph by Eugene Hunn, used with permission.

Figure 5. *Cucurbita moschata* varieties. Photograph by Rafael Lira Saade, used with permission.

Figure 6. Tzeltal woman cleaning **ch'um**, *Cucurbita moschata,* 1960s. Photograph by Brent Berlin, used with permission.

Figure 7. Tzeltal woman with **ch'um**, *Cucurbita moschata*, 1960s. Photograph by Brent Berlin, used with permission.

Figure 8. *Cucurbita maxima* (Barbieri 2007).

Figure 9. *Cucurbita pepo*. Photograph by Javier Castrejón Reyna. Courtesy of Comisión Nacional para el Conocimiento y Uso de la Biodiversidad (CONABIO).

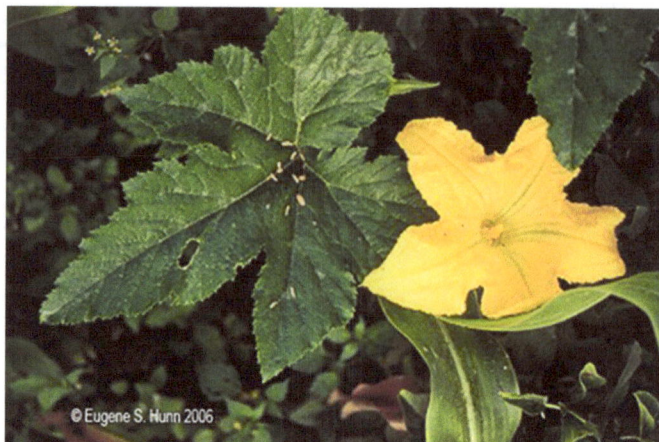

Figure 10. *Cucurbita pepo,* Oaxaca, Mexico. Photograph by Eugene Hunn, used with permission.

Precontact Crop Salience

Crop-origin research rarely includes detailed data on the extent of human interest in a target crop. While archaeobotany uses sophisticated technical approaches for locating and dating the earliest remains of a crop, determining the degree to which the crop was significant to a precontact people is considerably more difficult. It would be interesting to know, for example, how the earliest domesticated *C. pepo* was used (Figures 9, 10). Was it eaten or did it have some other function, for example, as a container or fishnet float? If consumed, what parts were eaten, seeds or flesh; was it consumed only on feasting occasions, or as a regular component of a group's diet; if the latter, what proportion of a diet did it constitute? Due to the vagaries of the archaeological record, such discussions in the crop-origin literature are typically limited to speculation, albeit often of a highly revealing nature (e.g., Hayden 1990; Piperno 2011:461–462).

An example in which archaeologists have developed some detailed evidence relating to crop salience involves domesticated *Zea mays* L. (henceforth, maize). Macro-remains of maize from Guilá Naquitz cave in Oaxaca have been dated directly through accelerator mass spectrometry to roughly 6200 BP (Piperno and Flannery 2001). Evidence in the form of indirectly dated maize phytoliths and starch grain from the Xihuatoxtla rock shelter in the Balsas River Basin of Mexico indicates an even older age for domesticated maize at around 8700 BP (Ranere et al. 2009). In addition, new genetic studies (van Heerwaarden et al. 2007) suggest c. 9000 BP for maize's domestication. Despite maize's great antiquity in the New World, stable carbon isotope studies of human bone collagen samples from a number of archaeological sites in Mexico and other parts of Latin America brought together by Smalley and Blake (2003) indicate that for most precontact peoples, maize became an important component of diets only thousands of years after its initial domestication. In general, the collected studies show that consumption of maize in Latin America begins to become significant for most groups starting around 3000 BP (cf. Brown 2006a).

Paleobiolinguistics provides for an assessment of when domesticated species acquired substantial salience for precontact groups. If a word for a biological species reconstructs for a proto-language, this is evidence that the species was known to and probably of considerable importance for speakers of the language. Berlin et al. (1973) compile data from two closely related Mayan languages of Mexico, Tzeltal and Tzotzil (Tzeltalan), showing that words for plants of high salience tend to be retained by daughter languages of proto-languages, whereas those for plants of low salience tend to be replaced over time. This is documented by a robust positive correlation between lexical retention (stability) of Tzeltalan plant names and the cultural significance of the plants they designate, where plant salience is measured from high to low respectively on the following scale: (1) cultivated plants, (2) protected plants, (3) wild-useful plants, and (4) wild-insignificant plants. The Berlin et al. findings have been replicated by Balée and Moore (1991) in a study of plant names in five Eastern Amazonian Tupi-Guaraní languages.

Plant term reconstruction is possible for a proto-language when words for a particular species are retained by daughter languages (see below discussion of the reconstructive method). The implication of the Berlin et al. investigation for paleobiolinguistics is that plant names that reconstruct for proto-languages tend strongly to designate plants that were of substantial cultural significance for speakers of those languages. If the proto-language involved were spoken by agriculturists, plausibly many plants whose names reconstruct are likely to have been important cultigens. On the other hand, failure of a plant name to reconstruct for a proto-language does not necessarily mean that the plant was not present in the habitat of speakers; it could mean that, if present, it was not highly salient. Alternatively, if originally highly salient, it could have diminished in significance for a people over time for different reasons and, thus, the proto-word for the plant may not have survived in daughter languages.

In this study, we examine New World proto-languages for the presence of words for squash in their reconstructed vocabularies. An assumption, based on the Berlin et al. (1973) and Balée and Moore (1991) findings, is that if a word for squash reconstructs for a proto-language, the designated referent was of considerable use to and known by most adult speakers of the language. This approach does not support determination of whether a reconstructed squash word designated either a wild or domesticated species. However, if other evidence (archaeological and/or linguistic) should indicate that speakers of a proto-language were farmers, a reasonable conclusion is that the squash named in the language was domesticated.

Methods

Reconstruction involves comparing terms for squash from a set of modern genetically related languages (which form a language family). If found to be phonologically similar, they may be cognate, or, in other words, derived from a single squash term found in the language family's proto-language.[1] If cognate, knowledge of phonological regularities allows reconstruction of the proto-language's squash term (see Brown 2006a, 2006b and Mithun 1984 for non-technical descriptions of the reconstructive method). Many of the reconstructed squash words referred to in this paper have been extracted from the literature. Others have been reconstructed by the authors based on assembling comparative evidence from lexical sources (e.g., ethnobotanies, dictionaries, vocabularies).[2]

Whether or not a squash term reconstructs for a proto-language depends in part on the upper chronological limit of historical linguistics for recovering proto-words. Steady changes in languages over time accumulate such that eventually daughter languages will in no way resemble their ancient parent language. How much time must pass before the lexicon of a proto-language is no longer recoverable is highly debated by historical linguists. Our non-systematic evaluation is that many historical linguists would agree to the conservative proposal that the vocabulary of a proto-language older than around 8000 BP cannot be recovered.

Tables 3 through 6 present squash-term reconstructions for proto-languages of four major regions of the New World: (1) Eastern North America (Table 3); (2) Western North Amer-

Table 3. Squash-term reconstruction for proto-languages of Eastern North America.

Years (BP)	Proto-Language	Proto-Word for Squash (NR = Not Reconstructable)	Homeland Center (Lat/Long)	Family Affiliation	Reconstruction Source
6178	Siouan-Catawba	NR	43.83, −101.83	Siouan-Catawba	
5944	Iroquoian	NR	42.75, −76.17	Iroquoian	
5554	Algic	NR	42.67, −73.5	Algic	
4828	Caddoan	NR	33.33, −97.33	Caddoan	
3343	Algonquian	NR	42.67, −73.5	Algic	
3176	Northern Iroquoian	NR	42.75, −76.17	Iroquoian	
3169	Siouan	NR	43.83, −101.83	Siouan-Catawba	
3035	Northern Caddoan	NR	33.33, −97.33	Caddoan	
2678	Central Algonquian	NR	43, −83	Algic	
1926	Southeastern Siouan	NR	36.03, −89.39	Siouan-Catawba	
1880	Cree-Montagnais-Naskapi	NR	52, −65	Algic	
1850	Missouri River Siouan	*kakúwi	47, −108	Siouan-Catawba	1
1839	Ofo-Biloxi	*ąthą́	30.5, −88.67	Siouan-Catawba	1
1809	Pawnee	*wahuks	41, −98.67	Caddoan	2
1798	Mississippi Valley Siouan	NR	43.83, −101.83	Siouan-Catawba	
1720	Muskogean	*šoksiCaai	34, −85	Muskogean	3
1673	Five Nations	NR	42.75, −76.17	Iroquoian	
1526	Fox-Kickapoo-Sauk	*wapikon	43, −83	Algic	Authors
1378	Mohawk-Onieda	*onuʔuselaʔko	43.5, −74.25	Iroquoian	Authors
1295	Ojibwa	*okosimaan	47, −89	Algic	Authors
1173	Seneca-Onondaga	*ohniohsaʔ	42.75, −76.75	Iroquoian	Authors
1005	Dhegihan	*wathą́	36.17, −94.42	Siouan-Catawba	1
737	Dakota	*wagmu	43.83, −101.83	Siouan-Catawba	4
345	Western Muskogean	*osito	34, −88	Muskogean	Authors

Reconstruction Source:
1. Carter et al., in preparation
2. Douglas Parks, pers. comm.
3. Booker 2005
4. Robert Rankin, pers. comm.

ica and Northern Mexico (Table 4); (3) Southern Mexico and Northern Central America, (henceforth Mesoamerica) (Table 5); and (4) Southern Central America and South America (Table 6). The only New World regions not covered are Arctic and Subarctic parts of Alaska and Canada where squash is found only as a historical introduction.

The four tables list most major proto-languages of the Americas. Excluded are highly controversial proposals such as Proto-Hokan and Proto-Penutian, which have yet to be demonstrated by historical linguistics. Proto-Macro-Ge, while controversial, is included since many if not most parts of the proposal have been demonstrated. Some proto-languages, e.g., Proto-Kiowa Tanoan and Proto-Tupian, are not included because lexical information from daughter languages is not sufficiently available for drawing either positive or negative conclusions about squash-term reconstruction.

In addition to identifying proto-languages with squash terms, the tables identify proto-languages for which squash terms are "not reconstructable" (NR). NR is a designation used when terms for squash are present in all or most languages of a family, but, nonetheless, are not cognate and, hence, do not attest to a squash term in their shared ancestral language. NR, then, never indicates non-reconstructibility because of missing data.

Table 4. Squash-term reconstruction for proto-languages of Western North America and Northern Mexico.

Years (BP)	Proto-Language	Proto-Word for Squash (NR = Not Reconstructable)	Homeland Center (Lat/Long)	Family Affiliation	Reconstruction Source
4018	Uto-Aztecan	NR	27.5, −110.25	Uto-Aztecan	
3827	Salishan	NR	49.25, −122.5	Salishan	
3472	Southern Uto-Aztecan	*ayaw	27.5, −110.25	Uto-Aztecan	1
2980	Interior Salish	NR	48, −117	Salishan	
2725	Sahaptian	NR	46, −116	Sahaptian	
2576	Northern Uto-Aztecan	*pa-taŋa	39, −109	Uto-Aztecan	1
2500	Yukian	NR	38.5, −122.5	Yukian	
2459	Central Salish	NR	49.25, −122.5	Salishan	
2400	Sonoran	*ayaw	27.5, −110.25	Uto-Aztecan	1
2062	Athabaskan	NR	53.75, −123.5	Athabaskan	
1865	Yuman	*xamta	32.67, −116.17	Yuman	2
1864	N. Interior Salish	NR	50.75, −122	Salishan	
1737	Numic	*ayaw	39, −109	Uto-Aztecan	1
1724	S. Interior Salish	NR	48, −117	Salishan	
1587	Cupan	NR	33.17, −116.5	Uto-Aztecan	
1573	Southern Numic	*pa-taŋa	39, −109	Uto-Aztecan	1
1241	Eastern Miwokan	NR	38, −121	Miwokan	
1213	Tarahumaran	*ayaw, *kama	27.75, −108.67	Uto-Aztecan	1
1148	Central Numic	*pa-taŋa	37, −117	Uto-Aztecan	1
899	Tepiman	*ʔimai	29, −111	Uto-Aztecan	3
718	Apachean	NR	36.58, −104	Athabaskan	
534	River Yuman	*xamt	32.83, −114.33	Yuman	Authors

Reconstruction Source:
1. Stubbs 2011
2. Mauricio Mixco, pers. comm.
3. Bascom 1965

Table 5. Squash-term reconstruction for proto-languages of Mesoamerica (Southern Mexico and Northern Central America).

Years (BP)	Proto-Language	Proto-Word for Squash (NR = Not Reconstructable)	Homeland Center (Lat/Long)	Family Affiliation	Reconstruction Source
6591	Otomanguean	*-kʷe-, *hku	18, −96.92	Otomanguean	1, 2
5976	Eastern Otomanguean	*-kʷen	18, −96.92	Otomanguean	1
5498	Popolocan-Zapotecan	*-kʷen	17.17, −96.17	Otomanguean	2
5357	Amuzgo-Mixtecan	*lauken	16.92, −97.58	Otomanguean	1, 2
4542	Mixtecan	*kʷel/*ken	16.92, −97.58	Otomanguean	2
4274	Totozoquean	NR	19.92, −97.42	Totozoquean	
3654	Otopamean	*mǫ, *mǫih-ʔ	20.08, −100.08	Otomanguean	3
3149	Zapotecan	*ke, *kettu	17.17, −96.17	Otomanguean	2, 4
3140	Mixtec-Cuicatec	*yɔ-kïm/*yɔ-kʷï	16.92, −97.58	Otomanguean	Authors
3036	Popolocan	*-ku,*-kʷen	18, −96.92	Otomanguean	2
2220	Mayan	*k'uhm	15.42, −91.83	Mayan	5
2214	Otomian	*muʔu	20.08, −100.08	Otomanguean	Authors
2209	Chocho-Popolocan	*ču	17.67, −97.42	Otomanguean	Authors
1935	Chinantecan	*má:ʔᴸ	17.92, −96.5	Otomanguean	6
1783	Popoloca	*čuᴬ	18, −96.92	Otomanguean	7
1676	Zapotec	*yetu	17.17, −96.17	Otomanguean	Authors
1649	Quichean-Mamean	*k'uum	15.42, −91.83	Mayan	5
1520	General Aztec	*ayoh-	18.35, −99.83	Uto-Aztecan	8
1492	Greater Mamean	*k'uum	15.42, −91.83	Mayan	5
1437	Mixtec	*yikiʔ	16.92, −97.58	Otomanguean	9
1435	Totonacan	*nípši'	19.92, −97.42	Totozoquean	10
1432	Cholan-Tzeltalan	*č'uhm	16.83, −92.83	Mayan	5
1407	Mixe-Zoquean	*pasoŋ	17.95, −95	Totozoquean	11
1225	Kanjobalan-Chujean	*k'uum	15.83, −91.83	Mayan	5
1198	Corachol	*soci	22.17, −104.83	Uto-Aztecan	12
1148	Cholan	*čuhm	14.81, −89.38	Mayan	5
1058	Chujean	*k'um	15.92, −91.58	Mayan	5
997	Chatino	*kyòjò	16.25, −97.38	Otomanguean	4
981	Greater Quichean	*k'uum	14.78, −91.5	Mayan	5
948	Subtiaba-Tlapanecan	*di	17.08, −99	Otomanguean	Authors
900	Mixe	*ciʔwa	17.02, −96.07	Totozoquean	11
802	Kanjobalan	*k'uum	15.83, −91.83	Mayan	5
790	Yucatecan	*k'uum	20, −89	Mayan	5
787	Zoque	*pasoŋ	16.9, −94.68	Totozoquean	11
741	Otomi	*mu	20.08, −100.08	Otomanguean	Authors
511	Tzeltalan	*č'um	16.83, −92.83	Mayan	5

Reconstruction Source:
1. Kaufman 1990
2. Rensch 1976
3. Bartholomew 1965
4. Campbell 2012
5. Brown and Wichmann 2004
6. Rensch 1989
7. Matteson 1972
8. Campbell and Langacker 1978
9. Josserand 1983
10. Brown et al. 2011
11. Wichmann 1995
12. Stubbs 2011

Table 6. Squash-term reconstruction for languages of Southern Central America and South America.

Years (BP)	Proto-Language	Proto-Word for Squash (NR = Not Reconstructable)	Homeland Center (Lat/Long)	Family Affiliation	Reconstruction Source
7266	Macro-Ge	NR	−11.3, −53	Macro-Ge	
4701	Mataco-Guaykuru	NR	−22.5, −62.58	Mataco-Guaykuru	
4461	Southern Arawakan	NR	−10.33, −74.33	Arawakan	
4400	Chibchan	*api' ~ api's	9.75, −83.42	Chibchan	1
4134	Arawakan	NR	1, −69.17	Arawakan	
4085	N Arawakan	NR	1, −69.17	Arawakan	
3943	Panoan-Tacanan	NR	−7.5, −75	Panoan-Tacanan	
3518	Caribbean N. Arawakan	NR	12, −72	Arawakan	
3310	Salivan	NR	5, −67	Saliva	
3178	Zaparoan	NR	−3.25, −74	Zaparoan	
3124	Nadahup	NR	0, −69	Nadahup	
3023	Ge	NR	−15, −52.5	Macro-Ge	
2903	Witoto-Ocaina	NR	−2.75, −71.75	Witoto-Ocaina	
2774	Misumalpan	*ĩwã	13, −84.5	Misumalpan	2
2731	Talamancan	*apí	9.75, −83.42	Chibchan	1
2699	Tucanoan	NR	0.33, −70.25	Tucanoan	3
2593	Inland N. Arawakan	NR	1, −69.17	Arawakan	
2404	Matacoan	NR	−22.5, −62.58	Mataco-Guaykuru	
2362	Cariban	*(k)awayama	10.17, −72.75	Cariban	4
2258	Chocoan	NR	6.83, −77.17	Chocoan	
2156	Western Tucanoan	NR	−2.83, −72.5	Tucanoan	
1672	Panoan	NR	−7.5, −75	Panoan-Tacanan	
1634	Mainline Panoan	*wara	−7.5, −75	Panoan-Tacanan	5
1780	Mascoian	*yaktepa	−23.2, −58	Mascoian	Authors
1764	Arauan	NR	−6.00, −70.50	Arauan	
1717	Quechuan	*sapallu	0.33, −78	Quechuan	6
1590	Tacanan	*xemi	−13.33, −66.5	Panoan-Tacanan	7
1550	Tupi-Guarani	NR	−8, −62	Tupi	
1519	Kampan	*kemi	−10.33, −74.33	Arawakan	8
1419	Cayapa-Colorado	*ʔu	0.67, −79	Barbacoan	Authors
1319	Yanomam	NR	3.5, −62.83	Yanomam	
1241	Eastern Tucanoan	NR	0.33, −70.25	Tucanoan	
1185	Kawapanan	*kun	−5.5, −77	Kawapanan	9
678	Jivaroan	*yuwi	−2.5, −78	Jivaroan	Authors
398	Mayoruna Panoan	NR	−4.42, −70.25	Panoan-Tacanan	

Reconstruction Source:
1. Constenla 1981, 1990
2. Constenla 1987
3. Thiago Chacon, pers. comm.
4. Sérgio Meira, pers. comm.
5. Shell 2008
6. Willem Adelaar, pers. comm.
7. Key 1968
8. Lev Michael, Frank Seifart, and Mary Ruth Wise, pers. comm.
9. Pilar Valenzuela, pers. comm.

Dates for proto-languages presented in the tables are intended to be the latest dates at which these languages were spoken (just before breaking up into daughter languages). These are calculated through use of ASJP (Automated Similarity Judgment Program) chronology, a computational dating approach based on the lexical similarity of languages and a set of 52 calibration dates for proto-language breakups documented through historical, epigraphic, and archaeological records (see Holman et al. 2011). The discrepancies between ASJP estimated dates and the 52 calibration dates are on average 29% as large as the estimated dates themselves, a figure that does not differ significantly among language families of the world; also, younger dates tend to be more accurate than older ones (Holman et al. 2011). The 29% average difference between an estimated date and its calibration date should be viewed as the estimated date's margin of error. Since an ASJP date indicates the latest date at which a proto-language was spoken, plausibly any proto-language could have been spoken hundreds of years if not more before its ASJP date. Possible geographic coordinates for proto-language homeland centers given in the tables are produced through automation using an algorithm for identifying the maximum lexical diversity within a language family (see Wichmann et al. 2010). The geographic center of lexical diversity of a family is assumed to correlate with where the family's proto-language was spoken.

The information reported in Tables 3 through 6 is plotted in Maps 1, 2 and 3 to give a visual perspective on both the chronological and geographic distributions of reconstructed squash terms. These distributions are discussed next.

Findings

Eastern North America

Squash terms are reconstructable for 11 of the 24 proto-languages of Eastern North America (Map 1; Table 3). (Information from Tables 3 and 4 are combined on Map 1.) No squash terms are reconstructable for the eight proto-languages older than 3000 BP, and none for five of the proto-languages younger than the latter date. The oldest proto-language for which a squash term reconstructs is Proto-Missouri River Siouan (1850 BP).

The oldest crop-origin date for domesticated squash in Eastern North America is 5000 BP (Table 3), based on *C. pepo* remains from the Phillips Spring site in Missouri, USA (Smith 2006). None of the proto-languages of Eastern North America with reconstructed squash terms show pre-5000 BP dates. Indeed, the earliest date for such a proto-language, 1850 BP (Missouri River Siouan), is more than 3000 years younger than the crop-origin date. In addition, all of the other proto-languages of the region having squash terms show dates younger than 2000 BP. These linguistic data suggest that domesticated squash did not become widespread in Eastern North America until thousands of years after squash was first domesticated in the region.

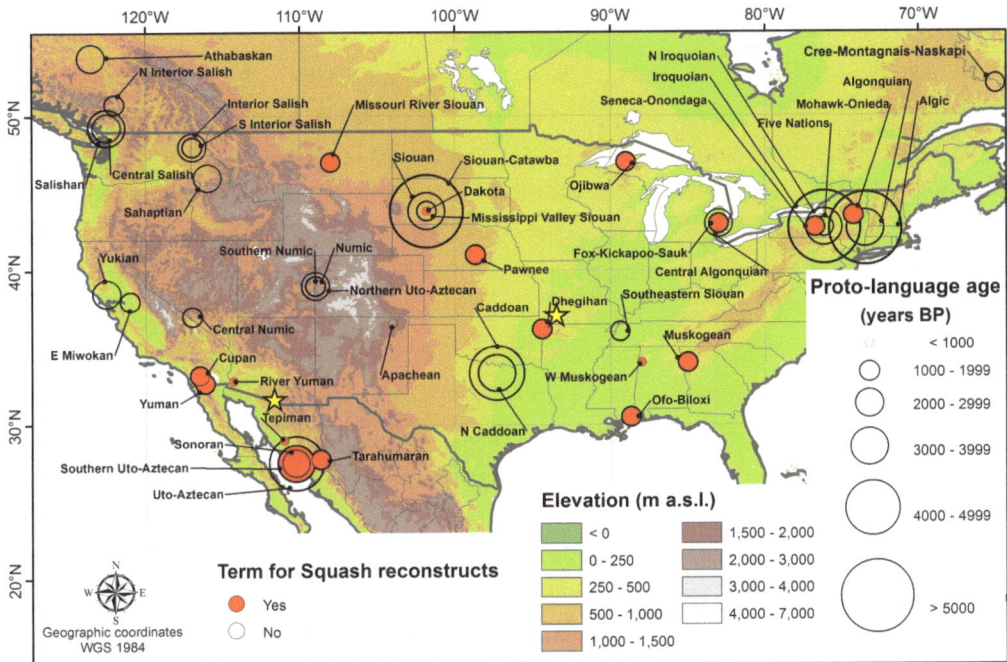

Map 1. Squash-term reconstruction information from Tables 3 and 4 plotted on map covering Eastern North America and Western North America/Northern Mexico. Yellow stars indicate sites of earliest archaeobotanical evidence of domesticated squash respectively for Eastern North America and Western North America/Northern Mexico. Centers of circles locate homeland centers of proto-languages (see geographic coordinates of Tables 3 and 4) and circle size indicates proto-language age (see "years before present" of Tables 3 and 4), with larger circles indicating older proto-languages and smaller circles, younger ones. Circles are red filled if a squash term reconstructs for a proto-language, and transparent if not.

Western North America and Northern Mexico

Squash terms reconstruct for ten of 22 proto-languages of Western North America and Northern Mexico (Map 1; Table 4). The oldest of these ten is Proto-Southern Uto-Aztecan with a date of 3472 BP, followed by Proto-Northern Uto-Aztecan (2576 BP), and Proto-Sonoran (2400 BP). The remaining seven of the ten show dates younger than 2000 BP.

The oldest crop-origin date for domesticated squash in the region is 4000 BP (Mexican/US Desert Borderlands [Fritz 2011]). None of the ten proto-languages with reconstructed squash terms show dates older than 4000 BP. Unlike Eastern North America, there is not a large gap between the date of the region's earliest archaeobotanical evidence for domesticated squash and the earliest paleobiolinguistic date (3472 BP). Archaeological evidence (Fritz 2011:507) indicates that *C. pepo* squash, along with maize, diffused about 4000 years ago from its place of domestication in Southern Mexico northward into the Desert Borderlands, eventually spreading further north into the U.S. Great Basin and abutting areas.

Mesoamerica

Squash terms reconstruct for all but one of the 36 proto-languages of Mesoamerica, the oldest of which is Proto-Otomanguean with a date of 6591 BP (Map 2; Table 5). The only proto-language of the region for which a squash term does not reconstruct is Proto-Totozoquean[3], dated to 4274 BP. Proto-Otomanguean has the most ancient date for a proto-language with a squash term in the New World. The earlist archaeobotanical date for squash (*C. pepo*) in the region is 10,000 BP, documenting the oldest *Cucurbita* remains recovered anywhere in the Americas (from Guilá Naquitz cave in eastern Oaxaca State, Mexico [Smith 2001]). As in Eastern North America, there is a substantial gap in time between the date for the region's earliest archaeobotanical domesticated squash (10,000 BP) and the oldest paleobiolinguistic date for the crop (6591 BP). The homeland center for Proto-Otomanguean (Map 2) is located in the northwestern corner of Oaxaca, only some 200 kilometers removed from Guilá Naquitz cave.

Otomanguean ancestral languages make up 18 of the 36 proto-languages of the region (Table 5). The oldest proto-language not belonging to the Otomanguean family for which a squash term reconstructs is Proto-Mayan with a date of 2220 BP. Thus, the earliest non-Otomanguean date for squash in the region is 4371 years younger than the oldest paleobiolinguistic date for the area (6591 BP). This chronological difference suggests that speakers of

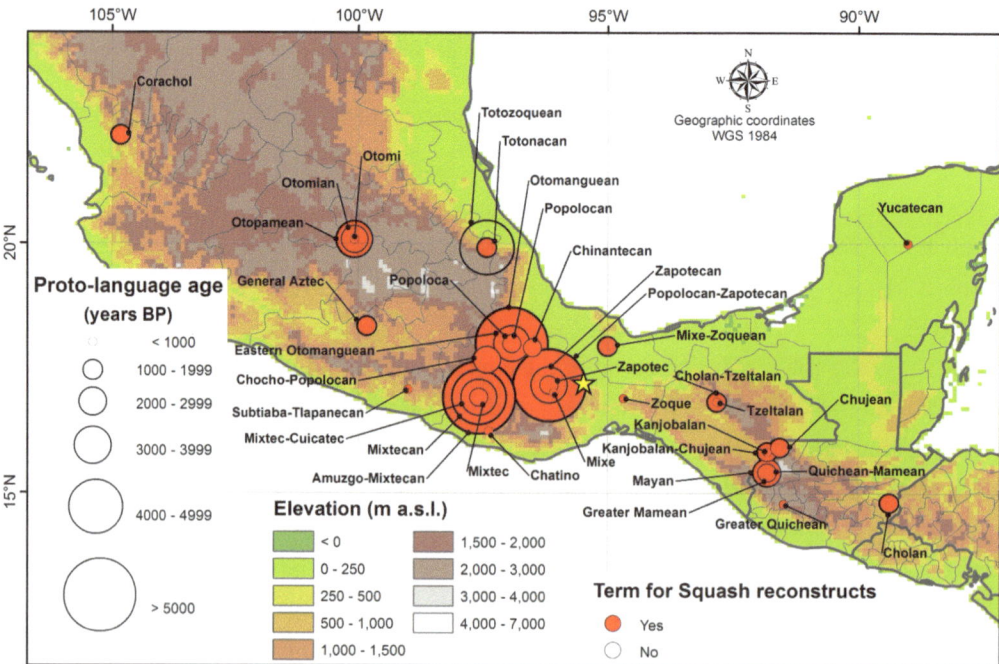

Map 2. Squash-term reconstruction information from Table 5 plotted on map of Mesoamerica (Southern Mexico and Northern Central America). Yellow star indicates site of earliest archaeobotanical evidence of domesticated squash. Symbols are as in Map 1.

Proto-Otomanguean were the first or, at least, among the first prehistoric people of Meso-america for which squash was of substantial salience.[4] Indeed, such an early apparent interest in squash may have its origins in early Otomanguean participation in the domestication of squash. This tentative proposal is bolstered by the proximity of the Proto-Otomanguean homeland to Guilá Naquitz cave from which remains of the earliest domesticated squash have been recovered.

Southern Central America and South America

Squash terms reconstruct for 12 of the 35 proto-languages of Southern Central America and South America (Map 3; Table 6). The oldest ancestral language showing squash is Proto-Chibchan of Southern Central America with a date of 4400 BP. The next three oldest with squash are Proto-Talamancan (2731 BP, a daughter language of Proto-Chibchan), Proto-Misumalpan (2774 BP), and Proto-Cariban (2362 BP), all of which are spoken in southern Central America and northern South America near the Isthmus of Panama (the northern region of Map 3).The oldest archaeological squash is from Northern Peru (9240 BP, Map 3).

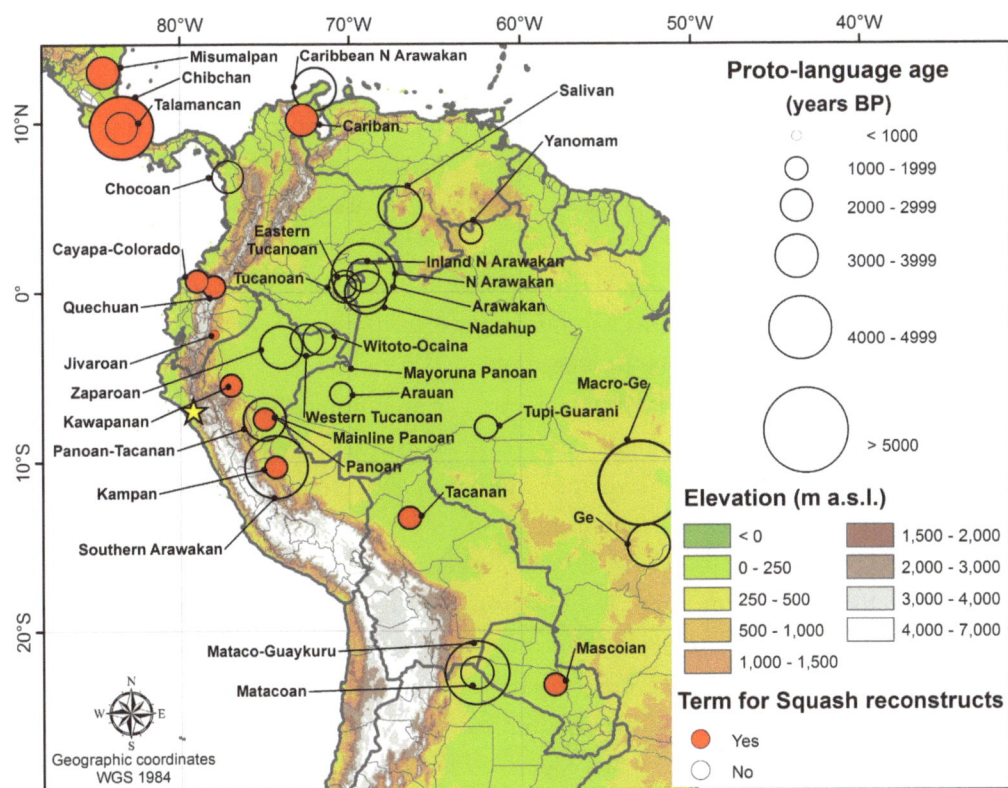

Map 3. Squash-term reconstruction information from Table 6 plotted on map covering Southern Central America and South America. Yellow star indicates site of earliest archaeobotanical evidence of domesticated squash. Symbols are as in Map 1.

Very early squash remains (8600 BP) have also been recovered in southern Central America (Piperno 2011) close to homeland centers for Proto-Chibchan, Proto-Talamancan, and Proto-Misumalpan. The remaining eight proto-languages with squash are all younger than 1700 BP. These are all located in western regions of South America, largely along or close to the eastern slope of the Andes.

Oldest archaeobotanical dates for the three squash species domesticated in South America, *C. ficifolia* (Figures 2, 3, 4), *C. moschata* (Figures 5, 6, 7), and *C. maxima* (Figure 8), are respectively 9300–8000 BP, 5100 BP, and 4400–3200 BP (Table 2). There is a 4900-year gap between the earliest archaeobotanical date (for *C. moschata*) and the age of the oldest proto-language with a squash term (4400 BP) suggesting that a substantial period of time elapsed between early squash domestication in the region and squash's acquisition of considerable salience. Paleobiolinguistic evidence indicates that domesticated squash developed widespread salience in western South America only after around 2000 BP (Map 3). Apparently, interest in the crop did not extend to proto-languages of eastern regions of South America in precontact times.

Discussion and Conclusion

In all four New World regions there is a lapse in time between the earliest domesticated squash remains and the date of the oldest proto-language with a squash word (Table 7). This chronological gap is greatest for Southern Central America and South America (4900 years) and smallest for Western North America and Northern Mexico (528 years). The average difference for all the Americas is 2997 years. Throughout the New World, then, squash seems to have been domesticated considerably before gaining enough salience to register on the paleobiolinguistic radar screen. This is reminiscent of and analogous to the archaeological finding involving stable carbon isotope measurement of human bone collagen discussed earlier, a measurement indicating that maize became an important component of precontact diet in much of Latin America around 3000 BP, thousands of years after its domestication. Like maize, squash seems to have developed significant widespread salience for New World groups several millennia after initial domestication.

Smalley and Blake (2003) propose that maize was domesticated for its sugary pith or other edible parts rather than for its grain. They propose that the stalk sugar of maize was its initial major attraction for groups, possibly used for making alcoholic beverages. According to them, at around 3000 BP maize kernels surpassed stalk sugar in importance and *Zea mays* widely became a dietary staple. While only limited direct evidence for this hypothesis has emerged since its proposal (Michael Blake, pers. comm.), it is nonetheless of special interest in the context of Brian Hayden's (1990) accumulator/feasting hypothesis.

The accumulator/feasting hypothesis proposes in part that initial domestication of some crops has been in response to the drive of "complex hunter-gatherers" (who are similar to traditional hunter-gatherer groups of the Pacific Northwest Coast) to accumulate and display wealth. Such crops develop as feasting delicacies to aggrandize people, and not, initially at least, to be used by group members at large. Comparable crops of the modern world would include foods such as truffles and caviar. According to Hayden (1990:61), this hypothesis "explains the nature of the first domesticates and the full range of domesticates: the condiments, the containers, the intoxicants, the lipid rich foods, the carbohydrates, and even dogs." If maize were managed initially for stalk sugar to make intoxicating beverages for feasting, and only much later to have its kernels used widely as a dietary staple, this would explain the considerable time gap between the earliest archaeobotanical date for domesticated maize (8700 BP), and when stable carbon isotope measurement indicates the beginning of broad consumption of maize in Latin America (c. 3000 BP). The same hypothesis might also account for the similar time gap involving archaeobotanical and paleobiolinguistic dates for domesticated squash (Table 7). One possibility is that early squash was domesticated for use as containers, or as fishnet floats rather than for widespread consumption of its fruit by the general populace (Hart et al. 2004).

The dates for the beginning of squash's broad salience in three of the four New World regions (Table 7) are similar to one another, ranging from 2500 to 2000 BP. In the case of Mesoamerica, paleobiolinguistic evidence suggests that squash developed substantial significance all over the area some four millennia earlier, around 6500 BP (Table 7), this being the same date as that for the oldest proto-language of the region with a squash term, i.e., Proto-Otomanguean. Subsequent to 6500 BP, squash terms reconstruct for all Mesoamerican proto-languages but

Table 7. Summary of findings (based on information from Tables 2–6).

	Eastern North America	Western North America and Northern Mexico	Mesoamerica (Southern Mexico and Northern Central America)	Southern Central America and South America
Crop-Origin (Archaeobotanical) Date for Earliest Squash	5000 BP	4000 BP	10,000 BP	9300–8000 BP
Date for Oldest Proto-Language with Squash Term	1850 BP	3472 BP	6591 BP	4440 BP
Chronological Gap	3150 years	528 years	3409 years	4900 years
Date of Beginning of Widespread Salience of Squash[1]	2000 BP	2500 BP	6500 BP	2000 BP
Percent of Highest-order Proto-languages with Squash Term[2]	17% (1/6)	14% (1/7)	75% (3/4)	38% (8/21)

1. Earliest date after which the vast majority of proto-languages of a region are found to have a squash term.
2. A "highest-order proto-language" of a region is an ancestral language that is not a daughter language of any other proto-language of that region. For example, Proto-Otomanguean of Mesoamerica is a highest-order proto-language, while its daughter language, Proto-Eastern Otomanguean, is not. The pertinent percent for Mesoamerica is the number of highest order proto-languages of the area with squash terms (3) divided by the total number of highest order proto-languages of the area (4).

one. Squash, then, seems to have acquired considerable salience and broad distribution in Mesoamerica much earlier than it did in the other three regions. This is also attested by the fact that the percentage of higher-order proto-languages of Mesoamerica having squash terms is 75%, while those for the other three New World regions are all below 40% (Table 7).

Proto-Otomanguean of Mesoamerica has the distinction of being among the very oldest demonstrated proto-languages in the New World. It is also the oldest proto-language in the Americas for which a squash term reconstructs. Perhaps not coincidentally, the ancestral language's homeland center is located only some 200 kilometers from Guilá Naquitz cave in Oaxaca, Mexico (see yellow star, Map 2) where the earliest dated archaeobotanical squash for the New World has been recovered.

Proto-Otomanguean is also the oldest New World proto-language with reconstructed terms for four or more botanical species that constitute important crops today. These include in addition to squash, maize (*Zea mays*), chile (*Capsicum* spp.), avocado (*Persea americana* Mill.), century plant (*Agave* spp.), and prickly pear (*Opuntia* spp.) (Brown 2010), and, possibly, common bean (*Phaseolus vulgaris* L.) and sweet potato (*Ipomoea batatas* (L.) Lam.) (Kaufman 1990), and maybe even others (Rensch 1976). Paleobiolinguistic evidence, then, suggests that the economy of Proto-Otomanguean speakers entailed a robust food-producing component, advanced beyond early incipient farming, but falling short of a settled agrarian way of life described as full village farming (Smith 1992) that was to emerge in Mesoamerica more than two millennia after the proto-language's breakup. It seems appropriate to dub speakers of Proto-Otomanguean "advanced incipient farmers" who were probably among the earliest of their kind in the New World (cf. Amador Hernández 1979; Hopkins 1984).

Otomangueans may have advanced incipient farming by expanding food production from the management of one or two domesticated crops, for example, those tended by elites for feasting events, to the conscious collection in their immediate area of all domesticated species occurring in the abutting greater region. The latter might include different crops tended in household gardens in diverse locations. This may have involved making these crops available to all speakers of the language. The subsequent emergence of full village farming in Mesoamerica beginning some four thousand years ago (Smith 1992) may not have been possible without such a development. A further consequence of this may have been a substantial general increase in the salience of crops for the group as a whole, ultimately rendering crop names stable over great periods of time and, thus, facilitating the eventual recovery of such words through modern paleobiolinguistic analysis.

Notes

1. If not cognate, similarities could be due to other factors such as borrowing (most likely), universal tendencies, or chance.

2. Limitations of lexical data only very rarely permit identification to species of reconstructed squash terms. In addition, in some instances, reflexes of reconstructed terms denote bottle gourd instead of or in addition to squash, making semantic reconstruction problematic. Great caution has been taken to sort through such semantic issues and to reconstruct squash as referents of proto-terms only when clearly justified by the data.

3. A term reconstructs for Proto-Totozoquean (**nkʸwip*) with reflexes in some languages that designate squash (*Cucurbita* spp.) and reflexes in others denoting chayote vine (*Sechium edule* (Jacq.) Sw.) (Brown et al. 2011). Consequently, squash cannot be definitively reconstructed as the proto-term's referent.

4. Since 2220 BP is the *latest date* at which Proto-Mayan was spoken, plausibly the language has a much greater antiquity and, therefore, squash could have been of significance to its speakers considerably earlier than that date.

Acknowledgements

A number of scholars have made contributions to this study for which we are grateful. John P. Hart suggested the project to Brown over six years ago. Other earlier contributors include Gene Anderson, Michael Blake, Pamela Brown, Wallace Chafe, Deena S. Decker-Walters, Richard Ford, Gayle J. Fritz, Eugene Hunn, Timothy K. Perttula, Dolores Piperno, Bruce D. Smith, Linda Wessel-Beaver, and Richard A. Yarnell. For supplying information used in the current version of this paper, we would like to thank Willem Adelaar, William Balée, Brent Berlin, Michael Blake, Thiago Chacon, Richard Ford, Carlos Galindo, Eric Holman, Eugene Hunn, Rafael Lira S., Sérgio Meira, Lev Michael, Mauricio Mixco, Douglas Parks, Robert Rankin, Eduardo Ribeiro, Frank Seifart, Pilar Valenzuela, Mary Ruth Wise and Felice Wyndham. Comments on the present version of the paper have been provided by William L. Balée, David Beck, Michael Blake, Thiago Chacon, Charles Clement, Geo Coppens, Catherine S. Fowler, John P. Hart, Eric Holman, and Frank Seifart.

References Cited

Amador Hernández, M., and P. Casasa García. 1979   Un Análisis Cultural de Juegos Léxicos Reconstruidos del Proto-otomangue. In *Estudios Lingüístico en Lenguas Otomangues*, eds. N.A. Hopkins and J.K. Josserand, pp. 13–19. Instituto Nacional de Antropología e Historia, México, D.F.

Balée, William L., and Denny Moore. 1991   Similarity and Variation in Plant Names in Five Tupi-Guarani Languages (Eastern Amazonia). *Bulletin-Florida Museum of Natural History* 35(4):209–262.

Barbieri, Nino. 2007   Cucurbita Maxima 03, Pumpkin. Wikimedia Commons. Available at: http://commons.wikimedia.org/wiki/File:Cucurbita_maxima_03.jpg (verified 15 May 2012).

Bascom, Burton William. 1965   Proto-Tepiman (Tepehuan-Piman). Ph.D. Dissertation. University of Washington, Seattle.

Berlin, Brent, Dennis E. Breedlove, Robert M. Laughlin, and Peter H. Raven. 1973   Cultural Significance and Lexical Retention in Tzeltal-Tzotzil Ethnobotany. In *Meaning in Mayan Languages*, ed. Munro S. Edmonson, pp. 143–164. Mouton, The Hague.

Blench, Roger M. 2008   Using Linguistics to Reconstruct African Subsistence Systems: Comparing Crop Names to Trees and Livestock. In *Rethinking Agriculture: Archaeological and Ethnoarchaeological Perspectives*, eds. Timothy P. Denham, José Iriarte, and Luc Vrydaghs, pp. 598–644. Left Coast Press, California.

Booker, Karen. 2005   Muskogean Historical Phonology. In *Native Languages of the Southeastern United States,* eds. Heather Hardy, and Janine Scancarelli, pp. 246–298. University of Nebraska Press, Lincoln, NE.

Brown, Cecil H. 2006a   Glottochronology and the Chronology of Maize in the Americas. In *Histories of Maize: Multidisciplinary Approaches to the Prehistory, Biogeography, Domestication, and Evolutions of Maize*, eds. John E. Staller, Robert H. Tykot, and Bruce F. Benz, pp. 648–663. Elsevier, San Diego.

Brown, Cecil H. 2006b   Prehistoric Chronology of the Common Bean in the New World: The Linguistic Evidence. *American Anthropologist* 108:507–516.

Brown, Cecil H. 2010   Development of Agriculture in Prehistoric Mesoamerica: The Linguistic Evidence. In *Pre-Columbian Foodways: Interdisciplinary Approaches to Food, Culture and markets in Ancient Mesoamerica*, ed. John E. Staller and Michael D. Carrasco, pp. 71–107. Springer Science+Business Media, Berlin.

Brown, Cecil H., and Søren Wichmann. 2004   Proto-Mayan Syllable Nuclei. *International Journal of American Linguistics* 70:128–186.

Brown, Cecil H., David Beck, Grzegorz Kondrak, James K. Watters, and Søren Wichmann. 2011   Totozoquean. *International Journal of American Linguistics* 77: 323–372.

Campbell, Eric. 2012   The Internal Diversification and Subgrouping of Chatino. Forthcoming in *International Journal of American Linguistics*.

Campbell, Lyle, and Ronald W. Langacker. 1978   Proto-Aztecan Vowels: Part III. *International Journal of American Linguistics* 44:262–279.

Carter, Richard T., A. Wesley Jones, John E. Koontz, Robert L. Rankin, and David S. Rood. In Preparation. Comparative Siouan Dictionary. Computer database from the University of Colorado.

Constenla-Umaña, Adolfo. 1981   Comparative Chibchan Phonology. Ph.D. Dissertation, University of Pennsylvania.

Constenla-Umaña, Adolfo. 1987   Elementos de Fonología Comparada de las Lenguas Mis-umalpas. *Filología y Lingüística* 13(1):129–161.

Constenla-Umaña, Adolfo. 1990   Una Hipótesis sobre la Localización del Protochibcha y la Dispersión de sus Descendientes. *Revista de Filología y Lingüística de la Universidad de Costa Rica* 16:111–123.

Decker-Walters, Deena S. 1993   New Methods for Studying the Origins of New World Domesticates: The Squash Example. In *Foraging and Farming in the Eastern Woodlands*, ed., C. Margaret Scarry, pp. 91–97. University Press of Florida, Gainesville.

Decker-Walters, Deena S., Terrence W. Walters, C. Wesley Cowan, and Bruce D. Smith. 1993   Isozymic Characterization of Wild Populations of *Cucurbita pepo*. *Journal of Ethnobiology* 13:55–72.

Diebold, A. Richard, Jr. 1985. The Evolution of Indo-European Nomenclature for Salmonid Fish: The Case of 'Huchen' (*Hucho* spp.). *Journal of Indo-European Studies* Monograph Series Number Five, Washington, D.C.

Dillehay, Tom D., Jack Rossen, Thomas C. Andres, and David E. Williams. 2007   Preceramic Adoption of Peanut, Squash, and Cotton in Northern Peru. *Science* 316:1890–1893.

Duncan, Neil A., Deborah M. Pearsall, and Robert A. Benfer, Jr. 2009   Gourd and Squash Artifacts Yield Starch Grains of Feasting Foods from Preceramic Peru. *Proceedings of the National Academy of Sciences* 106 (32):13202–13206.

Fowler, Catherine S. 1972   Some Ecological Clues to Proto-Numic Homelands. *Desert Research Institute Publications in the Social Sciences* 8:105–117.

Fowler, Catherine S. 1983   Some Lexical Clues to Uto-Aztecan Prehistory. *International Journal of American Linguistics* 49:224–257.

Friedrich, Paul. 1970   *Proto-Indo-European Trees*. The University of Chicago Press, Chicago.

Fritz, Gayle J. 1990   Multiple Pathways to Farming in Precontact Eastern North America. *Journal of World Prehistory* 4(4):387–435.

Fritz, Gayle J. 2011   The Role of "Tropical" Crops in Early North American Agriculture. In *Subsistence Economies of Indigenous North American Societies*, ed. Bruce D. Smith, pp. 503–516. Rowman Littlefield.

Hart, John P., and Nancy Asch Sidell. 1997   Additional Evidence for Early Cucurbit Use in the Northern Eastern Woodlands East of the Allegheny Front. *American Antiquity* 63(3):523–537.

Hart, John P., Robert A. Daniels, and Charles J. Sheviak. 2004   Do *Cucurbita pepo* Gourds Float Fishnets? *American Antiquity* 69:141–148.

Hart, John P., Hetty Jo Brumbach, and Robert Lusteck. 2007   Extending the Phytolith Evidence for Early Maize (*Zea mays ssp. mays*) and Squash (*Cucurbita sp.*) in Central New York. *American Antiquity* 72(3):563–583.

Hayden, Brian. 1990   Nimrods, Piscators, Pluckers, and Planters: The Emergence of Food Production. *Journal of Anthropological Archaeology* 9:31–69.

Hill, Jane H. 2001   Proto-Uto-Aztecan: A Community of Cultivators in Central Mexico? *American Anthropologist* 103:913–934.

Holman, Eric W., Cecil H. Brown, Søren Wichmann, André Müller, Viveka Velupillai, Harald Hammarström, Sebastian Sauppe, Hagen Jung, Dik Bakker, Pamela Brown, Oleg Belyaev, Matthias Urban, Robert Mailhammer, Johann-Mattis List, and Dmitry Egorov. 2011   Automated Dating of the World's Language Families Based on Lexical Similarity. *Current Anthropology* 52:841–875.

Hopkins, N.A. 1984   Otomanguean Linguistic Prehistory. In *Essays in Otomanguean Culture History*, eds. J. Kathryn Josserand, Marcus Winter, and Nicholas A. Hopkins, pp. 25–64. Vanderbilt University, Nashville, Tennessee.

Kaufman, Terrence S. 1990   Early Otomanguean Homeland and Cultures: Some Premature Hypotheses. *University of Pittsburgh Working Papers in Linguistics* 1:91–136.

Key, Mary Ritchie. 1968   *Comparative Tacanan Phonology: With Cavineña Phonology and Notes on Pano-Tacanan Relationship*. Mouton, The Hague.

Lema, Verónica S. 2011   The Possible Influence of Post-Harvest Objectives on *Cucurbita maxima* subspecies *maxima* and subspecies *andreana* Evolution under Cultivation at the Argentinean Northwest: An Archaeological Example. *Archaeological and Anthropological Sciences* 3:113–139.

Lira, Rafael. 1995   *Estudios Taxonómicos y Ecogeográficos de las Cucurbitaceae Latinoamericanas de Importancia Económica: Cucurbita, Sechium, Sicana y Cyclanthera*. Systematic and Ecogeographic Studies on Crop Gene Pools: 9. International Plant Genetic Resources Institute. Rome, Italy.

Lovis, William A., and G. William Monaghan. 2008   Chronology and Evolution of the Green Point Flood Plain and Associated *Cucurbita pepo*. In *Current Northeast Paleoethnobotany II*, ed. John P. Hart, pp. 141–150. New York State Museum Bulletin 512. The University of the State of New York, Albany.

Matteson, Esther. 1972   Toward Proto Amerindian. In *Comparative Studies in Amerindian Languages*, eds. Esther Matteson, Alva Wheeler, Frances L. Jackson, Nathan E. Waltz, and Diana R. Christian, pp. 21–89. Mouton, The Hague.

Mithun, Marianne. 1984   The Proto-Iroquoians: Cultural Reconstruction from Lexical Materials. In *Extending the Rafters: Interdisciplinary Approaches to Iroquoian Studies*, eds. Foster K. Michael, Jack Campisi, and Marianne Mithun, pp. 259–282. State University of New York Press, Albany.

Pearsall, Deborah M. 1992   The Origins of Plant Cultivation in South America. In *The Origins of Agriculture: An International Perspective*, eds. C. Wesley Cowan and Patty Jo Watson, pp. 173–205. Smithsonian Institution Press, Washington, D.C.

Piperno, Dolores R. 2011   The Origins of Plant Cultivation and Domestication in the New World Tropics: Patterns, Process, and New Developments. *Current Anthropology* 52(S4):S453–S470.

Piperno, Dolores R., and K.V. Flannery. 2001   The Earliest Archaeological Maize (*Zea mays* L.) from Highland Mexico: New Accelerator Mass Spectrometry Dates and Their Implications. *Proceedings of the National Academy of Sciences* 98(4):2101–2103.

Piperno, Dolores R., and Deborah M. Pearsall. 1998   *The Origins of Agriculture in the Lowland Neotropics.* Academic Press, San Diego.

Piperno Dolores R., Thomas C. Andres, and Karen E. Stothert. 2000   Phytoliths in *Cucurbita* and other Neotropical Cucurbitaceae and their Occurrence in Early Archaeological Sites from the Lowland American Tropics. *Journal of Archaeological Science* 27:193–208.

Piperno, Dolores R., and Tom D. Dillehay. 2008   Starch Grains on Human Teeth Reveal Early Broad Crop Diet in Northern Peru. *Proceedings of the National Academy of Sciences* 105(50):19622–19627.

Piperno, Dolores R., Irene Holst, Linda Wessel-Beaver, and Thomas C. Andres. 2002   Evidence for the Control of Phytolith Formation in *Cucurbita* Fruits by the Hard Rind (Hr) Genetic Locus: Archaeological and Ecological Implications. *Proceedings of the National Academy of Sciences* 99(16):10923–10928.

Piperno, Dolores R., and Karen E. Stothert. 2003   Phytolith Evidence for Early Holocene *Cucurbita* Domestication in Southwest Ecuador. *Science* 299(5609):1054–1057.

Ranere, Anthony J., Dolores R. Piperno, Irene Holst, Ruth Dickau, and José Iriarte. 2009   The Cultural and Chronological Context of Early Holocene Maize and Squash Domestication in the Central Balsas River Valley, Mexico. *Proceedings of the National Academy of Sciences* 106(13):5014–5018.

Rankin, Robert L. 2006   Siouan Tribal Contacts and Dispersions Evidenced in the Terminology for Maize and other Cultigens. In *Histories of Maize: Multidisciplinary Approaches to the Prehistory, Biogeography, Domestication, and Evolutions of Maize,* eds. John E. Staller, Robert H. Tykot, and Bruce F. Benz, pp. 563–575. Elsevier, San Diego.

Rensch, Calvin R. 1976   *Comparative Otomanguean Phonology.* Indiana University Publications, Bloomington.

Rensch, Calvin R. 1989   *An Etymological Dictionary of the Chinantec Languages.* Summer Institute of Linguistics, Arlington, Texas.

Sanjur, Oris I., Dolores R. Piperno, Thomas C. Andres, and Linda Wessel-Beaver. 2002   Phylogenetic Relationships among Domesticated and Wild Species of *Cucurbita* (Cucurbitaceae) Inferred from a Mitochondrial Gene: Implications for Crop Plant Evolution and Areas of Origin. *Proceedings of the National Academy of Sciences* 99(1):535–540.

Shell, Olive A. 2008   *Estudios pano III: Las lenguas pano y su reconstrucción.* Instituto Lingüístico de Verano, Lima, Perú.

Shepard, G.H., and H. Ramirez. 2011   "Made in Brazil": Human Dispersal of the Brazil Nut (*Bertholletia excelsa,* Lecythidaceae) in Ancient Amazonia. *Economic Botany,* 65(1):44–65.

Siebert, Frank T., Jr. 1967   The Original Home of the Proto-Algonquian People. Anthropological Series 78. *National Museum of Canada Bulletin* 214:13–47.

Smalley, John, and Michael Blake. 2003   Sweet Beginnings: Stalk Sugar and the Domestication of Maize. *Current Anthropology* 44(5):675–703.

Smith, Bruce D. 1992   *Rivers of Change: Essays on Early Agriculture in Eastern North America.* Smithsonian Institution Press, Washington, D.C.

Smith, Bruce D. 1997   The Initial Domestication of *Cucurbita pepo* in the Americas 10,000 Years Ago. *Science* 276:932.

Smith, Bruce D. 2001   Documenting Plant Domestication: The Consilience of Biological and Archaeological Approaches. *Proceedings of the National Academy of Sciences* 98(4):1324–1326.

Smith, Bruce D. 2006   Eastern North America as an Independent Center of Plant Domestication. *Proceedings of the National Academy of Sciences* 103(33):12223–12228.

Stubbs, Brian D. 2011   *Uto-Aztecan: A Comparative Vocabulary.* Shumway Family History Services, Flower Mound, Texas.

Van Heerwaarden, Joost, John Doebley, William H. Briggs, Jeffrey C. Glaubitz, Major M. Goodman, Jose de Jesus, Sanchez Gonzalez, and Jeffrey Ross-Ibarra. 2011   Genetic Signals of Origin, Spread, and Introgression in a Large Sample of Maize Landraces. *Proceedings of the National Academy of Sciences* 108(3):1088–1092.

Whistler, Kenneth W. 1977   Wintun Prehistory: An Interpretation Based on Linguistic Reconstruction of Plant and Animal Nomenclature. In *Proceedings of the 3rd Annual Meeting of the Berkeley Linguistics Society*, ed. Kenneth W. Whistler, p. 157–174.

Wichmann, Søren. 1995   *The Relationship among the Mixe-Zoquean Languages of Mexico.* University of Utah Press, Salt Lake City.

Wichmann, Søren, A. Müller, and V. Velupillai. 2010   Homelands of the World's Language Families: A Quantitative Approach. *Diachronica* 27(2):247–276.

Zizumbo V., Daniel. 1986. Aspectos Etnobotanicos de las Calabazas Silvestres y Cultivadas (*Cucurbita* spp.) de la Peninsula de Yucatan. *Boletín de la Escuela de Ciencias Antropológicas de la Universidad de Yucatán* 13(77):15–29.

The Wild, the Domesticated, and the Coyote-Tainted: The Trickster and the Tricked in Hunter-Gatherer versus Farmer Folklore

Gary Paul Nabhan[†]

Abstract

Folklore regarding (biological) coyotes and (the mythic) Old Man Coyote the Trickster is rich in both hunter-gatherer and farmer-herder societies in Western North America, and apparently not restricted to language group, socioeconomic status, or subsistence strategy. To date, there has yet to be a systematic comparison of hunter-gatherer versus farmer uses of 'Coyote' as a modifier in the secondary lexemes used to name plants and invertebrates, or in associated oral narratives. While these folk taxa may be called "coyote's biota" for shorthand, it is necessary to discern whether they all share some common diagnostic features or characteristic values in the cultures which name them. I propose that the values embedded in any particular culture's view of coyote's biota can to some extent be inferred from the rich body of narratives in which other animals and plants have been associated with one of three entities: a) the biological coyote (*Canis latrans*); b) the mythic Coyote, the Trickster found commonly in the stories of farming cultures, or c) Coyote the Tricked, found more commonly in the stories of hunter-gatherer cultures. This initial comparison of Comcáac (Seri) versus O'odham (Northern Piman) names, morality plays, and narratives suggest that O'odham farmers have traditionally viewed the domain of Coyote's plants as those which have been tainted, tricked or corrupted by the lazy, or inattentive behavior of their (Coyote-like) stewards, whereas the Comcáac use of Coyote as a marker in secondary lexemes for miniaturized or other peculiar lifeforms indicate that he has been "tricked" into thinking these lifeforms are as beautiful or useful as others.

Introduction

The science of ethnoecology (Berkes 1999) does not merely document the species engaged in ecological relationships among cultures, plants, animals and microbes; it also includes narratives which elucidate cultural values and perceptions—symbolic, moral or otherwise—about those relationships (Nabhan 2000). This insight was first brought home to me by my mentor

† Southwest Center, University of Arizona, 1052 N. Highland Ave., Tucson, AZ 85721-0185
  [gpnabhan@email.arizona.edu]

Amadeo M. Rea while we were collaboratively documenting Northern Piman ethnobiological knowledge in the 1970s. Our simultaneous, sometimes co-managed fieldwork resulted in his classic ethnobotany of the Gila River Pima, *At the Desert's Green Edge* (Rea 1997), as well as my still-unpublished dissertation (which he advised) and its more readable complement, *The Desert Smells Like Rain* (Nabhan 1982).

Amadeo Rea has always been fastidious in documenting the identities of the foods and medicines that Piman speakers have used for the welfare of their communities, so much so that some of his readers may assume that his brand of ethnobiology is largely an applied science focused on utilitarian issues. However, as a student of how language, myth and religion influence indigenous peoples' stewardship of the natural world, Amadeo Rea was the first ethnobiologist I knew who asked larger philosophical, moral, and spiritual questions with the rigor of a well-trained ethnobiologist.

Amadeo first convinced me that such inquiries were not only plausible but necessary while we stood around a desert campfire one evening after recording wonderful commentaries from our O'odham (Pima and Papago) colleagues about a number of plants whose names were marked with the term *ban* as part of secondary lexemes. *Ban* appears to be a pan-Tepiman term, included as a modifier in secondary lexemes that allude to relationships with biological coyotes (*Canis latrans*) or to the mythic tricksters often referred to in vernacular English as Old Man Coyote.

Both Amadeo and I were aware that the use of 'Coyote,' *'Coyotl'* (or its many native equivalents) as a modifier in the secondary lexemes was not at all restricted to the O'odham, but that it is widespread among the indigenous cultures of Western North America. Bright (1999) suggests that the pervasiveness of Old Man Coyote narratives in Canada, the United States, and Mexico may indicate that Coyote is among the oldest archetypal characters in American folklore, so it is not surprising that he appears in a number of origin narratives regarding plants (Nabhan 1982). At least since the nineteenth century, Coyote has been used as a marker in the vernacular names of plants among Hispanic and Anglo residents of the continent as well, supposedly through diffusion from native cultures (Cassidy 1985; Moerman 1998). In fact, this marker is one of the few ethnosystematic elements which have diffused linguistically from the many indigenous languages of North America into the *linguas francas* of American regional English and Mexican regional Spanish used in these regions today (Table 1).

When contrasting some of these plants associated with Old Man Coyote with their highly useful counterparts—such as domesticated tobacco, melons, gourds, or squashes—it is clear that those marked with Coyote in their names are often smaller, wilder or more unruly, more bitter or less useable than their unmarked counterparts (Nabhan 1982; Rea 1997). The implications of that trend were not lost on either Amadeo or myself. We were aware that over the last quarter century, tremendous progress has been made in understanding cultural values embedded in "folk taxonomies" or ethnosystematic classifications of biodiver-

Table 1. Plants with names associated with Coyote in vernacular English or Spanish.

Common English &/or Spanish name	Scientific name(s)	States of occurrence	Source
Coyote berries	*Ribes* cf. *sanguineum*	OR	Cassidy (1985)
Coyote brush	*Baccharis pilularis*	CA	Moerman (1998)
Coyote cactus	*Opuntia leptocaulis*	AZ, CHIH, NM, SON, TX	Cassidy (1985)
Coyote gourd, *Calabacilla del coyote*	*Cucurbita digitata*	AZ, CA, SON, BCN, BCS	Cassidy (1985); Hodgson (2001)
Coyote melon, *Melón de coyote*	*Apodanthera undulata*	AZ, BCN, NM, SON	Cassidy (1985), Hodgson (2001)
Coyote mint, Mountain coyote mint	*Monardella odoratissima*	CA, NV	Moerman (1998)
Coyote's rope	*Clematis lasiantha*	CA	Moerman (1998)
Coyote's tail	*Cirsium pastoris*	NV, UT	Moerman (1998)
Coyote thistle	*Eryngium armatum*, *E. vaseyi*	CA, OR	Cassidy (1985)
Coyote's tobacco, *Tabaco del coyote*	*Nicotiana attenuata*, *N. clevelandii*, *N. rustica*, *N. trigonophylla*	AZ, CHIH, NM, SON, UT	Cassidy (1985)
Coyote willow	*Salix exigua*	AZ, CO, ID, MT, ND, NM, OR, UT, WY	Cassidy (1985)

sity (Berlin 1992; see also Harmon 2002). All cultures—whether foraging, farming-based, or highly industrialized—not only name various plants and animals within their reach, but infer patterns of kinship between wild and cultivated organisms (Berlin 1992). The distinctions made by naming organisms and grouping them into hierarchical categories also guide the habitat management and genetic selection of populations of these organisms (Nabhan and Rea 1987).

For instance, agricultural societies may "over-classify" certain domesticated plants and animals that they intensively manage. They may name many varieties or ethno-taxa that are economically important to them even though these taxa may be below the level of biological species recognized by Western-trained bio-systematists. At the same time, both industrialized and wild-foraging societies may "under-classify" these same domesticated species. Finally, some hunter-gatherer societies over-classify mythically and economically-important organisms like mesquite or sea turtles (Nabhan 2003) at the same time they show less interest in domesticated animals and plants. This insight begs the question that is the subject of this inquiry: Are the values embedded in associating a particular plant with Old Man Coyote in a hunting and gathering culture different than those in a farming culture?

The responses to this question suggest that this arena remains contested. Berlin (1992) in particular has proposed that there are structural similarities among the folk taxonomies of all agricultural peoples, similarities that do not necessarily extend to the folk taxonomies of hunter-gatherers. There remains considerable debate over the universal patterns Berlin has devised to discern hunter-gatherer from agricultural folk taxonomies (Nabhan 2003). Nevertheless, it is clear that the plants or animals essential to the major energy flows coursing through a particular cultural community tend to be over-classified, whether they be wild or domesticated. The more intensively certain biota are managed or utilized as food, the greater the probability is that their cultural stewards notice and mark morphological, ecological, and behavioral distinctions along them. Indigenous agriculturalist's taxonomies encode these distinctions in names, narratives and "scripts" that guide the management and utilization of these organisms (Alcorn 1989).

The rather anecdotal comparisons we have of hunter-gatherer and agricultural folk taxonomies may not necessarily shed sufficient light on a fundamental question: How do various cultures value wild organisms (especially those in their natural habitats) relative to the more highly-managed domesticated organisms that have become increasingly abundant in this world? Does their culture's ecological relationship with the wild organisms carry more weight in their naming processes and narratives that define them as a distinctive culture, or is their cultural identity more bound up with domesticated organisms such as horses, camels, cassava, maize, or wheat?

For the purposes of this discussion, I wish to draw attention to some profoundly-different values regarding the wild and the managed that are encoded in the lexicons of two neighboring cultures in the Sonoran Desert of North America with whom Amadeo Rea and I have visited and worked among: the Seri (Comcáac) and the Northern Pima (O'odham). In terms of their subsistence strategies, the Seri of the Sonoran coast and midriff islands and River Pima (Akimel O'odham) fall close to two poles of the continuum from nomadic forager to sedentary agriculturalist, with the Desert Papago (Tohono O'odham) and Sand Papago (Hia C-ed O'odham) falling somewhere between (Table 2). The Seri Indians, who call themselves the Comcáac, live along the desert coast of the Gulf of California, where their economy has remained steadfastly based on fishing, hunting, gathering, and wildcrafting, albeit with some crop plants and meats historically stolen or imported into their territory. The Northern Pima, composed of River Pima, Papago, Sand Papago and Lowland Pima, collectively call themselves O'odham. They live inland from the Comcáac, but his-

Table 2. Simplified comparison of the ecological niches of the O'odham and Comcáac.

Cultural group	O'odham	Comcáac
Major calorie-getting subsistence activities	Ranching, farming, gathering, hunting & wildcrafting	Fishing, gathering, clamming, hunting & wildcrafting
Habitats from which energy is extracted/harvested	Desert-scrub, thorn-scrub, oak woodlands, desert grasslands, & riparian zones/springs	Desert-scrub, mangrove estuaries, eelgrass beds, open seats, thorn scrub & springs
Territorial range	Southwest Arizona, USA, Northwest & Eastern Sonora, Mexico	Coastal Sonora, adjacent islands & Baja California, Mexico
Cultural keystone species	Tepary beans, mesquite, maize, saguaro cactus, amaranth greens, & Creosote Bush	Sea turtles, estuarine fish, ironwood, mesquite, shellfish, chuckwallas, organpipe and cardón cacti
Language family	Uto-Aztecan	Hokan?
Historic % of foods from wild sources	40–80%	95–100%

torically made pilgrimages to the Gulf, while practicing various mixes of farming, herding, foraging, hunting, and wild crafting; they are now engaged in commercial ranching and welfare food economies as well (Table 2). For a deeper understanding of the interactions of these people with the biodiversity of the desert and sea, refer to the ethnobiologies of the O'odham (Nabhan et al. 1989; Rea 1997, 1998, 2007); and of the Comcáac (Felger and Moser 1985; Nabhan 2003).

In contrasting the views of the Seri and Northern Pima of the wild and the domesticates encoded in their indigenous languages, I will give special attention to the ways each culture group identifies plants and animals associated with the rather ambivalent mythic figure of Coyote, who may be either the Trickster, the Tricked or both (Bright 1999). Coyote features prominently in many of the narratives of cultural emergence among indigenous cultures of western North America, including the O'odham and the Comcáac (Felger and Moser 1985; Rea 1997). I will specifically focus on the Coyote marker in secondary lexemes as a means of understanding their classification and thus perceptions of wild versus domesticated taxa.

As William Bright (1978, 1999) and Karl Luckert (1984) have cogently summarized, Old Man Coyote is a multi-faceted and therefore ambiguous character that both reflects and challenges the values of the cultures that tell his stories. He can be a clown, a creator, a culture hero, a lawgiver, a spoiler, a lazy steward, a thief, a trickster, a victim, or a hapless loser who has been tricked. "At the same time, Coyote provides a 'horrible example' of how people should not behave; he breaks every taboo, and frequently 'dies' as a result, but regularly reappears for new escapades" (Bright 1978:1–2). As I will make clear in the subsequent discussion, Coyote leaves an indelible mark on certain (formerly sacred or perfect) plants and animals, tainting them with his urine, saliva, or irreverent neglect. I hypothesize that each culture's list of plants and animals tainted by Coyote may reveal its peculiar perception of and preoccupation with the differential values of the wild versus domesticated.

Contrasting Energy Flows Through O'odham and Comcáac Societies

As neighbors for centuries, the O'odham and Comcáac do not form mutually-exclusive populations or spheres of influence. While their languages are mutually unintelligible and belong to different linguistic families, there are perhaps 10–20 loan words between the two, due to historic trade and at least two bilingual villages. Most relevant to this discussion are the facts that O'odham and Comcáac have: 1) exchanged stories and songs about commonly shared biota (such as desert bighorn sheep) over centuries; 2) exchanged genes through sporadic intermarriage; and 3) traded marine goods from the Comcáac for agricultural goods of the O'odham for centuries. Although their homelands share much of the same desert biodiversity, the Comcáac retain a larger lexicon for marine biodiversity (Moser and Marlett 2005; Nabhan 2003), while the O'odham retain a larger lexicon from agro-biodiversity (Mathiot

1973; Nabhan 1982). As noted earlier, both cultures have narratives about Coyote the trick-ster/tricked one, and name specific plants and animals with which he is associated.

Defining Wild, Domesticated and Feral in O'odham and Comcáac Culture and Language

In this section, I compare and contrast certain terms in the languages known as O'odham Ha-Nioki and the Cmique Iitom of the Comcáac to provide insight into their cultural per-ceptions of wild and domesticated. The terms come from both currently available lexicons in published dictionaries and ethnobiological monographs cited above. In general, this com-parison shows much more discernment of wild versus feral in O'odham than in Comcáac dis-course, and much more discourse regarding domesticated biota among the O'odham as well.

For the O'odham, the core condition of a healthy life is wildness, but paradoxically, do-mesticated plants and animals are given considerable attention and are seen as having been present in a perfect form at the time of their emergence as a culture. Their verb, *doajk*, means 'to be wild, untamed or unbroken.' It is related to the terms *doa*, 'to be healthy,' *doak*, 'whole, having integrity,' and *doaj*, 'to cure, heal restore or recover' (Mathiot 1973). Thus *daokud*, 'the condition of healthfulness,' and *doakam*, 'something whole and full of life,' or 'lively animals of a single species,' are not merely etymologically related. Rather, they suggest an underlying relationship between health and wildness. In contrast, this assumption of health is not extended to a domesticated animal such as a horse when it is intentionally "broken" and becomes *maaxo*, that is, 'tamed, muzzled or trammeled.' In addition, the O'odham term *ha'icu doakam*, 'something alive' is frequently used as 'unique beginner,' describing the entire domain of what we might call "the animal kingdom" in vernacular English (Mathiot 1973; Rea 1998). This term includes wild, domesticated, and even feral animals, the latter being labeled as *misciñ*, a loan word derived from the Spanish *mesteño*, in much the same way that the American English term *mustang* is derived from the same cognate. As Rea (1997) rightly observed, all of these terms are "unequivocally utilitarian rather than morphological" in na-ture, describing the organism's condition based on access for use, rather than on anatomical, physiological, or evolutionary similarities.

At the same time that the O'odham lexicon suggests a relatively positive view toward wild/ unmanaged species, a countervailing sentiment is embedded in O'odham creation and emer-gence narratives, especially in those within which Coyote the Trickster appears. In these narratives, certain domesticated (as well as wild) plants are given to the O'odham at the time of their emergence as a distinctive culture. However, in subsequent episodes of these mythic narratives, certain domesticated plants that were perfectly useful in every way were spoiled by neglect, laziness, greed, or misuse at the hand of Coyote the Trickster. They then "degener-ate" into the forms that botanists recognize today as wild relative crops. O'odham narratives suggest that this degeneration process resulted in marginally-useful wild forms of tobacco, devil's claw, and gourds that grow naturally in Sonoran Desert, for these are considered inferior to their domesticated kin (Nabhan 1982).

In essence, these narratives suggest that without appropriate human management, these domesticated species go feral and then lose some of their economically-important traits. One can make a loose and very limited comparison with the Judeo-Christian-Moslem narratives which suggest a "fall from grace" that contaminated the perfect plants and animals (including humans) with sins, flaws, or imperfections. As I will explain in the next section, these degenerated crop relatives are among those that the O'odham label as Coyote's plants, because they have been tainted by his foolhardiness and negligence.

In contrast to O'odham agriculturalists, the Comcáac hunter-gatherers do not necessarily place such pejorative connotations on wild relatives of crops that grow without human management in the desert, nor on other wild plants and invertebrates associated with Coyote. As Cathy Moser Marlett (pers. comm.) has suggested to me, the narratives she remembers from growing up among the Seri often treat him as a buffoon who is easily tricked rather than as the Trickster *per se*:

"… the coyote is greedy and takes some things as his own because he thinks it is pretty or nice (as humorously noted by others, it is NOT [nice], i.e., not the real thing), so it is rather funny that he ends up with something inferior."

By inferior items, Cathy Moser Marlett refers to lifeforms that appear miniaturized or minor in value compared to other, more commonly used or seen ones. These lifeforms may have meager fat and meat, soapier flavors, or smaller bodies than their counterparts, which are named by primary lexemes, even when these counterparts are also wild species.

Over many years of meals with the Comcáac, some of them have hinted to me that a few domesticated species such as beef, wheat, peas, and chickpeas are of inferior value when compared to wild species in both flavor and texture (However, Cathy Moser Marlett does not sense that this can be inferred across the board). For example, the domesticated chickpea (*Cicer arietinum* L.) introduced by Jesuit missionaries to the Sonoran desert is called **paar icomitin**, 'the padre's ironwood seed' and the domesticated pea (*Pisum sativum* L.) is called **paar icomible**, 'padre's mesquite seeds' (Felger and Moser 1985). Although somewhat similar in appearance to the seeds of the wild ironwood and mesquite that historically sustained the Comcáac, these domesticated legumes must be sown, weeded, irrigated, and uprooted to obtain a similar food product. In contrast, mesquite and ironwood grow on their own, without human intervention, and their pods and seeds are simply harvested.

Curiously, the term the Comcáac use for 'domesticated'—**quiixz**—is etymologically derived from their term that means both pet and parasite, **iixz** (Moser and Marlett 2005). In fact, at least eight ectoparasites on particular species or genera of animals that are economically important to the Comcáac include the term **iixz**, 'pet or parasite' in their folk binomials (Moser and Marlett 2005). In contrast, the closest term used by the Comcáac for 'wild'—

catol—also means fearless, uncivilized, or untamed. This sentiment is found embedded in their compound lexeme, **yequim catoli**, which refers to their Yaqui or Yoeme neighbors to the south, who have remained undefeated and defiant of Spanish and Mexican control in their territory. There is thus the positive connotation in this term that someone described as **catol** has not been subjugated or dominated, but lives with an unbroken spirit.

Thus, the lexicons of both the Comcáac and the O'odham reveal positive values associated with wildness. However, the O'odham place more value in domesticated plants and animals, whereas the Comcáac suggest relationships among tamed or domesticated organisms and parasites. One might speculate that both cultigens and parasites demand human energy in return for their products. The O'odham—whose economy has perhaps been based on balancing domesticated and wild resources for their survival in the desert for over four millennia (Mabry 2008) seem to treat some wild relatives of crops and feral animals with ambivalence. I suggest that an association with Coyote may be linked to the Comcáac and O'odham perceptions of wild and domesticated resources.

Coyote-Tainted Organisms and Their Significance

In both the Comcáac and O'odham cultures, the ethnobiological lexicon includes organisms that have been associated with Coyote the Trickster or the Tricked (Tables 3 and 4). However, there is a key difference among these organisms in the two cultures. Of the nine ethnotaxa of plants and invertebrates associated with Coyote by the Comcáac, none are wild relatives of crops. In contrast, half of the six ethnotaxa of plants affiliated with Coyote by the O'odham are wild relatives of crops (3) and the others are either diminutive look-alikes or close kin to other economically-important plants. In neither case are we sure that any of these taxa are ecological associates of *Canis latrans*.

Table 3. Secondary lexemes used by the O'odham that refer to Coyote the Trickster.

O'odham Ethnotaxon	Scientific name	Traits	Untainted Analog
Ban 'ihug-ga, *Ban xuuxk*	*Proboscidea altheafolia*	Dried fruit's claws too small for basket fiber	*Proboscidea parviflora* var. *hohokamiana**
Ban viiv-ga, Itahes	*Nicotiana clevlandii* and/or N. trigonophylla (current name?)	High nornicotine content, too harsh to smoke	*Nicotiana tabacum** & *N. rustica**
Baaan 'auppa-ga	*Acourtia nana*	Plants too small to offer timber, beams	*Populus fremontii*#
Ban bavi, Ban cexenig, Cepulina bavi	*Phaseolus acutifolius* var. *tenuifolius* & *P. filiformis*	Beans too small, pop out of pods	*Phaeolus acutifolius* var. *acutifolius**
Ban cepla, Ban ha-mauppa, Baaban ha-'iiswigi, Ban cekida	*Mammillaria thornberi* & *M. grahamii*	Fruit too small, too few	*Echinocereus fasciculatus*#, *E. fendleri,* & *E. Fasciculatus*
Ban toki	*Gossypium thurberi*	Barely any cotton in boll	*Gossypium hirsutum* var. *puncttum*

* = domesticated species, # = historically-cultivated species.

Table 4. Secondary lexemes used by the Comcáac that refer to Coyote the Tricked.

Comcáac ethnotaxon	Scientific name	Traits	Inferior Analog
Oot asáac	*Myceroperca jordani*	A large grouper called son of Coyote, troublesome, lacking in edible meat and fat	*Epinephelus itajara* & *E. labriformis*
Oot icáanaj	*Rypticus bicolor* & *R. nigriprimis*	Smaller and "soapier" than giant groupers	*Epinephelus itajara* & *E. labriformis*
Oot iháxöl	Not known	Smaller, rarer and less edible than several commercially-harvested clams	*Agropecten circularis*
Oot ijöeene	*Passiflora arida*	Disagreeable taste of small fruit	*Passiflora palmeri*
Oot iqéepl	*Petrilisthes armatus*	Smaller than the most common porcelain crab	*Petrolisthes cintipes*
Oot iquéjöc	*Jatropha cinerea*	Fuel wood too dry to light well and produces too much smoke; basketry fiber not pliant	*Jatropha cuneata*
Oot ixpaléemelc	*Olivella dama*	Half the length of those used by Indian artisans	*Oliva incrassate* & *O. spicata*
Oot izámt	*Cronius ruber*	Miniature of blue-eating crab	*Calinectes bellicosus* & *C. arctuatus*
Oot yacmolca	*Morum tuberculosum*	A tiny helmet shell, too small to use as shaman amulet or in necklaces	*Cassis* spp.

In both languages, Coyote's biotas are smaller, less useful or somehow inferior compared to their counterparts named with primary lexemes. As Felger and Moser (1985:53) have summarized for the Comcáac, "false items and things of little use or value were commonly associated with coyote [including] *Bursera microphylla* A. Gray, *Jatropha cinerea* and *Passiflora arida*." For instance, the Comcáac call the ashy limberbush (*Jatropha cinerea* (Ortega) Müll. Arg.) by the nickname **Oot iquéjöc** ('Coyote's firewood') because its dead, dried branches are nearly worthless as fuel (Felger and Moser 1985). Similarly, 'Coyote's passion vine' (*Passiflora arida* (Mast. & Rose) Killip) produces fruit with a disagreeable taste compared to those of other wild passion vines. Likewise, the O'odham call a desert-holly (*Acourtia nana* (A. Gray) Reveal & King) by the name **Baaban auppa-ga** ('Coyote's cottonwood') because its small prickly leaves superficially resemble cottonwood seedlings. When Gila River Pima elder George Kyyitan once saw a patch of desert-holly, he exclaimed, "Ha **Baaban auppa-ga**! Can't make no house with it … no beams with it; it's good for nothing, just like the owner [Coyote]" (Rea 1998).

A similar commentary has been made by Tohono and Hia C-ed O'odham elders about the wild devil's claw that Coyote is said to vomit up after eating (Nabhan 1982). Sometimes called **Ban xuuxk** ('Coyote's shoe or sandal') because of the shape of its green fruit, this desert plant is a relative of one that the O'odham themselves domesticated in historic times for its exceptional basketry fiber (Nabhan and Rea 1987). While the domesticated form is called **'ihug**, both its wild progenitor and a related wild species are commonly called **Ban 'ihug-ga** ('Coyote's devil's claws'). According to Tohono O'odham lore, "those other ones are **Ban 'ihuga-ga** because Coyote left them out in the desert, uncared for. Now they are no good for making baskets with—those fibers are too small, too brittle. They just snap. You can't make anything out of them."

Two O'odham stories about Coyote's tobacco make a similar moral point—that crops given to their ancestors must be cared for, or else Coyote will get them, neglect or defile them, and the resulting feral forms will be degenerate. In one story, Coyote's carelessness in sowing, singing to, and tending maize resulted in it being transformed into Coyote's tobacco (Saxton and Saxton 1973). In a second narrative, Coyote stole sacred tobacco from the grave of a mythic woman and tried to use it in a sacred smokehouse without sharing it with others; that is when it degenerated into a wild tobacco so harsh that it is difficult to smoke (Underhill 1946).

Camcáac narratives about Coyote collected by Mary Beck Moser and Stephen Marlett (2005), Cathy Moser Marlett (pers. comm.), and by myself, suggest that Coyote's mythic character has been tricked by mirages, duped by beetles, and by rabbits. What is most interesting, however, is that none of the wild relatives of crops within Comcáac territory are referred to as Coyote's plants in their native language. Although the Comcáac may now call wild tobacco *tabaco del Coyote* in Spanish, they never do so when speaking in their own language. Lacking an agricultural heritage, such comparisons of closely-related wild and domesticated organisms may have traditionally been less engaging for the Comcáac. In at least four cases, their comparisons are sometimes with economically-important wild species. It appears that in their tradition as desert hunter-gatherers and marine fishers, they have focused their humor and delight in anything in miniaturized or gigantized form, or anything of dubious value in the wild.

Discussion

Farmers and herders in many agricultural societies tell mythic narratives that speak to the value of domesticated plants and animals as cultural keystone species essential to their society's identity and survival (Harlan 1995). However, genetic manipulation of plants and animals under domestication creates organisms that some hunter-gatherer societies such as the Comcáac liken to parasites, in that they are dependant upon diverting human energy for their survival. Perhaps their lexicons and narratives offer us hilarious reminders of the sometimes parasitic aspects of the co-dependence among domesticated crops, livestock, and humans. Their underlying message may be a caution to us all: an overly-managed world with genetically-manipulated organisms dependent on human energy investment may be less interesting, less tasty, and less liberating.

The era of the Homogocene—one of overly-managed farmlands, forests, and trawled sea beds replete with invasive species—is clearly upon us, in that a larger proportion of the surface of the earth and its offshore waters is under human management than ever before in history (Jackson 1998; Vitousek et al. 1986; Watling and Norse 1998). This comparison of folk taxonomies for wild, domesticated, and feral organisms may, if nothing else, remind us that wildness has its own intrinsic value, one that all of us need to recognize and celebrate. Wildness, like diversity itself (Harmon 2002), provides humankind with benchmarks by which to measure the impacts of our actions. One remarkable legacy of Amadeo Rea's fieldwork and archival documentation is that it will provide a lasting benchmark by which future generations can measure the degree to which we have tolerated and fostered such diversity and wildness, or alternatively, suffocated it out of existence.

Acknowledgements

Special thanks to Amadeo Rea for years of patient, insightful and humorous mentorship. I am also grateful to Stephen Marlett, Jim Hills and Laurie Monti for their insights, and to Cathy Moser Marlett for sharing contents of her forthcoming book (A Seri Ethnography of Mollusks). Amalia Astroga, Adolfo Burgos, Manuel Monroy, Efrain Estrella, Maria Luisa Astorga, Laura Kerman, Phillip Salcido, Delores Lewis, and Frances Manuel offered extraordinary guidance and insights regarding Coyote, his shellfish, and his plants.

References Cited

Alcorn, Janice B. 1989   Process as Resource. In *Resource Management in Amazonia: Indigenous and Folk Strategies,* eds. Darrell A. Posey and W. Balee, pp. 63–77. New York Botanical Garden, The Bronx.

Anderson, M. Katherine. 2005   *Tending the Wild: Native American Knowledge and the Management of California's Natural Resources.* University of California Press, Berkeley.

Berkes, Fikret. 1999   *Sacred Ecology: Traditional Ecological Knowledge and Resource Management.* Taylor and Francis, Philadelphia.

Berlin, Brent. 1992   *Ethnobiological Classification: Principals of Categorization of Plants and Animals in Traditional Societies.* Princeton University Press, Princeton.

Bright, William. 1978   *Coyote Stories.* Native American Text Series (IJAL-NATS Monograph 1). University of Chicago Press, Chicago.

Bright, William. 1999   *Nature, Culture and Old Man Coyote.* Lecture presented at the Free University, Berlin, Germany. Available at: www.americanindianonline.

Brody, Hugh. 2001   *The Other Side of Eden: Hunters, Farmers, and the Shaping of the World.* North Point Press, New York.

Cassidy, Frederic G. 1985   *Dictionary of American Regional English.* Belknap Press of Harvard University Press, Cambridge.

Felger, Richard S., and Mary B. Moser. 1985   *People of the Desert and Sea: Ethnobotany of the Seri Indians.* University of Arizona Press, Tucson.

Harlan, Jack. 1995   *The Living Fields: Our Agricultural Heritage.* Cambridge University Press, New York.

Harmon, David. 2002   *In Light of Our Differences: How Diversity in Nature and Culture Makes Us Human.* Smithsonian Institution Press, Washington, D.C.

Hodgson, Wendy. 2001   *Sonoran Desert Food Plants.* University of Arizona Press, Tucson.

Jackson, Laura L. 1998   Agricultural Industrialization and the Loss of Biodiversity. In *Protection of Global Biodiversity: Converging Strategies*, eds. Lakshman D. Guruswamy and Jeffrey A. McNeely, pp. 66–86. Duke University Press, Durham, NC.

Luckert, Karl W. 1984   Introduction. In *Navajo Coyote Tales*, Father Berard Haile, pp. 3–19. University of Nebraska Press, Lincoln.

Mabry, Jonathan B. 2008   *Las Capas: Early Irrigation and Sedentism in a Southwestern floodplain.* Center for Desert Archaeology Anthropological Papers 28. Tucson, AZ

Mathiot, Madeline. 1973   *A Dictionary of Papago Usage.* Indiana University Publications Language Science Monographs 5. Bloomington, IN

Moerman, Daniel E. 1998   *Native American Ethnobotany.* Timber Press, Portland, OR.

Moser, Mary Beck, and Stephen A. Marlett. 2005   *Comcáac Quih Yaza Quih Hant Ihip Hax: Diccionario Seri-Español-Inglés.* Universidad de Sonora, Hermosillo, SON.

Nabhan, Gary Paul. 1982   *The Desert Smells Like Rain: A Naturalist in Papago Indian Country.* North Point Press, San Francisco.

Nabhan, Gary Paul, and Amadeo Michael Rea. 1987   Plant Domestication and Folk Biological Change: The Upper Pima/Devil's Claw Example. *American Anthropologist* 89:57–75.

Nabhan, Gary Paul, Wendy Hodgson, and Frances Fellows. 1989   A Meager Living in Lava and Sand? Hia-ced O'odham Food Resources and Habitat Diversity in Oral and Written Histories. *Journal of the Southwest* 31:508–533.

Nabhan, Gary Paul. 2000   Interspecific Relationships Affecting Endangered Species Recognized by O'odham and Comcáac Cultures. *Ecological Applications* 10(5):1288–1295.

Nabhan, Gary Paul. 2003   *Singing the Turtles to Sea: The Comcáac (Seri) Art and Science of Reptiles.* University of California Press, Berkeley.

Nelson, Richard. 1983   *Make Prayers to the Raven: A Koyukon View of the Northern Forest.* University of Chicago Press, Chicago.

Rea, Amadeo M. 1997   *At the Desert's Green Edge: An Ethnobotany of the Gila River Pima.* University of Arizona Press, Tucson.

Rea, Amadeo M. 1998   *Folk Mammology of the Northern Pimans.* University of Arizona Press, Tucson.

Rea, Amadeo M. 2007   *Wings in the Desert: A Folk Ornithology of the Northern Pimans.* University of Arizona Press, Tucson.

Saxton, Dean, and Lucille Saxton. 1973   *O'otham Hoho'ok A'agitha: Legends and Lore of the Papago and Pima Indians.* University of Arizona Press, Tucson.

Underhill, Ruth. 1946   *Papago Indian Religion.* Columbia University Press, New York.

Vitousek, Peter M., Paul R. Ehrlich, Anne H. Ehrich, and Pamela A. Matson. 1986   Human Appropriation of the Products of Photosynthesis. *BioScience* 36(6):368–373.

Watling, Les, and Elliott A. Norse. 1998   Disturbance of the Seabed by Mobile Fishing Gear: A Comparison to Forest Clearcutting. *Conservation Biology* 12(6):1180–1197.

"Dog" as Life-Form[1]

Eugene S. Hunn[†]

Abstract

The Berlinian framework for analyzing folk biological classification and nomenclature is best understood as a flexible cognitive tool rather than as a rigid structure of universal taxonomic ranks. I analyze vernacular English dog names to show that "dog" may be interpreted both as a folk generic taxon and a life-form taxon depending on the frame of reference. I analyze two samples, each including approximately 100 named "kinds of dogs"—the first from 19 respondents to a free-listing task, the second from the American Kennel Club (AKC) list of officially recognized dog breeds—to show that the set of categories so-named exhibit the characteristics considered definitive of life-form taxa by Berlin. I conclude that this result is "an exception that proves the rule," affirming the basic validity of the Berlinian perceptual-taxonomic theory.

Introduction

Berlin's (1992) taxonomic theory of universal folk biological classification and nomenclature is now firmly established in the ethnobiological literature (Anderson 2011:5–6). This foundation allows us to navigate the bewildering chaos of an initial encounter with the natural history of an unfamiliar language. Yet, those of us who have over the past four decades helped elaborate and refine the Berlinian paradigm know well that reality is too complex and varied to fit neatly within any single analytic frame, including Berlin's.

One substantial difficulty derives from the definition of universal taxonomic ranks. Berlin's framework requires that each and every folk biological taxon should fit uniquely within one and only one rank. Berlin's universal ranks are "kingdom," "life-form," "intermediate," "generic," "specific," and "varietal," in descending order of inclusion. These ranks are defined by strategic (perhaps "artful") combinations of nomenclatural, structural, and biological characteristics of taxa (cf. Hunn 1982; Berlin 1992:23–24; Figure 1). For example, taxa at the specific rank are characteristically named by "secondary names," which typically are binomial, composed of a generic head noun plus a modifying attributive, a nomenclatural characteristic (Berlin 1992:34, principle II-3). However, secondary names must be distinguished from "productive primary names"—which are also binomial—by reference to the "contrast

† Department of Anthropology, University of Washington, Seattle, WA (204 Fair Ave., Petaluma, CA 94952) [enhunn323@comcast.net]

set" to which they are assigned, which is a structural characteristic. So "bald eagle" is of specific rank, contrasting with "golden eagle," within the folk generic contrast set "eagle," while "mockingbird" is of generic rank, as it contrasts with such categories as "robin," "crow," and "owl," within the life-form "bird," a more broadly inclusive category, a biological characteristic. Thus deciding the rank of a particular category is not automatic but may require careful weighting of diverse factors (Figure 1).

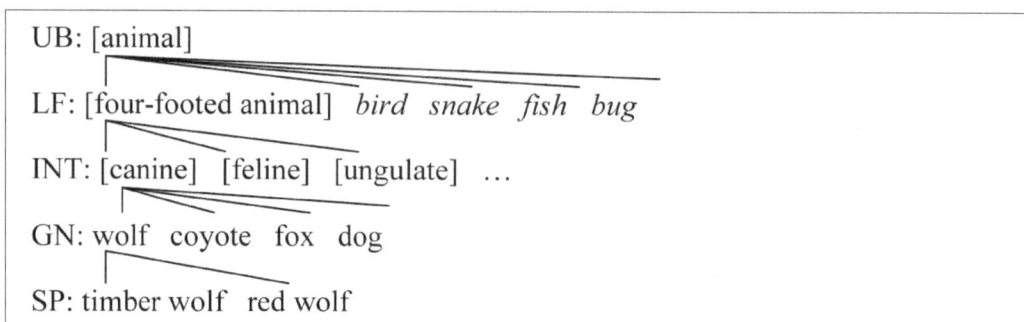

Figure 1. Standard taxonomic representation following Berlin (1992) (from Hunn and Brown 2011:329, Figure 19.3).

I propose here a modest complication of this basic scheme to accommodate an anomaly. This anomaly is most apparent, but not limited to, the classification of highly domesticated animals. A case in point elaborated below, is vernacular English "dog." "Dog" is a single Linnaean species, but a species so modified culturally as to exhibit a degree of phenotypic variety to be expected of a Linnaean genus or family. I argue that the resulting folk biological nomenclatural elaboration is best understood by a simple extension of the Berlinian framework. I call this extension <u>taxonomic elevation</u>.

Vernacular English "Dog"

My prime example of this anomaly is the American English vernacular nomenclature for breeds of dogs, each a member of the species *Canis (lupus) familiaris*, human camp follower for at least the past 15,000 years (Morey 2010). "Dog" in the English folk classification is a folk generic taxon within the animal domain or "kingdom," sharing this rank and contrasting with an extensive inventory of mammal categories, most of which are named with "simple primary names" or familiar elaborations thereof. Examples of contrasting folk generic animal categories include "cat," "rat," "coyote," "raccoon," "whale," "seal," "cougar," "rabbit," "cow," "pig," "camel," and "elephant," among the furry (or not so furry) beasts known more technically as "mammals." At this same generic rank we find as well such feathered fauna as "robin," "duck," "owl," "seagull," "sparrow, " "blackbird," and "starling"; plus, in other life-forms, "cobra," "boa," "rattler," "turtle," "lizard," "frog," "salmon," "shark," "spider," "bee," "ant," and "wasp," to suggest the quantity and quality of English folk generic animal taxa.

According to Berlin, the generic rank encompasses the great majority of all named folk biological taxa (Berlin 1992:23–24). Most of these folk generic taxa—perhaps in excess of 80% (Berlin 1992:129)—will be monotypic, that is, they will include no named subcategories, for example, "cougar." Some folk generic taxa, however, will be polytypic, that is, they will include folk specifics. An example is "whale" which includes subcategories such as "blue whale" and "humpback whale." Vernacular English "dog" is one such polytypic generic taxon. However, "dog" is extraordinarily elaborated in comparison to the polytypic generics encountered in most other languages (Berlin 1992:122–133).

In more "natural" folk taxonomies—that is, those recorded from oral traditions of rural, subsistence-based communities—polytypic folk generics rarely include more than five to ten folk specific subcategories. The rare exceptions include major staple cultivars such as manioc for the Aguaruna Jívaro of Peru (Boster 1985) or for rice, taro, sweet potatoes, or plantains in certain Southeast Asian societies (Berlin 1992:124–125), or horses (late historical introduction) for the Sahaptin-speaking Indians of the Columbia River Plateau of western North America (Hunn and Selam 1990:330–331). I believe such "super-polytypic" taxa pose interesting challenges for the Berlinian theory and thus warrant close scrutiny.

In my view, vernacular English "dog" breeds cannot be readily analyzed as either folk specific or varietal taxa, as defined by the Berlinian framework (Berlin 1992:31–35). Instead, "kinds of dogs" exhibit all the distinguishing nomenclatural and structural characteristics we should expect of taxa subordinate to a life-form (Berlin 1992:33–34); that is, most are breed generics, and may be either simple or polytypic, the latter including breed specifics (Figure 2), which also may be polytypic, and these include varietals. We even find breed intermediates, which group multiple breed generics. None of this fits the standard model if "dog" is treated as a generic. To accommodate these nomenclatural elaborations for naming "kinds of dogs", one would need to invent new folk taxonomic ranks, adding a second "intermediate" rank between the folk generic and specific ranks and a sub-varietal rank. It would also be necessary to detail a large number of exceptions to Berlin's original principles to take account of the conceptual and nomenclatural complexities. On the other hand, no such ad hoc theoretical manipulations are required and it all makes perfect sense if "dog" is analyzed as if it were both a folk generic and a life-form.

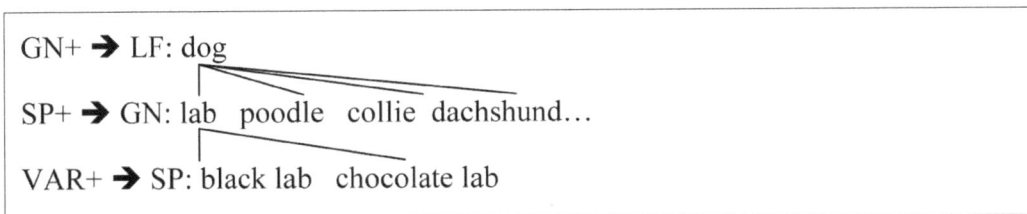

GN+ ➔ LF: dog

SP+ ➔ GN: lab poodle collie dachshund…

VAR+ ➔ SP: black lab chocolate lab

Figure 2. Dog as life-form (from Hunn and Brown 2011:329, Figure 19.4).

Methods

An analysis of a folk biological classification system in any language should be based on a sample of terms in use which is as nearly comprehensive as possible. These terms are then organized into contrast sets at the appropriate taxonomic rank, applying Berlin's criteria.

I rely for my analysis here on two data sets. First is an inventory of "kinds of dogs" elicited from 19 respondents as a class project of my winter 2003 University of Washington Cognitive Anthropology seminar. Second is an alphabetical listing of the American Kennel Club's officially recognized dog breeds, which is posted on the internet (American Kennel Club 2012). This data set listed 174 official dog breeds.

In my class project sample, students were asked to write down (or freelist) the names of as many "kinds of dogs" as they could recall, up to a total of 25, without consulting external references. They were also invited to request the same of one or more friends or relatives. Ten of the nineteen lists submitted included the limit of 25 names. Three more included 20–24, four more 15–19, with just two shorter lists. These names were then alphabetized by head noun to produce the master list. The 36 most frequently named were then used for a pile sorting task, which is beyond our purview here.

Results

The class project elicited 89 kinds of dogs, once the data were "cleaned" for inadmissible, fanciful, or anomalous terms, such as "Lassie," "hot dog," and "coyote" (see Appendix 1). The 19 respondents recorded a total of 60 "generic" dog names, of which approximately 15 were polytypic (Appendix 1). The polytypic breed names include at least 44 "specific" dog names. Polytypic breeds ranged from binaries to highly polytypic taxa. Binaries break into two "specifics," as in "standard poodle" and "toy poodle" or "Australian sheepdog" and "English sheepdog." [2] Highly polytypic categories contain several specifics such as "terrier," which included eight named "specifics," such as "fox terrier," "Jack Russell terrier," and "Scottish terrier," which might be abbreviated as "Scottie." One term appeared to label an "intermediate" taxon: this is "hound" and its exotic cognates such as "hund," as in "dachshund" (a.k.a. "wiener dog"), which included breeds such as "wolfhound," "greyhound," "bloodhound," and Afghan (hound), each best treated, in my judgment, as a "generic" breed.

One particularly complicated case is that of "retriever." Respondents listed "Chesapeake Bay retriever," "golden retriever," and "Labrador retriever." However, "Labrador retrievers" (Figure 3) are better known as "labs," which would appear to be a generic breed in its own right, as it includes such varieties as "black lab," "chocolate lab," and "yellow lab" (Figure 4). Alternatively, we might treat these various "labs" as dog breed "varietals

Above: Figure 3. My wife, Nancy, with our late favorite Ella, black lab with a bit of Australian Shepherd. As is said of labs, she was a puppy until three days after the day she died.

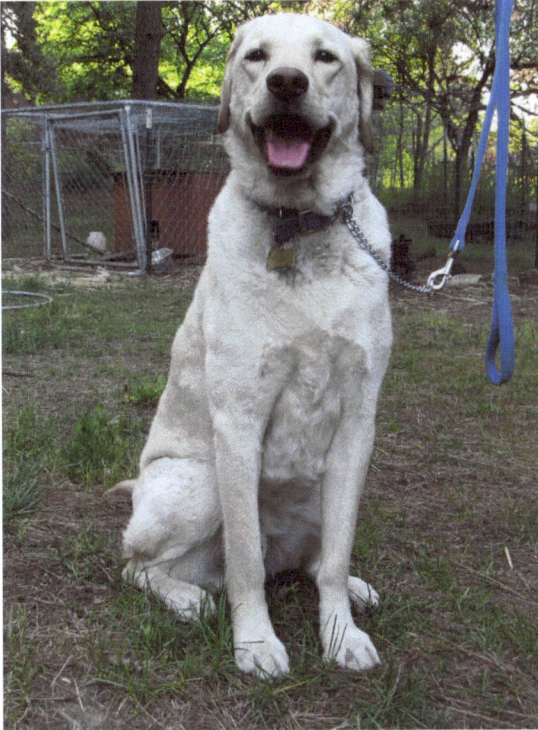

Left: Figure 4. A "yellow lab," Gaius. Photograph by Maggie Quinlan, used with permission.

(that is, as subdivisions of the breed specific "lab," which in turn is a subdivision of the breed generic "retriever") as it is not unusual for folk specific names to be abbreviated when employed as the head noun for a varietal term. A non-dog example of this is "tiger swallowtail (butterfly)."

Or we might analyze "lab" as an example of Brown's "folk subgenus" (Brown 1987), a nomenclatural response when a generic must expand to include a wider range of organisms, often as a consequence of historic species introductions. Examples include deer as "forest sheep" (Tzeltal Mayan in Hunn 1977:227–228), wheat as "Castillian corn" (Zapotec in Hunn 2008:87), or dog as "little horse" (Sahaptin in Hunn and Selam 1990:329). These examples expand the semantic range of the original generic. An additional example is "pit bull." This seems best treated as a breed generic rather than as a kind of terrier, e.g., "pit-bull terrier," as in the official AKC breed list.

There are a few terms which I suggest name <u>residual</u> generic categories. A residual category is "… defined negatively, i.e., an organism is perceived to be a member of X but **not** a member of any distinctive kind of X." For example, a "mutt" or mongrel is any dog that is not a particular "kind of dog" (Hunn 1977:57). We also find analogs of <u>special purpose</u> categories (Anderson 2011:5), such as "guard dog" and "seeing-eye dog."

Finally, it is noteworthy that some respondents included as "kinds of dog" wild relations, such as "wolf," "coyote," "dingo," and "African wild dog." This suggests a polysemous higher order concept inclusive of all "canines." Thus, some English speakers, at least, conceive of "dog" not only as equivalent to the Linnaean species *Canis familiaris* (dog$_1$) but also as equivalent to the Linnaean family Canidae (dog$_2$). Berlin refers to these polysemous supergeneric taxa as "intermediates" (Berlin 1992:139–141), which would be an appropriate rank for "dog" as a folk generic but not as a life-form, unless we invent yet another taxonomic rank superordinate to the life-form yet subordinate to kingdom. I would argue against this alternative as unnecessarily complicating.

The more formally-specified "official" American Kennel Club (AKC) dog breed nomenclature exhibits many of these same features, with added elaboration (see Appendix 2). There are 33 recognized "terrier" breeds in the AKC, all with binomial or more elaborate names, and 13 "spaniel" breeds, including three polytypic specifics, for example, "water spaniel" which includes "American" and "English water spaniel" varietals. There are six types of "retrievers," four types of "shepherd" (Figures 5 and 6), and five each of "sheepdog" and "coonhound." The intermediate status of "hound" is again apparent, as there are not only "coonhounds" but also "deerhounds," "fox hounds," "greyhounds," plus "dachshunds" and "keeshonds," in addition to "Afghan" and "Pharoh hounds." Of the 174 AKC recognized breeds, 93 are "generic breeds." Of these, 19 are polytypic, including a total of 72 "specific breeds." Five of these are in turn polytypic, including a total of 14 "varietal breeds." This degree of elaboration is fully comparable to that of the largest life-forms in any language (Brown 1984).

Above: Figure 5. A German shepherd, Maggie May. Photograph by Charles Snyder, used with permission.

Left: Figure 6. An Australian shepherd, Jada. Photograph by Alissa Miller, used with permission.

Discussion

That the vernacular English "dog" classification and nomenclature exhibits all the features to be expected of a life-form does not argue against the utility and power of the Berlinian taxonomic framework. On the contrary, this is an "exception that proves the rule" in that "dog" fits neatly the criteria Berlin has specified for life-form taxa, despite its dual status as a folk generic taxon. It does suggest that we need to understand folk taxonomies not as rigid structures but as flexible cognitive mechanisms that may be adapted in predictable ways to varied cultural contexts and the life experiences that follow. Perhaps we should imagine not taxonomic trees, but rather taxonomic fractals[3], structures which are self-replicating, exhibiting the same complex patterns even as we "zoom in" to focus more closely on some particular salient corner of our world's biodiversity. In modern urban America, dogs have been genetically manipulated to the point that the available phenotypes exhibit a large number of "perceptual discontinuities" (Hunn 1977) ripe for naming as folk generics. It is a matter of perspective. "Dog" is still a folk generic taxon in the context of the animal domain, but a life form when dogs are at the center of cultural attention (e.g., Figure 7). I suggest we call this phenomenon "generic elevation." A parallel, if opposite phenomenon has already been noted and designated "life-form devolution," as in the case of vernacular English "tree," which has been trimmed to the size of a folk generic shrub for many urban Americans (Dougherty 1978:67; Rosch 1978). Both taxonomic elevation and life-from devolution make sense as flexible cultural responses to urban realities.

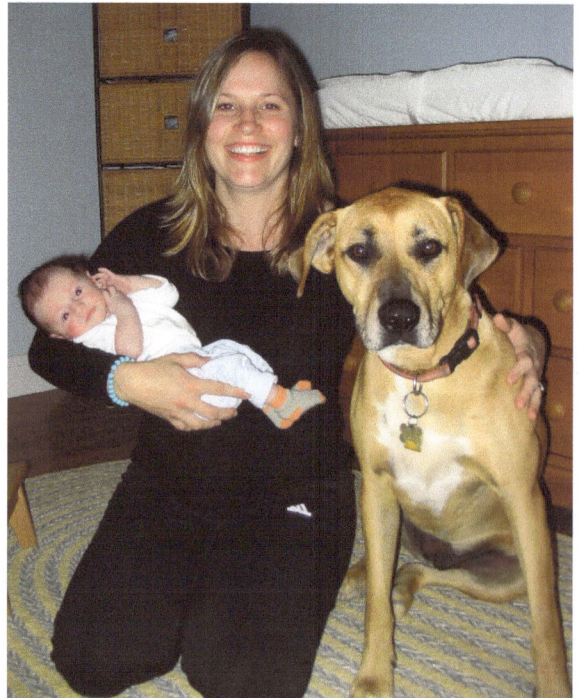

Figure 7. My daughter, Serena Stark, and grandson, Ethan, with gentle Mollie, a Rhodesian Ridgeback, a shelter orphan. Deeply insecure at first, once when left alone she caused a thousand dollars in damage to the house in her desperate efforts to escape.

Notes

1. I briefly introduced this example in *Ethnobiology* (Anderson et al. 2011) in a chapter on "Linguistic ethnobiology" co-authored with Cecil H. Brown (Hunn and Brown 2011:329).

2. Note that "sheepdog" here is analogous to "mockingbird" and "tulip tree," both "productive primary names" which typically name folk generics (Berlin 1992:28). Other examples here include "bulldog" and "mountain dog."

3. "Fractals are typically self-similar patterns, where *self-similar* means they are 'the same from near as from far.' Fractals may be exactly the same at every scale, or … they may be *nearly* the same at different scales. The definition of *fractal* includes the idea of a **detailed pattern** repeating itself." (Wikipedia 2012)

References Cited

American Kennel Club (AKC). 2012   Complete List of AKC Recognized Breeds. Available at: http://www.akc.org/breeds/complete_breed_list.cfm (verified January 2012).

Anderson, E.N. 2011   Ethnobiology: Overview of a Field. In *Ethnobiology*, eds. E.N. Anderson, Deborah M. Pearsall, Eugene S. Hunn, and Nancy J. Turner, pp. 1–14. Wiley-Blackwell, Hoboken, N.J.

Anderson, E.N., Deborah M. Pearsall, Eugene S. Hunn, and Nancy J. Turner, eds. 2011   *Ethnobiology*. Wiley-Blackwell, Hoboken, N.J.

Berlin, Brent. 1992   *Ethnobiological Classification: Principles of Categorization of Plants and Animals in Traditional Societies*. Princeton University Press, Princeton, N.J.

Boster, James Shilts. 1978   "Requiem for the Omniscient Informant": There's Life in the Old Girl Yet. In *Directions in Cognitive Anthropology*, ed. Janet W.D. Dougherty, pp. 177–198. University of Illinois Press, Urbana and Chicago.

Brown, Cecil H. 1984   *Language and Living Things: Uniformities in Folk Classification and Naming*. Rutgers University Press, New Brunswick, N.J.

Brown, Cecil H. 1987   The Folk Subgenus: A New Ethnobiological Rank. *Journal of Ethnobiology* 7:181–192.

Dougherty, Janet W.D. 1978   Salience and Relativity in Classification. *American Ethnologist* 5:66–80.

Hunn, Eugene S. 1977   *Tzeltal Folk Zoology: The Classification of Discontinuities in Nature*. Academic Press, New York, N.Y.

Hunn, Eugene S. 1982   The Utilitarian Factor in Folk Biological Classification. *American Anthropologist* 84:830–847.

Hunn, Eugene S., and Cecil H. Brown. 2011   Linguistic Ethnobiology. In *Ethnobiology,* eds. E. N. Anderson, Deborah M. Pearsall, Eugene S. Hunn, and Nancy J. Turner, pp. 319–333. Wiley-Blackwell, Hoboken, N. J.

Hunn, Eugene S., with James Selam and family. 1990   *Nch'i-Wána, The Big River: Mid-Columbia Indians and Their Land.* University of Washington Press, Seattle.

Morey, Darcy. 2010   *Dogs: Domestication and the Development of a Social Bond.* Cambridge University Press.

Rosch, Eleanor. 1978   Principles of Categorization. In *Cognition and Categorization,* eds. Eleanor Rosch and Barbara Lloyd, pp. 28–49. Lawrence Erlbaum Associates, Hillsdale, N.J.

Wikipedia. 2012   Fractals. Available at: http://en.wikipedia.org/wiki/Fractal (verified May 2012).

Appendix 1: Vernacular English "Kinds of Dog" Class Project

(Data from: Anthropology 542 - Cognitive Anthropology, Winter 2003, University of Washington, Seattle, WA; N = 19 respondents).

Afghan
airedale
akita
basset [hound]
beagle
bichon frise
boxer

bulldog
hairless chihuahua
chihuahua
chow
cockapoo
blue collie
border collie
rough collie
collie
Pembroke Welsh corgi
corgi
coyote
dachshund
dalmation
dingo
miniature doberman
doberman [pinscher]
African wild dog
Aztec hairless dog, synonym
of xoloitzcuintle
bird dog
Burmese mountain dog
hot dog (*sic.*)
junkyard dog
hound dog

fox
great dane
greyhound
Australian blue heeler
Queensland heeler
blood-hound
blue tick hound
wolfhound

hound [dog]
Siberian husky
husky
skipper key
black lab
chocolate lab
golden lab, synonym of
yellow lab
yellow lab
labrador [retriever]
Lassie
Lhasa Apso
[Alaskan] malamute
maltese
bull mastiff
Tibetan mastiff
mastiff
mutt
pekinese
pinscher
pit-bull
pointer
pomeranian
French poodle
standard poodle
toy poodle
poodle

Prince Charles
pug
Chesapeake Bay retriever
golden retriever
labrador retriever

retriever
rottweiler
Saint Bernard
salchicha
samoyed
schnauzer
scottie [dog]
English setter

Gordon setter
Irish setter
red setter
setter
sharpai/sharpei
Australian sheepdog
English sheepdog

sheepdog
blue sheltie
sheltie
Australian shepherd
Belgian shepherd
German shepherd
shepherd
shi[a]tzu
Brittany spaniel
cocker spaniel
springer spaniel
spaniel
spitz
Australian terrier
Boston terrier
Brittany terrier
fox terrier
Jack Russell terrier
rat terrier

Scottish terrier
Yorkshire terrier
terrier
weimeraner
weiner [dog], synonym for
dachshund
westie
timber wolf
Irish wolfhound
Russian wolfhound
wolfhound
xoloitzcuintli

Appendix 2: AKC Officially Recognized Dog Breeds

(From American Kennel Club, 2012, see http://www.akc.org/breeds/complete_breed_list.cfm.)

Affenpinscher
Afghan Hound
Airedale Terrier
Akita
Alaskan Malamute
American English Coonhound
American Eskimo Dog
American Foxhound
American Staffordshire Terrier
American Water Spaniel
Anatolian Shepherd Dog
Australian Cattle Dog
Australian Shepherd
Australian Terrier
Basenji
Basset Hound
Beagle
Bearded Collie
Beauceron
Bedlington Terrier
Belgian Malinois
Belgian Sheepdog
Belgian Tervuren
Bernese Mountain Dog
Bichon Frise
Black and Tan Coonhound
Black Russian Terrier
Bloodhound
Bluetick Coonhound
Border Collie
Border Terrier
Borzoi
Boston Terrier
Bouvier des Flandres
Boxer
Boykin Spaniel
Briard
Brittany
Brussels Griffon
Norwich Terrier
Nova Scotia Duck Tolling Retriever
Old English Sheepdog

Bull Terrier
Bulldog
Bullmastiff
Cairn Terrier
Canaan Dog
Cane Corso

Cardigan Welsh Corgi
Cavalier King Charles Spaniel
Cesky Terrier

Chesapeake Bay Retriever
Chihuahua
Chinese Crested
Chinese Shar-Pei
Chow Chow
Clumber Spaniel
Cocker Spaniel
Collie
Curly-Coated Retriever
Dachshund
Dalmatian
Dandie Dinmont Terrier
Doberman Pinscher
Dogue de Bordeaux
English Cocker Spaniel
English Foxhound
English Setter
English Springer Spaniel
English Toy Spaniel
Entlebucher Mountain Dog
Field Spaniel
Finnish Lapphund
Finnish Spitz
Flat-Coated Retriever
French Bulldog
German Pinscher
German Shepherd
German Shorthaired Pointer
German Wirehaired Pointer
Giant Schnauzer
Redbone Coonhound
Rhodesian Ridgeback

Rottweiler

Glen of Imaal Terrier
Golden Retriever
Gordon Setter
Great Dane
Great Pyrenees
Greater Swiss Mountain Dog
Greyhound
Harrier
Havanese

Ibizan Hound
Icelandic Sheepdog
Irish Red and White Setter
Irish Setter
Irish Terrier
Irish Water Spaniel
Irish Wolfhound
Italian Greyhound
Japanese Chin
Keeshond
Kerry Blue Terrier
Komondor
Kuvasz
Labrador Retriever
Lakeland Terrier
Leonberger
Lhasa Apso
Löwchen
Maltese
Manchester Terrier
Mastiff
Miniature Bull Terrier
Miniature Pinscher
Miniature Schnauzer
Neapolitan Mastiff
Newfoundland
Norfolk Terrier
Norwegian Buhund
Norwegian Elkhound
Norwegian Lundehund
Staffordshire Bull Terrier
Standard Schnauzer

Sussex Spaniel

Otterhound
Papillon
Parson Russell Terrier
Pekingese
Pembroke Welsh Corgi
Petit Basset Griffon Vendéen

Pharaoh Hound
Plott
Pointer
Polish Lowland Sheepdog
Pomeranian

Poodle
Portuguese Water Dog
Pug

Puli
Pyrenean Shepherd

Saint Bernard
Saluki
Samoyed
Schipperke
Scottish Deerhound
Scottish Terrier

Sealyham Terrier
Shetland Sheepdog
Shiba Inu
Shih Tzu
Siberian Husky

Silky Terrier
Skye Terrier
Smooth Fox Terrier

Soft Coated Wheaten Terrier
Spinone Italiano

Swedish Vallhund
Tibetan Mastiff
Tibetan Spaniel
Tibetan Terrier
Toy Fox Terrier
Treeing Walker
Coonhound
Vizsla
Weimaraner
Welsh Springer Spaniel
Welsh Terrier
West Highland White
Terrier
Whippet
Wire Fox Terrier
Wirehaired Pointing
Griffon
Xoloitzcuintli
Yorkshire Terrier

The *Kasaga'yu*: An Ethno-Ornithology of the Cattail-Eater Northern Paiute People of Western Nevada

Catherine S. Fowler[†]

Abstract

The Cattail-Eater Northern Paiute people have lived near the marshes of the Carson Basin in western Nevada for many generations. During this time, they have come to recognize and name over 100 bird species in and around the marsh ecosystems, and have incorporated many of them into their subsistence system and ideology. Some of the uses they made of birds for food and examples of references to them in story, song and sacred contexts are reviewed, along with their principles of bird nomenclature and categorizations. The data were collected from two elderly Cattail-Eater women between 1949 and1978. Their names for birds are also compared to those from other Northern Paiute-speaking regions, and more broadly, from other Uto-Aztecan languages. Unfortunately the comparative data are too scant overall to derive conclusions about the linguistic prehistory of Cattail-Eater people. But they do suggest that their ancestors have been around marsh ecosystems for a long period of time.

Introduction

The role of birds in the lives of indigenous peoples is of considerable interest in the growing literature on Traditional Ecological Knowledge (TEK).[1] In the Great Basin of western North America, data on indigenous knowledge of birds are richest for the **Toidikadi**[2] or 'Cattail-Eater' people of the Carson Basin of western Nevada (Figure 1). Their traditional homeland contains and has contained over several thousand years, shallow lakes, fresh and salt water marshes, and upland and lowland ecosystems attractive to a wide variety of resident and migratory avifauna. Over countless generations Cattail-Eater people have observed the seasonal habits of numerous species of waterfowl, shore birds and others, come to understand their nesting and food choices, sorted visitants from residents, learned to recognize and duplicate their calls, and much more. In addition, Cattail-Eater people have witnessed the partial destruction of this important and productive bird habitat (especially Stillwater Marsh) due to periodic drought, and more recently, upstream

† University of Nevada, Department of Anthropology (096), Reno, NV 89557 [csfowler@unr.edu]

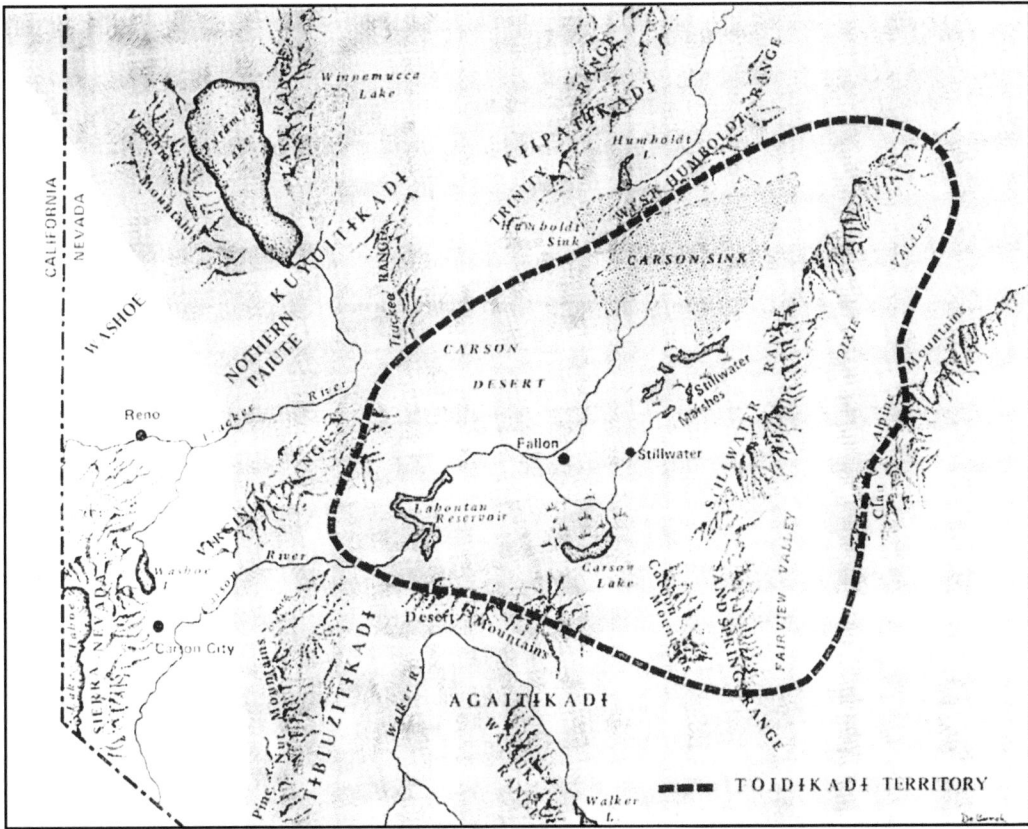

Figure 1. Cattail-Eater or ***Toidikadi*** Northern Paiute territory, ca. 1860. Masked area shows adjacent Northern Paiute groups. Map by Patricia DeBunch.

water diversion for agriculture and urban growth. And they also have seen parts of the marsh habitats come back remarkably during wet cycles, and, especially within the past 70 years, through concerted management efforts by federal, state and private agencies (especially the US Fish and Wildlife Service). In this paper, I review selected aspects of Cattail-Eater traditional knowledge of birds. Included is a list of the birds they named, some examples of their uses for subsistence (especially waterfowl), and the overall place of birds in their lives. I also review some of the principles by which they named birds in their language and how they saw the relationships among them. And I note some of the changes that elders have witnessed through the years for some species, including in numbers, habits and habitats. Finally I look at cognates shared by groups linguistically related to the Cattail-Eater people for possible clues to their linguistic prehistory. The comparative data are offered to further discussions of these important topics within ethno-ornithology and TEK generally.

The Cattail-Eater People and Their Region

The *Toidikadi*, or Cattail-Eater people, speak a dialect of the Northern Paiute language, one of six or seven member languages of the Numic Branch of the Uto-Aztecan language family (Miller 1986). They have lived in the Carson Basin in western Nevada for at least the last 1000 years and perhaps longer (Kelly 2000). Prior to contact and disruption of their lifeways by Euro-American incursion in the 1820s to 1840s and settlement in the 1860s to 1880s, they were hunters and gatherers subsisting on a variety of biotic resources, including plants, birds (principally waterfowl), large and small mammals and a few fish species. Given that the wetlands of the Carson Basin (especially Carson Lake and Stillwater Marsh) were the most productive of the habitats within their territory, the people remained tethered to these locations, leaving them only periodically to collect special food resources characteristic of the adjacent valley zones or mountains (see Fowler 1992 for details).

For the most part, the Cattail-Eater homeland is a dry, upland locality (roughly 1160 m base elevation), with much of the land being part of the Carson Desert. This desert is within the rain shadow of the Sierra Nevada and receives on average slightly less than 120 mm of precipitation annually, with three-fourths of this falling in the winter season. Summer temperatures often reach 40°C+ and plummet to −18°C and below in the winter, with a common diurnal of 10°C (Morrison 1964:5–6). Water resources are controlled by the Sierran snow pack, and are provided largely by the Carson River which flows eastward from the Sierra Nevada to terminate in the area. It feeds the three shallow water bodies (Carson Lake, Stillwater Marsh, Carson Sink), the first two literally oases in the desert. Together they form one large system that becomes progressively more saline as it drains to the north (Figure 2). In good winter precipitation years there may be more than 82,000 hectares of wetlands in the system, while in bad there may be less than one-tenth of that. The area is a key stopping place on the Pacific Flyway, often accommodating more than 1,000,000 migrating and resident birds (Anglin and Shellhorn 1992). But the variation places considerable stress on the biotic resources, and periodically in the past, on the people (Kelly 2000). The wetlands support a variety of emergent and submergent vegetation, including cattail (*Typha latifolia* L., *T. domingensis* Pers., *T. angustifolia* L.), hardstem and alkali bulrush (*Scirpus acutus* Bigelow, *S. maritimus* L.), and pondweeds (*Potamogeton* spp., *Rorippa* spp., etc.). The *Toidikadi*, literally 'Cattail-Eater' people, take their name from the many uses they made of cattail, especially for food, but also shelter and material culture (Wheat 1967).

Surrounding the wetlands are various valley, foothill and mountain regions with biotic zones generally characteristic of drier portions of the Great Basin and intermontane west (Cronquist et al. 1972). Lowlands in the Carson Desert generally support sparse vegetation dominated by a little greasewood—shadscale association (*Sarcobatus vermiculatus* var. *baileyi* (Cov.) Jeps.—*Atriplex confertifolia* (Torr.& Frem.); Figure 3). Foothills and slopes of ranges, depending on soil types, are characterized by Big Sagebrush (*Artemesia tridentata* Nutt.),

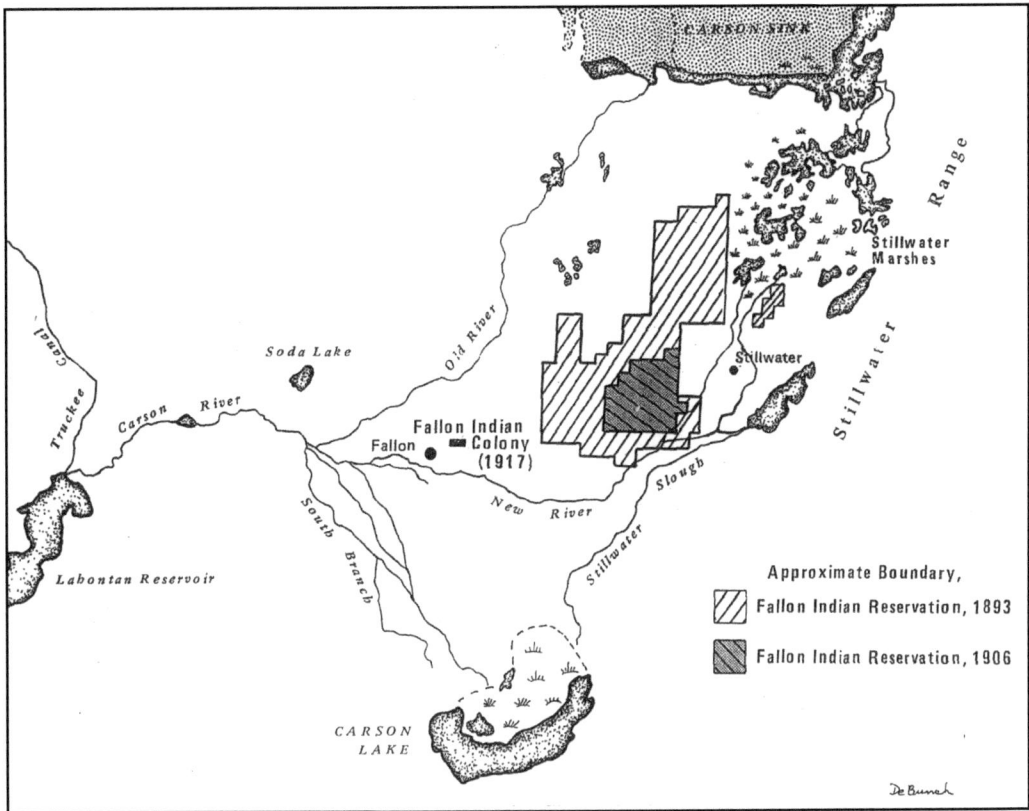

Figure 2. Carson Basin marsh ecosystem (Carson Lake, Stillwater Marsh, Carson Sink), ca. 1880. Includes historic and present-day Fallon Indian Reservation boundaries. Map by Patricia DeBunch.

Figure 3. Little Greasewood-Shadscale association, Carson Desert, 1952. Photograph by Dave Marshall. Courtesy of US Fish and Wildlife Service, Stillwater National Wildlife Refuge.

especially where fresh water is close to the surface (Cronquist et al. 1972:90), and a variety of grasses (*Elymus, Agropyron, Eragrostis, Achnatherum*, etc.). Mountain ranges reaching 1800 to 2500 m, although limited in extent (Stillwater Range, Clan Alpine Range), support scattered scrub forests of pinyon pine (*Pinus monophylla* Torr. & Frem.) and Utah Juniper (*Juniperus osteosperma* [Torr.] Little; Figure 4), as well as a variety of root vegetables (*Lomatium, Claytonia*, etc.) and berry-producing plants (*Prunus, Sambucus*, etc.). They also shelter birds and mammals attractive to **Toidikadi** hunters and collectors. But by far the richest resources are to be found in the wetlands, with their complex series of fresh water and alkaline ponds and marshes, associated vegetation and wildlife (Anglin and Shellhorn 1992). Cattail-Eater people chose places close to the wetlands to establish their temporary and semi-permanent family camps, and spent a considerable amount of time living and working around them (Figures 5, 6).

Left: Figure 4. View of Stillwater Marsh from the Stillwater Range, 1952. Pinyon-juniper association in foreground. Photograph by Dave Marshall. Courtesy of US Fish and Wildlife Service, Stillwater National Wildlife Refuge.

Data and Methods

The primary data on Cattail-Eater ethno-ornithology that follow were obtained in general and specific ethnographic/linguistic interviews with two remarkably knowledgeable **Toidikadi** women, Mrs. Wuzzie George and Mrs. Alice Steve, of the Fallon Indian Reservation, both of whom spent all or a significant portion of their lives near Stillwater Marsh. In 1949, Margaret Wheat, talented local amateur anthropologist, began interviewing Mrs. Steve, then approximately 70 years old, about the ways of her ancestors as part of a larger study focused on Northern Paiute "survival arts" (Wheat 1967). Within a year or two, they were joined by Mrs. Steve's friend, Wuzzie George, who was also roughly 70 years old. Wheat recorded approximately 150 hours of tape with the women (Mrs. Steve died in 1964), and photographed them and other

Figure 5. Stillwater Marsh with the Stillwater Range in the background, 1952. Photograph by Dave Marshall. Courtesy of US Fish and Wildlife Service, Stillwater National Wildlife Refuge.

Figure 6. Wuzzie George collecting immature spikes of cattails as green food, ca. 1956. Photograph by Margaret Wheat, Stillwater Marsh. Courtesy of Special Collections Department, University of Nevada Reno Libraries.

Northern Paiute people in many indigenous pursuits (see Wheat 1967). In the early 1960s, Sven Liljebald, a Swedish linguist, began working with the women and also reviewing Wheat's tapes for lexical data. I joined Wheat and Liljeblad in the late 1960s, and independently and together, we recorded an additional 50 hours with Mrs. George until her death in 1978 (see Fowler 1992 for details).[3]

Some of the interviews over the years related specifically to local flora and fauna while others focused on other topics. Wheat and I also traveled with Mrs. George throughout her homeland, and especially in and around the marshes, observing and talking about the region and its resources, including the plants, mammals, reptiles, insects, and particularly birds. Mrs. George was an ardent bird watcher, and seemed happiest in the Stillwater Marshes where she spent her childhood years and could watch the birds. Together we made field iden-tifications of birds, and especially waterfowl, but also spent hours going through photographs in field guides. We also viewed taxidermy mounts or birds at the Churchill County Museum (Fallon, NV) and the Nevada State Museum (Carson City, NV) where we also went through some of their study skins. For this paper, the data on Cattail-Eater birds were extracted from these multiple interviews and the field and museum visits, and were then checked for accu-racy against local field guides (Alcorn 1988; Nevada Division of Wildlife 1999; US Fish and Wildlife Service 1982). Changes in bird nomenclature since that time have been incorporated from the American Ornithologists' Union (2011) and through the kindness of reviewers.[4] Comparative data in other sections of the paper are from other sources that are referenced in those sections.

The Birds of the Cattail-Eaters

Recognizing the Birds

Checklists of birds for Stillwater Marsh, Carson Lake and the larger Carson Desert list rough-ly 175 species, including a dozen or more rare or single sightings (see especially Alcorn 1988; Nevada Division of Wildlife 1999; US Fish and Wildlife Service 1982). Of these, Mrs. George and Mrs. Steve were able to name roughly 100 (see Tables 1–4). Although both of these women had remarkable memories and were very familiar with the region and its avifauna, their knowledge is likely not exhaustive of Cattail-Eater names for local birds. Both had been involved at least in part in traditional subsistence systems into adulthood, but what they knew already had been affected by a century of cultural and language erosion. It had also been affected by restricted access to many parts of the region and its resources due to private and federal property rights. In addition, our elicitation procedures were not fully systematic, es-pecially for smaller birds. Yet both women without doubt were true Native ornithologists and recognized cultural experts by their community (Fallon Reservation). They freely shared their knowledge with us in the hope that it would be preserved for their descendants and others.

Within the general category waterfowl, Mrs. George and Mrs. Steve named 32 of 43 species listed as occurring in the region, five of the remaining being taxa that they did not differentiate or which were known from rare sightings only (see Table 1). They named 11 of the 27 listed shorebirds and gulls, with differences being accounted for based on classification differences, rarity, and possibly some confusion in elicitation procedures (see Table 2). They named 13 of the 18 birds of prey and owls, with the discrepancy being primarily in differences in generic taxa recognized (they merged some of the owls and some of the hawks and falcons; see Table 3). Of the remaining categories of birds, they named most of the woodpeckers, all the corvids, merged the hummingbirds under one taxon, and knew fewer of the small perching birds (89 listed; 47 named; see Table 4). Again, lack of in-depth questioning,

Table 1. Waterfowl and other marsh birds.*

	Used as food:	
Species, Northern Paiute Name	**Eggs**	**Young**
Common Loon (*Gavia immer*), **pawa animiwaa, patiiti, pabuku**, 'water pet'	+	
Pied-billed Grebe (*Podilymbus podiceps*), **witi'i**	+	
Western Grebe (*Aechmophorus occidentalis*), **kwibui'idi**	+	
American White Pelican (*Pelecanus erythrorhynchos*), **paannusa**	(+)	+
Double-crested Cormorant (*Phalacrocorax auritus*), **patsigwai'yu**		
Great Blue Heron (*Ardea horodias*), **wassa**	+	+
Great Egret (*Ardea alba*), **tohaggwassa**, 'white heron'	+	+
Snowy Egret (*Egretta thula*), **tohaggwassa**, 'white heron'	+	
Sandhill Crane (*Grus canadensis*), **koda'a**		
Black-crowned Night-heron (*Nycticorax nycticorax*), **kwangidi**	+	
American Bittern (*Botaurus lentiginosus*), **tabapunikadi'i**, 'sits looking at the sun'		
White-faced Ibis (*Plegadis chihi*), **panatannga'a**	+	+
American Coot (*Fulica americana*), **saya**	+	+
Tundra Swan (*Cygnus columbianus*), **wohidda, tamawohidda**		
Canada Goose (*Branta canadensis*), **nagvta**	+	+
White-fronted Goose (*Anser albifrons*), **pibuggwaza'a**		
Snow Goose (*Chen caerulescens*), **saigossa**		
Ross's Goose (*Chen rossii*), **saigossa**		
Green-winged Teal (*Anas crecca*), **sogobihi**, 'earth duck'	+	+
Mallard (*Anas platyrhynchos*), **kudaa**	+	+
Northern Pintail (*Anus acuta*), **wigwassi**	+	
Cinnamon Teal (*Anas cyanoptera*), **atsasogobihi**, 'red-earth duck'	+	+
Northern Shoveler (*Anas clypeata*), **igommobi'i**, 'tongue nose'	+	+
Gadwall (*Anas strepera*), **izikudaa**, 'gray mallard'	+	
American Wigeon (*Anas americana*), **imuduyu**	+	+
Canvasback (*Aythya valisineria*), **tohatsakwaadi**, 'white-side'		
Redhead (*Aythya americana*), **ohaa'idi**	+	+
Common Merganser (*Mergus merganser*), **hubaggwi**, 'dace'		
Double-crested Cormorant (*Phalacrocorax auritus*), **patsigwai'yu**		
Common Goldeneye (*Bucephala clangula*), **pui'oabino'o**, 'yellow-eye-inside'		
Bufflehead (*Bucephala albeola*), **annawo'o**, 'long head'	+	
Ruddy Duck (*Oxyura jamaicensis*), **nobaba'a**, 'big egg'	+	

* Includes Loons, Grebes, Pelicans, Cormorants, Herons and Bitterns, Ibises, Rails.

Table 2. Shorebirds, plovers and gulls.[*]

Species, Northern Paiute name	Used as food:	
	Eggs	Young
Killdeer *(Charadrius vociferus)*, **patitsinngi'i**, 'water bent-leg'	+	
Black-necked Stilt *(Himantopus mexicanus)*, **tuukwiidi'na'a**	+	
American Avocet *(Recurvirostra americana)*, **kwiidi'na'a**		+
Long-billed Curlew *(Numenius americanus)*, **todoggwiu'u**	+	+
Semipalmated Plover *(Charadrius semipalmatus)*, **timmassana'a**	+	
Wilson's Snipe *(Gallinago delicta)*, **saahidi**	+	+
Wilson's Phalarope *(Phalaropus tricolor)*, **paadduisi**, 'water pet'	+	
California Gull *(Larus californicus)*, **toha'ada**, 'white crow'	+	+
Caspian Tern *(Hydroprogne caspia)*, **kicazaia**	+	+
Forster's Tern *(Sterna forsteri)*, **kitsaza'a**	+	+
Black Tern *(Chlidonias niger)*, **tuukitsaza'a**, 'Black Tern'	+	

[*] Adults of most sometimes eaten; confusion on naming small wading birds.

Table 3. Vultures, hawks and falcons and owls.

Species, Northern Paiute name
Turkey Vulture *(Cathartes aura)*, **wiho**
Cooper's Hawk *(Accipiter cooperi)*, **tuukini'i**, 'Black Swainson's Hawk'
Red-tailed Hawk *(Buteo jamaicensis)*, **nakai'i**
Swainson's Hawk *(Buteo swainsoni)*, **kini'i**, also Sharp-shinned Hawk *(Accipiter velox)*, **kini'i**
American Kestrel *(Falco sparverius)*, **kidid'i**
Northern Harrier *(Circus cyaneus)*, **saibazo'o**
Golden Eagle *(Aguila chrysaetos)*, **kwi'naa'a**
Bald Eagle *(Haliaeetus leucocephalus)*, **pazia, tohatsopigiga'yu kwi'naa'a**, 'white-headed eagle'
Osprey *(Pandion haliaetus)*, **paggwidikadi**, 'fish-eater'
Great Horned Owl *(Bobo virginianus)*, **muhu**
Western Screech-Owl *(Otus kennicotti)*, **potopodo'o**
Barn Owl *(Tyto alba)*, **sigummuhu**
Burrowing Owl *(Athene cunicularia)*, **kuhu'u**

especially in the latter category, may be a contributing factor, although their classification scheme appears to generally merge most small birds into a few taxa (see further discussion under Bird Nomenclature). Small birds are only occasionally differentiated by color or some other feature. Rea (2007:43) and Hunn (1990:144) note similar trends in naming among the Northern Piman and Sahaptin peoples, and my comparative data from other Numic-speaking groups reflect the same (Fowler 1972).

Birds and Subsistence

Of the various birds recognized by Mrs. George and Mrs. Steve, by far those hunted most commonly for food were the waterfowl, marsh and shorebirds. In addition to the adults, people collected immature birds and eggs of several nesting species. Tables 1 and 2 list the species the women verified as used for food, including whether their eggs or young were also collected. Mrs. George was quite clear as to which waterfowl and shore birds were exempt

Table 4. Other upland and small birds.*

Species, Northern Paiute name	Used as Food	
	Eggs	Young
Greater Sage Grouse (*Centrocercus urophasianus*), **huuzi**	+	+
Sooty Grouse (*Dendragapus obscurus*), **kahi'i**	+	+
California Quail (*Callipepla californica*), **sikiggi'i** (non-native)	+	
Mountain Quail (*Oreortyx pictus*), **tuhuta'a**	+	+
Belted Kingfisher (*Ceryle alcylon*), **paggwitsanannagi'i**, 'fish-swallower'		
Mourning Dove (*Zenaida macroura*), **ihobi**	+	+
Common Nighthawk (*Chordeiles minor*), **tinnabbiuzu**		
Common Poorwill (*Phalaenoptilis nuttallii*), **todigwa, tabutsigwi'i**		
Northern Flicker (*Colaptes auratus*), **atsabanna**		
Hairy Woodpecker (*Diocoides villosus*), **wibibbana'a**		
Acorn Woodpecker (*Melanerpes formicivorus*), **atsaka'yu wibibbana'a**		
Western Scrub Jay (*Aphelocoma coerulescens*), **witsimmi, iza'a padi**, 'coyote's daughter'		
Steller's Jay (*Cyanocitta stelleri*), **wogowi'atsimmi**, 'pine scrub jay'		
Pinyon Jay (*Gymnorhinus cyanocephalus*), **aa'a**		
American Crow (*Corvus brachyrhynchos*), **ada**		
Common Raven (*Corvus corax*), **kwii'ada**		
Black-billed Magpie (*Pica hudsonia*), **kwidagaga'i**, 'defecates a lot'		
Say's Phoebe (*Sayornis saya*), **togwi'u**		
Gray Flycatcher (*Empidonax wrightii*, + others), **yituggisi**		
Horned Lark (*Eremophila alpestris*), **tsidunna**	+	+
Barn Swallow (*Hirundo rustica*), **sogobbina'a**, 'earth + ?'		
Cliff Swallow (*Hirundo pyrrhonota*), **toyawatsiddono'o**, 'mountain + ?'		
Mountain Chickadee (*Poecile gambeli*), **tsitsibi'i**		
Juniper Titmouse (*Parus inornatus*), **yadakaasi**, 'has a winnowing tray'		
Red-breasted Nuthatch (*Sitta canadensis*), **sannaki'i**, 'pitch + ki, ki'		
Broad-tailed Hummingbird (*Selasphorus platycercus* + others), **songoi'i**		
Marsh Wren (*Cistothorus palustris*), **totokwizizi'I**	+	+
Sage Thrasher (*Oreoscoptes montanus*), **iwa'yawaha**, 'lots of ?'		
American Robin (*Turdus migratorius*), **sugu**		
Mountain Bluebird (*Sialia currucoides*, + *S. mexicana?*), **pidu'yu**		
Loggerheaded Shrike (*Lanius ludovicianus*), **tsonumma**		
Western Meadowlark (*Sturnella neglecta*), **pazidono**	+	+
Yellow-headed Blackbird (*Xanthocephalus xanthrocephalus*), **saibakodobba**, 'tule blackbird'		
Brewer's Blackbird (*Euphagus cyanocephalus*), **pakodobba**		
Red-winged Blackbird (*Agelaius phoneceus*), **atsakassaga'yu pakodobba, atsapakodobba**, 'has red wings blackbird,' 'red blackbird'		
Bullock's Oriole (*Icterus bullockii*), **wanawini'i**, 'net maker'		
Black-headed Grosbeak (*Pheucticus melanocephalus*), **yuniguiti**		
American Goldfinch (*Spinus tristis*), **oahuziba**, 'yellow little bird'		
Lazuli Bunting? (*Passerina amoena*), **puihuzi'i**, 'blue little bird'		
Brewer's Sparrow (*Spizella breweri*), **tonohuziba**, 'greasewood small bird' or **izihuziba**, 'gray little bird'		
White-crowned Sparrow (*Zonotrichia leucophyrys*), **puitsitsi'i**		
Black-throated Sparrow (*Amphispiza bilineata*), **wutuzizi**		
Sage Sparrow (*Amphispiza belli*), **tokitsiwa**		
Song Sparrow (*Melospiza melodia*), **siihuziba**, ? + 'little bird'		
Unidentified sparrow (?), **yuhuhuziba**, 'fatty little bird'		
Dark-eyed Junco (*Junco hyemalis*), **nibadono'o**, 'snow carrier'		
Purple Finch (*Carpodacus purpureus*), or House Finch (*Carpodacus mexicanus*), **widuzi'i**		

* Small birds somewhat confusing and likely confused, especially the sparrows. Names do not always agree with Ridgway or with Merriam's identifications.

from egg collecting, most because they did not nest locally. Of non-nesting species, she remarked: "she not make egg here—make egg someplace else." In addition to the waterfowl and shorebirds listed, both women also collected the eggs of certain other birds that habitually nested in the marshes, such as Red-winged Blackbird, Yellow-headed Blackbird, Marsh Wren and others (see Table 4). It is likely that other people did the same, although there were undoubtedly preferences involved in these and other patterns of bird hunting and egg collecting (see also below).

A variety of techniques were used by Cattail-Eater people in hunting adult waterfowl, including the use of duck decoys (**pihi ti'a**), the bodies of which were made of hardstem bulrush or 'tule' and occasionally cattail leaves covered with duck skins (Fowler 1990; Wheat 1967; Figure 7); bows and special bulbous-tipped duck arrows (**pihipongossa**); linear nets set on stakes at water line or just above the water and largely designed to take ducks that have to patter or run across the water surface to get airborne (e.g., the Pochards and their allies [Wilke and Thompson 1989]); tethered and baited hooks; and hunters concealed under floating blinds who pulled ducks underwater by their feet and then dispatched them. Drives of waterfowl either with or without nets and using tule balsa boats and wading drivers were also frequent during periods of molt for adult birds (especially the American Coot) and for fully fledged hatchlings. These drives are well described for the 19th Century by early observers (DeQuille 1963:38–9; Henshaw 1879:2304; Scott 1966:24–5). Different techniques were used depending on season, conditions and species sought.

The two peak seasons for hunting waterfowl and shorebirds were the spring and fall migration periods when the wetlands were teeming with thousands of birds. Numbers often approached and exceeded 100,000 for several waterfowl species according to mid 20th Century census figures (Fowler 1992:Tables 3, 4; Stillwater Wildlife Mangement Area, 1950-55). As Mrs. George said, when all other foods failed, "there was always ducks."

Figure 7. Jimmy George, husband of Wuzzie George, with two of his Canvasback duck decoys, 1936. Photograph by Omer C. Stewart. Courtesy of the author.

Waterfowl hunting was largely the work of men, while women and children were the primary egg collectors. Everyone participated in duck drives, although the women were the ones responsible for skinning and drying the large catch, and for cooking or otherwise preparing waterfowl for food. Eggs were collected daily during the nesting season, and special but expedient twined tule bags (***noho mago'o***, 'egg bag') were used to hold and transport a dozen or two eggs on each trip to and from the marshes (Figure 8). Sometimes entire clutches of eggs were taken, as people observed that most waterfowl would lay another clutch (see also Hunn, Johnson, Russel and Thornton 2003). However, when there were any hatchlings in a nest, remaining unhatched eggs were generally bypassed in favor of other nests. But some people, especially "old people," prized eggs with fully formed birds inside. Mrs. George was not fond of these, but her grandmother liked them best. Eggs were also buried in the damp and cool mud to preserve them for a few weeks, thus lengthening the egg collecting season. Eggs were ordinarily boiled in baskets using hot stones, and eaten with other foods or as snacks (Fowler 1992:54–6). Eggs of birds other than waterfowl were similarly treated.

Birds in Ceremony

The feathers of some bird species were specifically sought by Cattail-eater people because of their religious connotations. In particular, the primaries of the Golden Eagle and immature Bald Eagle were important to doctors or shamans through their association with power (***puha***). They were often attached to wands placed at the head of a patient during a doctoring or curing ceremony (Park 1938:134). Eagle down was considered to be a powerful preventative for illness, and was often placed above a person's sleeping place to ward off ghosts or other spirits that might do the person harm. Similarly, the tail feathers of the Black-billed Magpie were associated with power by some doctors, and frequently used in wands prepared for doctoring. Magpie feathers also decorated dance plumes, headdresses, and the tips of cords wound with eagle down that made up dance skirts and arm and leg bands used especially in the South Dance (see Fowler and Liljeblad 1986). Red-tailed

Figure 8. Wuzzie George, ca. 1960, and one of her hardstem bulrush egg collecting bags. Photograph by Margaret Wheat. Courtesy of Special Collections Department, University of Nevada Reno Libraries.

Hawk tail feathers also could be used in dance outfits, according to an individual's preference, as could those of the Great Horned Owl. Willard Park (1934) collected several examples of headdresses made with California Gull tail and wing feathers for Harvard's Peabody Museum, but does not specifically describe the dances or ceremonies in which they were used.

Any large or medium-sized bird might be a source of power to an aspiring doctor or shaman. Particularly important again were the eagles and magpies, but also specifically mentioned in addition by Park (1938:16–18) were hawks, crow, owl, another unidentified bird and possibly loon. Hummingbird was an important power for Mrs. George's husband, Jimmy George, who doctored into the early 1960s (Fowler 1990). Mr. George interpreted the bird's hovering behavior specifically as an offering of power. Mrs. George also told of stories and songs that were specific to the power held by the American Coot, the Long-billed Curlew and the Pinyon Jay. Birds, however, were by no means the only power sources for doctoring: technically any living thing could have power and offer it for curing (Park 1938).

Birds in Other Cultural Contexts

The women (and other Northern Paiute people) also spoke of other associations with and for various birds. The corvids, for example, were known to be particularly talkative, keeping up a constant chatter with people whenever they saw them. Their messages were not considered to be either good or bad—merely messages. Owls, on the other hand, and especially the Great Horned Owl and the Western Screech Owl, were primarily associated with bad news, communicated either through their calls or by a person seeing one in the daytime. The cry of the Common Poorwill also was considered to convey bad news, especially when heard at night. And Northern Flickers brought messages, usually by dropping a wing or tail feather: finding one was a sign of news to come. Owls could also do harm through sorcery, especially at night, and doctors with owl power were sometimes suspect.

Several smaller birds were considered friendly and their songs and chatter were often interpreted as speaking. To hear bird song brought pleasure, and Mrs. George, in particular, always enjoyed watching and listening to birds either in the marsh or along the Carson River where many smaller birds nested in the large trees. People often monitored the health of the land and safety of a situation by listening to birds singing. If they were singing, things were going well in that place. More specifically, during pine nut season people talked to the Mountain Chickadee, asking, "how is your mother?" S/he replies "*chi, chi, bi, bi, bi,*" meaning "she is good, good, good." At the same time, the Red-breasted Nuthatch goes about saying "*ki, ki, ki, ki,*" and people answered back. (The bird is called *sanaki'i*, pitch *ki ki*, partly for its call and partly for its use of pitch (*sanabi*) in nest building [see below]). People also sang to the Pinyon Jay at this time, and it answered back, as this bird is considered to doctor the pine nuts and produce a good crop for the people to harvest. Similarly, the Western Scrub Jay, also seen at this time, yells at people to leave its pine nuts alone. It is referred to as coyote's daughter (*iza'abadi*) in addition to its regular name (*wiatsimmi*), for its habit of stealing pine nuts from camp sites.

In the spring when women were out gathering seeds in the valley, the Western Meadow Lark is said by Mrs. George to continually "scold everybody" with its calls, and people often joked about this habit. Similarly, she said, "Killdeer gives you hell when you come too close to her eggs." The Northern Shrike once dreamed of becoming an eagle, so it could snatch human children so people would know how it feels to have their children (eggs) stolen and eaten. And the Mourning Dove is thought to be able to call and send the rattlesnake after people who bother her eggs. The eggs of all four species were harvested for food.

Birds in Tales

Additional associations for birds are referenced in traditional stories, wherein birds as well as other animals in the distant past set about making the world ready for people to inhabit. The tales told by Mrs. George and other Cattail-Eater people included several birds (Fowler 1992:228ff). "Black" woodpecker, Northern Harrier, mouse and coyote are specifically involved in the story of the Theft of Pine Nuts, wherein pine nuts are brought to their present locations. Hummingbird is the only one who can fly high enough and long enough to visit the Sun when others, including the Golden Eagle, fail. She[5] can do this because she stores tiny seeds in her crop to sustain her on the journey. Great Blue Heron is a chief, and with the help of Steller's Jay and Black-billed Magpie, defeats frog and his allies. The American Bittern becomes the sun's guardian after other animals try to harm her; she continues to stand looking at the sun to the present (concealing posture). American Coot doctors several other birds and ultimately foretells her own death. Golden Eagle gets to choose its habitual food (rodents, rabbits) after a long race with weasel. The son of White-crowned Sparrow became a doctor and was twice-born. Again, as with potential power sources, birds are not the only actors in stories, but they are consistently involved, often in prominent roles. Doubtless many additional references to them occur in the rich oral tradition of the region (see Liljeblad 1986).

Cattail-Eater Bird Nomenclature

An analysis of the bird names with transparent etymologies reveals several principles used in Cattail-Eater bird nomenclature. Included are names that refer to a (usually obvious) morphological feature of a bird species, a behavioral feature, season of appearance or other seasonal association, and the characteristic onomatopoeic call (see also Rea 2007:39). Bird names with less transparent etymologies may follow the same principles, but their origin is less obvious due to changes in the language. Some bird names are very old within the Numic branch of the language family and also within Uto-Aztecan itself (see below).

Examples of bird names referring to morphological features include the following: 1) Common Goldeneye, ***pui'oabino'o***, 'eye-yellow-inside'—for its bright yellow eye; 2) Canvasback, *tohatsakwaadi*, 'white-side'—for its coloring; 3) Northern Shoveler, *igommubi'i*, 'tongue-nose'—for its bill shape; and 4) Northern Pintail, *wigwassi*, 'sharp-tail'—again for an obvious morphological feature. Note that similar observations are apparently behind the common names for these waterfowl in English (see also Rea 2007:38).

Behavioral features leading to naming include: 1) Bullock's Oriole, *wanawini'i*, 'net-maker'—based on its bag nest construction; 2) Ruddy Duck, *nobaba'a*, 'makes big egg' which it does; 3) Black-billed Magpie, *kwidagaga'i*, 'defecates a lot'—again an accurate observation; 4) American Bittern, *tabapunikadi'i*, 'sits looking at the sun'—for its concealing posture; and 5) Red-breasted Nuthatch, *sannaki'i*, pitch-*ki ki*—for its habit of surrounding its nest cavity with pitch as well as its call.

Imitations of the bird's call are recognized as the source for the names of several birds including the Mountain Chickadee, *tsitsibi'i*; the Marsh Wren, called *totokwizizi'i*; the California Quail, *sikiggi'i*, and several more. Fall migration and association with snow falls leads to the name of the Dark-eyed Junco as *nibadono'o*, 'snow carrier'—"she always brings the snow." Immature Tundra Swan that often arrive late in the spring are called *tamawohidda*, 'spring Trundra Swan.' A few other names with obvious etymologies are less easily explained: Wilson's Phalarope is called *paatuissi*, 'water pet,' and the Juniper Titmouse is *yaddakaassi*, 'has pine nut roasting tray.' The latter may have something to do with this bird's appearance in the hills during pine nut gathering time, although no one is quite sure at present. Wilson's Phalarope is a water bird, but only one of several that could be water pets.[6] The Common Loon is also sometimes called *pabuku*, 'water pet'—with *puku* in this case being a different term for pet, now mostly equated with 'horse,' but sometimes to other domestic animals.

Cattail-Eater equivalents of species names for birds are commonly compounds with one transparent morpheme: usually color or some other attributive. Some examples are: 1) Great Blue Heron, called *wassa*, with the Great Egret and Snowy Egret both called *tohaggwassa* or 'white Great Blue Heron;' 2) Golden Eagle, called *kwi'naa'a*, while the Bald Eagle is *tohatsopigi kwi'naa'a*, 'white-headed Golden Eagle;' 3) American Avocet, called *kwiidi'na'a* while the Black-necked Stilt is *tuukwidi'na'a*, 'black American Avocet.' Of this pair Mrs. George said of the stilt that "she's the same but with different clothes on." The triplet Brewer's Blackbird is called *pakodobba*, Red-winged Blackbird, is *atsapakodobba* or 'red Brewer's Blackbird,' and the Yellow-headed Blackbird is *saipakodobba*, or 'tule Brewer's Blackbird.' Although possibly not a true specific, but rather a name that calls attention to certain similar behaviors, is American Crow, called *ada*, and the Common Raven called *paba'ada*, 'big American Crow' or *kwii'ada* (*kwii*- ?? + 'American Crow'), and the California Gull, called *toha'ada*, 'white American Crow.' Mrs. Steve remarked of the latter, "they are always talking like crows."

Something of the process of bird name formation through compounding can be illustrated by one of the examples just cited as well as by another. As noted, Red-winged Blackbird, called *atsapakodobba*, literally 'red Brewer's Blackbird,' has been shortened from *atsakassaga'yu pakodobba*, literally 'has red wings Brewer's Blackbird.' A similar name for the Brewer's Sparrow, *tonohuziba*, 'greasewood little bird,' started as *tonobinakati huziba*, 'greasewood-sitter little bird,' with the loss of the plant name classifier -*bi* and the verb -*kati*, 'to sit (singular).' Given these processes, some bird names that are by length obvious compounds through time have become partly or wholly unanalyzable. Other examples may be Northern Harrier (*saibazo'o* < *sai*- 'bulrush' + -*pa*- 'water' + -*zo'o* 'to crush, grind'), Barn Swallow (*sogobbina'a*, < *sogo*- 'soil' + *pina'a* ??), and the Western Screech Owl (*tabutsigwi'i* < *tabu*- 'cottontail rabbit' + *tsigwi'i* ??).

In sum, of the various bird names, roughly a third (11 of 32) of the names for waterfowl are not analyzable, with a quarter (3 of 11) of the shorebird names, two-thirds (8 of 13) of the names for birds of prey, and a bit less than half (21 of 47) of the names for others also falling into this category. The birds of prey form the category with the highest percentage of unitary lexemes. While there are probably many reasons why these birds stand out (morphology, behavior, sacredness), it is certainly not because they are used as food. Most are tabooed as food for several reasons, but according to Mrs. George, a major one is that they are meat-eaters. Historical linguistic comparisons of cognates for bird names at various language/branch levels within the Uto-Aztecan family also indicate that birds of prey have been recognized and named for a long time (see below).

Cattail-Eater Bird Taxonomies

Cattail-Eater bird taxonomies, especially when compared to the limited data from other groups speaking Numic languages, suggest some interesting environmental influences on how the people view the relationships among the birds of their world. Like groups speaking other Numic languages, Cattail-Eater people segregate birds from other fauna as *kasaga'yu*, 'those with wings[7] (or feathers),' after first determining whether their primary habitat is 'in the water' (*paawaiti*) or 'on the land' (*tiipiwaiti*) (Fowler and Leland 1967). Speakers of sister languages and Northern Paiute speakers in other areas further segregate birds into 'large birds' vs. 'small birds.' For large birds (mainly birds of prey) they usually elevate the term for Golden Eagle (*kwi'naa'a*) to mark this intermediate category, with the regular term for 'small birds' (*huziba*, or *witsitsi* in Southern Paiute) marking the second (Fowler 1972). Or they have a concept such as 'high flyers' (again primarily the birds of prey) vs. 'low flyers' (primarily upland game birds and perching birds) as intermediate categories. Mrs. George, however, had a more complicated view of the 'water birds,' further segregating them into 'waders' (*kwa'nidi*, < *kwa'ni*- 'to wade'), 'ducks' (*pihi*), 'diving ducks' (*pihi kumi'i* < *pihi* + *kumi'i*, 'to dive') and 'water doves' (*paahiyoba* < *paa*- + *iyoba*, from *iyoba*, 'Mourning Dove'). These four categories are roughly equivalent to 1) shorebirds; 2) loons plus coots and other surface feeding ducks; 3) diving ducks, grebes + small dabblers; and 4) small birds that are marsh nesters. These divisions appear to reflect the unique environmental position of the

Cattail-Eaters. Unfortunately, there are no comparative data on taxonomies for Northern Paiute groups in similar marsh ecosystems (e.g., Harney Basin of Malheur, Oregon) to see if these categories are common or unique. Nor are there other Cattail-Eater elders with the wide range of knowledge of birds that Mrs. George had to question further on taxonomies. Her views of relationships, however, seem quite reflective of the unique environmental position of the Cattail-Eaters in their marsh ecosystem.

The term 'little bird' (*huziba*) seems to be used rather freely for all small, named and un-named birds, and within the marsh, appears to overlap some of the water doves, including the blackbirds and the Marsh Wren. As Mrs. George understood its use, *huziba* covered any small bird no matter where found or whether or not named, but nothing as large or larger than the Pinyon Jay. She noted when questioned directly that she would not use the term *huziba* to refer to an eagle, pelican, goose, magpie, or woodpecker. Given that many of the smaller, plain birds are not easily differentiated unless they are seen up close, this category is of great use, often employed, and may well be a universal in bird taxonomies (see also Rea 2007)—something equivalent to a "dicky bird" or "little brown bird" (LBB) in English nomenclature.

Changes in the Marsh Ecosystems and Their Birds

Mrs. George and Mrs. Steve often commented on changes that they had seen through their lifetimes in the extent of the marshes of their homeland (Carson Lake, Stillwater Marsh, Carson Sink) and also in the bird life. Upstream diversion of the Carson River and its tributaries for agriculture began in the 1890s, but was intensified with dams and reclamation after 1906. Given that these water bodies are end-points for the river, Carson Lake and Stillwater Marsh, especially, have been severely reduced since that time. Also, since the 1930s, portions of the system have been incorporated into private waterfowl hunting clubs as well as into federal and state preserves. At present, Cattail-Eater people have even less access to the marshes that remain than they did prior to the 1950s, and are often in conflict with authorities and/or accused of trespass if they use any of the area's resources (Fowler 1992; Reno Gazette-Journal 2011).

In spite of difficulties of access that began early, both Mrs. Steve and Mrs. George remained familiar enough with the wetlands that they had observed a number of changes, especially into the 1950s. For example, both women felt that water levels and vegetation patterns had changed significantly, especially by the 1950s. They estimated that by then, hardstem bulrush (associated with deep water) was half as common as it had been around 1900, while cattail (associated with shallow water) was three times more common. They estimated that alkaline areas at the terminus of the marsh that once supported alkali bulrush (a favored seed food) had been reduced by one-third (Fowler 1992:Table 1). Most of the large cottonwood trees

(*Populus fremontii* S.Wats.) had been eliminated by the 1950s. These had been used as roosts for some species of birds. They were likely victims to die-offs from age as well as harvesting by non-Natives for firewood and fencing. Cattle grazing in and near the marshes had all but eliminated new seedling trees.

These changes in turn affected the mix of bird species in the marshes, with the White-fronted Goose, Tundra Swan and American Bittern being much less common by the 1950s than in 1900, likely due to changes in water depths and vegetation type. Shore bird populations had also generally declined. The Canada Goose, although still common, no longer nested as often in the area, and Sandhill Cranes were rarely seen. Mrs. George named the Surf Scoter but observed that it had always been rare at Stillwater, as was the Double-Crested Cormorant. She knew both were more common at Pyramid Lake to the north, however. The Wood Duck was also rare and remained so in the 1950s. On the other hand, Redhead and Cinnamon Teal were common nesters and that had not changed by the 1950s. American Coots were more common by that time as were White-faced Ibis, the latter being happy to glean in recently plowed farmlands. The women knew of only one heron rookery in 1900, and there remains only one today, although now it is frequented mostly by Black-crowned Night-heron. Great Blue Heron, who also nested there, had taken up nests in the few remaining cottonwoods near the town of Stillwater by the 1950s. The women also claimed that in the past with more water flow, American Pelicans often nested on an island at the end of the "Old" Carson River (a branch that flowed directly into Carson Sink; see Figure 2), whereas after the 1950s as well as presently, there is an island there except in very high water years. They still come to feed in the area, while nesting at Pyramid Lake (see Fowler 1992:50–54 for further details).

Both women also commented on changes for various other birds, especially small bird species. Not seen before were American Goldfinch, Starling, English Sparrow, and various 'little gray birds,' most of which remain unidentified. In addition, they commented that the California Quail was recent in the region. It was actually introduced into western Nevada near Reno, and later spread to the Carson Desert (Alcorn 1988). There had also been changes in some of the mountain birds, but unfortunately the data on these are too scant to evaluate.

Comparisons to Other Regions

Northern Paiute

Unfortunately, although there are lists of bird names for a few other Northern Paiute-speaking groups, none is comparable in depth to the lists or the other data available for the **Toidi-kadi** of western Nevada—especially those provided by Mrs. Steve and Mrs. George. One area with a similar ecosystem for waterfowl and shorebirds is the Harney Lake—Malheur Basin of east-central Oregon, home to the **Wadadikadi,** or 'Seepweed Seed-Eaters' [(Suaeda depressa (Pursh)]. However, only a handful of bird names have been recorded from them, mostly in the early 20th Century (Marsden, n.d.), and no ethno-taxonomic data are available. The best data from the rest of Northern Paiute territory come from the Pyramid Lake district, where Robert Ridgway (1877) collected bird specimens and recorded Northern Paiute names in 1867–9, and from the Walker Lake area where C. Hart Merriam collected 63 bird names in 1935 (Heizer 1979). A number of the names on these lists can be correlated with those elicited from Mrs. George and Mrs. Steve, and also are suggestive of some additional points of interest for ethno-taxonomy.

For example, Merriam (Heizer 1979:202) identifies the Sharp-shinned Hawk as "ke-ne" (**kini'i**; see Table 3); and Cooper's Hawk as "too-Ke-ne" (**tuukini'i**, 'black Sharp-shinned Hawk'). He also lists both the Prairie Falcon and the Red-tailed Hawk as "NaK-Ki-e" (**nakai'i**), whereas Mrs. George did not specifically name the Prairie Falcon. He also gives the Great Horned Owl as "ko-hoo" (instead of **muhu**), Burrowing Owl as "ko-ho-o" (**kuhu'u**) and Spotted Owl[8] as "se-vo mo-ho," suggesting some sort of attributive designation for the latter. Also, both Merriam and Ridgway reverse the terms for American Crow and Raven. Given that each man was an excellent ornithologist, it might suggest that in more recent times, as the American Crow became more common, a marking reversal has occurred, so that **ada**, once Raven, became American Crow, thereby requiring a modifier for the term for raven (**paba'ada** 'big crow' or **kwii'ada** ?? + 'American Crow'). Marking reversals are not uncommon in situations of lexical acculturation (Brown 1999). There are additional discrepancies in the lists that remain to be fully explored.

Other Numic Languages

There are a few additional data on bird ethno-taxonomies for other Numic languages worth reviewing (see also Fowler 1972). Northern Paiute, Southern Paiute and Western Shoshone languages and peoples share several cognates in bird names and nomenclature, and also at least in some general principles in categorization. All three languages, although from different sub-branches within the Numic branch of the Uto-Aztecan language family, have a life form term for "bird" and follow the distinctions of "land vs. water" birds, and "large vs. small" or alternatively, "high vs. low flyers" as subcategories. None of these designations are cognates across these languages however. These categories may instead be common principles in constructing ethno-taxonomic systems with broader implications to be investigated (Berlin 1992). Again, Mrs. George's more elaborate taxonomy for 'water birds' may illustrate the role that special environmental features play in these processes.

Numic and Uto-Aztecan Cognates for Bird Names

There are some bird name cognates within the Numic branch and also more broadly within the Uto-Aztecan language family that invite speculation about aspects of the region's linguistic prehistory. Bird names that can be reconstructed within the branch and the family are given in Table 5. As is evident, there is a small legacy of names from Proto-Uto-Aztecan times, and thus, Proto-Numic speakers would have shared the terms for Great Blue Heron and Sandhill Crane among the water birds, as well as a few terms for birds of prey and others. From Proto-Northern Aztecan times, they would have retained a term for American Coot, two additional birds of prey, and a few upland species. And by Proto-Numic times, they would have added terms for Canada Goose, an unidentified shorebird, Red-tailed Hawk, and a few others. These data are presently incomplete, and need to be reviewed in light of more recent work on Uto-Aztecan and Numic cognate sets (i.e., Stubbs 2008), as well as current speculation as to the overall prehistory of the language family (i.e., Hill 2011). However, based on these few comparisons it was suggested earlier that water birds and likely marsh ecosystems were a component of early homelands for Proto-Numic peoples and perhaps earlier ancestors (Fowler 1983). At present, these and other data are insufficient to establish when the Cattail-Eater people began to live near the marshes of the Carson Basin, beyond suggestions that they have been there for at least 1000 years (see Cabana, Hunley and Kaestle 2008; Madsen and Rhode 1996). Archaeological evidence indicates that the area has been occupied by indigenous peoples for much longer (9000+ years [Kelly 2000]). Whenever they arrived, the Cattail-Eaters began an intimate and culturally significant association with the birdlife of these marshes, likely building upon experiences with marsh species in the more distant past.

Table 5. Reconstructed bird names*

Proto-Uto-Aztecan:	
Common Name	Reconstructed Name
Great Blue Heron	**kwasa*
Sandhill Crane	**koda*
Golden Eagle	**kwaa, **kwaCa*
Great Horned Owl	**muhu*
Screech Owl	**tuku*
Turkey Vulture	**wiko*
Hawk (Accipiter sp.)	**kwisa*
A woodpecker	**tsuutu*
A small bird	**witsi*
Proto-Northern Uto-Aztecan (all of the above plus):	
Common Name	Reconstructed Name
American Coot	*saya*
Swainson's Hawk	*kini-*
Burrowing Owl	*kuku*
American Crow	*ata*
A bluebird/jay	*tsai-*
Mourning Dove	*howi*
Mountain Quail	*kaka*
Proto-Numic (all of the above plus):	
Common Name	Reconstructed Name
Canada Goose	*nagi*
A shorebird	*patitsi*
Red-tailed Hawk	*naka'i*
American Robin	*suku*
A blue jay	*tsogo*

* Based on data from Fowler (1972; 1983)

Summary and Conclusions

The data collected from two remarkable women, Mrs. Alice Steve and Mrs. Wuzzie George between 1949 and 1978 clearly show that they, and likely other Cattail-Eater people of the Carson Basin of western Nevada, were keenly aware of the birds of their homeland. These women were especially familiar with the area's marshes—Carson Lake, Stillwater Marsh and Carson Sink—the end points of the Carson River, and unique oases in the Carson Desert. They and their ancestors routinely utilized resident and migrant species (especially waterfowl) for food, but also gave many other birds prominent places in their lives and lifeways. They were keen observers of the region's ecosystems, and of the habits and habitats of the birds. They named and classified birds based on detailed observations, including of their morphology, behavior, calls, and other attributes. They gave birds important roles in their everyday life, including in traditional stories and ceremonial contexts, and they looked forward to specific interactions with them during various seasons of the year. They also carefully watched and listened to the local birds in order to monitor the health of their homeland.

These women were likewise aware of the changes that occurred in their region after Euro-American settlement, and especially how these affected the marshes and the bird life. Changes noted by Mrs. Steve and Mrs. George from roughly 1900 to the 1950s were largely the result of altered stream flow of the Carson River into the wetlands, but also the privatization of much of the land base in the area. Although their own traditional knowledge of the area likely had been affected by these and other changes in their own lives, including disruption of former subsistence systems and access to their former homelands, as well as the many other changes associated with the transition to reservation life, they nonetheless retained a significant legacy of ethno-ornithological knowledge. They kindly shared this knowledge to be passed on to future generations of their own people as well as others. Their words provide a wealth of indigenous wisdom for present and future Native and non-Native people, especially as to the significance of this region's avifauna.

In addition, the materials are useful in other comparative inquiries, including within Numic and Uto-Aztecan linguistic studies, and studies of ethno-ornithology and Traditional Environmental Knowledge. Although the data on cognate relationships for bird names within the language branch and family are preliminary at present, additional work may provide more clues to aid in unraveling questions of regional linguistic prehistory. These in turn and in combination with other data may provide additional information as to the role of marshes and other ecosystems in that prehistory, and possibly lead to a more accurate definition of the character and location of the original homeland of the Cattail-Eater people and their ancestors. Those interested in the area and its unique natural and cultural history, as well as in these wider topics, remain in debt to Mrs. Steve and Mrs. George.

Notes

1. This paper was originally written in 2005 as part of a volume honoring Amadeo Rea, and appears here in a slightly revised and updated form. Rea has contributed vigorously through the years to the literature on TEK, especially documenting the ethnobiological knowledge of the Northern Piman peoples of the Sonoran Desert of North America (Rea 1983, 1997, 1998, 2007). Particularly significant for the present paper is his *Wings in the Desert: A Folk Ornithology of the Northern Pimans* (Rea 2007), a model for the presentation of data on this area of knowledge.

2. The orthographic conventions followed here are derived from a modified version of the International Phonetic Alphabet applied to writing the Northern Paiute language (Liljeblad, Fowler and Powell 2012), with some exceptions for practicality: glottal stop is written '; fortis voiced consonants, especially nasals and sibilants, are doubled, except that **ngng**, velar nasal, is shortened to **nng**; *i* is a high mid vowel (often *y* in IPA); doubled vowels are long, not pronounced twice (ex. *a:* in IPA).

3. Most of these taped interviews, along with partial to complete transcripts and Wheat's remarkable photographs, are deposited in the Special Collections Department, University of Nevada Reno Libraries.

4. I also thank Society of Ethnobiology members Cecil Brown, Eugene Hunn and Eugene Anderson for comments and corrections provided, especially for the lists of birds.

5. Several, but not all birds in stories were referred to in English by Mrs. George as "she." However, the Northern Paiute language does not specify gender in its third person singular pronoun, and this may be a carryover into her English. "She" was Mrs. George's preferred gender category in English.

6. Cecil Brown (pers. comm. 2011) observed that this bird may be called this based on its spin feeding behavior—like a pet dog chasing its tail.

7. Most Northern Paiute speakers and speakers of other Numic languages, classify bats (**pigahana'a**) as birds because they fly. However, they also recognize and often comment on them being "mouse-like."

8. This is likely an error in identification, as the Spotted Owl does not occur east of the Sierra Nevada within the state of Nevada. The Spotted Owl, however, does occur east of Nevada in parts of Arizona, New Mexico, Utah and Colorado, and broadly in Mexico (Eugene Hunn, pers. comm. 2011).

Acknowledgments

Special thanks to Alana Cordy-Collins for inviting me to participate in this collection of essays honoring Amadeo Rea, and also to Marsha Quinlan and Dana Lepofsky for seeing this volume through to publication. In addition to the editorial comments provided by Marsha and

Dana, I also thank Eugene Hunn, Cecil Brown and Eugene Anderson for reading drafts of this manuscript and providing additional comments, especially on changes in bird nomenclature in recent years. A portion of the original research for this paper was supported by Contract No. 14-16-0001-89537 from the US Fish and Wildlife Service, Region 1, Stillwater National Wildlife Refuge. This funding and the many kindnesses of their staffs are gratefully acknowledged, as is permission to use Dave Marshall's photographs. Margaret Wheat's photographs appear through the courtesy of the Special Collections Department, University of Nevada Reno Libraries.

References Cited

Alcorn, J.R. 1988   *The Birds of Nevada.* Farview West Publishing, Fallon, NV.

American Ornithologist's Union. 2011   Checklist of North American Birds. Available at: http://www.aou.org/checklist/north/results.php (verified 2 February 2012).

Anglin, Ron, and Gary Shellhorn. 1992   Great Basin Wetlands: A Concept Paper. U.S. Fish and Wildlife Service, Stillwater Wildlife Management Area, Fallon, NV.

Berlin, Brent. 1992   *Ethnobiological Classification: Principles of Categorization of Plants and Animals in Traditional Societies.* Princeton University Press, Princeton, NJ.

Brown, Cecil H. 1999   *Lexical Acculturation in Native American Languages.* Oxford Studies in Anthropological Linguistics 20. Oxford University Press, New York.

Cabana, G.S., K.L. Hunley, and F.A. Kaestle. 2008   Population Continuity or Replacement? A Novel Computer Simulation Approach and Its Application to the Numic Expansion (Western Great Basin, USA). *American Journal of Physical Anthropology* 135:438–447.

Cronquist, Arthur, Arthur H. Holmgren, Noel H. Holmgren, and James L. Reveal, eds. 1972   Geological and Botanical History of the Region, Its Plant Geography and a Glossary; the Vascular Cryptograms and the Gymnosperms. In *Intermountain Flora: Vascular Plants of the Intermountain West, U.S.A.*, Vol. 1. Hafner, New York.

DeQuille, Dan (William Wright). 1963   *Washoe Rambles.* Introduction by Richard E. Lingenfelter. Westernlore Press, Los Angeles.

Fowler, Catherine S. 1972   Comparative Numic Ethnobiology. Ph.D. Dissertation (Anthropology). University of Pittsburgh, Pittsburgh.

Fowler, Catherine S. 1983   Some lexical clues to Uto-Aztecan prehistory. *International Journal of American Linguistics* 49(3):254–257.

Fowler, Catherine S. 1990   Tule technology: Northern Paiute Uses of Marsh Resources in Western Nevada. *Smithsonian Folklife Studies* No. 6. Washington.

Fowler, Catherine S. 1992   In the Shadow of Fox Peak: An Ethnography of the Cattail-Eater Northern Paiute People of Stillwater Marsh. *Cultural Resource Series* No. 5. Fish and Wildlife Service, Region 1, Stillwater National Wildlife Refuge, U.S. Department of the Interior, Washington.

Fowler, Catherine S., and Joy Leland. 1967   Some Northern Paiute Native Categories. *Ethnology* 6(4):381–404.

Fowler, Catherine S., and Sven Liljeblad. 1986   Northern Paiute. In *Handbook of North American Indians*, Vol. 11 (*Great Basin*), eds. William C. Sturtevant and Warren L. d'Azevedo, pp. 435–65. Smithsonian Institution, Washington.

Henshaw, H.W. 1879   Ornithological Report from Observations and Collections Made in Portions of California, Nevada, and Oregon. Appendix L. In *Annual Report Upon Geographical Surveys of the Territory West of the 100th Meridian*, ed. G.W. Wheeler, Appendix OO of the Annual Report of the Chief of Engineers for 1879. U.S. Government Printing Office, Washington.

Heizer, Robert F., assembler and annotator. 1979   Indian Names for Plants and Animals Among Californian and Other Western North American Tribes by C. Hart Merriam. *Ballena Press Publications in Archaeology, Ethnology and History* No. 14. Socorro, NM.

Hill, Jane H. 2011   Linguistic Paleontology and Migration. In *Rethinking Anthropological Perspectives on Migration,* eds. Graciela S. Cabana and Jeffery J. Clark, pp. 175–190. University Press of Florida, Gainesville.

Hunn, Eugene S. with James Selam and Family. 1990   *Nich'i-Wana "The Big River: Mid Columbia Indians and Their Land.* University of Washington Press, Seattle.

Hunn, E.S., D.R. Johnson, P.N. Russell, and T. Thornton. 2003   Huna Tlingit Traditional Knowledge, Conservation, and the Management of a "Wilderness" Park. *Current Anthropology* 44(Supplement):157–169.

Kelly, Robert L. 2000   Archaeological Survey and Excavations in the Carson Desert and Stillwater Mountains, Nevada. *University of Utah Anthropological Papers* No. 123. Salt Lake City.

Liljeblad, Sven. 1986   Oral Tradition: Content and Style in Verbal Art. In *Handbook of North American Indians*, Vol. 11 (*Great Basin*), eds.William C. Sturtevant and Warren L. d'Azevedo, pp. 641–659. Smithsonian Institution, Washington.

Liljeblad, Sven, Catherine S. Fowler, and Glenda Powell. 2012   *Northern Paiute— Bannock Dictionary, with an English—Northern Paiute—Bannock Finding List and a Northern Paiute—Bannock—English Finding List.* University of Utah Press, Salt Lake City.

Madsen, David B., and David Rhode, eds. 1994   *Across the West: Human Population Movement and Expansion of the Numa.* University of Utah Press, Salt Lake City.

Marsden, W.L. n.d.   Burns [OR] Northern Paiute Linguistic Manuscript Collection, Department of Anthropology Archives, University Archives, Bancroft Library, University of California, Berkeley.

Miller, Wick R. 1986   Numic languages. In *Handbook of North American Indians*, Vol. 11 (*Great Basin*), eds. William C. Sturtevant and Warren L. d'Azevedo, pp. 98–106. Smithsonian Institution, Washington.

Morrison, Roger. 1964   Lake Lahontan: Geology of Southern Carson Desert, Nevada. *U.S. Geological Survey Professional Paper* 401. Washington.

Nevada Division of Wildlife. 1999   Checklist: Birds of Northwestern Nevada. Nevada Division of Wildlife, Carson City.

Park, Willard Z. 1934   Notes Accompanying Paviotso collection. Accession 34-110, Peabody Museum of Archaeology and Ethnology Archives, Harvard University, Cambridge.

Park, Willard Z. 1938   Shamanism in western North America: A study in cultural relationships. *Northwestern University Studies in the Social Sciences* 2. Evanston.

Rea, Amadeo M. 1983   *Once a River: Bird Life and Habitat Changes on the Middle Gila.* University of Arizona Press, Tucson.

Rea, Amadeo M. 1997   *At the Desert's Green Edge: An Ethnobotany of the Gila River Pima.* University of Arizona Press, Tucson.

Rea, Amadeo M. 1998   *Folk Mammalogy of the Northern Pimans.* University of Arizona Press, Tucson.

Rea, Amadeo M. 2007   *Wings in the Desert: A Folk Ethno-ornithology of the Northern Pimans.* University of Arizona Press, Tucson.

Reno Gazette-Journal. 2011   Paiute Craftsman, Cited for Collecting Cattails, Wins Federal Case. Available at: http://pqasb.pqarchiver.com/rgj/access/2502448931.html (verified 2 February 2012).

Ridgeway, Robert. 1877   Part 3: Ornithology. In *United States Geological Exploration of the Fortieth Parallel*, ed. Clarence King, geologist-in-charge. Government Printing office, Washington.

Scott, Lalla. 1966   *Karnee: A Paiute Narrative.* Charles R.Craig, annotator. University of Nevada Press, Reno.

Stillwater Wildlife Management Area. 1950–55   Narrative Reports. Archives, Stillwater Wildlife Management Area, U.S. Fish and Wildlife Service, Fallon, NV.

Stubbs, Brian D. 2008   *A Uto-Aztecan Comparative Vocabulary* (Third Preliminary Edition). Privately Printed, Blanding, UT.

U.S. Fish and Wildlife Service. 1982   Birds: Stillwater Wildlife Management Area, Nevada. Department of the Interior, Washington. (Pamphlet)

Wheat, Margaret M. 1967   *Survival Arts of the Primitive Paiutes.* University of Nevada Press, Reno.

Wilke, Philip, and Steven W. Thompson. 1989   Waterfowl Decoys and Waterfowling in the Aboriginal Western United States. Paper presented at the 12th Annual Meeting of the Society of Ethnobiology, Riverside, CA.

People of the Sky: Birds in Chumash Culture

Jan Timbrook[†] and John R. Johnson[‡]

Abstract

Since ancient times, birds have been an integral part of life for California's native peoples, including the Chumash of the Santa Barbara region. Ethnographic data show that birds figured prominently in Chumash place names, myths, ceremonies, symbolism, and even medicinal practices. Regalia made from feathers were particularly important in dances and other rituals. Archaeological avian remains, indicating both dietary and material culture uses, are among the earliest evidence of human occupation on the Santa Barbara Channel Islands. These remains document prehistoric changes in species distribution as well as subsistence differences between island and mainland peoples. Many of these special relationships with birds continue among Chumash descendants today.

Introduction

As many studies of indigenous cultures around the world have found, birds play prominent roles often disproportionate to their abundance, diversity and biomass in the environment (e.g., Krech 2009, Rea 2007, Tidemann and Gosler 2010). Birds are conspicuous visually and aurally and have distinctive behaviors. Their utility as resources for food and tool making is often eclipsed by the importance of their feathers in ceremony. Bird names and behaviors are incorporated into place names, and particular species serve as hunting aids, augurs and omens. Linking the terrestrial realm with the sky, birds serve as powerful symbols in myth, religion and art. So ethno-ornithology—the study of the entire complex of interrelationships between humans, birds, and everything else—can provide many cultural insights. Through birds, we can learn about both environmental and cultural changes, gain insight into other philosophies and world views, and enrich our understanding of the relationships between people and the natural world.

In this paper we describe the role of birds in the culture of Chumash peoples of coastal south-central California, from recent times extending back into prehistory. We begin with the rich oral tradition recorded by John P. Harrington in the early 20th century. Stories, myths,

† Department of Anthropology, Santa Barbara Museum of Natural History, 2559 Puesta del Sol Road, Santa Barbara, CA 93105 [jtimbrook@sbnature2.org]

‡ Department of Anthropology, Santa Barbara Museum of Natural History, 2559 Puesta del Sol Road, Santa Barbara, CA 93105 [jjohnson@sbnature2.org]

and cosmology are followed by the characterization of birds in Chumashan languages, including patterns of nomenclature and place names. Hunting techniques and the use of birds for food are briefly discussed. We describe diverse material cultural items the Chumash made from birds, with particular attention to regalia used in ritual practices. Some of these continue in use among Chumash descendants today. With these ethnohistorical data to provide context, we then turn to the archaeological record to see what can be learned about the role of birds among earlier Chumash peoples and their ancestors farther back in time.

Chumash Peoples

Today, several thousand people whose ancestors spoke Chumashan languages continue to live in their ancient homeland, the south central coast of California in the vicinity of San Luis Obispo, Santa Barbara, and Ventura Counties and the Northern Channel Islands (Map 1). Archaeological evidence points to a Native American presence in this region for at least 13,000 years (Johnson et al. 2002), and a cultural pattern ancestral to that practiced by Chumash Indians arose by the end of the Middle Holocene (Glassow et al. 2007; Kennett 2005;

Map 1. The Chumash and their neighbors.

King 1990). The Chumashan languages are not related to any other known language. Evidence of an ancestral Chumashan language can also be traced back at least 5000 years and was probably spoken long before that, further indicating a very long presence of Chumash ancestors in this region (Golla 2011).

These peoples made their living solely by hunting, gathering and fishing. Partly because of the area's abundance and rich diversity of natural resources of land and sea, but also due to the skill and ingenuity of the people themselves, the Santa Barbara coast and offshore islands became among the most densely populated places in North America north of central Mexico (Brown 1967; Cook 1976; Ubelaker 2006). Some coastal towns had as many as a thousand inhabitants. A thriving regional trade network, facilitated by seagoing canoes and shell beads used as currency, helped to support a high standard of living and a degree of cultural complexity rarely found among non-agricultural societies (Arnold 2001; Gamble 2008).

Although many Chumash descendants are still with us, much of their traditional culture has been altered or lost as a result of Spanish missionization in the late 18th century and subsequent colonization by American settlers. Most of what we know about their past comes from archaeological research, historical documents left by explorers and missionaries, and early ethnographic studies, especially interviews by the linguist John Peabody Harrington. These sources reveal that, among the many kinds of plants, mammals, fish, reptiles, insects and other living creatures with which Chumash peoples shared their world, birds played several essential roles.

The Ethnographic Record

Considerable data on bird use among the Chumash in the recent past can be found in ethnographic and ethnohistoric sources. Of particular importance is the information recorded by John P. Harrington from Chumash elders in the early 20th century (Harrington 1986). Over the course of nearly fifty years, he conducted extensive interviews with about a dozen speakers of several Chumashan languages from throughout the region, including individuals whose ancestors had lived on the offshore islands. Harrington's notes include details on subsistence and material culture, as well as on less tangible aspects such as language, place names, myth, cosmology, and symbolism.

In this section we first present some of the Chumash oral narratives that feature birds, including "just-so" stories accounting for the appearance of things, tales that reflect Chumash social and political roles, and myths describing the structure of the universe. Next we examine Chumashan languages' words for birds, their appearance in place names and the use of onomatopoeia in naming many species.

We briefly describe how the Chumash acquired birds for food and for their skins, feathers, bones, and claws as raw materials for diverse kinds of material culture items. In reviewing the numerous material culture items that the Chumash made from bird parts, we see that dance regalia and ritual uses were by far the most important.

Oral Traditions

The rich oral tradition of the Chumash includes stories and myths featuring birds. Some tales describe the structure and nature of the cosmos and explain how certain things came to be the way they are. Some were told merely for amusement. Many of them illustrate social roles and expectations for proper behavior (see Blackburn 1975 for a thorough analysis of Chumash oral narratives). Here we have italicized the names of mythical characters and supernatural beings to distinguish them from creatures in the everyday world.

According to a story passed down in a Santa Barbara Chumash family, *Condor* was once an all-white bird. Curious about a fire he saw burning in a village, he flew too close and was burned all black except for his armpits (McCall and Perry 2002:61). In another story, *Acorn Woodpecker,* tired of *Coyote* incessantly asking him about his beautiful red head, said, "Well, stick a live coal on your head and you'll have a red head too." *Coyote* did it, burned his head, and *Woodpecker* just laughed (Blackburn 1975:231).

Woodpeckers are prominently featured in stories of the Flood among various indigenous cultures in the American Southeast (Krech 2009:169–170) and Southwest (Rea 2007:198– 199, 202). *Woodpecker* also appears in the Chumash Flood myth, as in this story told by María Solares of Santa Ynez:

> Maqutikok, *Spotted Woodpecker,* was the only one saved in the flood. He was Sun's nephew. María doesn't know why the flood came or how it started, but it kept raining and the water kept rising higher and higher until even the mountains were covered. All the people drowned except Maqutikok, who found refuge on top of a tree that was the tallest in the world. The water kept rising until it touched his feet, and the bird cried out, "Help me, Uncle, I am drowning, pity me!" Sun's two daughters heard him and told their father that his kinsman was calling for help. "He is stiff from cold and hunger," they said. Sun held his firebrand down low and the water began to subside. Maqutikok was warmed by the heat. Then Sun tossed him two acorns. They fell in the water near the tree and Maqutikok picked them up and swallowed them. Then Sun threw two more acorns down and the bird ate them and was content. That is why he likes acorns so much – they are still his food. And after the water was gone only Maqutikok remained [Blackburn 1975:94–95].

Some of these stories have been remembered by an older generation of California Indians. For example, two stories told by José Juan Olivas, a Ventureño Chumash elder, were related by his stepdaughter's son, Catarino Montes, who was born and raised at the Tejón Indian ranchería, southeast of Bakersfield:

> When we were little, [my grandfather] told stories about this and that. [One story is about how *Mourning Dove* got] its little spots, little black spots. [The animals] were all people at one time. This dove married this woman's son. This [dove] was awful lazy and was just waiting for the mother-in-law to cook so she could eat, sitting by the fire there. Her mother-in-law got mad at her, because she didn't do anything. [She took] this piece of stick with embers on it, and [the mother-in-law] hit her with it. See, that is the reason [the dove] has spots, burn marks. It looks like it has been burned with all those little spots there.

> And there was another little bird you'd see him around every once in awhile. It was a little bitty kind of a bird. … It's got a red spot, right on top of his head [*Ruby-Crowned Kinglet*]. This little bird trapped a big old bird. It wasn't too big. Anyway, he trapped it, and he killed it or thought he did. So this little bird was going around singing a song and dancing around the old [bird], and then that big bird came to and swallowed that little bird. That old bird took off and flew around the earth two or three times. The little bird had a little, bitty knife made out of flint. The little bird had a song [which my grandfather sang]. When that big bird swallowed that little bird he went clear inside there and saw this big old object that was [the big bird's] heart. He said, "I have to get out that way," so he got his little knife and started sawing away on that heart. Finally he sawed it off. When he did, blood from where he cut the heart fell on his head. That's how he got the little red spot on top of his head [Montes 1993].

Reflections of Chumash Society

Social and political aspects of Chumash culture are also illuminated in oral traditions involving birds. Many of these stories took place long ago before humans appeared in the world, "when animals were people." In the time of these First People, the animals had a society organized much like that of the Chumash who came after them. *Golden Eagle* (**slo'w**) was chief of all the animals. *Eagle's* sister's son was *Falcon* (**xelex**), who was said to be second in authority to *Eagle*. This might be interpreted to mean that accession to political office could be inherited matrilineally. Further, the relationship between uncle and nephew appears to be more prominent than that between father and son (Blackburn 1975:35, 50). The flood story, where Sun saves his sister's son, *Woodpecker* (**maqutiko'k**), from the rising waters and gives him food, demonstrates this strong connection (Johnson 1988:242).

Coot, or *Mudhen,* was the messenger for the chief or ceremonial leader (Blackburn 1975:35–36). Among the Chumash themselves, the ceremonial messenger was called **k'sen** (coot) and when acting in official capacity wore body paint that symbolized the bird's markings, white over black (Hudson and Blackburn 1985:316). In mythic times, *Pelican* and *Cormorant* were known as fishermen and canoe owners (Blackburn 1975:36). Although one of Harrington's Chumash consultants spoke of clans named for eagle, falcon, Snow Goose and raven, all highly respected birds (Johnson 1988:222–230), we suspect that this information may have pertained to the central Californian Yokuts side of this woman's family, with whom she had lived for a time when she was young. It therefore remains unclear whether the Chumash were among California Indian societies that were organized into clans.

Spirituality

Throughout south-central California, including among Chumash peoples, a person was believed to have a better chance of success in life if he developed a relationship with a personal spirit guide, or "dream helper," often contacted through *Datura*-induced visions. Many of these dream helpers were animals, and some of them were birds. The prominence of any animal in myth is not necessarily reflected in its role as a dream helper, but *Eagle* and *Hawk* were among the helpers considered to be particularly strong. *Falcon* could confer skill in gambling, and *Hummingbird* granted courage, agility and speed. Shamans often had *Owl* as a helper (Applegate 1978:19–20). Ventureño Chumash elder Fernando Librado told of an actual disaster at sea, where the captain and crew of a canoe in danger of sinking in a storm were saved through the intervention of the captain's dream helper, *Peregrine Falcon* (Hudson et al. 1978:158–159).

World View

Birds were conceptualized in Chumash astronomy and cosmology. The star cluster we call the Big Dipper has been hypothesized to be associated with a story in which seven boys turned into geese, flying in a clockwise direction, higher and to the north each night (Hudson and Underhay 1978:105). The cosmos is made up of three superimposed worlds, with the Chumash at the center. The Upper World is supported on the wings of the giant *Eagle* of the Sky. The movements of his wings cause the phases of the moon and eclipses of both sun and moon (Blackburn 1975:91–92). Thus, birds were deeply intertwined with the very structure of the Chumash universe.

Language, Taxonomy, and Naming

Harrington's principal interest was language, and he recorded it with far greater precision than earlier interviewers, who included Pinart (1952), Henshaw (1955), and Merriam (1979). He recorded names of birds and other animals and plants, but, not being very familiar with biological species himself, he consulted scientific experts to aid in identification, either from specimens or from verbal descriptions. His "slip files" of animal names (Harrington 1986, Reel 71) indicate that he took at least one of his consultants, Juan de Jesús Justo, to California Academy of Sciences where they apparently looked at taxidermy bird specimens in order to link Chumash vernacular names with scientific species. He appears to have gone through a local collection at the Bard Hospital in Ventura with another consultant, Candelaria Valenzuela. Nonetheless, it has not been possible to accurately identify every kind of bird mentioned in his notes. Our best efforts, derived from Harrington's original notes and from two dictionaries based on them (Applegate 2007; Whistler 1980), are shown in Table 1. Although Californian and Mexican Spanish are not always congruent, Schoenhals (1988) was a helpful reference for translating bird names.

We found insufficient data to determine whether any hierarchical structure existed in Chumash folk taxonomy. Harrington did record a few life form terms related to birds, such as Ineseño *'axonowon* (flier). In Ventureño, *'iyalxoyoyon* (flier) included birds and bats, while *'alqapach* (feathered) referred to birds in general. Terms for categories of birds—carrion eaters, birds of prey, insect eaters, diving birds, edible birds, etc.—were also recorded in some Chumashan languages, but these all seem to be descriptive phrases translated from Spanish or English. The Ineseño intermediate term **wits'** for 'small bird' is very similar to the Barbareño Chumash word **wit** (condor)—the largest bird in North America. Such inversion may be an example of the Chumash sense of humor.

In many indigenous languages, names for birds often reflect the sound the bird makes. Berlin and O'Neill (1981) suggest that onomatopoeic bird names are quite common in languages spoken by peoples of small-scale, non-literate societies, where the sounds offer a useful mnemonic device. More recent ethno-ornithological studies invariably mention onomatopoeia as a common basis for bird naming (Berlin 1992:259; Forth 2010:232–233; Hunn and Thornton 2010:207; Krech 2009:29; Rea 2007:38–39). This pattern is quite apparent in Chumashan bird names, as can be seen in Table 1, where onomatopoeic names are marked with an asterisk. It appears particularly true for vocal species like ducks and geese, owls, hawks, pigeons and doves, woodpeckers, and corvids (jays, magpies, crows and ravens). Other examples include **takak** (quail), **ts'iyukqwili** (Western Meadowlark), and **yuxnu'ts** (hummingbird) in Ineseño Chumash.

Features other than voice inspired some names. As other studies have found, bird names may describe some aspect of appearance or distinctive behavior. The Long-billed Curlew, **ku'y** in Ventureño, got its name from the resemblance of its bill to the curved scratcher, **ku'y**, made from the rim of an abalone shell (Harrington 1986:R71, F 478). Northern Flicker, which has red-orange feather quills, is given the same name as the dark orange base of *Juncus* rush stalks used in basketry, **syit**. A Ventureño man said that they called this bird **syit** for its color, but its real name is **chulakak'** (Harrington 1986:R71, F569).

Another commented, "Strange to say, some things have two names" (Harrington 1986:R71, F351). The example given was Mourning Dove (Barbareño **'ayu'wi**, **tukutuk'u**), but it also

Table 1. Chumashan names for birds.

Birds are not equally represented in these three languages, due to differences in the data recorded from Chumash consultants and in the expertise and focus of the linguists who compiled the word lists. We have used only two special symbols for Chumash language terms: the apostrophe represents a glottal stop; the barred *i* represents a sound similar to the schwa *ə*. Vowels and *x* are pronounced as in Spanish. Birds whose Chumashan names resemble their calls are marked with an *asterisk.

Bird species	Barbareño[1]	Ineseño[2]	Ventureño[3]	Comments
Bird (life form)	------	ʔaxonowon (flier)	ʔalapach (feathered) ʔiyalxoyoyon (fliers)	V. ʔiyalxoyoyon 'fliers' = birds and bats
night bird, any kind			xʔox	"When you hear a night bird and do not know what kind it is, call it xʔox."
DUCKS, GEESE, AND WATERFOWL – *ANSERIFORMES ANATIDAE*				
*Goose spp. (undiff.)	waʔwau [1a]	wawaʔw	wauwau	"used to be many at Castle Rock in SB… A white goose with black on tips of wings… In the squawk it calls its name."
Snow Goose *Chen caerulescens*			waʔwaʔw	JPH note: "all other goose species [besides *puluy*] seem to be *waʔwau*."
Canada Goose *Branta canadensis*	puluy [1a]		------	B. *waʔwau* also recorded as white goose.
Swan (e.g. Tundra Swan) *Cygnus columbianus*	waʔwau [1a]	ʔalexlelen	tuhuy	B. *ʔoxwoshkolol* 'any duck'
Duck (undiff.)	ʔoxwoshkolol [1a]		------	
flies very low over water		ʔalikwetete'	------	
medium-sized		ʔaliwi	------	
*small duck sp.		qwa'	------	
small with blue crest		ʔanutswa	------	
undescribed duck		cholo	------	
Mallard *Anas platyrhynchos*		ʔoloxwoshkoloy	ʔanixwoshkoloy	V. *ʔanixwoshkoloy* 'Mallard'
Blue-winged Teal *Anas discors*			leʔle	V. *lele* "white stripes on cheeks, breast blended reddish &brown, back black & gray."
Green-winged Teal *Anas crecca*	kchon [1a]		------	B. *kchon* "a small duck with brown head and blue-black eyes." Identified from specimen.
White-winged Scoter *Melanitta fusca*	mut [1a]		hoti	B. *mut* "goes along shore, pure black. It can't fly, and when a wave comes it dives into it … 1½ ft long, blackish brown color with a duck-like bill." Identified from specimen. V. *hoti* "same bird as the SB call *mut*."
NEW WORLD QUAIL – *GALLIFORMES ODONTOPHORIDAE*				
*California Quail *Callipepla californica*	takak [1a] taqtaq [1b]	takak	ʔikɨy	JPH note: "B. *takak* name for all quail spp." The two B. names may reflect individuals' varying pronunciation.
LOONS – *GAVIIFORMES GAVIIDAE*				
Common Loon *Gavia immer*	mut [1a]		------	"2 ½ ft long, white belly, gray back, slenderish beak; bigger than the *mut*. Identified from specimen, [B. *mut* 'White-winged Scoter']."

Bird species	Barbareño[1]	Ineseño[2]	Ventureño[3]	Comments
GREBES – *PODICIPEDIFORMES PODICIPEDIDAE*				
Grebe (e.g. Western Grebe) *Aechmorphus occidentalis*	ʼalqintap[1a]	-------	ʼalqiltap	JPH note: "B. **ʼalqintap** Western Grebe, all grebes called by this name."
PELICANS – *PELECANIFORMES PELECANIDAE*				
Brown Pelican *Pelecanus occidentalis*	xeʼw[1b]	hew	hew	
CORMORANTS AND SHAGS – *PELECANIFORMES PHALACROCORACIDAE*				
Cormorant, (e.g. Double-crested Cormorant) *Phalacrocorax auritus*	-------	-------		B., V. **mut** has previously been identified as Cormorant, but B. **mut** = White-winged Scoter, identified from specimen; V. **hoti** = B. **mut**.
HERONS, EGRETS, AND BITTERNS – *CICONIIFORMES ARDEIDAE*				
*Great Blue Heron *Ardea herodias*	pelepel[1a]	xʼox	xwas	B. **pelepel** 'big blue heron' V. **xwas** 'garza morena.' "Same size as the *garza morena* [Egret], the latter called **pelepel**. F has seen some **xwas** with a small crest. Never noticed that the **pelepel** has a crest."
Great Egret *Ardea alba*	pelepel[1b]	pelepel	pelepel	V. **pelepel** "white as snow all over."
"small heron" Black-crowned Night Heron? *Nycticorax nycticorax*	kwak[1a]	waqʼ	kwas	B. **kwak**, V. **kwas** 'night heron' I. **waqʼ** 'heron species'
NEW WORLD VULTURES – *FALCONIFORMES CATHARTIDAE*				
Turkey Vulture *Cathartes aura*	ʼonoq[1a]	ʼonoq	ʼonhoq	
California Condor *Gymnogyps californianus*	puyaʼwiʼt[1a] wit[1b]	ʼalmiyiʼ	puʼyawit	
HAWKS, EAGLES, AND KITES – *FALCONIFORMES ACCIPITRIDAE*				
Hawk sp. (unid.)	xelex[1b]	takimiʼ	------	I. **takimiʼ** "hawk species, medium sized, dark."
White-tailed Kite *Elanus leucurus*	ʼalqolokin[1a]	------	------	B. **ʼalqolokin** "foot-long grayish hawk - whitish tail"
Bald Eagle *Haliaeetus leucocephalus*	------	maxiwo	maxiwo	
Sharp-shinned Hawk *Accipiter striatus*	matiwayaʼway[1b]	ʼanichʼapapa	------	
*Red-shouldered Hawk *Buteo lineatus*	------	woy (?)	------	I. **woy** "hawk, large and dark, cries **woy woy woy**."
*Red-tailed Hawk *Buteo jamaicensis*	kwich[1a]	ʼatimasiq (?)	tsin; kwich (?)	B. **kwich** "this kind is big …some have a red tail and some haven't." Identified from specimen. I. **ʼatimasiq** "hawk with a dark band around the waist." V. **tsin** "that is the **tsin** that has the red tail. The tail and all of the **kwich** is whitish." Immature Red-tailed Hawk?

Table 1 continued.

Bird species	Barbareño[1]	Ineseño[2]	Ventureño[3]	Comments
Golden Eagle *Aquila chrysaetos*	slo'w[1a]	slo'w	slo'w	
FALCONS AND CARACARAS – *FALCONIFORMES FALCONIDAE*				
Falcon sp. (unid.)	------	kwich	------	
*American Kestrel *Falco sparverius*	------	kilik	------	
Peregrine Falcon *Falco peregrinus*	kwich[1b]	xelex	------	I. *xelex* "hawk species, possibly Peregrine Falcon."
RAILS, GALLINULES, AND COOTS – *GRUIFORMES RALLIDAE*				
Clapper Rail *Rallus longirostris*	wak[1a]	------		B. *wak* 'Clapper Rail' identified from specimen. "Good to eat."
American Coot *Fulica americana*	kse'n[1a]	kse'n	kse'n	
CRANES – *GRUIFORMES GRUIDAE*				
Crane (e.g. Sandhill Crane) *Grus canadensis*	x'ox[1b]	puluy	puluy	Sandhill Crane winters in Chumash area.
PLOVERS AND LAPWINGS – *CHARADRIIFORMES CHARADRIIDAE*				
*Killdeer *Charadrius vociferus*	tstutu[1a] t'u'u[1b]	------	tsiyitsi'y	V. *tsiyitsi'y* "It has a collar of 3 stripes & stripe on its head ... like a necklace & headband."
SANDPIPERS AND ALLIES – *CHARADRIIFORMES SCOLOPACIDAE*				
Long-billed Curlew *Numenius americanus*	'alp'inoqsh[1b]	pi'nu'nun	ku'y	V. *ku'y* "got its name from resemblance of bill to abalone scratcher."
GULLS – *CHARADRIIFORMES LARIDAE: LARINAE*				
Gull (undiff.) *Larus* spp.	'aniso[1a]	'aniso	'aniso	B. *'aniso* "any kind of gull."
Gull sp. (unid.) *Larus* sp.	'ono'myo[1b]	'ono'myo'	------	
PIGEONS AND DOVES – *COLUMBIFORMES COLUMBIDAE*				
Band-tailed Pigeon *Patagioenas fasciata*	yok'[1a] wele'wel[1a]	wele'wel		
Mourning Dove *Zenaida macroura*	'ayu'wi[1a] tukutuk'[1a]	'anuwe'	shukushuk	B. *'ayuwi, tukutuk'* "Strange to say, some things have two names." I. *'anuwe'* "they cry their name - *'anúwe' hu hu hu hu.*" V. *shukushuk* = 'turtle dove, *paloma del monte*' [=mourning dove?].
CUCKOOS – *CUCULIFORMES CUCULIDAE*				
*Greater Roadrunner *Geococcyx californianus*	pupu'[1a]	p'up'u'	pu'pu	
BARN-OWLS – *STRIGIFORMES TYTONIDAE*				
*Barn Owl *Tyto alba*	she'w[1a]	she'w	she'w	

Bird species	Barbareño[1]	Ineseño[2]	Ventureño[3]	Comments
OWLS – STRIGIFORMES STRIGIDAE				
*Western Screech-Owl Megascops kennicottii	wonono[1a]	wonono	wonono	I. *wonono* 'screech owl, pygmy owl' Name resembles Western Screech Owl's call.
*Great Horned Owl Bubo virginianus	muhu[1a]	muhu	muhu	B. *muhu* identified from specimen.
*Northern Pygmy-Owl Glaucidium gnoma	wonono[1b]	puk	------	I. "*pukú pukú pukú pukú* = call of the *puk'* (gray owl)." Resembles Pygmy Owl's call.
*Burrowing Owl Athene cunicularia	tspokoy[1a] pewyoko'[1b]	pokoy	kokok	B. *tspokoy* "a small owl species, lives in squirrel holes." V. *kokok* 'ground owl'
NIGHTJARS AND ALLIES – CAPRIMULGIFORMES CAPRIMULGIDA				
Lesser Nighthawk? Chordeils acutipennis	------	te'	tspilnowo 'i sulku	I. *te'* "hawk species, grayish, flies at twilight." V. *tspilnowo 'i sulku* "*brinca en la noche* – name of night-hawk."
*Common Poorwill? Phalaenoptilus nuttallii	------	po'yoko'	------	I. *po'yoko'* "hawk species, flies at twilight."
HUMMINGBIRDS – APODIFORMES TROCHILIDAE				
*Hummingbird (e.g. Anna's Hummingbird) Calypte Anna	yuxnuts[1b]	yuxnuts'	yuxnuts	
KINGFISHERS – CORACIIFORMES ALCEDINIDAE				
*Belted Kingfisher Megaceryle alcyon	'ayuwanchánchak, xa'yxa'y 1b	'ayuwinch'áchaq	'ayuwinchachaq	B. *'ayuwanchánchak* 'kingfisher'[1b] B. *xa'yxa'y* 'western belted kingfisher'[1b]
WOODPECKERS – PICIFORMES PICIDAE				
*Acorn Woodpecker Melanerpes formicivorus	pulakák[1a]	pulaká'k maqutiko'k	woltot	B. *pulakak* "the only bird that puts acorns in trees." I. *maqutiko'k* 'Pileated Woodpecker'[2] but that species is not known to have occurred in the Chumash region.[4] *maqutiko'k* is said to be fond of acorns (Blackburn 1975:95). This is probably another name for Acorn Woodpecker. V. *woltot* "red-headed, dark-bodied woodpecker, the only kind seen storing acorns in trees."
*Northern Flicker Colaptes auratus	syit[1a]	syit'	syit', chulakak	V. *syit* 'red juncus' used for design accents in basketry. "They call this bird *syit* for its color, but its real name is *chulakak*."
PERCHING BIRDS – PASSERIFORMES				
Small songbird (generic)	chwi'w[1a]	wits'	------	cf. B. *wit* 'condor.' Irony?
CROWS, JAYS, AND MAGPIES – PASSERIFORMES CORVIDAE				
Western Scrub-Jay Aphelocoma californica	cha'y[1b]	cha'y	chay	V. "the jay says *chay chay chay chay*."
*Yellow-billed Magpie Pica nuttallii	cha'i[1a] 'achach[1b]	kishki'sh	áchach	

Table 1 continued.

Bird species	Barbareño[1]	Ineseño[2]	Ventureño[3]	Comments
*American Crow *Corvus brachyrynchos*	*à'*[1b]	*à'*	*à*	V. *à* "the cry signifies an applause."
*Common Raven *Corvus corax*	*qaq'*[1b]	*qaq'*	*qliw*	V. *qliw* 'raven' i.e. 'big crow'
SWALLOWS – *PASSERIFORMES HIRUNDINIDAE*				
Swallow spp. (undiff.)	*'anipe*[1a]	------	*'anipe*	
*Northern Rough-winged Swallow *Stelgidopteryx serripennis*	*'ansut'uy*[1b]	------	------	B. *'ansut'uy* 'Bank Swallow'[1b] - a species that does not occur in Chumash area. Rough-winged Swallow is similar.
Barn Swallow *Hirundo rustica*	------	------	*chopoyo*	JPH: V. *chopoyo* "resembling *'anipe* but bigger wings, bigger body and blue back, makes a mud nest like ½ abalone shell".
Cliff Swallow *Petrochelidon pyrrhonota*	*'à'nippey*[1b]	*'anipe'*		
WRENS – *PASSERIFORMES TROGLODYTIDAE*				
*House Wren *Troglodytes aedon*	*tissit*[1b]	*'anaxsuhu'y*	------	B. *tissit* "Jenny wren" = House Wren
THRUSHES AND ALLIES – *PASSERIFORMES TURDIDAE*				
Western Bluebird *Sialia mexicana*	------	*yol*	------	
American Robin *Turdus migratorius*	*chaq'wa*[1b]	------	------	
MOCKINGBIRDS AND THRASHERS – *PASSERIFORMES MIMIDAE*				
Northern Mockingbird *Mimus polyglottos*	*'alsunaxyit*[1a] *ch'u'*[1b]	*ch'u'*	*chiyo'i* *yopyop*	B. *'alsunaxyit* 'singer of the morning' V. *chiyo'i* "There are two kinds of bird called *chiyo'i*. One is the mockingbird, the other has a reddish crown on its head."
California Thrasher *Toxostoma redivivum*	*xuy*[1b]	*xuyxuy*	*chiyo'i*	B. *xuy* "the blackberry eater" V. *chiyo'i* "There are two kinds of bird called *chiyo'i*. One is the mockingbird, the other has a reddish crown on its head."
NEW WORLD WARBLERS – *PASSERIFORMES PARULIDAE*				
Warbler (e.g. Yellow-rumped Warbler) *Dendroica coronata*	------	*hochhoch*		
BUNTINGS, SPARROWS, SEEDEATERS – *PASSERIFORMES EMBERIZIDAE*				
Spotted Towhee *Pipilo maculatus*	*chopil'*[1a]	------	------	
California Towhee *Pipilo crissalis*	------	*ts'ilikaka*	------	

Bird species	Barbareño[1]	Ineseño[2]	Ventureño[3]	Comments
Sparrow (e.g. Song Sparrow) *Melospiza melodia*	*yo'y*[1b]	------	-------	
TROUPIALS AND ALLIES – *PASSERIFORMES ICTERIDAE*				
*Blackbird (unid.)	*choq*[1a]	*chòq'*	------	cf. B., I. *shoqsh* 'feather down'
*Red-winged Blackbird *Agelaius phoeniceus*	------	*syuts'alan*	------	
*Western Meadowlark *Sturnella neglecta*	*tsiyuqwili*[1a]	*ts'iyuqwili'*	*chyuq'wili*	
Oriole sp. (e.g. Bullock's Oriole) *Icterus bullockii*	*wontot*[1b]	*chakachak chàxa'w*	------	B. *wontot* "probably Bullock's Oriole, Mr. Loomis says. Cal. Acad. Sciences" I. *chàxa'w* 'small oriole species.'
SISKINS, CROSSBILLS, AND ALLIES – *PASSERIFORMES FRINGILLIDAE*				
House Finch *Carpodacus mexicanus*	------	*à'luqayas*	*chiyo'y*	I. *à'luqayas* "very small bird with red neck, brown body." V. *chiyo'y* "a small bird, male & female always go together, the female is (mixed brown & black) and the male has red on his head."

Sources

[1a] Harrington 1986 Reel 71: Frames 284-683 ("Ch. Gen. on Birds")

[1b] Whistler 1980

[2] Applegate 2007

[3] Harrington 1986 Reel 71: Frames 284-683 ("Ch. Gen. on Birds")

[4] Paul Collins, Curator of Vertebrate Zoology, Santa Barbara Museum of Natural History (pers. comm. 2011)

seems to be the case for Acorn Woodpecker (Ineseño *pulak'a'k*, *maqutiko'k*), as we will discuss in relation to bird behavior. One term may mimic the bird's call and the other may refer to the bird itself.

Birds were acknowledged in the names that Chumashan peoples gave to places in the world around them (Table 2). Many of these place names reflect occurrence of particular species, geographical features of the landscape, or elements of myth (Applegate 1974). For example, María Solares said that as the soul prepares for its journey after death, it passes some rocks where two giant ravens peck out its eyes (Blackburn 1975:99–100). This spot, near Point Conception, is called *humqaq'*, 'the raven comes' (Applegate 1975:29).

Particular birds recognized in Chumashan place names include American Kestrel, Golden Eagle, Peregrine Falcon, Great Blue Heron, Turkey Vulture, scrub jay, Greater Roadrunner, and gull—sometimes just the bird itself, in other cases its nest. Another feature of birds is acknowledged in the Santa Rosa Island town of *qshiwqshiw*, 'lots of bird droppings' (Johnson 1999:63). Although there are many place names of Chumash origin still in use today, unfortunately none of the bird-based ones are among them.

Bird Behavior and Omens

Harrington's notes show that Chumash people were keen observers of the appearance and behavior of birds in both the terrestrial and marine environment, and that they often linked bird

Table 2. Birds in Chumashan place names.

Chumashan languages: (B) Barbareño; (Cr) Cruzeño or island language; (I) Ineseño; (O) Obispeño; (P) Purisimeño; (V) Ventureño.

Place name	Language	Translation	Location
ch'oloshush[1]	Cr.	'seagull gathering place'	village at Christy Beach, Santa Cruz Island
humqaq'	I.	'the raven comes'	Point Conception
huspat hulkilik	B.	'nest of the kestrel'	Eagle Canyon, west of Santa Barbara
kachukuchuk	V.	'the little dove'	Cañada Larga, north of Ventura
kaspat kaxwa	V.	'nest of the heron'	place northwest of Ojai
kaspat kaslo'w	V.	'nest of the eagle'	mountain west of San Fernando Valley
lexlele	P.	'swan'	village at Guadalupe Lake
maspat aslo'w	I.	'nest of the eagle'	alder grove north of Santa Ynez
pat 'akwich	P.	'nest of the falcon'	place near Mission La Purísima
pi'awa p^{h}ew	Cr.	'house of the pelican'	island at east end of Anacapa Island
qshiwqshiw	Cr.	'lots of bird droppings'	village on east end of Santa Rosa Island
qwa'	B.	'kind of duck'	place on Goleta Slough
siyo kinik.	B	'water of the little songbird'	place in Arroyo Burro, Santa Barbara
siyo'kilik	I.	'water of the kestrel'	spring on Alamo Pintado Creek
sonoq	P.	'at the buzzard'	place near Nojoqui Falls
s'uw mach'a'y	I.	'the scrub jay eats'	mouth of de la Cuesta Canyon

[1] Johnson 1999:59; all others, Applegate 1975.

behavior to effects on other creatures, including humans. This is exemplified in the following passages, the first of which also demonstrates Harrington's efforts at species identification:

> **mut**, the bird that goes along shore … *prieto no mas, puro negro y no se puede volar, y cuando viene la ola se embuta allá* [= just dark, pure black and it cannot fly, and when a wave comes it dives there]. **mut** = a small duck that never leaves the ocean beach. Cal. Acad. Sciences. At last we found the **mut**. It is Oidemia deglandi [=*Melanitta fusca*, White-winged Scoter]. A shag 1½ ft long, blackish brown color with a duck-like bill…. **mut**, a kind of black duck [Harrington 1986:R71, F517–518, 517].
>
> (note: "*se embuta*" was probably an incorrect transcription of *zambulle*, 'it dives')

As previously noted, **k'sen** referred to coot, or mudhen, and was also the name for the chief's or ceremonial leader's official messenger. It was said that for a **k'sen** (messenger) "they always select somebody who will come back again … They select some lazy person so he will go no farther than he has to, and the mud-hen is lazy, never going to the islands but staying in the sloughs" (Harrington 1986:R71, F479).

Harrington's Chumash consultants observed that **pulakak** is the only woodpecker that puts acorns in trees—an obvious description of Acorn Woodpecker, the only woodpecker species that eats acorns. In the Flood story, Sun saved *Woodpecker* (**maqutiko'k**) by throwing down acorns for him to eat: "That is why he likes acorns so much—they are still his food." Therefore, both terms must refer to the same species, the former name echoing its raucous call.

Referring to Red-tailed Hawk, which makes a distinctive prolonged hoarse whistling cry, "Old Indians said that when this hawk whistles, it is good news for some and for others it is the contrary … When the **kwich** whistles, all stop stupefied. The **kwich** catches rattlesnakes and *conejos* [rabbits] and eats them, also mice and rats" (Harrington 1986:R71, F487).

Bird behavior was thought to have meaning for other birds as well as for humans. "The buzzard from midnight on knows whether there is something in sight or not by listening to the crow, whose call is a rejoicing … When they [canoemen] saw a crow in mid-channel nearly falling into the water, they used to row fast, lest a storm overtake them" (Harrington 1986:R71, F330–331). A Rhinoceros Auklet, if seen circling around, was also a bad omen for canoemen (Harrington 1986:R71, F369).

Fernando Librado was told that if a kingfisher hovered over a person, it meant that something bad was going to happen. If it alighted nearby, then fell from the tree as if dead, one should never touch that bird, and if any trouble were to arise after this, there would be danger. One should pay no attention and walk away (Harrington 1986:R71, F353–354).

Acquiring Birds

California Indians in general hunted birds from blinds, used decoys to attract them, trapped them with snares, nets or maze traps, placed traps over nest holes, captured them by hand at roosts, and sometimes raised captured nestlings (Lightfoot and Parrish 2009:27).

Among the Chumash, Harrington's consultants talked about hunting quail, ducks and geese for food. The Chumash caught quail with nets or maze traps and herded ducks into bulrush enclosures. Sometimes they killed small birds like blackbirds with a device consisting of a horizontal pole designed to pivot on a stationary post when pulled with a long rope. They also made duck decoys, shot the birds with plain wood-pointed arrows, or stunned them with special arrows that were tipped with a small lattice of crossed sticks. The arrows themselves were stabilized in flight by their fletching of Red-tailed Hawk, eagle, crow, raven, or condor feathers. (See Hudson and Blackburn 1982 for more complete descriptions of Chumash bird hunting and trapping techniques.)

Food

The "animals eaten" category in Culture Element Distribution checklist filled out by Harrington (1942) includes only seven birds as food options. Of these, dove and mudhen (American Coot) were checked as eaten by Barbareño, Ineseño and Ventureño Chumash; the Ventureño also ate hawk and eagle but probably not buzzard, raven and owl, according to the checklist. We are not certain that Chumash people actually used hawks and eagles as food, unless for ritual reasons. There are many discrepancies between the checklist and the information Harrington recorded from interviews; it is thought that he filled out the questionnaire from memory, without consulting his notes. And the checklist is severely limited because it omits many common species of birds that surely provided food for the Chumash, including quail, pigeons and doves, ducks and geese, other waterfowl and seabirds.

Fernando Librado (Ventureño) said he had never seen Indians eat pelicans or seagulls, but he had seen them eat mudhens (Harrington 1986:R71, F448). Also said to be good to eat was 'enek'wetete, a kind of small duck that is whitish from its duck-like bill down to the belly and with a mottled gray and black back; it dives and is seen in estuaries (Harrington 1986:R71, F433). Juan de Jesús Justo (Barbareño) identified a specimen of Clapper Rail as a bird that was good to eat (Harrington 1986:R71, F638).

It has been suggested that bird meat may have been an important protein substitute for fish during winter, a relatively lean time of year when rough weather might prevent venturing out in canoes but migratory waterfowl are abundant in coastal estuaries (Landberg 1965:77).

Material Culture

The diversity of Chumash material culture is well documented (Hudson and Blackburn 1982, 1983, 1985, 1986, 1987). Table 3 enumerates the many kinds of items Chumash people made from bird parts. We describe them in some detail here, beginning with secular clothing and

Table 3. Bird parts used in Chumash material culture.

Part	Item(s)	Species (if known)	Comments
Whole body	talisman	hummingbird	
Skull / head	talisman	hawk, eagle	worn as pendant
Beak	necklace		
Bones	hairpin		
	necklace beads	vulture, condor	
	whistle	albatross, heron, hawk, pelican, goose, cormorant	
	Flute	pelican	
Claws/Talons	talisman	eagle, vulture, crow, condor, raven	worn as pendant
Skin	dress, cape	gull, duck, waterfowl	whole or sewn pieces
Feathers	cordage (with plant fiber)		
	woven blanket		
	dance skirt pendants		
	netted dance skirt / robe	woodpecker, magpie, gull, vulture, hawk, crow, eagle, condor	ethnographic and cave cache
	topknot dance headdress	magpie, roadrunner, crow, turkey	
	headdress / hair pin tassel	woodpecker	
	dance chest band	blackbird, crow, magpie	in Swordfish Dance
	dance wand	crow, white goose, hawk, woodpecker	
	medicine	eagle	to administer ants
	offertory pole	vulture, crow, condor, raven, eagle	black feathers
Quills	dance forehead band	flicker, woodpecker	trimmed feathers
	banner/ flag	flicker, woodpecker, magpie, crow, pelican, condor, hawk, egret, eagle, jay, pigeon	ethnographic and cave cache
	basket material	flicker, other unidentified sp.	rare
Down	cordage (with plant fiber)	goose, eagle	
	down-cord dance skirt		white down
	down-cord headband / crown	eagle	
	ritual offering	goose, egret	white down
	medicine	eagle	to administer ants

jewelry followed by ceremonial regalia and various ritual paraphernalia and practices involving birds. One use of feathers that does not fit into any of these categories is the very rare appearance of trimmed feather quills as weft material in coiled basketry. Although this is commonly seen in baskets of other California Indian peoples, only four Chumash examples are known, each of which has only a few quill stitches subtly interspersed among the *Juncus* or sumac (*Rhus trilobata* Torrey & A. Gray) sewing material (Dawson and Deetz 1965:plates 7a, 16a; Smith 1987:15; and one unpublished example, examined by Timbrook, in a private collection). In two of the baskets the quills are flicker; the other two are as yet unidentified.

Secular Clothing and Ornamentation

Living in a mild climate, the Chumash people wore little clothing, but in colder weather they did use capes made from animal skins. Feathered garments were made in three ways: (1) by sewing large pieces of bird skins together; (2) by cutting strips of bird skin, twisting the strips around plant-fiber cordage so that the feathers were outside, then twining them together in the same manner as weaving a rabbit skin blanket; or (3) by twisting feathers or feather down into the plant fibers while making the cordage, then weaving that (Hudson and Blackburn 1985:46–47, 55). An example of the sewn bird skin garment was recorded as having been worn by an Indian woman who lived alone on San Nicolas, one of the Southern Channel Islands, from 1835 to 1853. When discovered by sea otter hunters, she was wearing a long, sleeveless dress made from squares of cormorant skins sewn together, the feathers all pointing downward to form a continuous sheen of iridescent green-black (Heizer and Elsasser 1973:4, 12, 28, 32–33). This type of garment may also have been used among the Chumash of the Northern Channel Islands (Hudson and Blackburn 1985:39). Several known examples of thick, plush-like feather blankets, woven from soft downy feathers incorporated into both warp and weft cordage, are thought to have been made by peoples to the north of the Chumash (McLendon 2002).

Ornaments and jewelry made with bird parts included hairpins of bird bone, mammal bone or wood, often decorated with feathers, worn by both men and women. Hollow bird bones were cut into segments and worn as necklace beads. Another kind of necklace was made with strands of beads threaded through and held separate by segments of Turkey Vulture or California Condor feather quill, so that the necklace would lie flat. Terms in three Chumash languages were recorded for a necklace made of bird beaks, but no further data were gathered (Henshaw 1955:99; Hudson and Blackburn 1986:143). Eagle claws were sometimes perforated for wearing as pendants (Gifford 1940:185, 234; Orr 1947:118, 129; see Hudson and Blackburn 1985 for further details on ornament types).

Ceremonial Regalia

One of the most important ways the Chumash utilized birds was in making ceremonial or dance regalia from feathers. Dances were performed for both religious and secular purposes, and similar types of regalia were worn for many dances. Most dancers wore a skirt fashioned from lengths of dogbane (*Apocynum cannabinum* L.) or milkweed (*Asclepias* spp.) cordage twisted together with eagle down, the strands hanging from a waistband and tipped with whole feathers (Hudson and Blackburn 1985:117–118). This type of skirt appears in the only known photographs of a Chumash Indian wearing traditional clothing (Figure 1).

Another type of feathered skirt consisted of a net made from cordage of nettle (*Urtica dioica* L. subsp. *holosericea* (Nutt.) Thorne), milkweed, or dogbane. This netting hung from the waist to the knees or mid-calf and was covered with four or five overlapping layers of feathers, with the longest at the bottom. Species used for the feathered net skirt included woodpecker, magpie, gull, vulture, and hawk (Hudson and Blackburn 1985:119–123). These skirts were used by other tribes, not just the Chumash; the Luiseño people of southern California made them with feathers of Golden Eagle and California Condor (Bates et al. 1993:41–42).

Figure 1. Rafael Solares, leader of the Santa Ynez Chumash community, wearing dance regalia, 1878. Photograph by Leon de Cessac (collection Musée du quai Branly, Paris), used with permission.

Much longer feathered net robes that covered the dancer from head to toe were made by some native peoples, as seen in a Nisenan (Northern California) example from the Museum of Anthropology and Ethnography in St. Petersburg, Russia (Figure 2). This may be similar to what the Chumash made for the *xolxol*, or condor impersonator (Hudson and Underhay

Figure 2. Northern Californian feather regalia exhibited in the Museum of Anthropology and Ethnography in St. Petersburg, Russia (Muzej Antropologii i Etnografii). The Chumash may have made similar regalia. *(Left)* The whole skin of a California Condor worn in a dance to honor the bird, attributed to Valley Nisenan (cat. no. 570-2). *(Right)* An enveloping cloak of crow feathers attached to a net, with Turkey Vulture wing feathers mounted on willow shoots thrust into the head piece, attributed to Valley Nisenan (cat. no. 570-1). This cloak is incorrectly displayed to reveal the dancer's face. Photograph given to Travis Hudson, Santa Barbara Museum of Natural History. Courtesy of the Museum of Anthropology and Ethnography, St. Petersburg.

1978:91). A whole California Condor skin worn to enfold the dancer is also in the museum in St. Petersburg (Bates 1983).

Two principal kinds of feather headdresses were worn by Chumash dancers. For a flexible forehead band, they trimmed the feathers, pierced and threaded them together with transverse rows of fine string so that the quills lay closely parallel. Longer bands made in the same way were worn hanging down the back or served as banners or flags to decorate outdoor dance enclosures (Hudson and Blackburn 1985:169–173; 1986:61–64). Throughout California, the favorite feathers for these bands and banners were the bright orange quills of the Northern Flicker, a kind of woodpecker. An ethnographic example from Yosemite of such a banner, 66 cm long, was made with 412 flicker feathers, representing wings and tails of at least 14 individual birds (Elsasser and Heizer 1963:14).

The other common type of dance headdress was a topknot formed from short feathers mounted onto a framework, with a much longer projecting central bunch of Black Magpie or roadrunner tail feathers. It was held in place with a headdress pin, also feathered (Hudson and Blackburn 1985:180–188). This type is shown in the historic photos of Chumash leader Rafael Solares (Fig. 1). In the Santa Barbara Museum of Natural History is a similar headdress in which the crown framework is covered with split feathers of Wild Turkey—a bird introduced to the Chumash in historic times—with the central topknot of magpie tail feathers.

Dances and Music

Not only did the dancers wear feather regalia and carry feathered dance wands, but some of the dances themselves were based on bird appearance and behavior. Chumash elder Fernando Librado told Harrington that in the Blackbird Dance, the dancers "imitated the blackbird with singing, bathing, and whistling [and making] backward steps like the blackbird when he is scratching for things." The dancer was painted to resemble the blackbird, he said, with a speckled face and red patches on the shoulders (Hudson et al. 1977:84–85). There was also a Condor Dance, in which the dancer held sticks that the condor struck together, enabling him to fly long distances quickly (Hudson and Blackburn 1985:212; Hudson and Underhay 1978:90). In many cases the dancer was believed no longer to be a person but transformed into the spirit he was depicting. These dances continued to be performed throughout the Mission Period and as late as the 1870s (Hudson et al.1977:91–93). Descriptions recorded by Harrington have been used by modern descendants to revive the dances of their ancestors.

Bird bone whistles are very commonly used by native people throughout California. They are often worn suspended from a cord around the dancer's neck, held between the teeth, and blown to accompany the dance movements. Members of the Portolá expedition, who journeyed through Chumash territory in 1769–1770, were kept awake at night by these "very disagreeable" whistles, "the noise of which grated upon our ears" (Costansó 1911:37, 43). Chumash whistles were made from a short section of bird bone with one end plugged and a transverse slit on one side, through which air was expelled to produce a single note. Sometimes two or more such whistles of differing lengths were bound together as a sort of panpipe (Corbett 2004:66; Hudson and Blackburn 1986:349–350). Whistles made from several different species of birds are commonly found in archaeological sites in the Chumash region.

Ritual Paraphernalia and Practices

Birds figured in various religious practices, both public and personal. Prayers were said and offerings left at shrines, which were marked with tall poles painted red and embellished with tufts of black feathers from Turkey Vulture, crow, condor, raven, or eagle (Hudson and Blackburn 1986:93–98). A claw from one of these birds, a whole hawk or eagle skull or stuffed head, or a dried hummingbird might be worn suspended from a cord around one's neck as a personal talisman (Hudson and Blackburn 1986:142–148).

Effigy carvings that resemble birds like pelican or cormorant (Figure 3) may have been personal talismans intended to bring their owners success in fishing (Hudson et al. 1978:126–127,156–157), although they are also recorded to have been used in more public ceremonies. According to Justo, a Santa Barbara Indian, twenty such stones were arranged in a square, five on each side, around a bowl of water. The "medicine man" blew smoke from an herb resembling southernwood (probably *Artemisia californica* Less.) burning in his stone pipe toward the water and then toward the stones. The people came and moistened their faces with this now-holy water. This ceremony was believed to bring rain, cause death to enemies, and various other things (Yates 1890:28). Elderly Chumash consultants interviewed by the French anthropologist Leon de Cessac in 1878 (Cessac 1951) called these effigies *pajaritos*, meaning 'little birds' in Spanish.

Vultures and condors were considered to be expert at finding lost objects, since they fly so high and can spot things on the ground. Special stones collected from the nests of these birds could confer these same powers on the finder. To collect such a stone, Fernando Librado told Harrington:

> When the vulture lays eggs in her nest, find the nest and steal one egg. Boil the egg hard and then return it to the nest. Do all this when the vulture doesn't see you. She sits on the eggs and then after a while discovers that something is wrong with one of these eggs. She then starts off for the mountains. All this time you are watching carefully. She comes back with a rock and places it right against the egg and the chick hatches at once. As soon as the vulture leaves the nest, you go and take the stone, for with that stone you can get whatever you want. You can get hidden things that are pretty far away, though not too far away [Blackburn 1975:278].

Feather down was deposited as an offering at shrines, scattered to bring rain, and used to "feed" ritual objects. A cord with down twisted into it was used in divination (Blackburn

Figure 3. "Pelican stones" are bird-like effigy carvings, possibly intended as talismans for fishermen. Photograph by Jan Timbrook. Courtesy of Santa Barbara Museum of Natural History..

1975:283, 285). Among the Ventureño Chumash, twelve plummet-shaped charmstones were arranged in a circle around a central disk-like stone and sprinkled with chia seed (*Salvia columbariae* Benth.) mixed with white goose down followed by red ochre. Accompanied by singers and rattles, dancers circled the pile. This was done to cure the sick, bring rain, put out fires in the mountains, call fish up the streams, and make war (Henshaw 1885:110–111). This ceremony was very similar in intent to the Barbareño practice described above (Yates 1890), but distinct in using charmstones rather than the bird-like effigies, in omitting the consecrating smoke, and in adding a sprinkling of feather down.

Chumash and Kitanemuk Indians kept ritual stones called *toshaawt* in their homes, wrapped up with feather down, chia seed, money, and tobacco, in order to protect the house from weather and to use in treating illness. The down and other ritual "food" was burned and replaced each year (Hudson and Blackburn 1986:166–170; Timbrook 2002:634–636). The ceremonial sunstick used in winter solstice rituals was also kept in a redwood box filled with white egret or goose down (Hudson et al. 1977:57).

Medicine

Birds also had a role in medical treatments. The flesh of Red-tailed Hawk was believed to be medicinal, and was given to a sick person to eat (Harrington 1986:R71, F487). For serious illnesses that did not respond to folk herbal remedies, the Ant Doctor might be consulted. This doctor would take the patient to an anthill in the mountains. There she would use the down feather of an eagle to pick up four or five red ants at a time and wrap this up into a ball. Fifty or more of these eagle-down balls filled with ants were given like pills for the patient to swallow one at a time. The ants were induced to bite, and the patient would faint and have visions. After regaining consciousness, the sick person underwent the same treatment at intervals for several days. This was believed to be a powerful cure (Walker and Hudson 1993:60). An extensive review of ethnographic evidence pertaining to ant ingestion for therapeutic and religious purposes has been undertaken by Groark (1996).

The Archaeological Record of Birds in the Chumash Region

What is known of the ancient antecedents of these ethnographically-known relationships with birds? Archaeological evidence for exploitation of avian fauna in this region extends far back into prehistory. As we have noted, Chumashan peoples have been living in south central California for millennia, but it is unknown when their direct ancestors first arrived. Human remains from Santa Rosa Island are 13,000 years old, among the earliest in the Americas (Johnson et al. 2002). Because there exists a gap in the archaeological record between this Late Pleistocene individual and sites dating to the Early Holocene (Kennett 2005), it cannot be established with certainty whether that individual was a member of a group related to later Chumash peoples, or from some other unrelated early population. In any case, it is common-ly accepted by archaeologists and linguists that an ancestral proto-Chumash population did become established quite early in prehistory (e.g., Golla 2011; King 1990), a hypothesis that is gaining empirical support from molecular anthropological research (Johnson and Lorenz 2006; Johnson et al. 2012). With environmental fluctuations and technological innovations, surely the relationships of humans—whoever they were—with avian and other species living in this area changed over time.

It is also worth noting that the archaeological record does not offer a complete or accurate representation of local bird species exploited by people. First, bird bone usually comprises a relatively tiny fraction—often 1% or less—of recovered bone at most sites in the Chumash area (e.g., Braje 2010:95; Colten 2001:203; Erlandson 1994:260; Glassow 1996:59). Second, bird bones are relatively delicate and often fracture into small pieces unidentifiable to species or even genus, a fact mentioned in nearly every report on faunal remains (e.g., Glassow et al. 2008:37). Third, the presence of bird bone in archaeological deposits, especially of smaller species, may be misleading as these birds are subject to predation and deposition by owls or other raptors (Guthrie 1993b:157). Finally, absence of remains may or may not indicate absence of species. While some birds, like mallard and band-tailed pigeon, may have been less common in Chumash times, cultural practices for handling others such as eagles and condors might prevent their remains being found in trash deposits. The occurrence and preservation of avian remains in Chumash-area archaeological deposits has been discussed by Guthrie (1980, 1993a, 1993b, 1998).

The Northern Channel Islands

Some of the very earliest evidence of human occupation in North America has been found on San Miguel Island and Santa Rosa Island, the two westernmost of the California Channel Islands. On San Miguel, the archaeological deposits in Daisy Cave, which was occupied from about 11,600 until 700 years ago, contain very early evidence of humans using birds on the Channel Islands (Erlandson et al. 1996).

On Santa Rosa Island, well-preserved bird bone, charcoal and stone tools were found in deeply buried strata at CA-SRI-512. Distinctive Channel Island barbed projectile points and crescents found at the site are thought to have been used in hunting birds. The faunal assemblage is dominated by bird bone, including Canada Goose, Snow Goose, cormorant, and albatross. Dates obtained from three samples of goose bone range from 11,970 to 11,355 calendar years before present (Erlandson et al. 2011).

The faunal remains from both these sites include bones of an endemic species of flightless sea duck, *Chendytes lawi*, which was the size of a goose and formerly nested in great numbers on the islands. These remains—some of them burned—indicate that *Chendytes* continued to live on the islands after the arrival of humans and coexisted with them for several thousand years until it disappeared, apparently due to hunting as the human population increased (Guthrie 1993a:414, 1993b:162; Jones et al. 2008).

On Santa Cruz Island, bird bone was sparse throughout Late Holocene deposits (after 3000 B.P.), representing a maximum of 1.57% of meat weight and declining to 0.45% in the Historic Period. Not surprisingly, this assemblage was dominated by marine birds, predominantly cormorants, pelicans, gulls and ducks (Colten 2001).

Collins (2009) has compiled a comprehensive list of avian remains found in archaeological sites on the six largest Channel Islands (three islands are outside the Chumash area), noting that only about 40% of the bone elements were identifiable. About 80% of these were from marine/shore/aquatic/wading birds. The most abundant species—and among the most abundant remains overall—were cormorants, gulls, albatrosses, Cassin's Auklet, Northern Fulmar, and *Chendytes lawi* (Collins 2009:20).

Archaeological bird remains can provide clues about the past distribution and abundance of other bird taxa. Snow Goose bones are common in archaeological deposits, but these birds are relatively rarely seen today (Collins and Jones 2012). Snow Geese wintered in grasslands on the Northern Channel Islands historically, but changed their migratory destination to wetlands in California's Central Valley after the development of wildlife refuges near agricultural fields that provided abundant food resources (Guthrie 1993b:162–163). Populations of Short-tailed Albatross were formerly abundant on the California coast and this is reflected in their numerous remains in archaeological deposits on the Channel Islands. This species was drastically reduced by egg collecting on its Pacific island breeding grounds in the early 1900s (Guthrie 1993b:161). It is only an accidental visitor to the islands today (Collins and Jones 2012).

Double-crested, Pelagic, and Brant's Cormorants are very common to abundant residents and breed on several of the islands today (Collins and Jones 2012). Cormorant bones from all three species are likewise abundant in the archaeological deposits. Many of the bones are burned, indicating that these birds were cooked and eaten. Their abundance shows that cormorants were clearly a preferred food of prehistoric peoples, who probably captured them on their island rookeries at night. Cormorants were probably also important for non-food uses such as skins or feathers (Guthrie 1980:696, 1993b:164). One site on Santa Cruz Island, which contained abundant evidence for exploitation of a nearby cormorant rookery, was characterized by archaeologist Phil C. Orr as having been a seabird "poultry market" (Berger and Libby 1966:469).

Artifacts from San Miguel Island sites indicate that bird bones were a valued raw material for a variety of tools. The artifacts include cormorant bone awls, a kittiwake bone whistle, tubes made from goose, albatross and gull bones, and a scraper made from an albatross or goose ulna (Guthrie 1980:696). Archaeological collections in the Santa Barbara Museum of Natural History from Northern Channel Islands sites include whistles made from bones of short-tailed albatross, Great Blue Heron, Red-tailed Hawk, Brown Pelican, Canada Goose and cormorant, as well as a rare 4-holed flute made from the wing of a Brown Pelican. Only two other examples of bird bone flutes with multiple finger holes are known from the Chumash area (Hudson and Blackburn 1986:366–368).

The Chumash Mainland

The variety of bird species whose bones have been reported from several archaeological deposits on the Northern Channel Islands, a few coastal mainland sites, and one interior site is shown in Table 4. The zooarchaeological record from mainland sites has been much less extensively studied but includes many of the same species found on the islands. For

Table 4. Presence of bird bone in archaeological deposits in the Chumash region.

Marine, shore, and freshwater species	San Miguel Island[1]	Santa Rosa Island[1]	Santa Cruz Island[1]	Mainland Coast[2]	Inland[3]
DUCKS, GEESE, AND WATERFOWL – *ANSERIFORMES ANATIDAE*					
Goose spp. (undiff.)	x		x	x	
Snow Goose	x		x	x	
Chen caerulescens					
Canada Goose				x	
Branta canadensis					
Duck sp. undiff.			x	x	
American Wigeon			x	x	
Anas americana					
Mallard			x	x	
Anas platyrhynchos					
Teal spp. (undiff.)			x	x	
Anas discors, A. cyanoptera, A. crecca					
Scoter sp. (unid.)			x	x	
Melanitta sp.					
Surf Scoter	x			x	
Melanitta perspicillata					
White-winged Scoter	x		x	x	
Melanitta fusca					
Extinct sea duck	x		x	x	
Chendytes lawi					
LOONS – *GAVIIFORMES GAVIIDAE*					
Loon sp. (undiff.)	x		x	x	
Gavia sp.					
Common Loon	x		x	x	
Gavia immer					
Pacific Loon	x				
Gavia pacifica					
GREBES – *PODICIPEDIFORMES PODICIPEDIDAE*					
Grebe sp. (undiff.)			x	x	
Eared Grebe	x		x	x	
Podiceps nigricollis					
Western/Clark's Grebe	x	x	x	x	
Aechmophorus occidentalis, A. clarkii					
ALBATROSSES – *PROCELLARIIFORMES DIOMEDEIDAE*					
Albatross sp. (undiff.)			x	x	
Short-tailed Albatross	x			x	
Phoebastria albatrus					
SHEARWATERS AND PETRELS – *PROCELLARIIFORMES PROCELLARIIDAE*					
Sooty Shearwater	x				
Puffinus griseus					
Black-vented Shearwater	x				
Puffinus opisthomelas					
Leach's Storm-petrel	x				
Oceanodroma leucorhoa					
Ashy Storm-petrel	x				
Oceanodroma homochroa					

Table 4 continued.

Marine, shore, and freshwater species	San Miguel Island[1]	Santa Rosa Island[1]	Santa Cruz Island[1]	Mainland Coast[2]	Inland[3]
PELICANS – *PELECANIFORMES PELICANIDAE*					
Brown Pelican *Pelecanus occidentalus*	x		x	x	
CORMORANTS AND SHAGS – *PELECANIFORMES PHALACROCORACIDAE*					
Cormorant sp. (undiff.)	x	x	x	x	
Brandt's Cormorant *Phalacrocorax penicillatus*	x		x	x	
Double-crested Cormorant *Phalacrocorax auritus*	x		x	x	
Pelagic Cormorant *Phalacrocorax pelagicus*	x		x	x	
HERONS, EGRETS, AND BITTERNS – *CICONIIFORMES ARDEIDAE*					
Great Blue Heron *Ardea herodias*				x	
Great Egret *Ardea alba*				x	
Snowy Egret *Egretta thula*				x	
OSPREY – *FALCONIFORMES PANDIONIDAE*					
Osprey *Pandion haliaetus*	x		x	x	
RAILS, GALLINULES, AND COOTS – *GRUIFORMES RALLIDAE*					
American Coot *Fulica americana*	x			x	
CRANES – *GRUIFORMES GRUIDAE*					
Sandhill Crane *Grus canadensis*	x			x	
GULLS – *CHARADRIIFORMES LARIDAE*					
Black-legged Kittiwake *Rissa tridactyla*	x		x		
Gull spp. (undiff.) *Larus* spp.	x	x	x	x	
AUKS, MURRES, AND PUFFINS – *CHARADRIIFORMES ALCIDAE*					
Common Murre *Uria aalge*	x		x	x	
Xantus's Murrelet *Synthiboramphus hypoleucus*	x		x		
Cassin's Auklet *Ptychoramphus aleuticus*	x		x	x	
Rhinoceros Auklet *Cerorhinca monocerata*	x		x	x	
Tufted Puffin *Fratercula cirrhata*	x		x	x	
Terrestrial species					
NEW WORLD QUAIL – *GALLIFORMES ODONTOPHORIDAE*					
California Quail *Callipepla californica*				x	x
NEW WORLD VULTURES – *FALCONIFORMES CATHARTIDAE*					
Turkey Vulture *Cathartes aura*				x	

Terrestrial Species	San Miguel Island[1]	Santa Rosa Island[1]	Santa Cruz Island[1]	Mainland Coast[2]	Inland[3]
California Condor *Gymnogyps californianus*	x			x	
HAWKS, EAGLES, AND KITES – *FALCONIFORMES ACCIPITRIDAE*					
Bald Eagle *Haliaeetus leucocephalus*				x	
Hawk (undiff.) *Buteo* sp.			x	x	x
Red-tailed Hawk *Buteo jamaicensis*	x			x	
Golden Eagle *Aquila chrysaetos*				x	
FALCONS AND KESTRELS – *FALCONIFORMES FALCONIDAE*					
American Kestrel *Falco sparverius*	x				
Peregrine/Prairie Falcon *Falco peregrinus / F. mexicanus*			x	x	
PIGEONS AND DOVES – *COLUMBIFORMES COLUMBIDAE*					
Mourning Dove *Zenaida macroura*			x		
BARN-OWLS – *STRIGIFORMES TYTONIDAE*					
Barn Owl *Tyto alba*	x			x	
OWLS - *STRIGIFORMES STRIGIDAE*					
Western Screech-Owl *Megascops kennicottii*					x
Great Horned Owl *Bubo virginianus*				x	
Burrowing Owl *Athene cunicularia*	x			x	
Short-eared Owl *Asio flammeus*	x				x
CROWS, JAYS, AND MAGPIES – *PASSERIFORMES CORVIDAE*					
Island Scrub-Jay *Aphelocoma insularis*			x		
American Crow *Corvus brachyrhynchos*				x	x
Common Raven *Corvus corax*	x		x	x	
TROUPIALS AND ALLIES – *PASSERIFORMES ICTERIDAE*					
Western Meadowlark *Sturnella neglecta*	x				
Brewer's Blackbird *Euphagus cyanocephalus*	x				
PASSERINES – PASSERIFORMES (GENERAL)					
Passerine spp. (undiff.)	x		x	x	x

Sources

[1] Selected spp. from a compilation by Collins 2009; far more numerous studies have been conducted on San Miguel than on the other islands.

[2] Glassow 1996, Howard and Dodson 1933.

[3] Hildebrandt 2004.

example, bones from the flightless sea duck *Chendytes* occur in several mainland sites as late as 2400 B.P. (Jones et al. 2008), and cormorant bones are also common in some coastal mainland sites (Glassow 1996:128).

Two Late-Period sites adjacent to the mouth of the Santa Ynez River contain enormous numbers of waterfowl bones, as much as 39% of bone weight in one excavated unit, and large amounts were also found in an earlier site a short distance away. The principal reason for occupation of this location may have been for intensive harvest of freshwater birds in the nearby lagoon (Glassow 1996:132). Such estuarine habitats are common at stream mouths on the mainland but are less widespread on the islands.

Excavations at the historic coastal Chumash town of ***muwu***, near the vast wetlands at Point Mugu in Ventura County, found large amounts of bone from Double-crested and Brandt's Cormorants, loons, Brown Pelican, gulls, scoters and other ducks. About 250 artifacts were made from bones of cormorant, albatross, pelican, gull and large loon. Very small numbers of remains from land birds included Red-tailed Hawk, Turkey Vulture, crow, raven and Barn Owl (Howard and Dodson 1933). It appears that birds constituted a significant part of the diet in coastal estuary locations, which were also centers for large concentrations of the human population in the late prehistoric and early historic period.

Different birds were being utilized by peoples who lived in the inland valleys, no doubt largely due to differences in local availability. Relatively little recovery or analysis of bird bone has been undertaken in archaeological projects there. A Late Period (post-AD 1300) interior site in the Santa Ynez Valley contained very small amounts of identifiable bird bone; most numerous were quail, with one or two pieces from crow, owls, buteo hawk, and a passerine (Hildebrandt 2004:86).

Bones from a number of other birds that were probably not significant food sources are also found, including woodpeckers, blackbirds, hawks and owls (Guthrie 1998). These species were known to have been used for feather regalia and other ritual purposes in historic times.

Two notable discoveries of archaeological caches of feather regalia have been made in and near the Chumash area. A netted skirt made with crow and Golden Eagle feathers, found in a cave cache in the Cuyama area, is similar to ethnographically-described dance skirts (Grant 1964:4–5, 25). A cave cache of ceremonial regalia found over a hundred years ago in Los Angeles County, not far from territory inhabited by Ventureño Chumash groups, contained 33 feather bands from 60 cm to 180 cm in length. These bands, like those described ethnographically, were made from partially-stripped feathers laid parallel, pierced and sewn together. They included wing and tail feathers of many different birds: flicker as well as American Crow, Brown Pelican, California Condor, Red-shouldered Hawk, Snowy Egret, Bald Eagle, jay, and Band-tailed Pigeon (Elsasser and Heizer 1963:13-17).

Bird-like stone effigy carvings (Figure 3) have been found in archaeological sites in the Chumash area as well as on the Southern Channel Islands, which were occupied by non-Chumashan peoples. As we noted above, ethnohistoric information suggests some possible functions of these enigmatic objects, either as personal talismans or as part of ceremonies to bring rain or other benefits to the community.

Rock Art

The truly pervasive importance of birds in Chumash life may provide clues to interpreting one of the most fascinating legacies of Chumashan peoples—their mysterious and compelling rock paintings. Thought to have been created by shamans for religious purposes, the paintings were held to be spiritually dangerous to the uninitiated. Because of this potency, very little knowledge of their meaning was passed on to the individuals that Harrington and other early anthropologists interviewed (Hudson 1982:19–21). Most surviving pictographs are believed to have been created in the last thousand years, some only a few hundred years ago (Grant 1993:96; Hudson 1982:22).

Rendered in red, black and white, the complex designs include geometric, anthropomorphic, and zoomorphic figures. Among the latter, very few resemble identifiable biological species. Some definitely appear bird-like, however, with clearly depicted wings and feathers such as the namesake figure at Condor Cave (Hudson and Underhay 1978:fig. 13). Some appear strikingly similar to costumed dancers wearing fringed down cordage skirts and/or feather topknot headdresses (Figure 4; see also Grant 1993:plates 20, 24, 25). And there are some that combine human and avian features. Although we cannot be certain what the painter intended, it would be consistent with what we know of Chumash world view if these figures represented the spiritual transformation of the dancer or shaman into a bird—literally becoming one of the People of the Sky.

Figure 4. Chumash rock painting of a winged anthropomorphic figure that appears to be wearing a topknot-style feather headdress. Photograph by Kathleen Conti. Courtesy of Santa Barbara Museum of Natural History.

Discussion

As we have seen, birds were woven into nearly every aspect of Chumash life—food, clothing, tools, ritual, medicine, and more. Their vocalizations, appearance and behavior were embedded in language: following a pattern seen in many cultures worldwide, the Chumash named many birds according to their calls. In oral traditions, birds were here before there were humans, and their roles echo many social and political aspects of Chumash society. With the sky held up on the wings of a giant eagle, birds were essential to the very structure of the Chumash universe. This picture has emerged principally from the detailed linguistic and ethnographic notes of interviews conducted by John P. Harrington in the early 20th century.

Archaeological evidence for human-bird relationships extends far back into prehistory in the Chumash region. Much of it is consistent with what is described for Chumash peoples during the post-European contact period, but it also fills in some blanks. The archaeological record actually contains more detailed and quantifiable information about probable food species than are described in ethnographic accounts. Birds seem to have been a much less significant food source than fish and shellfish, particularly on the islands, but may have increased in importance over time as human populations grew and became concentrated around large estuaries on the mainland coast where waterfowl were abundant.

It is apparent that many birds were also taken for their feathers or skins rather than for food. Feather regalia identical to that described by Harrington's Chumash consultants have been found in cave caches in the region, and bird bone whistles are common in many sites.

Conversely, ethnographic data have shed light on the function of certain artifacts, such as the bird effigy carvings used in particular ceremonies or as talismans. Descriptions of dances, shamanism, and interactions with the spirit world suggest possible interpretations for some of the esoteric rock paintings.

Bird remains also reveal changes in species abundance and distribution over time, due to human exploitation, environmental changes, or both. The extinction of the goose-sized, flightless sea duck *Chendytes* on the Channel Islands and mainland coast was surely a result of prolonged hunting pressure. Without archaeological evidence, we would not have realized that Short-tailed Albatross once occurred in great abundance on our shores. Other species such as Mallards are rare in archaeological contexts but are abundant in the area today. The migratory patterns of Snow Geese—birds once common on the Channel Islands and a food source for Native people there—changed due to habitat alterations in the 20th century.

Although there is a long (millennia-old) tradition of bird use among the Chumash and their ancestors, like other aspects of culture it was also fluid. As the human population increased, birds apparently became a more significant food source, at least in some areas, and a variety of hunting and trapping methods were devised. After Wild Turkeys were introduced to California in historic times, their feathers were quickly adopted for making the traditional style of dance headdresses.

When all these pieces are put together, there emerges a complex—though still incomplete—picture of Chumash interrelationships with birds. Ethnobiology is not restricted to the uses people make of other organisms but also how people think about the other creatures with whom they share their world: how they name and classify them, weave stories about them, how each is intertwined with the other, and how their actions affect one another. For the Chumash, birds were sustainers of life, providers of materials for daily use and in religious practices, key players in the world before humans, symbols in art and ritual, and links between the worlds of earth and sky. We hope this study contributes to a deeper understanding of California Indian peoples and their long presence as part of the environment.

Postscript: Birds and Chumash People Today

Indigenous cultural traditions have changed over the course of history, beginning with Spanish explorations in the 16th century, through the Mission Period 1779–1834, followed by Mexican ranchos and American colonization. Still the Chumash have survived. Several thousand people of Chumash descent live in their ancestral homeland today. Most live dispersed among non-Indian communities but their identity is important to them.

Both of us have long relationships with many Chumash individuals as colleagues and friends. We are often invited to public festivals, private gatherings, and occasions of personal significance. Representatives of Chumash families and communities serve on the California Indian Advisory Committee at the Santa Barbara Museum of Natural History. We are honored to have their trust and be part of their lives.

Because of these personal relationships rather than formal fieldwork, we have observed that, although birds are less interwoven with everyday life now than in their ancestors' day, many Chumash descendants continue to hold birds in special regard. At cultural programs and ceremonial gatherings, for example, an eagle feather fan is often used to spread the smoke of burning sage for ritual purification.

Since the 1970s, Chumash people have begun to perform many of the dances again and to make their own regalia, largely based on the information that Harrington had recorded from their forebears. Among the first of these practitioners were Antonio Romero (Chumash) and his associate Pete Zavalla (Comanche), who developed a Crane Dance in which they blew bird-bone whistles while re-creating the movements of Sandhill Cranes. On being queried about its origin, Romero told the senior author that he had received this dance in a dream (pers. comm. 1977).

Feathers are still used in dance regalia, although permit requirements and legal restrictions on ownership of feathers of most wild birds have necessitated substitution of commercial turkey feathers in many instances. One notable exception occurred when Antonio Romero was granted a federal permit for ceremonial use of California Condor feathers molted from captive and wild birds. In re-creating the Condor Dance, Romero fashioned the feathers into a semblance of the whole skin which he wrapped around his body, holding the wings on his outstretched arms so that it seemed to fly. He performed this dramatic, culturally meaningful dance before a spellbound audience at the Santa Barbara Museum of Natural History in 1992. Plains-style feathered regalia are also prevalent at pan-Indian powwows in which Chumash people participate, but increasingly they are proudly donning more traditional dress from their own culture in these dances.

Language revival programs are instilling bird names into everyday thought. The stories that Chumash ancestors told to Harrington are still being kept alive too, in teaching of children and through public cultural presentations. *Coyote* and his red head may be brought to mind whenever people hear the sound of an *Acorn Woodpecker* laughing. If they observe an eclipse of the sun or moon, they speak of the giant *Eagle* that holds up the sky, who must be tired and is stretching his wings.

Acknowledgments

This paper is a considerably revised and augmented version of one presented at the Society of Ethnobiology 22nd annual conference in Oaxaca in 1999. We thank Paul Collins, Dan Guthrie, Javier Rivera, Steve Timbrook, the two anonymous reviewers, and especially the thoughtful editors Dana Lepofsky and Marsha Quinlan, whose invaluable suggestions made it a much better paper than it started out to be.

At my first Ethnobiology Conference in Tucson in 1980, Amadeo Rea gave a compelling presentation on the value of film in documenting cultural practices involving human relationships with plants, in this case arrow-making among the Pima. Since then, I have attended every annual conference of the Society of Ethnobiology and my admiration for Amadeo has continued to grow over these many years. Ethnobotany, ethnoecology, linguistics, taxonomy, folk mammalogy and ornithology, always combined with unfailing respect for his indigenous teachers and collaborators—these only begin to list his contributions to our field. With his wide-ranging interests, keen insight, thorough scholarship, infectious enthusiasm, and supreme kindness, Amadeo has been one of the key people who have altered the course of many peoples' lives in inspiring us to become ethnobiologists. We can hardly thank him enough for the adventures that resulted.   —JT

References Cited

Applegate, Richard. 1974   Chumash Placenames. *Journal of California Anthropology* 1(2):187–205.

Applegate, Richard. 1975   An Index of Chumash Placenames. In Papers on the Chumash. Occasional Paper No. 9, pp. 19–46. San Luis Obispo County Archaeological Society, San Luis Obispo, CA.

Applegate, Richard. 1978   *'Atishwin:* The Dream Helper in South-Central California. Ballena Press Anthropological Papers No. 13. Ballena Press, Socorro, NM.

Applegate, Richard. 2007 *Samala-English Dictionary: A Guide to the Samala Language of the Ineseño Chumash People*. Santa Ynez Band of Chumash Indians, Santa Ynez, CA.

Arnold, Jeanne E. (ed.). 2001 *The Origins of a Pacific Coast Chiefdom: The Chumash of the Channel Islands*. University of Utah Press, Salt Lake City.

Bates, Craig D. 1983 The California Collection of I.G. Voznesenski. *American Indian Art* 8(3):36–41, 79.

Bates, Craig D., Janet A. Hamber, and Martha J. Lee. 1993 The California Condor and California Indians. *American Indian Art* 19(1):40–47.

Berger, Rainer, and Willard F. Libby. 1966 UCLA Radiocarbon Dates V. *Radiocarbon* 8:467–497.

Berlin, Brent. 1992 *Ethnobiological Classification: Principles of Categorization of Plants and Animals in Traditional Societies*. Princeton University Press, Princeton, NJ.

Berlin, Brent, and John P. O'Neil. 1981 The Pervasiveness of Onomatopoeia in Aguaruna and Huambisa Bird Names. *Journal of Ethnobiology* 1(2):238–261.

Blackburn, Thomas C. 1975 *December's Child: A Book of Chumash Oral Narratives*. University of California Press, Berkeley.

Braje, Todd J. 2010 *Modern Oceans, Ancient Sites: Archaeology and Marine Conservation on San Miguel Island, California*. University of Utah Press, Salt Lake City.

Brown, Alan K. 1967 Aboriginal Population of the Santa Barbara Channel. University of California Archaeological Survey Reports 69:1–99.

Collins, Paul W. 2009 Historic and Prehistoric Record for the Occurrence of Island Scrub-jays (*Aphelocoma insularis*) on the Northern Channel Islands, Santa Barbara County, California. Technical Reports No. 5. Santa Barbara Museum of Natural History, Santa Barbara, CA.

Collins, Paul W., and Lee Jones. 2012 A Checklist of the Birds of the California Channel Islands. Santa Barbara Museum of Natural History, Santa Barbara, CA (in press).

Colten, Roger H. 2001 Ecological and Economic Analysis of Faunal Remains from Santa Cruz Island. In *The Origins of a Pacific Coast Chiefdom: The Chumash of the Channel Islands*, ed. Jeanne E. Arnold, pp. 199–219. University of Utah Press, Salt Lake City.

Cook, Sherburne F. 1976 *The Population of California Indians, 1769–1970*. University of California Press, Berkeley.

Corbett, Ray. 2004 Chumash Bone Whistles: The Development of Ceremonial Integration in Chumash Society. In *Foundations of Chumash Complexity*, ed. Jeanne E. Arnold, pp. 65–73. Perspectives in California Archaeology, Vol. 7. Cotsen Institute of Archaeology, University of California, Los Angeles.

Costansó, Miguel. 1911 Diary of Miguel Costansó: The Portolá Expedition of 1769–70, ed. Frederick J. Teggart. Publications of the Academy of Pacific Coast History 2(4). University of California, Berkeley.

Cessac, Leon de. 1951   Observations on the Sculptured Stone Fetishes in Animal Form Discovered on San Nicolas Island (California). Archaeological Survey Report 12:1–6. University of California, Berkeley.

Dawson, Lawrence, and James Deetz. 1965   A Corpus of Chumash Basketry. Archaeological Survey Annual Report 7:193–276. University of California, Los Angeles.

Elsasser, Albert B., and Robert F. Heizer. 1963   The Archaeology of Bowers Cave, Los Angeles County, California. Archaeological Survey Report 59:1–60. University of California, Berkeley.

Erlandson, Jon M. 1994   *Early Hunter-Gatherers of the California Coast.* Plenum Press, New York.

Erlandson, Jon M., Douglas J. Kennett, B. Lynn Ingram, Daniel A. Guthrie, Don P. Morris, Mark A. Tveskov, G. James West, and Phillip L. Walker. 1996   An Archaeological and Paleontological Chronology for Daisy Cave (CA-SMI-261), San Miguel Island, California. *Radiocarbon* 38(2):355–373.

Erlandson, Jon M., Torben C. Rick, Todd J. Braje, Molly Casperson, Brian Culleton, Brendan Fulfrost, Tracy Garcia, Daniel A. Guthrie, Nicholas Jew, Douglas J. Kennett, Madonna L. Moss, Leslie Reeder, Craig Skinner, Jack Watts, and Lauren Willis. 2011   PaleoIndian Seafaring, Maritime Technologies, and Coastal Foraging on California's Channel Islands. *Science* 331:1183–1185.

Forth, Gregory. 2011   What's in a Bird's Name: Relationships among Ethno-ornithological Terms in Nage and other Malayo-Polynesian Languages. In *Ethno-ornithology: Birds, Indigenous Peoples Culture and Society*, ed. Sonia Tidemann and Andrew Gosler, pp. 224–237. Earthscan, London and Washington, DC.

Gamble, Lynn H. 2008   *The Chumash World at European Contact: Power, Trade, and Feasting among Complex Hunter-Gatherers.* University of California Press, Los Angeles.

Gifford, Edward W. 1940   California Bone Artifacts. Anthropological Records 3:153–237. University of California, Berkeley.

Glassow, Michael A. 1996   *Purisimeño Chumash Prehistory: Maritime Adaptations along the Southern California Coast.* Harcourt Brace College Publishers, Orlando FL.

Glassow, Michael A., Lynn H. Gamble, Jennifer E. Perry, and Glenn S. Russell. 2007.   Prehistory of the Northern California Bight and the Adjacent Transverse Ranges. In *California Prehistory: Colonization, Culture, and Complexity*, eds. Terry L. Jones and Kathryn A. Klar, pp. 191–213. AltaMira Press, Lanham, NY.

Glassow, Michael A., Jennifer E. Perry, and Peter F. Paige. 2008   The Punta Arena Site: Early and Middle Holocene Cultural Development on Santa Cruz Island. Contributions in Anthropology No. 3. Santa Barbara Museum of Natural History, Santa Barbara, CA.

Golla, Victor. 2011   *California Indian Languages.* University of California Press, Berkeley.

Grant, Campbell. 1964   Chumash Artifacts Collected in Santa Barbara County, California. Archaeological Survey Reports 63:1–44. University of California, Berkeley.

Grant, Campbell. 1993   *The Rock Paintings of the Chumash*. Santa Barbara Museum of Natural History, Santa Barbara, CA.

Groark, Kevin. 1996   Ritual and Therapeutic Use of "Hallucinogenic" Harvester Ants (*Pogonomyrmex*) in Native South-central California. *Journal of Ethnobiology* 16(1):1–29.

Guthrie, Daniel A. 1980   Analysis of Avifaunal and Bat Remains from Midden Sites on San Miguel Island. In *The California Islands: Proceedings of a Multidisciplinary Symposium*, ed. D.M. Power, pp. 689–702. Santa Barbara Museum of Natural History, Santa Barbara, CA.

Guthrie, Daniel A. 1993a   New Information on the Prehistoric Fauna of San Miguel Island, California. In *Third California Islands Symposium: Recent Advances in Research on the California Islands*, ed. F.G. Hochberg, pp. 405–416. Santa Barbara Museum of Natural History, Santa Barbara, CA.

Guthrie, Daniel A. 1993b   Listen to the Birds? The Use of Avian Remains in Channel Islands Archaeology. In *Archaeology on the Northern Channel Islands: Studies of Subsistence, Economics, and Social Organization*, ed. Michael A. Glassow, pp. 153–167. Coyote Press Archives of California Prehistory No. 34, Coyote Press, Salinas, CA.

Guthrie, Daniel A. 1998   Avian Remains in Archaeological Sites. Presentation to Santa Barbara County Archaeological Society, 4 May 1998.

Harrington, John P. 1942   Cultural Element Distributions: XIX, Central California Coast. Anthropological Records 7(1):1–46. University of California, Berkeley.

Harrington, John P. 1986   *The Papers of John P. Harrington in the Smithsonian Institution 1907–1957, Vol. 3: Native American History, Language and Culture of Southern California/Basin*, eds. Elaine Mills and Ann J. Brickfield. Kraus International Publications, Reels 1–96, Millwood, NY.

Heizer, Robert F., and Albert B. Elsasser, eds. 1973   *Original Accounts of the Lone Woman of San Nicolas Island*. Ballena Press, Ramona, CA.

Henshaw, Henry W. 1955   California Indian Linguistic Records: The Mission Indian Vocabularies of H.W. Henshaw, ed. Robert F. Heizer. Anthropological Records 15(2). University of California, Berkeley.

Henshaw, Henry W. 1885   The Aboriginal Relics Called "Sinkers" or "Plummets." *American Journal of Archaeology* 1(2):105–114.

Hildebrandt, William R. 2004   *Xonxon'ata, in the Tall Oaks: Archaeology and Ethnohistory of a Chumash Village in the Santa Ynez Valley*. Contributions in Anthropology No. 2. Santa Barbara Museum of Natural History, Santa Barbara, CA.

Howard, Hildegard, and Leigh Marian Dodson. 1933   Bird Remains from an Indian Shellmound near Point Mugu, California. *Condor* 35(6):235.

Hudson, Travis. 1982   *Guide to Painted Cave*. McNally & Loftin, Santa Barbara, CA.

Hudson, Travis, and Thomas C. Blackburn. 1982   The Material Culture of the Chumash Interaction Sphere, Vol. 1: Food Procurement and Transportation. Anthropological Papers No. 25. Ballena Press, Los Altos, CA.

Hudson, Travis, and Thomas C. Blackburn. 1983   The Material Culture of the Chumash Interaction Sphere, Vol. 2: Food Preparation and Shelter. Anthropological Papers No. 27. Ballena Press, Los Altos, CA.

Hudson, Travis, and Thomas C. Blackburn. 1985   The Material Culture of the Chumash Interaction Sphere, Vol. 3: Clothing, Ornamentation, and Grooming. Anthropological Papers No. 28. Ballena Press, Menlo Park, CA.

Hudson, Travis, and Thomas C. Blackburn. 1986   The Material Culture of the Chumash Interaction Sphere, Vol. 4: Ceremonial Paraphernalia, Games, and Amusements. Anthropological Papers No. 30. Ballena Press, Menlo Park, CA.

Hudson, Travis, and Thomas C. Blackburn. 1987   The Material Culture of the Chumash Interaction Sphere, Vol. 5: Manufacturing Processes, Metrology, and Trade. Anthropological Papers No. 31. Ballena Press, Menlo Park, CA.

Hudson, Travis, Thomas Blackburn, Rosario Curletti, and Janice Timbrook, eds. 1977   *The Eye of the Flute: Chumash Traditional History and Ritual as Told by Fernando Librado Kitsepawit to John P. Harrington.* Santa Barbara Museum of Natural History, Santa Barbara, CA.

Hudson, Travis, Janice Timbrook, and Melissa Rempe. 1978   *Tomol:* Chumash Watercraft as Described in the Ethnographic Notes of John P. Harrington. Anthropological Papers No. 9. Ballena Press, Socorro, NM.

Hudson, Travis, and Ernest Underhay. 1978   Crystals in the Sky: An Intellectual Odyssey Involving Chumash Astronomy, Cosmology, and Rock Art. Anthropological Papers No. 10. Ballena Press, Socorro, NM.

Johnson, John R. 1988   Chumash Social Organization: An Ethnohistoric Perspective. Ph.D. dissertation (Anthropology). University of California, Santa Barbara.

Johnson, John R. 1999   The Chumash Social-Political Groups on the Channel Islands. In Cultural Affiliation and Lineal Descent of Chumash Peoples in the Channel Islands and the Santa Monica Mountains, eds. Sally McLendon and John R. Johnson, pp. 51–66. Report prepared for the Archeology and Ethnography Program, National Park Service, Washington, DC. Department of Anthropology, Hunter College, City University of New York, and Santa Barbara Museum of Natural History, Santa Barbara, CA.

Johnson, John R., Brian M. Kemp, Cara Monroe, and Joseph G. Lorenz. 2012   A Land of Diversity: Genetic Insights into Ancestral Origins. In *Contemporary Issues in California Archaeology*, eds. Terry L. Jones and Jennifer E. Perry, pp. 49–72. Left Coast Press, Walnut Creek, CA.

Johnson, John R., and Joseph G. Lorenz. 2006   Genetics, Linguistics, and Prehistoric Migrations: An Analysis of California Indian Mitochondrial DNA Lineages. *Journal of California and Great Basin Anthropology* 26:33–64.

Johnson, John R., Thomas Stafford, Henry Ajie, and Don Morris. 2002   Arlington Springs Revisited. In *Proceedings of the Fifth California Islands Symposium*, eds. David Browne, Kathryn Mitchell, and Henry Chaney, pp. 541–545. Santa Barbara Museum of Natural History, Santa Barbara, CA.

Jones, T. L., J. F. Porcasi, J. M. Erlandson, H. Dallas, Jr., T. A. Wake, and R. Schwaderer. 2008   The Protracted Holocene Extinction of California's Flightless Sea Duck (*Chendytes lawi*) and its Implications for the Pleistocene Overkill Hypothesis. *Proceedings of the National Academy of Sciences USA* 105(11): 4105–4108. Available at: http://www.ncbi.nlm.nih.gov/pmc/articles/PMC2393816/?tool=pmcentrez (verified 25 January 2012).

Kennett, Douglas J. 2005   *The Island Chumash: Behavioral Ecology of a Maritime Society.* University of California Press, Berkeley.

King, Chester D. 1990.   *The Evolution of Chumash Society.* Garland Publishing, New York.

Krech, Shepard III. 2009   *Spirits of the Air: Birds & American Indians in the South.* University of Georgia Press, Athens, GA.

Landberg, Leif C.W. 1965   The Chumash Indians of Southern California. Southwest Museum Papers 19. Southwest Museum, Los Angeles.

Lightfoot, Kent G., and Otis Parrish. 2009   *California Indians and their Environment: An Introduction.* University of California Press, Berkeley and Los Angeles.

McCall, Lynne, and Rosalind Perry, eds. 2002   *California's Chumash Indians* (rev. ed.). EZ Nature Books, San Luis Obispo, CA.

McLendon, Sally. 2001   California Feather Blankets: Objects of Wealth and Status in Two Nineteenth-Century Worlds. In *Studies in American Indian Art: A Memorial Tribute to Norman Feder,* ed. Christian F. Feest, pp. 132–161. University of Washington, Seattle.

Merriam, C. Hart. 1979   Indian Names for Plants and Animals among Californian and Other Western North American Tribes, ed. Robert F. Heizer. Publications in Archaeology, Ethnology and History No. 14. Ballena Press, Socorro, NM.

Montes, Catarino. 1993   Oral History Interview by John R. Johnson, February 24, 1993, Fellows, California. Unpublished transcript, Department of Anthropology, Santa Barbara Museum of Natural History, Santa Barbara.

Orr, Phil C. 1947   Additional Californian Bone Artifact Types in the Santa Barbara Museum of Natural History. Anthropological Records 9:115–132. University of California, Berkeley.

Pinart, Alphonse. 1952   California Indian Linguistic Records: The Mission Indian Vocabularies of Alphonse Pinart, ed. R.F. Heizer. Anthropological Records 15(1):1–84. University of California, Berkeley.

Rea, Amadeo. 2007 *Wings in the Desert: A Folk Ornithology of the Northern Pimans.* University of Arizona Press, Tucson.

Schoenhals, Louise C. 1988 *A Spanish-English Glossary of Mexican Flora and Fauna.* Summer Institute of Linguistics, Mexico City.

Smith, Lillian. 1987 A Fourth Chumash Inscribed Basket with Designs from Spanish Colonial Coins. *Ventura County Historical Society Quarterly* 32(4):12–23.

Tidemann, Sonia, and Andrew Gosler, eds. 2010 *Ethno-ornithology: Birds, Indigenous Peoples, Culture and Society.* Earthscan, London and Washington, DC.

Timbrook, Jan. 2002 Search for the Source of the Sorcerers' Stones. In *Proceedings of the Fifth California Islands Symposium*, eds. David R. Brown, Kathryn C. Mitchell, and Henry W. Chaney, pp. 633–640. Santa Barbara Museum of Natural History, Santa Barbara, CA.

Ubelaker, Douglas H. 2006 Population Size: Contact to Nadir. In *Handbook of North American Indians*, vol. 3: Environment, Origins, Population, ed. Douglas H. Ubelaker, pp. 694–701. Smithsonian Institution, Washington, D.C.

Walker, Phillip L., and Travis Hudson. 1993 *Chumash Healing: Changing Health and Medical Practices in an American Indian Society.* Malki Museum Press, Banning, CA.

Whistler, Kenneth W. 1980 *An Interim Barbareño Chumash Dictionary.* Unpublished manuscript on file, Department of Anthropology, Santa Barbara Museum of Natural History, Santa Barbara, CA.

Yates, Lorenzo. 1890 Charm Stones: Notes on the So-Called "Plummets" or "Sinkers." *Bulletin of the Santa Barbara Society of Natural History* 1(2):13–28. [Reprinted, with revisions and additions, from: *Smithsonian Institution Annual Report for 1886 (pt. 1)*, pp. 296–305.]

Upland Salado Resource Use

Charmion R. McKusick[†]

Abstract

Recent publications have considered the A.D. 1225–1440 settlements of the Globe-Miami Arizona as atypical appendages of the Tonto Basin Salado. In contrast, this article presents evidences of resource use from Besh-Ba-Gowah (AZ V: 9:11 ASM) and Gila Pueblos (AZ V: 9:52 ASM), and their respective outliers, Pinal Pueblo and the Hagen Site, as more consistent with those of Mogollon ancestral pueblos. Bone and shell artifacts from ceremonial contexts, which are the same as those depicted on Mimbres pottery, indicate conservatism over long periods of time. Considerations of resource use, fluctuation in rainfall, and loss of population resulting from raiding, contribute to an understanding of the extended length of the Upland Salado occupation, and its eventual end.

Introduction

In recent years there has been some debate about the identity of the Upland Salado, those people living in the Globe-Miami region of Arizona, during the period between A.D. 1225–1440 (Lincoln 2000:24–25; Wood 2000:125–126). One argument is that the settlements of this region are atypical appendages of the Tonto Basin Salado, who built huge sites at a lower altitude in the vicinity of what is now Roosevelt Lake and Tonto Creek. This argument is based on a similarity of the smaller sites in the Tonto Basin to those in the Globe-Miami area, and on the production in both areas of the Salado Polychromes. I concur with Crown (1994), who argues for a regional Southwestern Cult, expressed in iconography painted on the Salado Polychromes, which are not indicators of a Salado cultural identity, but rather were produced by widely varying groups in the Southwest United States and northern Mexico. An alternative view, and one that is proposed here, is that the Upland Salado people of the Globe-Miami region utilized resources common to a higher altitude environment, and were part of an exchange network involving larger Mogollon ancestral pueblos.

I make the latter argument in this paper by presenting an overview of resource use by the Upland Salado people living along Pinal Creek on the southern edge of Globe, Arizona (Figure 1), between A.D. 1225 and the 1440s. I suggest that these data can be used to infer an oc-

---

† Southwest Bird Laboratory, 9025 South Kellner Canyon Road, Globe, Arizona 85501.
  Phone: 928-425-5051

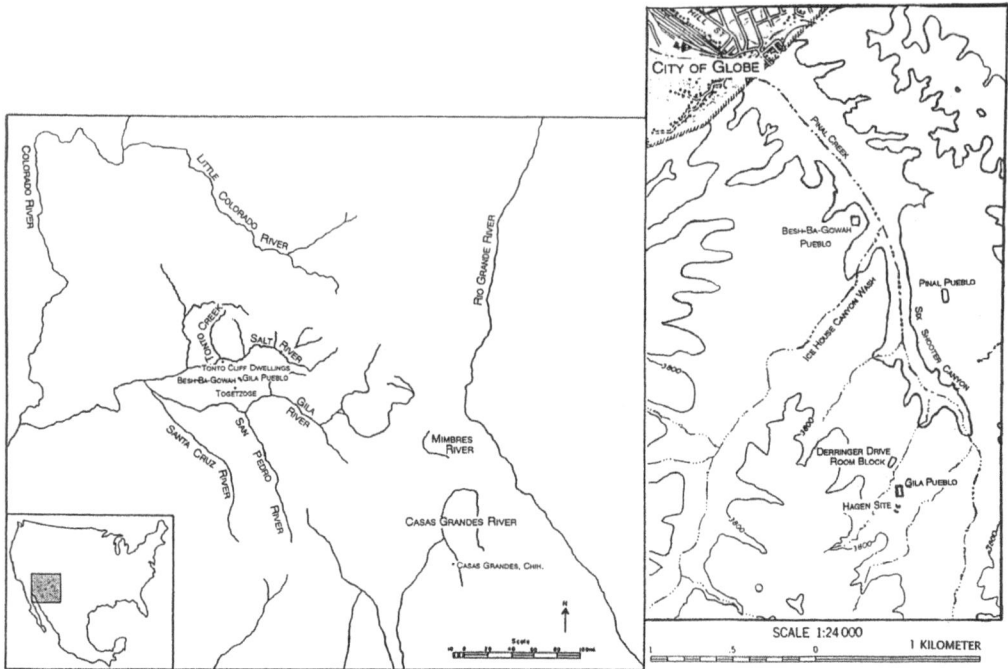

Figure 1. Location map. Left, general location of Upland Salado Sites. Right, detailed map of area, after McKusick and Young 1997:2.

cupational continuum influenced both by climatic ebb and flow, and by human activity, such as raiding, originating both within and without the immediate area. In particular, I review the evidence of resource use from Besh-Ba-Gowah (AZ V: 9:1 ASM) and Gila Pueblo (AZ V:9:52 ASM), and their outliers, Pinal Pueblo and the Hagen Site. The review focuses primarily on the use of vertebrate fauna, but I also briefly discuss the use of minerals, plants, and shells.

Besh-Ba-Gowah and Gila Pueblo are 200-room, hilltop room block structures located in east central Arizona north of the confluence of the San Pedro and Gila Rivers. They are located midway between the Gila River to the south and the Salt River to the north on the Pinal Creek Corridor (Figure 1). The trail between them, running from south to north up Dripping Springs Wash, across Pioneer Pass in the Pinal Mountains, and down Pinal Creek, is considered to be a trade route joining these rivers (Wood 2000:131). Besh-Ba-Gowah Archaeological Park is located at the confluence of Ice House Canyon Wash and Six Shooter Canyon Wash, which join to become Pinal Creek. Its outlier, Pinal Pueblo, is located across Six Shooter Canyon Wash, and slightly upstream. Gila Pueblo is located on the south side of Six Shooter Canyon Wash about 2 km upstream; its outlier, the Hagen Site was about a hundred meters farther upstream. Based on a combination of tree ring, archaeomagnetic, and radiocarbon dates (McKusick and Young 1997:14–23), and similarity in artifact styles among the sites, these four pueblos date between ca. 1225 to the mid 1400s. Gila Pueblo and the Hagen Site were probably the latest occupation of the area.

I begin the review by summarizing the resources, published and unpublished, which provide context for the discussion on the four sites considered in this paper. This is followed by reviews of ecological setting and of resource use at Besh-Ba-Gowah, Gila Pueblo, and their outliers. I discuss environment and warfare as factors, which contribute to the longevity of these sites on one hand, and to their final destruction on the other. Based on these data, I conclude the resources used at these four Upland Salado sites are more consistent with those of Mogollon ancestral pueblos than with Tonto Basin Salado.

Methods

This review of resource use is based on data from four sites in the Globe-Miami region. The data are of varying quality and quantity, but collectively, they provide insights on ancient resource used in the region.

The majority of the data in this review come from Besh-Ba-Gowah; much less comes from its outlier, Pinal Pueblo. In particular, Besh-Ba-Gowah data are derived from Irene S. Vickrey's excavation notes and photographs, all of which are on file at the Arizona State Museum, as well as a published source by the same author (1939:19–22). In addition, details presented in Vickrey's guided site tours come from personal communications with the late John Woody, and with Robert T. McKusick. Additional published sources used are Hohmann (1990), who outlines the history of the excavations, and summaries of the excavations at Besh-Ba-Gowah, Hohman (1992), Hohmann, Germick and Adams (1992), and Crary, Germick, and Golio (1992). There is no indication that Vickrey's excavations involved screening. The 1980s excavations employed ¼ inch (6.35 mm) mesh screens.

The only specimens I examined from Pinal Pueblo were those from high status burials given to me by pothunters. Boggess, Ajeman, Gilman, and Bozarth (1992:188–190) were able to determine, from surface room clearing, that the badly vandalized site was involved in the commercial production of shell jewelry.

Data from Gila Pueblo and its outlier, the Hagen Site, come from several sources. From Gila Pueblo, these include Harold Sterling Gladwin's unpublished results from the late 1930s, McGregor's (1945:423) brief summary of Gladwin's work, and the results of Joel L. Shiner's excavations of one room (Shiner 1961). Data from the Hagen Site come from John Nathan Young's salvage excavation of the Hagen Site in 1970 (McKusick and Young 1997). In the early 1970s, under the auspices of the Eastern Arizona College, I supervised excavations of a ceremonial/redistribution complex consisting of 12 rooms on the southern margin of the site (McKusick and Young 1997). Alan Ferg, of the Arizona State Museum, completed the excavation of a 13th room in 1974. The later excavations used primarily ¼ inch (6.35 mm) mesh screens. Sediments from occupation surfaces were screened with small mesh (4-mesh, [4.7 mm]). No flotation samples were collected. Given the use of large screens, and the absence of flotation, this review of the faunal and botanical remains is biased towards larger specimens.

I identified all the large carbonized specimens by comparing them with plants growing in the area today and with comparative specimens at Boyce Thompson Arboretum, Superior, Arizona. The Dendrochronology Laboratory at the University of Arizona identified the carbonized wood. Ronna J. Bradley (1999:213–228) presents a clear appraisal of Upland Salado Shell usage, which supports her inclusion of these sites in the Casas Grandes Trade Network.

In addition to these published excavations, which vary considerably in time, methods, and available technology, artifacts of local origin treasured in family collections for generations are occasionally donated to local museums, or brought for me to see. The most active local pothunter was William Underwood who excavated over 1000 burials on private land for a share of the proceeds of marketable pottery. It was he who established that Salado Red and San Carlos Red-on-Brown were preferred burial offering from the pre-polychrome beginning to the end of the occupation.

The ages of Gila Pueblo, Besh-Ba-Gowah, and their outliers are derived from a variety of sources. Gladwin's tree ring date analysis from Gila Pueblo date a major reconstruction following a fire at ca. 1345, and another at ca. 1385 (Gladwin, pers. comm. ca. 1972). Matting preserved in ash resulting from a devastating general fire following an attack on Gila Pueblo yielded a radiocarbon date of ca. 1260. An archaeomagnetic date of a hearth, which was sealed following what appears to be the same fire, was also dated ca. 1260. Archaeomagnetic dates of hearths in use at the time of the final destruction by fire are ca. 1440–1447 for Gila Pueblo and the Hagen Site (McKusick and Young 1997:14). Comparative ceramic end dates for all four sites are coherent, indicating an occupation extending from ca. 1225 to the mid 1400s. Polychrome pottery found at Pinal Pueblo was manufactured between 1300 and 1450 (Lyons 2004:373, 379; Wood 1987:42–46).

Late rooms built on to the south end of Gila Pueblo include a suite of four adobe walled rooms, one of which contained a watermelon-shaped bowl, and several others bearing the gaudy Tonto Polychrome designs characteristic of Pinal Pueblo. Big stone-based jacal, single-family rooms, built even later, contained large Cliff Polychrome bowls painted with designs characteristic of Besh-Ba-Gowah. Thus, it appears that Gila Pueblo and the Hagen Site were probably the latest Salado occupation of the area.

Ecological Setting

Besh-Ba-Gowah is located in the southern outskirts of the City of Globe on a hilltop just downstream from the junction of Ice House Canyon Wash and Pinal Creek (Figure 1). Gila Pueblo, and its outlier the Hagen Site, lie almost two kilometers up Six Shooter Canyon from Besh-Ba-Gowah on a gentle slope overlooking Pinal Creek. The pueblos are situated in the foothills on the northern slope of the Pinal Mountains. Long ridges extend from the mountains in a generally northerly direction, formed by canyons cut by washes and streams such as Ice House Canyon and Kellner Washes and Pinal Creek, which ran all year until 1929 when the canyons were drained by the accidental flooding of the Old Dominion Copper Mine.

On the sunny side of the canyons are grasses, Desert Prickly-pear Cactus (*Opuntia engelmannii* Salm-Dyck ex Engelm.), Cane Cholla (*Opuntia spinosior* Engelm.), Barrel Cactus (*Ferocactus wislizeni* (Engelm.) Britt. & Rose), Engelmann's Hedgehog Cactus (*Echinocereus engelmannii* (Parry ex Engelm.) Lem.), Squaw Bush (*Rhus trilobata* Nutt.), Algerita (*Berberis haematocarpa* Wooton), Palmer's Agave (*Agave palmeri* Engelm.), Banana Yucca (*Yucca baccata* Torr.), Black-tailed Jackrabbits (*Lepus californicus*), and Black-tailed Deer (*Odocoileus hemionus*). Across the canyon, where it is less sunny, are scrub oaks or Emory Oak (*Quercus emoryi* Torr.), Common Sotol (*Dasylirion wheeleri* S. Watson ex Rothr.), rabbits (*Sylvilagus* sp.), and White-tailed Deer (*Odocoileus virginianus*). Velvet Mesquite (*Prosopis velutina* Woot.) Net-leafed Hackberry (*Celtis reticulata* Torr.), Arizona Sycamore (*Platanus wrightii* S. Watson), Arizona Black Walnut (*Juglans major* (Torr.) A. Heller), elderberry (*Sambucus mexicana* Presl.), and wild grapes (*Vitis arizonica* Engelm.), grow next to the streams in the deep, rich, black soil of the canyon bottoms. Before the introduction of cattle, common reed (*Phragmites australis* (Cav.) Trin.) grew in quantity. Herbaceous food plants include Cat-tails, locally known as Tules (*Scirpus* sp.), amaranth (*Amaranth* sp.), goosefoot (*Chenopodium* sp.), Purslane (*Portulaca retusa* Engelm.), and Devil's Claw (*Martynia* sp.). Medicinals such as datura (*Datura wrightii* Regel.), tobacco (*Nicotiana* sp.), Prickly Poppy (*Argemone intermedia* Sweet), a slender gray wormwood (*Artemesia* sp.), and Mountain Evening Primrose (*Oenothera hookeri* Torr. & Gray) also flourish. Grasslands above the pueblos provided Juniper (*Juniperus monosperma* (Engelm.) Sarg.), and Piñon Pine (*Pinus edulis* Engelm.). Yellow pine (*Pinus ponderosa* Lawson), grows on the slopes of the Pinal Mountains (Baldwin 1965:58–63, 77; McKusick and Young 1997:61; Rätsch 2005:61–63; Rea 1997:103, 205; Tagg 1985:24–26; Welles 1964:13–24).

The region is well-watered. The streams in the canyons where the pueblos are situated likely ran all year round. In addition, three former Salado reservoirs may still be seen on the surface. They were in use as late as the early 1950s (Carman Blalack, pers. comm. 1954).

Along the base of the north slope of the Pinal Mountains runs the Miami Fault. This is a very active fault, which causes cracks in houses and walls in the area even today. It also produced fine, brown-firing pottery clay by its movement over thousands of years. Seams in the fault supply creamy white kaolin, and colorful metallic oxides, some of which may be mined, ground, and painted on Salado-type pottery without further alteration. There is turquoise mineralization throughout the area.

The altitude of Besh-Ba-Gowah and Gila Pueblos is about 1160 m. The Pinal Mountains rise to about 2135 m, and accumulate snow which was sufficient to supply small canyon bottom streams throughout the year. The last frost in the spring is about the first week of

May, and the first killing frost in the fall comes at the end of October. The foothills receive an average of about 41 cm of rainfall per year, but this can vary widely. While ditch irrigation is very successful, dry farming is not a practical endeavor.

The area is ideal for hunting and for gathering wild foods, and also provided firewood, juniper and pine for framing, and, in prehistoric times, common reed for roofing. Differences in solar exposure and in altitude provide a great deal of variety of resources available in close proximity to the pueblos. In addition, it is possible to descend a short distance into a more desert environment for resources not locally available, and also to follow a maturing harvest of natural foods to a higher altitude on the slopes of the nearby mountains.

Resource Use at Besh-Ba-Gowah and Gila Pueblo and their Outliers

In the following sections, I summarize the evidence for the use of minerals, plants, insects, shell, and a variety of terrestrial and aquatic vertebrate fauna. Both because of the data available, and because of my zooarchaeological interests, the review is largely focused on vertebrate fauna. While there is quantitative data for the fauna, the other information is qualitative.

Minerals

Jon Nathan Young presents a detailed analysis of lithic materials and artifacts recovered from the Hagen Site, which is representative of mineral usage at all four sites (McKusick and Young 1997:40–79).

Clay from the Miami Fault was used in the local Salado Red and Salado Polychromes. These were decorated with a naturally occurring creamy-white kaolin slip and a kaolin and red ochre mixture, both of which run in veins adjacent to the clay and can be used as mined without further preparation. The black color on Salado pottery is often organic, but firing tests performed by Robert T. McKusick indicate that mixtures of locally available magnetite and manganese dioxide were added to deepen the color.

A large room in the ceremonial/redistribution complex was given over to the manufacture of substantial quantities of finely ground pigments, which were packaged in fragments of cotton cloth. These included red, yellow, and black iron oxides (hematite, limonite, and magnetite); blue and green copper oxides (azurite and malachite); and a brilliant white, ground from crystalline selenite. The space devoted to pigment production, the grinding stones found, and the quantity of ground pigments imply that they were trade items. Local usage included thick impastos of red, blue, and green painted on baskets, on arrow shafts, and on wands included in high status burials. Vickrey notes that green pigment covered the top of the head of some high status female burials. Cockle shells painted on the exterior with blue azurite were found in ceremonial contexts (McKusick and Young 1997:82–84).

Local turquoise was made into tabular and disc beads, and tesserae for mosaic. Disc beads were ground from Pinal Schist, argillite, and steatite. Beads in the shape of amphibians, snakes, birds, mammals, and humans (Figure 2), as well as small to tiny figurines, were carved from argillite, serpentine, and steatite (Cheek 1994:137). A tiny figurine was carved in the shape of a Javelina, even though there are no Javelina bones represented in the southwestern archaeological record. Javelinas were present at Hispanic Contact in 1699 in the Sacaton area on the Gila (Rea 1998:237), but did not cross the Salt River in Upper Gila Country until 1916–1918 (Gila County ranchers, pers. comm. 1968). This species, like several others, is in the process of northern invasion. Apparently a local stone-carver traveled south far enough to become familiar with the species, and memorialized his trip by carving the unusual animal. The most beautiful stone bead of all is a green parrot pierced so it hangs from its cord by its beak.

Figure 2. Mimbres and Salado costumes and jewelry. Upper Left: man in bat costume with hair pins—Mimbres Polychrome bowl, after Cosgrove and Cosgrove 1932:Plate 212. Upper Right: woman wearing an apron overlaid with a shell bead stomacher—Mimbres Black-on-White bowl, after Bradfield 1929:Plate 79, No. 364. Center: argillite deer-masked human bead – local unprovenanced , scale: x1.Lower Left: Tonto Polychrome male effigy jar—Gila Pueblo, ca. 1440. Lower Right: Pinto Polychrome masked personage bowl—Besh-Ba-Gowah, dating between 1275 and 1325.

Apparent ceremonial use of stone is suggested by chalcedony and agate "desert rose" formations found in medicine pouches, quantities of quartz crystals, and a selenite crystal 40 cm long recovered from the ceremonial/redistribution center at Gila Pueblo. The Besh-Ba-Gowah collection includes a stalactite shaped like a flying goose, and fossil brachiopods.

A 19.4 cm long leaf-shaped, Tiger Chert, "wood grain" biface was recovered from a ceremonial setting at Gila Pueblo. It is one of eight such bifaces known from a scattering of Central Arizona sites dating to the 1300s and early 1400s. Its most probable origin is southeastern Utah or southwestern Colorado (Ferg 1988:214–218; McKusick and Young 1997:24, 55, 103).

Plants

As a result of the extensive burning associated with the final raid on Gila Pueblo, ca. 1440, plant remains are abundant at that pueblo. Since there was no systematic collection of flotation samples, the remains from Gila Pueblo and Besh-Ba-Gowah are the only botanical remains recovered at the four sites. The absence of fine-screening and flotation means that the inventory of remains is biased towards large specimens.

Among the remains recovered at Gila pueblo, carbonized specimens of domestic crops are particularly abundant. Most common was corn (*Zea mays* L.), with cotton seed, (*Gossypium hirsutum* L.), in almost equal volume, and Tepary Beans (*Phaseolus acutifolius* A. Gray var. acutifolius), bulking a little less. Single specimens of Sieva Beans (*Phaseolus lunatus*), and common beans (*Phaseolus vulgaris* L.), and Winter Squash (*Cucurbita* sp. L.), rinds and stems survived. Pumpkin (*Cucurbita moschata* Duchesne) effigy vessels were recovered from Besh-Ba-Gowah burials (Rea 1997:306, 321, 325, 327, 344; Vickrey burial notes).

At the time of the final fire at Gila Pueblo, corn on the cob was drying on the roof, and stored in a large jar. Shelled corn from a small jar was being ground on a metate situated on the roof, with the fine meal caught in a small bowl. Six kernels of corn were included with other items in a cotton medicine pouch tied to the right side of the belt of a high status male, and a large boot pot filled with shelled corn rested on the floor of an arrow-making room above the ceremonial room. A very large Gila Polychrome bowl with an allover, interior design of small, stylized flying bird motifs was spattered with carbonized gruel.

Although the raid was too early in the season for the cotton harvest, an entire upper story room in the ceremonial/redistribution complex at Gila Pueblo was filled with cotton in the boll, apparently left unspun from the previous year. Cotton was most commonly made into undecorated plain weave cloth, but there were also coarse twills, and twills woven in multi-colored stripes. A Tonto Polychrome human effigy jar, depicting a patterned shawl, loincloth, medicine pouch, and footless stockings (Figure 2), demonstrates the wide use of cloth. Cotton in the boll, as string, and as woven cloth are important in the manufacture of ceremonial paraphernalia used by the Katsina Cult, which was known at Besh-Ba-Gowah between 1275 and 1325 A.D., as indicated by the depiction of a katsina mask on a Pinto Polychrome bowl manufactured during that period (Figure 2; Clark and Reed 2011:253). The Upland Salados, who did not participate in the Katsina Cult, may still have supplied cotton for Katsina Cult paraphernalia. Cotton seed probably provided an important dietary supplement high in protein and oil (McKusick and Young 1997:99; Rea 1997:71, 309).

A variety of other wild plants were used for food and other purposes. Juniper posts supported pine roof framing, covered with reeds and adobe. A rectangular cradleboard was made from common reed, and matting was plaited from yucca and twined from Squaw Bush stems. Agave was an important source of food and fiber, as indicated by carbonized specimens of cordage, by the presence of earth ovens, and by the high number of mescal knives recovered from the 1970s excavations, totaling more than one per room at Gila Pueblo, and more than two per room at the Hagen Site (McKusick and Young 1997:41–49). The only other wild food part recovered at Gila Pueblo was a walnut shell.

Plants were used in a variety of contexts at the pueblos. Datura may have been used in some form. This is suggested as indicated by the presence on the floor of Gila Pueblo ceremonial complex Room 103 of a small Tonto Polychrome jar that is painted with representations of a spiny datura seedpod. This representation is identical to datura icons from Hawikuh (Smith et al. 1966:Figure 49, Plate 22; Figure 3).

Ferg recovered a tubular stone pipe from room 111 at Gila Pueblo[1] that appears to be a tobacco pipe (Alan Ferg, pers. comm.). Native tobacco in large quantities is potent enough to allow a shaman to enter a trance so deep that pulse and respiration are imperceptible (Van Pool and Van Pool 2006:81–84). Tobacco may also be laced with parts of plants such as datura, Prickly Poppy, and artemisia, for added effect (Rätsch 1998).

Insects

No insect parts were recovered at Gila Pueblo, but there is indirect evidence of their use and importance. A brilliant red fiber apron worn by a high status woman was protected from fire by a shell bead stomacher, and sealed from deterioration by ash. The color was much too bright for any vegetal colorant, and was definitely not red iron oxide. Cochineal insects are still common near the pueblos, and are the most probable source of the dye. In addition to the fiber apron, a hawk moth is depicted in the center of a Gila Polychrome bowl recovered from Besh-Ba-Gowah (Figure 3), and also on a Tonto Polychrome canteen Jar (Figure 4).

Shells

A variety of shell taxa were recovered from Besh-Ba-Bowah, Gila Pueblo, and Hagen Site (Table 1). The destruction of Pinal Pueblo by pothunters was so complete, that shell refuse was noted but not collected. No shellfish taxa at any of these sites resulted from food production. Instead, all represent shell bead production and elite artifacts made from imported shell, almost all of which came from the Gulf of Lower California. Shell artifacts were produced for trade at the Upland Salado pueblos, as indicated by the large quantities of debitage at each of the four sites. According to Bradley (1999:213–228), based on the large quantity of

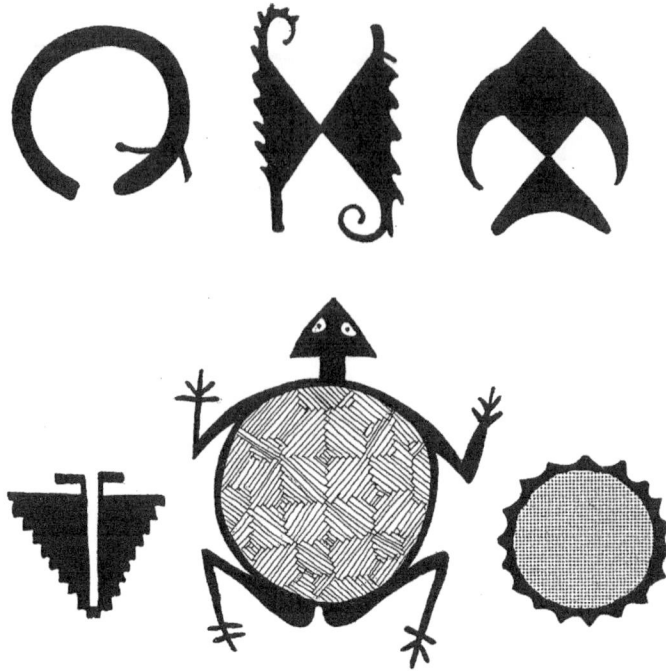

Figure 3. Life forms depicted on Salado pottery. Top (left to right): skink, opposed parrots, swallow—Gila Polychrome, Besh-Ba-Gowah. Bottom (left to right): hawk moth, frog/turtle/horned lizard—Gila Polychrome, Besh-Ba-Gowah; datura pod—Tonto Polychrome jar, Gila Pueblo, ca. 1440.

shell production at Gila Pueblo, the Upland Salado sites lie within the Casas Grandes Shell Distribution Network.

No ordinary inhabitants killed in the final attack at Gila Pueblo wore any jewelry. However, shell jewelry helped identify seven high status persons slain during the final attack. Particularly conspicuous were a 6–7000 *Laevicardiuim* shell disc bead stomacher, and a heavy graduated shell necklace worn by women. Also found was a *Nassarius* shell bracelet on a male left wrist. These bracelets are thought to be associated with warrior status (Fulton and Tuthill 1940:38). Besh-Ba-Gowah burial notes indicate necklaces of mixed disc and tabular beads, some with pendants. The burial of valuable jewelry with tiny infants suggests that it is "house jewelry," rather than personal property of the deceased. House jewelry among modern western pueblo peoples is owned by members of a matrilineage. Such items are not worn as every day adornment, but are available to dress family members, ranging from very old to very young, when they are costumed for a ceremonial occasion such as a Hopi Butterfly Dance (personal observation, 1966).

Fish, Amphibians, and Reptiles

The streams in the canyons where the pueblos are situated ran all year round, and there were three Salado reservoirs still in use as late as the early 1950s. All amphibian and reptile

Figure 4. a. Unprovenienced Tonto Polychrome canteen jar depicting hawk moth larva with horn curving to left and one eyespot on body. b. Same vessel, turned one quarter counter clockwise, showing adult hawk moth between hatching on rim. Photographs by Robert T. McKusick. Courtesy of Bullion Plaza Museum, Miami, Arizona.

Table 1. Upland Salado faunal identifications by species and minimum number of individuals count.

Species	Besh-Ba-Gowah	Gila Pueblo	Hagen Site	Total
MARINE SHELL, CALIFORNIA PROVINCE				
Haliotis, sp.	5	1		6
MARINE SHELL PANAMIC PROVICE				
Unidentified shell, mostly beads	20, 13*			20, 13*
Marine Tube Worm.—	1	1		2
Gastropods.—				
Turritella leucostoma Valenciennes	7	1		8
Hexaplex brassica Lamark "trumpet"		1		1
Melongena patula Broderip & Sowerby "trumpet"		1		1
Strombus sp.	1			1
Nassarius iodes Dall	4	2, ca. 35*		41
Oliva spicata Röding (carved)		1		1
Olivella sp.	32, 6*	4		36, 6*
Olivella dama Wood	1	2		3
Conus sp.	89	20	1	110
Conus perplexis Sowerby		1		1
Pelecypods.—				
Glycymeris, sp. (minute)	7			7
Glycymeris gigantea Reeve	86	18		104
Glycymeris maculata Broderip	16	13		29
Pinctada mazatlanica Hanley		1		1
Pecten sp.	4			4
Laevicardium elatum Sowerby (Beads)	15, 23*, 31*	23, 6–7000*		6600+
(Whole)	2			2
(Whole painted blue)			2	2
(Pendants)	1			1
(Tesserae)	1			1
(Debitage)	51	47		98
Chione californiensis Broderip	2			2
Dosinia ponderosa Gray	1, ca. 35*			36
PEARLY FRESH WATER SHELL				
Quadrula sp.	1	2		3
FISH, AMPHIBIANS, AND REPTILES				
Pisces sp. Trout–sized Fish		2		2
Scaphiopus holbrooki Spadefoot Toad	1	2		3
Hyla sp. Tree Frog		1		1
Reptilia sp. Small Snake	2			2
Kinosternon sonoriense Sonoran Mud Turtle	1	2		3
Phyrnosoma platyrhinos Desert Horned Lizard	1			1
BIRDS				
Cathartes aura Turkey Vulture	1^			1^
Accipiter cooperi Cooper's Hawk	1			1
Buteo sp. Buteonine Hawk	1			1

Species	Besh-Ba-Gowah	Gila Pueblo	Hagen Site	Total
Buteo jamaicensis Red-tailed Hawk	2	1		3
Aquila chrysaetos Golden Eagle	2			2
Haiaëtus leucocephalus Bald Eagle	1			1
Falco sparvarius Sparrow Hawk	1			1
Lophortyx gambellii Gambel's Quail	13	8		21
Meleagris gallopavo silvestris "Tularosa" Small Indian Domestic Turkey		1		1
Zenaidura macroura Mourning Dove	3			3
Ara macao Scarlet Macaw		(PINAL PUEBLO 2)		2
Geococcyx californianus Roadrunner	1			1
Colaptes auratus collaris Red-shafted Flicker group	2			2
MAMMALS				
Sylvilagus sp. Rabbit	257	50		307
Sylvilagus auduboni Desert Cottontail	3			3
Lepus californicus Black-tailed Jackrabbit	171	92	1	264
Ammospermophilus harrisii Harris' Antelope Squirrel		2		2
Spermophilus variegatus Rock Squirrel	5	4		9
Thomomys bottae Botta's Pocket Gopher		15		15
Peromyscus sp. White-footed Mouse	8	10		18
Neotoma albigula White-throated Wood Rat	23	4		27
Canis sp. Dog/Coyote		2, 1p		3
Canis latrans Coyote		1^		1^
Canis familiaris Medium Sized Dog	2	13, 5p		20
Procyon lotor Raccoon		1		1
Lyynx rufus Bobcat		1		1
Odocoileus sp. Unidentified Deer, bone and antler fragments	8, ?^	3, 14^	2^	11, 16^
Odocoileus hemionus Black-tailed Deer	62, ?^	13, 18^	3^	75, 21^
Odocoileus virginianus White-tailed Deer	52, ?^	10, 28^1		62, 18^

* = each * represents a separate multiple shell artifact

^ = bone artifact

p = puppy

species represented in the collection are present in the region today. Fish, and turtles were and still are used as food, and turtle shells are still used in the manufacture of rattles. The snake and the toads may have had burrows in the site. Horned Lizards are viewed with awe, since they avoid capture by spraying their assailants with a blood-red mist. In addition to the faunal remains, one Gila Polychrome bowl from Besh-Ba-Gowah depicts a frog/turtle/ horned lizard in the bottom. Another is painted with what appears to be a Western Skink (Figure 3).

Birds

Native Birds

A variety of bird taxa were recovered from these four sites (Table 1). All were used prehistorically at other southwestern sites, and the feathers of all are used by modern Pueblo Indians (McKusick 2001:Table 1, 7–10). Based on their recovery in food containers and in food refuse contexts, some taxa such as Gambel's Quail, (*Callipepla gambelii*), and Mourning dove (*Zenaidura macroura*), were used for food. The only Greater Roadrunner (*Geococcyx californianus*) bone in the collections was recovered from Room B/AB at Besh-Ba-Gowah, a small room with a walk-through door adjacent to the west plaza. The room also contained remains of Red-tailed Hawk (*Buteo jamaicensis*), American Kestrel (*Falco sparvarius*), Golden Eagle (*Aquila chrysaetos*), Bald Eagle, all of which are desirable for embellishing ceremonial costumes (Hohmnn et al. 1992:99–101). Greater Roadrunner remains in small numbers are not unusual in avian collections from the Southwest. Like parrots, the outer toe of the roadrunner turns back, giving it an X-shaped track, which is important in myth, art, and shamanism (Clara Lee Tanner, pers. comm. 1952).

The array of bird remains compares well with those of contemporary Mogollon ancestral pueblos such as Grasshopper Pueblo (McKusick 1982:88); AZ W: 10 50, Point of Pines (unpublished data); Gran Quivira (McKusick 1981:39–65); and Wind Mountain (McKusick 1996:407; Olsen and Olsen1996:282, 389–406).

Imported Birds

The Pinal Mountains lack suitable turkey habitat, and introduced wild turkeys have not survived. The only turkey bones recovered were from a habitation room which formed part of the ceremonial/redistribution complex at Gila Pueblo. They were neck bones from a young female domestic turkey which would have been in her first fall plumage. Since many turkey producing pueblos were deserted by the mid 1400s, I suggest that the probable source for this bird was Gran Quivira, which specialized in the breeding of the small phenotype represented (phenotype and taxonomy, McKusick 2001:109–125; genotype, Speller et al. 2010:2807–2812). Most likely it was imported along with Chupadero Black-on-White pottery (McKusick and Young 1997:33, Figure 22a; Wilcox et al. 2007:191).

Pothunters working Pinal Pueblo removed the bones of two Scarlet Macaws along with the burial of a high status older adult woman whose skull was covered with green paint. They brought the bones to me because they thought the burial included dogs, but the extraneous skeletons were actually those of young humans. The woman's burial was accompanied by the remains of a neonate, two infants under two, a three to four-year-old, and two children under six years of age. The skeleton of one Scarlet Macaw was mixed with the remains of the infants and children. The right ulna of an additional Scarlet Macaw accompanied the three to four-year-old, which was packaged separately. Since the burial was only being mined for salable pots, the remainder of the second macaw was probably left in the grave. The most likely hypothesis to account for this mass burial is that the burial represents the remains of humans and macaws that died of the same ailment. I have learned as a parrot keeper that parrots are also subject to common human ills, particularly respiratory ailments. Since pet parrots enjoy plucking morsels from their keeper's lips, disease could have been spread in this manner. The development of the macaw bones indicates that the burial was probably made in February, at least a month too early for the customary Spring Equinox Scarlet Macaw sacrifices of former times (McKusick 2001:78–89). After A.D. 1275, macaws were more often kept for their feathers, rather than for sacrifice (McKusick 2001:72–79). One Scarlet Macaw has been found buried with a human in the Mimbres Valley, and at another Salado site, the Freeman Ranch (Hargrave 1970:48; McKusick 2001:72, Table 2).

Mammals

Small Mammals

All mammalian species identified in the collections still remain in the region today. Although rabbits and hares are most numerous in the mammalian collection, they account for a relatively small portion of the available meat supply (Table 2). Ceremonial room B/AB at Besh-Ba-Gowah yielded food refuse of quail, roadrunner, rabbit, and packrat. A bowl on the roof of Gila Pueblo contained bones from a stew of quail and rabbit. The abdominal cavities of two inhabitants of the adobe rooms in Gila Pueblo contained crushed bones from a meal made from macerated rodents; a meal of macerated rodents is typical of Hohokam sites (McKusick1976:374).

Deer

Calculated meat weights suggest that Black-tailed Deer are the most important source of meat (Table 2). The importance of deer meat is a trend which begins in pithouse villages in the cooler parts of the Southwest about 200 B.C. (McKusick 1996:407). The proportion of White-tailed Deer to Black-tailed Deer remains is much higher at Besh-Ba-Gowah and Gila Pueblo than at other sites. This is probably mostly an expression of local availability. However, the inhabitants of Besh-Ba-Gowah and Gila Pueblo also took advantage of the fact that the

Table 2. Pounds of useable meat produced.

Species	No. of Individuals	Pounds of Meat Per Individual	Useable Meat	% of Total Meat
Black-tailed Deer	75	100.00	7500.00	51.00%
White-tailed Deer	62	70.00	4340.00	29.51%
Unidentified Deer	11	85.00	935.00	6.36%
Black-tailed Jackrabbit	264	3.00	792.00	5.30%
Dog	20	12.50	250.00	1.70%
Probable Dog	3	12.50	37.50	0.26%
Rabbit	310	1.75	542.50	3.69%
		TOTALS	14,397.00	97.91%

local subspecies of White-tailed Deer (*Odocoileus virginianus couesi*) has smaller bones that could be used to make finer artifacts. Deer tibia hair pins worn by the Mimbres bat-costumed man (Figure 2) and by the two high status men killed in the final attack on Gila Pueblo, could not have been made from the much larger and heavier bones of the Black-tailed Deer (McKusick and Young 1997:105). White-tailed deer is also depicted in the deer-masked human bead (Figure 2). A deer skull was found in a ceremonial context at Gila Pueblo, and may have been a Deer Dancer headdress. In his youth, Robert McKusick found bone finger rings manufactured from the femoral shafts of White-tailed Deer on the Besh-Ba-Gowah back dirt in a quantity which suggests that they may have been an item of commercial manufacture.

Dog/coyote

The only coyote bone in the assemblage was an ulnar awl found in Gila Pueblo. Although no dog bone artifacts were recovered, remains of very immature dogs were found on the roof of Gila Pueblo associated with the ca. A.D. 1440 terminal attack. These pups were in the vicinity of the bodies of slain children, as were both small brownware fired clay quadrupeds resembling dogs and tiny brownware pots.

Dogs may have been used for food and/or sacrifice at the Upland Salado pueblos. Both food and sacrificial animals were, and still are, skinned with the paws and tail vertebrae retained in the skin (McKusick 1981:61). At the fall of Gila Pueblo, three occurrences of paw and tail bones were recovered from the roof of the ceremonial/redistribution complex, suggesting three dog skins. A separate dog leg bone was found in room fill, suggesting food use of the carcass.

Resources, Rainfall, and Raiding

The Upper Pinal Creek Survey, conducted by Crary, Germic, and Golio (1992:1–5), identified 1276 structures: roasting pits, field houses, house clusters, and room blocks. In addition to the seven large pueblos, there were hamlets and farmsteads forming a rancheria-like settlement system. The authors expected, but did not find, flood plane and irrigation along Pinal Creek and its tributaries. The reason for their failure to find ditches was that the remains of the ditches lie within the modern residential area, along the canyon bottoms, and were not available to the survey. The ditches' owners proudly say that the ditches were "...built by the Hohokams, stone-lined by the Salados, and cemented by our grandfather," (JoNell Brantley, pers. comm. ca. 2005). Today they are filled with fallen leaves and used as a source for fishing worms.

Since 1951, I have had the experience of farming along Kellner Canyon Wash, about 5 km south of Besh-Ba-Bowah, and 152 m higher. I can verify that there is still evidence of reservoirs at the mouths of side canyons, and useable ditches in the canyon bottoms. In wet years, water rises from the ground at the bases of the ridges, and runs across the surface. Some ditches, which lead water from Kellner Canyon Wash in dry periods, are lengthened to drain excess water into the same wash during wet periods.

The survey provided information on rancheria settlements perhaps as early as the Hohokam Gila Butte Phase. The increase in population seems to follow the availability of surface water, with winter dominance in precipitation being an important factor. Prior to 1300, the population and settlement system were both small. Then, about 1295, began a rapid increase in population, peaking about 1330, and starting to decline by 1350. Similar patterns are defined for the Tonto Basin and for the Grasshopper/Forestdale areas and appear to be a function of a general southwestern rainfall pattern. Further, a switch to a summer dominant rainfall pattern would have caused flooding, destruction of water control devices, arroyo cutting, and lowering of the water table (Crary et al. 1992:6, 8). Crary, Germick, and Golio (1992:6–8) concluded that the Roosevelt Phase population of the Upper Pinal Creek area was insufficient to provide the personnel necessary to account for the seven large pueblos, and that population shifts were therefore involved. This is a marginal environment which could not support a large population indefinitely. Some have suggested that in times of crop failure, the inhabitants could forage in the hills. This is unrealistic. I cannot form any hypothesis for subsistence in this location which does not take full advantage of hunting and gathering as a regular part of the economy at all time periods. Living in the area, and digging wells and fence post holes, has made it apparent that by the time the Salado occupation ended the ridges had become so denuded of cover that much of the fertile canyon bottoms were, and still are, covered with up to a foot of adobe.

In addition to environmental degradation and rainfall fluctuations, the pueblos suffered devastating depopulation due to attacks. Another factor in the decline of the large pueblos may be associated with the consumption of cottonseed, which was found in quantity almost equal to corn. Although cottonseed is nutritious and is high in oil and protein it contains a yellow dye which serves as a male contraceptive, and may even cause male sterility if eaten in sufficient quantity (McKusick and Young 1997:99; see also Porat 1990). The Salado population may have dwindled from this cause.

Whether Gila Pueblo was destroyed first, or Gila Pueblo and the Hagen Site were destroyed in the same attack, someone was left in the area. Site-closing activities, such as breakage of some ceremonial goods, and protection of others with deliberately placed bodies, are evident. The attack on Gila Pueblo came at about the Fall Equinox, a time when great kettles of vultures gather, and roost in the trees downstream from Besh-Ba-Gowah for their seasonal migration, riding the last of the thermals south into Mexico. The condition of the burned bones indicates that the bodies lying on the Gila Pueblo roofs were quickly defleshed, probably by vultures, before the conflagration was set. Any remaining Salados probably slipped into the foothills, and took the trail over the Pinals to Dripping Springs, in the Arivaipa Population Cluster, a day's walk away.

Notes

1. Ferg finished the Eastern Arizona College excavation at Gila Pueblo in the 1970s, and found the pipe in the south half of room 111 (pers. comm.).

References Cited

Bradfield, Wesley. 1929   *Cameron Creek Village, Monograph No. 1.* School of American Research, Santa Fe.

Bradley, Ronna J. 1999   Shell Exchange within the Southwest: The Casas Grandes Interaction Sphere. In *The Casas Grandes World,* eds. Curtis F. Schaafsma and Carroll L. Riley, pp. 213–228. University of Utah Press, Salt Lake City.

Brody, J.J., Catherine J. Scott, Steven A. LeBlanc, and Tony Berlant. 1984   *Mimbres Pottery, Ancient Art of the American Southwest.* Hudson Hills Press, New York.

Cheek, Lawrence W. 1994   *Ancient Peoples of the Southwest, A.D. 1250.* Arizona Highways Books, Phoenix.

Clark, Jeffrey J., and Paul F. Reed. 2011   Chacoan Immigration and Influence in the Middle San Juan. *The Kiva* 77(2):251–274.

Cosgrove, Harriet S., and Cornelius B. Cosgrove. 1932   The Swarts Ruin: A Typical Mimbres Site in Southwestern New Mexico. *Papers of the Peabody Museum of Archaeology and Ethnology, vol. 15, no. 1.* Cambridge, Mass.

Crary, Joseph S., Stephen Germick, and Michael Golio. 1992   Late Mogollon Adaptations to the Upper Sonoran Desert: Examples from the Upper Pinal Creek Area, Arizona. Paper presented at the 1992 Mogollon Conference, Las Cruces, New Mexico.

Crown, Patricia L. 1994   *Ceramics and Ideology: Salado Polychrome Pottery.* University of New Mexico Press, Albuquerque.

Ferg, Alan. 1982   14th Century Kachina Depictions on Ceramics. In *Collected Papers in Honor of John W. Runyan,* ed. Gerald X. Fitzgerald, pp. 13–29. *Papers of the Archaeological Society of New Mexico 7,* Albuquerque Archaeological Society Press, Albuquerque.

Ferg, Alan. 1988   Appendix E: Exotic Artifacts and Shrines. In *Erich F Schmidt's Investigations of Salado Sites in Central Arizona: The Mrs. W. B. Thompson Archaeological Expedition of the American Museum of Natural History,* eds. John W. Hohmann and Linda B. Kelley, pp. 205–218. *Museum of Northern Arizona Bulletin 56.* Museum of Northern Arizona Press, Flagstaff.

Fulton, William Shirley, and Carr Tuthill. 1945   *An Archaeological Site near Gleeson, Arizona.* The Amerind Foundation, No.1. Dragoon, Arizona.

Hargrave, Lyndon L. 1970   *Mexican Macaws.* Anthropological Papers of the University of Arizona, Number 20. University of Arizona Press, Tucson.

Hohmann, John W. 1990   *Ruin Stabilization and Park Development for Besh-Ba-Gowah Pueblo.* Studies in Western Archaeology Number 2, Cultural Resource Group, Louis Berger & Associates, Inc., Phoenix.

Hohmann, John W. 1992   An Overview of Salado Heartland Archaeology. In *Proceedings of the Second Salado Conference Globe, AZ 1992,* eds. Richard C. Lange and Stephen Germick, pp. 1–16. Occasional Paper, Arizona Archaeological Society, Phoenix.

Hohmann, John W., Stephen Germick, and Christopher D. Adams. 1992   Discovery of a Salado Ceremonial Room. In *Proceedings of the Second Salado Conference,* eds. Richard C. Lange and Stephen Germick, pp. 92–102. Occasional Paper, Arizona Archaeological Society, Phoenix.

Lincoln, Thomas R. 2000   Introduction: The Salado Phenomenon. In *Salado,* ed. Jeffrey S. Dean. The Amerind Foundation, Dragoon.

Lyons, Patrick D. 2004   Cliff Polychrome. *The Kiva* 69(4):361–400.

McGregor, John C. 1965   *Southwestern Archaeology.* Southern Illinois University Press, Urbana.

McKusick, Charmion R. 1976   Appendix 6, Avifauna. In *The Hohokam,* ed. Emil W. Haury, pp. 374–377. University of Arizona Press, Tucson.

McKusick, Charmion R. 1981   The Faunal Remains of Las Humanas. In *Contributions to Gran Quivira Archaeolog,* ed. Alden C. Hayes, pp. 39–65. *Publications in Archeology 17.* National Park Service, U.S. Department of the Interior, Washington.

McKusick, Charmion R. 1982   Avifauna from Grasshopper Pueblo. In *Multidisciplinary Research at Grasshopper Pueblo Arizona,* eds. William A. Longacre, Sally J. Holbrook, and Michael W. Graves, pp. 87–96. Anthropological Papers of the University of Arizona, Number 40.

McKusick, Charmion R. 1996   An Analysis of Miscellaneous Faunal Materials from the Wind Mountain Locus and Analyses of Ridout Locus Faunal Materials. In *Mimbres Mogollon Archaeology,* eds. Anne I. Woosley and Allan J. McIntire, pp. 407–439. Amerind Foundation, Inc. Archaeological Series 10, Dragoon.

McKusick, Charmion R. 2001   Southwest Birds of Sacrifice. *The Arizona Archaeologist no. 31.* Arizona Archaeological Society, Phoenix.

McKusick, Charmion R., and Jon Nathan Young. 1997   *The Gila Pueblo Salados.* Salado Chapter, Arizona Archaeological Society, Globe, Arizona.

Moulard, Barbara L. 1984   *Within the Underworld Sky, Mimbres Ceramic Art in Context.* Twelvetrees Press, Pasadena.

Olsen, Sandra L., and John W. Olsen. 1996   An Analysis of Faunal Remains from Wind Mountain. In *Mimbres Mogollon Archaeology*, eds. Anne I. Woosley and Allan McIntire, pp. 389–406. The Amerind Foundation, Inc., Archaeologies Series, 10, Dragoon.

Porat, Offie. 1990   Effects of Gossypol on the Motility of Mammalian Sperm. *Molecular Reproduction and Development* 25(4):400–408.

Rätsch, Christian. Translated by John R. Baker. 1998   *The Encyclopedia of Psychoactive Plants.* Park Street Press, Rochester, Vermont.

Rea, Amadeo M. 1997   *At the Desert's Green Edge.* University of Arizona Press, Tucson.

Shiner, Joel L. 1961   A Room at Gila Pueblo. *The Kiva* 27(2):3–11.

Smith, Watson, Richard B. Woodbury, and Nathalie S. Woodbury. 1966   *The Excavation of Hawikuh by Frederick Webb Hodge.* Contributions, vol. 20, Museum of the American Indian, Heye Foundation, New York.

Speller, Camilla F., Brian M. Kemp, Scott D. Wyatt, Cara Monroe, William D. Lipe, Ursula M. Arndt, and Dongya Y. Yang. 2010   Ancient Mitochondrial DNA Analysis Reveals Complexity of Indigenous North American Turkey Domestication. *Proceedings of the National Academy of Sciences* 107(7):2807–2812.

Tagg, Martyn D. 1985   *Tonto National Monument, An Archaeological Survey.* Western Archeological and Conservation Center Publications in Anthropology, No. 31. U.S. National Park Service, Tucson.

VanPool, Christine S., and Todd L. VanPool. 2006   Casas Grandes Cosmology. In *Secrets of Casas Grandes,* ed. Melissa S. Powell, pp. 75–94. Museum of New Mexico Press, Santa Fe.

Vickrey, Irene S. 1939   Besh-Ba-Gowah. *The Kiva* 4:19–22.

White, Theodore E. 1953   A Method for Calculating the Dietary Percentage of Various Food Animals Utilized by Aboriginal Peoples. *American Antiquity* 18(4):396–398.

Wilcox, David R., David A. Gregory, and J. Brett Hill. 2007   Zuni in the Puebloan and Southwestern Worlds. In: *Zuni Origins,* eds. David A. Gregory and David R. Wilcox. University of Arizona Press, Tucson.

Wood, J. Scott. 1987   Checklist of Pottery Types for the Tonto National Forest: An Introduction to the Archaeological Ceramics of Central Arizona. *The Arizona Archaeologist* 21.

Wood, J. Scott. 2000   Vale of Tiers Palimpsest: Salado Settlement and Internal Relationships in the Tonto Basin Area. In *Salado,* ed. Jeffrey S. Dean, pp. 107–141. University of New Mexico Press, Albuquerque.

Amadeo M. Rea and the Case of a Vanishing Owl

Steven W. Carothers[†, ‡], Dorothy A. House[†, §], and R. Roy Johnson[¶]

Abstract

Amadeo M. Rea began his teaching career at the Gila River Indian Reservation near Phoenix, Arizona, in 1963. His subsequent studies on the natural history of the region demonstrated that the Cactus Ferruginous Pygmy-Owl (*Glaucidium brasilianum cactorum*) and many other plant and animal species had been extirpated along the entire middle Gila and lower Salt River decades before his studies began. These riparian species had apparently survived many centuries of pre-contact Native American occupation only to decline as a result of less than 100 years of Euro-American influence. Euro-Americans carelessly wrought changes that led to widespread destruction and desertification of riparian ecosystems throughout the Southwest, including the Gila River Indian Reservation. However, as evidenced by the environmental protection measures that have passed into law beginning in the 1960s, attitudes within American society have shifted toward an interest in preserving the natural world. Despite this evolving worldview, the losses in riparian ecosystems documented by Amadeo Rea on the Gila River Indian Reservation and decline of the Cactus Ferruginous Pygmy-Owl have not been reversed. Following in Amadeo's footsteps, we summarize the available evidence supporting the contention that the pygmy-owl was an obligate riparian species in south-central Arizona, and, because those habitats were largely destroyed due to Euro-American practices, the species has all but vanished from the state. This decline is likely to continue unless the natural riparian habitats necessary for the survival of this owl can be restored.

Amadeo Rea on the Gila River Indian Reservation

In 1963, 25-year-old Amadeo Michael Rea, a recent graduate of San Diego's San Luis Rey College, became an instructor at St. John's Indian School in Komatke Village on the Gila River Indian Reservation (Figure 1). Now called the Gila River Indian Community, this reservation was established at the confluence of the Salt and Gila Rivers near Phoenix, Arizona, as a homeland for members of two tribes: the Pima, "Akimel O'Odham" (River People) and the Maricopa, "Xalychidom Piipaash" (People Who Live Toward the Water).

† SWCA Environmental Consultants, 114 N. San Francisco St., Suite 100, Flagstaff, AZ 86001.
‡ [scarothers@swca.com]
§ [dhouse@swca.com]
¶ Johnson & Haight Environmental Consultants, 3755 S. Hunters Run, Tucson, AZ 85730.
   [rroylois@aol.com]

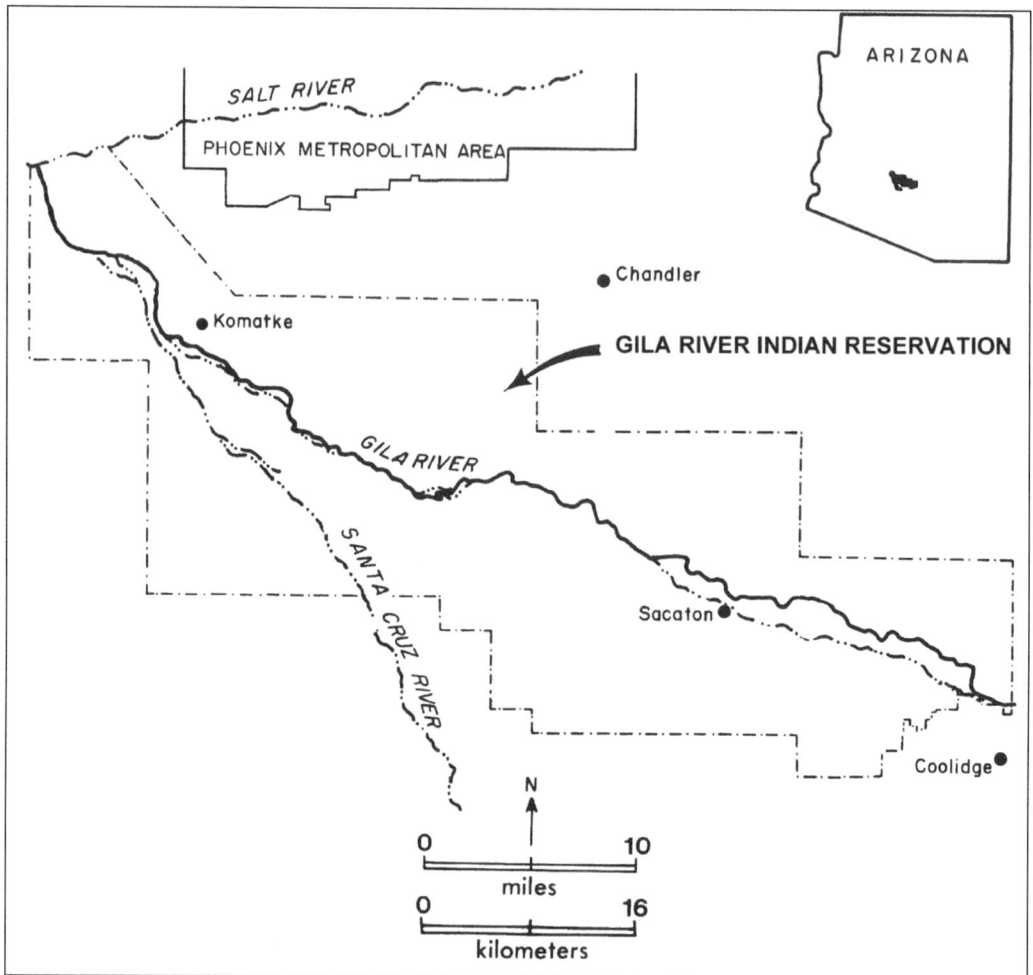

Figure 1. The Gila River Indian Reservation, now the Gila River Indian Community. Adapted from Rea (1983).

In addition to teaching general science, English, biology, and chemistry, Amadeo's major occupation while at the school was studying the natural history of the surrounding region. The Komatke area, with its Sonoran Desert biodiversity, was a unique location for biological investigations, especially studies of birds and plants. As it turned out, the fact that the Reservation straddles 105 km (65 miles) of the middle Gila River and a small portion of the lower Salt River proved to be of particular scientific interest to Amadeo. This area so intrigued him that by the time he published his first monograph, *Once a River: Bird Life and Habitat Changes on the Middle Gila*, in 1983 he had spent a total of a 1000 days doing fieldwork there, first during his residency at Komatke (1963–1969), and later as a visiting researcher (1970–1982) (Rea 1983).

Soon after Amadeo's arrival at Komatke, he realized that the riverine environment of the Gila and Salt Rivers, including its bird populations, had been drastically altered from its natural state. Oral histories gathered from Native American elders, as well as written accounts left by Euro-American travelers through the region in the mid to late 1800s and early 1900s, described an environment very different from the one he saw (Rea 1983). These sources mentioned flowing rivers, banks lined with dense riparian vegetation, and grassy meadows. What Amadeo saw, with few exceptions, was an arid landscape devoid of surface water and mostly devoid of vegetation. The Gila and the Salt Rivers had ceased to flow as perennial streams decades prior to his arrival. Former mesic, or water-loving vegetation that had once lined their banks had been replaced by more drought-tolerant plants, a process known today as desertification (Miksicek 1984). Animal populations that depended upon reliable water and riparian vegetation were either extirpated or drastically reduced.

Through his interviews with Pima elders on the Reservation, and a painstaking review of historical documents, Amadeo was able to paint a picture of the physical and biological environment that had once been occupied and maintained by the Pima and their indigenous antecedents (Rea 1983, 1997, 2007). At the same time, he began extensive fieldwork, collecting data on the existing environment on the Reservation, including its avifauna. Comparing his survey results with historical and ethnohistorical information, Amadeo was able to document the extirpation from the Reservation of many species of plants and birds, including a small diurnal owl, the Cactus Ferruginous Pygmy-Owl (*Glaucidium brasilianum cactorum*). This paper focuses on that owl (hereafter "pygmy-owl"[1]) and how its fate, not only on the Gila River Indian Reservation, but throughout its range in Arizona, reflects the displacement of one culture/worldview (that of the Pima and other indigenous people) by another (the evolving culture and ethos of Euro-Americans).

Contrasting Worldviews

The Pima, and the people who preceded them (termed "Hohokam" by archaeologists), farmed the floodplains along the Gila and Salt Rivers for more than a millennium (Haury 1976; Rea 1997). Certainly these farmers altered the natural environment to some extent, replacing acres of native plant communities with fields of non-native crops and a system of irrigation canals (Miksicek 1984; Periman and Kelley 2000; Redman and Kinzig 2008). But the indigenous inhabitants clearly valued and drew sustenance from the natural riparian ecosystem as well. When Euro-Americans first visited the area, riparian gallery forests dominated by Fremont Cottonwood (*Populus fremontii* Wats.) and Goodding Willow (*Salix gooddingii* Ball) lined the rivers, sharing rich bottomland with cultivated fields (Rea 1983, 1988, 1997). Together, the natural and cultivated riparian ecosystems supported an abundance and diversity of species (Rea 1988, 1997).

Intimately familiar with their physical and biological environment, aware of their dependence upon it, and limited by stone-age technology in their ability to control it, the Pima, and the Hohokam before them, lived successfully in this extreme environment for hundreds of years (Haury 1976; Rea 1997). The Pimas interviewed by Amadeo in the 1960s and 1970s communicated their beliefs about their cultural and physical landscape. They saw humans (O'odham) "as part of the natural world, not something separate from it" (Rea 1997:15). Moreover, they believed that all things in nature were created for a purpose, although that purpose may not be evident or useful to humans (Rea 1997). In other words, elements of the natural world were thought to have intrinsic value apart from their utility and should be treated with respect.

In contrast, the Euro-Americans who came to dominate the Southwest tended to see themselves as separate from and superior to nature and—aided by their more advanced technology—sought to master it (LaFreniere 2007; White 1967). Significantly, they brought to the Americas a scripture-based belief that the purpose of the natural world was to provide for human needs (White 1967). Encountering an abundance of what they perceived to be under-utilized natural resources, the newcomers commenced to use those resources in new ways and on an unprecedented scale. They put hundreds of thousands of head of cattle on the land, overgrazing and eroding the arid landscape. Beaver, whose dams had moderated the erosive power of stream flow, were trapped to near extinction. Riparian trees were cut to provide timber, and water was diverted from river channels to irrigate large-scale agricultural pursuits. Finally, the Gila and Salt Rivers were dammed with no regard for how the loss of natural stream flow would affect native plant and animal communities—let alone Native American communities. The result was the widespread destruction of riparian ecosystems throughout what is now south-central Arizona (Dobyns 1981; Rea 1983).

Throughout the period of Euro-American settlement, the Pima remained on their land, attempting to farm as they had always done, but white settlers upstream diverted the water of the Gila River, leaving little or none for the Native American fields and riparian habitat downstream. For the most part, farming became untenable. Forced to find alternative ways to subsist, the Pima hastened the desertification of their once productive bottomlands by converting woodlands to cordwood to sell to their non-Indian neighbors (Pima-Maricopa Irrigation Project 2012).

Desertification and its Effects on Avian Species

When Amadeo began his studies on the Gila River Indian Reservation he found a devastated ecosystem (Rea 1983). Where rivers once flowed, the only surface waters present were a few artificially established ponds and marshy areas created by irrigation ditch return flows, discharges from the Phoenix city sewage treatment facility, and a small wetland restoration project. Wells and reclaimed wastewater, rather than rivers, supplied much of the water that *was* available (Pima-Maricopa Irrigation Project 2012). Occasionally, abnormally heavy rains resulted in ephemeral runoff in the streambeds, but sustained natural river flow was nonexistent. As a result of desertification, a large number of riparian plant species that depended on river flow had been lost. Through his studies, Amadeo determined that at least 39 species of riparian/wetland plants had been extirpated from the Reservation along the middle Gila and lower Salt Rivers (Table 1; Rea 1983, 1988, 1997). Another seven plant species had disappeared from their natural setting but had later colonized or recolonized scattered localities after new sources of water (i.e., wells, reclaimed wastewater) created a few artificially watered areas (see Table 1). Amadeo uses the term "colonized" to refer to the occurrence of species in riparian and wetland habitats established by human activity in areas where such habitats had not existed before. He uses the term "recolonized" to refer to the return of species to the fragments of restored riparian and wetland habitats along the Salt and Gila River channels.

Table 1. Plant species collected in the early 20th century on the Gila River Indian Reservation that were subsequently either permanently or temporarily extirpated and later colonized or recolonized newly created riparian or wetland habitat (Modified from Rea 1997, Tables 6.2 and 6.4. C = colonized new riparian/wetland habitat; E = extirpated; R = recolonized restored riparian/ wetland habitats).

Common name Scientific name[1]	Status on reservation	Common name Scientific name	Status on reservation
Sea Purslane *Sesuvium verrucosum* Raf.	E	Buckhorn Plantain *Plantago lanceolata* L.	E
Arum-leaf Arrowhead *Sagittaria cuneata* E. Sheld.	E	Broadleaf Plantain *Plantago major* L.	E
False Daisy *Eclipta prostrata* (L.) L.	E, R	Redseed Plantain *Plantago rhodosperma* Decne.	E
Watercress *Nasturtium officinale* W.T. Aiton	E	Common Reed *Phragmites australis* (Cav.) Trin. ex Steud.	E
Curvepod Yellowcress *Rorippa curvisiliqua* (Hook.) Bessey ex Britton	E	Big Sacaton *Sporobolus wrightii* Munro ex Scribn.	E
Bog Yellowcress *Rorippa hispida* – now *Rorippa palustris* ssp. *hispida* (Desv.) Jonsell	E	Violet Dock *Rumex violascens* Rech. f.	E
Northern Marsh Yellowcress *Rorippa islandica* (Oeder) Borbás	E	Desert Rockpurslane *Calandrinia ciliate* (Ruiz & Pavón) DC.	E
Southern Marsh Yellowcress *Rorippa obtusa* – now *Rorippa teres* (Michx.) Stuckey	E	Sago Pondweed *Potamogeton pectinatus* – now *Stuckenia pectinata* (L.) Börner	E
Boraxweed *Nitrophila occidentalis* (Moq.) S. Watson	E	Western Rock Jasmine *Androsace occidentalis* Pursh	E
Desert Starvine *Brandegea bigelovii* (S. Wats.) Cogn.	E	Seaside Brookweed *Samolus parviflorus* – now *Samolus valerandi* L.	E
Pale Spikerush *Eleocharis macrostachya* Britton	E	Arizona Mousetail *Myosurus cupulatus* S. Watson	E
Hardstem Bulrush *Scirpus acutus* – now *Schoenoplectus acutus* var. *acutus* (Muhl. ex Bigelow) Á. Löve & D. Löve	E, R	Tiny Mousetail *Myosurus minimus* L.	E

Table 1 continued.

Common name *Scientific name*[1]	Status on reservation	Common name *Scientific name*	Status on reservation
Common Threesquare *Scirpus americanus* – now *Schoenoplectus pungens* var. *pungens* (Vahl) Palla	E	Celeryleaf Buttercup *Ranunculus sceleratus* L.	E,C
Cosmopolitan Bulrush *Scirpus maritimus* – now *Bolboschoenus* *maritimus* (L.) Palla	E, R	Coyote Willow *Salix exigua* Nutt.	E
Great Bulrush *Scirpus validus* now *Schoenoplectus* *tabernaemontani* (C.C. Gmel.) Palla	E	Yerba Mansa *Anemopsis californica* (Nutt.) Hook. & Arn.	E
Arizona Centaury *Centaurium calycosum* – now *Zeltnera* *calycosa* (Buckley) G. Mans.	E	Disc Waterhyssop *Bacopa rotundifolia* (Michx.) Wettst.	E
Catchfly Prairie Gentian *Eustoma exaltatum* (L.) Salisb. ex G. Don	E	Roundleaf Monkeyflower *Mimulus glabratus* Kunth	E
Parrot Feather *Myriophyllum aquaticum* (Vell.) Verdc.	E	Water Speedwell *Veronica anagallis-aquatica* L.	E, C
Inland Rush *Juncus interior* var. *arizonicus* – now *Juncus interior* Wiegand	E	Coyote Tobacco *Nicotiana attenuata* Torr. ex S. Watson	E
Longleaf Rush *Juncus macrophyllus* Coville	E	American Black Nightshade *Solanum americanum* Mill.	E, C, R
Field Rush *Juncus tenuis* var. *dudleyi* – now *Juncus* *tenuis* Willd.	E	California Caltrop *Kallstroemia californica* (S. Wats.) Vail	E
Inflated Duckweed *Lemna gibba* L.	E, R	Arizona Poppy *Kallstroemia grandiflora* Torr. ex Gray	E
Velvet Ash *Fraxinus velutina* Torr.	E	Warty Caltrop *Kallstroemia parviflora* J.B.S. Norton	E

[1] Current scientific names according to the Integrated Taxonomic Information System (ITIS)
(http://www.itis.gov). Common names and order are the same as in Rea 1997.

The impact of lost riparian habitat on the avifauna of the Gila River region became increasingly clear as Amadeo collected specimens in the field and searched the literature for biological, ethnographic, and archaeological information that would allow him to reconstruct the pre-contact avian community. He found that few ornithological papers had been published on the area around Phoenix despite the proximity of a major university nearby (Arizona State University, Tempe; see Anderson 1972, which lists early ornithological work in south-central Arizona and similar activities in the rest of the state). Notwithstanding a paucity of written records, Amadeo's investigations determined that 29 species of birds had been extirpated from the Reservation (Table 2; Rea 1983, 1988). Of these 29, 19 were breeding species. By the 1960s and 1970s, in addition to those extirpated, 25 other species of birds had experienced declining numbers on the Reservation, and only 12 of the 25 species were still breeding on the Reservation in limited numbers (see Rea 1983:82). Amadeo's findings were not all negative, however. The artificially created patches of riparian vegetation and open water allowed at least nine formerly extirpated riparian obligate birds to return to the Reservation as nesting species or migrants (see Table 2). He noted that birds had colonized a place he called Barehand Lane Marsh, where water draining from irrigated fields collected in a low-lying area to form a pond and wetland. Before the irrigation wastewater formed a wetland, Amadeo's Barehand Lane Marsh was upland desertscrub. Birds also recolonized a habitat restoration site at the confluence of the Salt and Gila Rivers and a stretch of once-dry river channel where effluent from a sewage treatment plant supported the regrowth of riparian vegetation.

Table 2. Species of birds that were either permanently extirpated from the Gila River Indian Reservation or temporarily extirpated and later colonized or recolonized newly created riparian or wetland habitat (from Rea 1983, 1988; additional information from Johnson et al. [2000] and Witzeman et al. [1997]).

Common Name[1] Scientific Name	Likely Former Status[2]	Status on Reservation[3]	Primary Habitat[4]
Greater White-fronted Goose Anser albifrons	W	E	Open water, fields
Snow Goose Chen caerulescens	W	E	Open water, fields
Canada Goose Branta canadensis	W	E	Open water, fields
Tundra Swan Cygnus columbianus	W	E	Open water
Northern Pintail Anas acuta	W	E	Open water
Common Merganser Mergus merganser	W	E	Open water
Pied-billed Grebe Podilymbus podiceps	B, W[5]	E, C	Dense marsh, open water
Least Bittern Ixobrychus exilis	B	E, C	Dense marsh
Great Blue Heron Ardea herodias	B, W	E	Riparian, open water, open marsh
Green Heron Butorides virescens	B	E, C, R	Riparian, open water, open marsh
Black-crowned Night-Heron Nycticorax nycticorax	B, W	E, R	Riparian, marsh
Harris's Hawk Parabuteo unicinctus	B, W	E	Riparian trees, Saguaros
Golden Eagle Aquila chrysaetos	B, W	E	Widespread
American Coot Fulica americana	B, W	E, R	Riparian, marsh, open water
Sandhill Crane Grus canadensis	W	E	Fields, cienegas, mudflats
Yellow-billed Cuckoo Coccyzus americanus	B	E, R	Riparian trees
Ferruginous Pygmy-Owl Glaucidium brasilianum	B, W	E	Riparian trees, Saguaros

Table 2 continued.

Common Name[1] Scientific Name	Likely Former Status[2]	Status on Reservation[3]	Primary Habitat[4]
Elf Owl *Micrathene whitneyi*	B	E	Riparian trees, Saguaros
Belted Kingfisher *Megaceryle alcyon*	B	E	Riparian, dirt banks
Vermillion Flycatcher *Pyrocephalus rubinus*	B	E	Riparian trees
Brown-crested Flycatcher *Myiarchus tyrannulus*	B	E	Riparian trees, Saguaros
Barn Swallow *Hirundo rustica*	B	E	Widespread, buildings, wells
Corvid, sp? *Corvus (brachyrhrynchos?)*	B, W	E	Widespread
Bridled Titmouse *Baeolophus wollweberi*	W	E	Riparian trees
Marsh Wren *Cistothorus palustris*	B, W	E	Marsh
Yellow Warbler *Setophaga petechia*	B	E	Riparian trees
Common Yellowthroat *Geothlypis trichas*	B	E, C, R	Marsh
Yellow-breasted Chat *Icteria virens*	B	E, C, R	Riparian scrub
Summer Tanager *Piranga rubra*	B	E, R	Riparian trees

[1] Names and order after AOU Checklist (1998) and following supplements published periodically in *The Auk*.

[2] W= Wintering, B = Breeding.

[3] E = Extirpated, R = Recolonized restored riparian/wetland habitat, C = Colonized new riparian/wetland habitat. Status after construction of upstream dams that resulted in desertification and loss of natural wet riparian and other wetland ecosystems along the Gila and Salt Rivers on the Reservation, and after the creation of artificial water sources.

[4] Note that most species are generally associated with wet riparian or other wetland ecosystems, such as those that existed before desertification of the Gila and Salt Rivers.

[5] "Breeding" and "winter" are used instead of "permanent resident" because it is not known if different individuals from the winter population replace or mix with the summer population.

The Cactus Ferruginous Pygmy-Owl in the Phoenix Area

One of the 19 breeding avian species that Amadeo identified as being extirpated from the Reservation was the Cactus Ferruginous Pygmy-Owl (Figure 2). This small owl (averaging approximately 16.5 cm in length) was once found from north of Phoenix, Arizona, down to southern Mexico (Monson 1998). It first joined the list of recorded avian species in the United States when it was discovered in 1872 by Charles E. Bendire along Rillito Creek, near Tucson (Bendire 1892; Coues 1872). Two ornithological papers published for the Phoenix area before 1900 mention this pygmy-owl (Breninger 1898; Fisher 1893). The first published

Figure 2. Cactus Ferruginous Pygmy-Owl, *Glaucidium brasilianum cactorum* (Jacobs 2007).

record for the species in that area was from 56 km north of Phoenix at New River, in 1892 (Fisher 1893). This is the northernmost record for not only the subspecies, *Glaucidium brasilianum cactorum*, but for the entire species (Proudfoot and Johnson 2000). At New River, the Cactus Ferruginous Pygmy-Owl was described as "quite common … among the mesquit [sic] and other shrubbery scattered through the groves of giant cactus" (Fisher 1893:199). In 1895, a pygmy-owl and eggs were collected at Cave Creek by R.D. Lusk, a few miles north of Phoenix, and by the end of the 1890s several pygmy-owls and their eggs had been collected in the Phoenix region, mainly along the Salt River (Johnson et al. 2003).

Breninger (1898:128) reported the Cactus Ferruginous Pygmy-Owl to be "of common occurrence" on the Salt and Gila Rivers in the Phoenix region. He collected 11 pygmy-owls and six sets of eggs between 1896 and 1899, and one additional pygmy-owl in 1905 at Phoenix (Johnson et al. 2003). Most or all of Breninger's specimens were apparently from the Salt River (egg labels examined by R. Roy Johnson), which enters the Gila River near Phoenix. However, this small owl was not mentioned by Breninger in his list of 86 species along the Gila River on the Gila River Indian Reservation (Breninger 1901). It is possible that the pygmy-owl was just overlooked by Breninger during his short time on the Reservation, or it was simply not in residence at the time. It has been suggested that the Cactus Ferruginous Pygmy-Owl may be migratory at the northern extreme of its range (Russell and Monson 1998), or at least that there may be some seasonal movements, especially in view of so few winter records from the Phoenix and Gila River regions (Johnson et al. 2003). Alternatively, it is possible that the owl was already declining in the Phoenix area and extirpated from the Reservation.

In 1920, Swarth (1920) did not record the species at Papago Saguaro National Monument (now Papago Park, a City of Phoenix facility) on the north bank of the Salt River, upstream from Phoenix, nor was it mentioned in an early book on birds of the Phoenix area (Robinson 1930). The last two specimens taken in the Phoenix region were collected in 1949 and 1951 by Allan Phillips in a remnant patch of riparian habitat at Blue Point Cottonwoods, on the

Salt River upstream from Phoenix (Johnson et al. 2003). Located in an abandoned meander, Blue Point Cottonwoods consisted of a large stand (approximately 100 ha [250 acres]) of mature cottonwoods and scattered Goodding Willow, with an understory of mesquite and wet riparian plants (Johnson and Simpson 1971). The final record for the region was also at Blue Point Cottonwoods. It consisted of a single calling pygmy-owl heard in 1971 (Johnson and Simpson 1971; Johnson et al. 2000; Millsap and Johnson 1988). The pygmy-owl no longer occurs in the Phoenix region (Johnson et al. 2004; Proudfoot and Johnson 2000; Witzeman et al. 1997).

A Vanishing Owl and Changing American Worldview

At the beginning of the 20th century, Pimas living along the Gila River still knew the Cactus Ferruginous Pygmy-Owl (Gilman 1909); they called it **koo-ah-kohld**. But by the time Amadeo arrived on the Reservation, this little owl had ceased to be part of the Piman world. When Amadeo showed his consultants pictures and skins of the owl in the 1960s, they did not recognize it; they had no name for it (Rea 1983). The cottonwood trees that had once lined the river and provided nesting habitat for the pygmy-owl were long gone; so was the owl. In fact, the Cactus Ferruginous Pygmy-Owl was disappearing throughout most of its range in Arizona.

While Fisher called the species "quite common" in Arizona in 1893 and Breninger stated that it was "of common occurrence" in 1898, only 41 Cactus Ferruginous Pygmy-Owls were collected in the state between the subspecies' discovery in 1872 and 1953. Most specimens were taken early in the period, prior to the wholesale destruction of riparian gallery forests in the region (Johnson et al. 2003). After 1953, the bird largely disappeared from the record for more than two decades. We believe that the small number of specimens collected in the 20th century is evidence of the decline of the species rather than a failure of ornithologists to detect the owl. The late 1800s and early 1900s was a period of active ornithological fieldwork in the region. Collectors were gathering thousands of birds in Arizona at this time, often taking a dozen or more birds each of several species in a single collecting trip (Johnson et al. 2003). Collecting records during the same period do not indicate that other owls in the region (e.g., the Elf Owl *Micrathene whitneyi*) experienced similar declines (Glinski 1998). Moreover, the Cactus Ferruginous Pygmy-Owl is a conspicuous diurnal species that is not likely to have been overlooked by the professional collectors.

In the 1960s, references to the decline of the Cactus Ferruginous Pygmy-Owl began to appear in the scientific literature (Johnson et al. 1979; Monson and Phillips 1981; Phillips et al. 1964). Ornithologists became increasingly aware that the northern edge of the pygmy-owl's range was receding southward toward the Mexican border. In fact, by 1997, the Arizona population of Cactus Ferruginous Pygmy-Owls had declined so much that it was listed as endangered under the Endangered Species Act of 1973 (USFWS 1997). Critical habitat designation followed in 2002 (USFWS 2002). Only the Arizona population was listed; pygmy-owls in Texas and Mexico were unaffected. This listing action reflected a fundamental change within the American culture regarding the relationship between human society and the natural world. While certainly not universal, the modern environmental movement that began in the 1960s fostered a worldview more in line with that of traditional Pimas. Conservation of natural resources became of sufficiently high priority within the general public that the U.S. Congress was moved to pass a series of landmark environmental laws, beginning with the National Environmental Policy Act in 1969. Other environmental laws initiated during this period include, among others, the Clean Air Act (1970), the Clean Water Act (1972), the Endangered Species Act (1973), and the Archaeological and Historic Preservation Act (1974).[2]

The Cactus Ferruginous Pygmy-Owl has the unusual distinction of being listed by the Federal Government as an endangered species only to be delisted a few years later (USFWS 2006). The species was delisted because the U.S. Fish and Wildlife Service, acting on a federal court order, re-evaluated the best available scientific data and found that the Arizona population was not sufficiently significant to the taxon as a whole to warrant listing. Among other significance criteria, the Arizona population was found to represent too small a proportion of the total population of the species and too small a proportion of the total range of the species, which still extends from southern Arizona south through western Mexico, to the States of Colima and Michoacán, and from southern Texas south through the Mexican States of Tamaulipas and Nuevo Leon (USFWS 1997). The species was petitioned for relisting in 2007 by environmental groups claiming to have new information on genetics, taxonomic classification, and threats to the species (Center for Biological Diversity and Defenders of Wildlife 2007). In October of 2011, the U.S. Fish and Wildlife Service announced that they had evaluated this new information and determined that:

> While threats to pygmy-owls may be substantial on a local scale, threats throughout the majority of the pygmy-owl's range are not of sufficient imminence, severity, or magnitude to indicate that the pygmy-owl is in danger of extinction (endangered), or likely to become endangered within the foreseeable future (threatened), throughout all of its range [USFWS 2011].

Cactus Ferruginous Pygmy-Owl Habitat Controversy

There is general agreement that the Cactus Ferruginous Pygmy-Owl has disappeared from most of Arizona except for regions near the border with Mexico; however, there is disagreement about what must be done to restore the owl. The difference of opinion centers on the issue of what constitutes the historical and current preferred habitat for the species in Arizona. We contend that the species' preferred habitat differs in different parts of the state. In the extreme southern portions of Arizona and in northern Mexico, the pygmy-owl is found in upland habitats in desertscrub, semidesert grassland, and xeroriparian habitats (Flesch and Steidl 2006; Richardson et al. 2000). However, at the northern periphery of its range, where climatic conditions and other factors are different (Brown 1982), the historical breeding records for the pygmy-owl are overwhelmingly from riparian habitats (Johnson and Carothers 2003). The notable exceptions are those where the habitat was not clearly stated either in print or on the specimen label. Almost every specimen of pygmy-owls obtained before 1940 was along a stream, often in cottonwood-willow (*Populus-Salix*) gallery forest with an attendant mesquite (*Prosopis* spp.) woodland understory (Johnson 2003). Most early museum skins and eggs were taken along Rillito Creek and the Salt and Gila Rivers. If Cactus Ferruginous Pygmy-Owls had inhabited upland and xeroriparian habitats, the numerous cross-country expeditions during the late 1800s and early 1900s (Fischer 2001) should have detected them.

It is significant that the decline of the pygmy-owl in Arizona and its extirpation from the south-central portion of the state, including the Gila River Indian Reservation, paralleled the extensive loss of riparian ecosystems described above (Johnson et al. 2000, 2003, 2004). Amadeo's conclusion that loss of riparian habitat along the Gila and Salt Rivers caused the extirpation of the pygmy-owl, along with the other 28 species, from the Gila River Indian Reservation is supported by the available historical records on pygmy-owl breeding. For example, six clutches of eggs collected by Breninger from the lower Salt River in 1896 and 1899 were all from cottonwoods (Johnson et al. 2003). Pygmy-owl use of cottonwoods along the Gila River was also mentioned by Gilman (1909), while Bendire (1872, 1892) wrote of their occurrence in mesquites along Rillito Creek in the Tucson area. Apparently these early pygmy-owls in the Gila River and Phoenix areas generally nested in cottonwood trees in cavities excavated by woodpeckers, but foraged in nearby mesquite bosques in a manner similar to the Gray Hawk (*Buteo nitidus*) in Arizona today (Bibles et al. 2002; Glinski 1988, 1998; Monson 1998). Breninger (1898:128) further wrote of the Phoenix area:

> … since trees planted by man have become large enough to afford nesting sites for woodpeckers, this owl has gradually worked its way from the natural growth of timber bordering the rivers to that bordering the banks of irrigating canals, until now it can be found in places ten miles from the river. I have never known it to use holes in giant cacti as does the little Elf Owl.

As noted above, when Amadeo arrived on the Gila River Indian Reservation in 1963, the Gila and Salt Rivers were already very different from the free-flowing river systems and attendant riparian vegetation that existed during the 1800s. The huge Fremont Cottonwood and Goodding Willow trees that had grown in magnificent riparian gallery forests had been replaced with scraggly Velvet Mesquites (*Prosopis velutina* Wooton) and the introduced Salt-cedar (*Tamarix* sp.) (Johnson and Simpson 1988; Rea 1983, 1988, 1997, 2007). Loss of cottonwood and willow trees would have particularly affected cavity-nesting species such as the pygmy-owl. We maintain, as did Amadeo in his meticulously researched publications, that the loss of riparian ecosystems along the Salt and Gila Rivers was a death knell for the species in that part of the state. The same is true for the Tucson area as well.

The opposing view is that upland desert is suitable habitat for the Cactus Ferruginous Pygmy-Owl throughout its historic range in Arizona, and the owl is not a riparian obligate species in any part of its range. The logical extension of this view is that conservation of the pygmy-owl in the state can be achieved by preserving upland desert habitat. Notably, the U.S. Fish and Wildlife Service's critical habitat designation for the species (USFWS 2002), now withdrawn (USFWS 2006), included over a million acres of primarily upland desert vegetation, from the Mexican border to just north of the Phoenix area. This designation focused on upland desert rather than riparian habitats in part because the pygmy-owl is known to occupy desertscrub in the absence of riparian habitat in the southern parts of its range. But perhaps the most compelling justification for the designation was the fact that, in the late 1990s and early 2000s, the only known nesting pygmy-owls in Arizona were associated with developed desert upland habitats in northwest Tucson. While these records may appear to support the supposition that desertscrub constitutes suitable habitat for the pygmy-owl throughout its range, such a conclusion overlooks the fact that all records from northwest Tucson are in association with irrigated landscape in human developments. We are unaware of any previous nesting records in upland desert habitats in south-central Arizona, including the Tucson area, that were not associated with some sort of wetland or riparian area, either natural or artificial, (e.g., springs, irrigation ditches, and stock tanks; Burton 1984; Johnson et. al 2000, 2003, 2004; Monson 1998; Proudfoot and Johnson 2000).

As early as the 1890s, the Cactus Ferruginous Pygmy-Owl was known to have used artificial riparian habitats (Breninger 1898). And Amadeo documented the use by avian species of artificial water sources and the creation of riparian habitats in formerly desert habitats (Barehand Lane Marsh) on the Gila River Indian Reservation. While the pygmy-owl was not one of the species that returned to the Reservation, Amadeo's observations resonate with the recent history of the pygmy-owl in the watered landscapes of Tucson. The presence of the Cactus Ferruginous Pygmy-Owl in areas of residential development was first documented in 1948 by a specimen collected by Allan Phillips from a subdivision in the foothills of the Santa Catalina Mountains outside of Tucson (Johnson et al. 2003). In the 1970s, a "cluster" of breeding pairs was recorded in large-lot residential developments surrounded by upland desertscrub in northwest Tucson, where exotic trees and shrubs were admixed with native vegetation (Johnson and Carothers 2003; Monson 1998). It is significant that in recent times all known pygmy-owl territories in northwest Tucson were associated with some form of human development (Wilcox et al. 1999).

We maintain that the owls, in the absence of natural riparian ecosystems, were drawn to the artificial, or cultivated, riparian habitats (irrigated landscaping, fountains, ponds, etc.) associated with residential development. The owls were likely attracted by the increased prey base enabled by these watered environments, and by thick, cultivated vegetation that provided cover and nesting and roosting habitat. Interestingly, while in 1898 Breninger commented that he had never found pygmy-owls nesting in Saguaro cacti, in northwest Tucson the only nesting records are from Saguaros associated with the cultivated landscapes. Unfortunately, in these cultivated landscapes, the pygmy-owls also encountered increased levels of predation, disease, and other anthropogenic hazards (windows, cats and dogs, automobile traffic, etc.). These hazards resulted in high levels of mortality in the pygmy-owls (pers. com., Dennis Abbate, Arizona Game and Fish Department) and other urban raptors (Boal 1997; Boal and Mannan 1998, 1999; Mannan et al. 2000).

When systematic studies began in 1996, the northwest Tucson population of pygmy-owls included over a dozen breeding birds (Abbate et al. 1996). Since that time, the documented population apparently succumbed to the inimical nature of the human habitat and dwindled to a single male that was captured from the wild in 2006 (pers. com., Dennis Abbate, Arizona Game and Fish Department). It is likely that the northwest Tucson population is now extirpated.

The future of the Cactus Ferruginous Pygmy-Owl in the Tucson area, let alone points farther north in Arizona, does not rest with the artificial riparian-like habitats associated with urban development. Nor will it be aided by the restriction of residential and commercial development in dry upland deserts. There is an alternative, however. Amadeo noticed that, where riparian habitat was incidentally restored along the Gila River in response to human activities, numerous avian species recolonized after a period of extirpation. His observation suggests a promising, if economically and politically difficult, scenario. A program of riparian restoration along the as yet undeveloped washes and streambeds of southern and central Arizona may be the best hope for Arizona's remnant population of Cactus Ferruginous Pygmy-Owls. If sufficient riparian habitat were available in suitable areas, pygmy-owls may disperse northward from Mexico, where they are more common, and colonize the restored habitats. Fluctuations in the historical records for this species in Arizona may reflect past, periodic dispersals of owls from their core population centers in Mexico to peripheral habitats farther north in Arizona (Flesch and Steidl 2006). Such dispersals will likely occur again if suitable breeding habitats are available. There is reason to be hopeful. Reflecting an interest in protecting and preserving natural ecosystems that has gained broad-based support in the American culture over the last 50 years, numerous riparian habitat restoration projects are proposed or underway throughout the Cactus Ferruginous Pygmy-Owl's historical range in Arizona, including efforts within the Gila River Indian Community (DeSemple 2006; Elkins 2011; Fred Phillips Consulting 2008; Megdal 2005; RECON Environmental 2007).

The Legacy of Amadeo Rea

If not for Amadeo's works (Rea 1983, 1997, 2007) the cause and timing of the demise of numerous plant and animal species, including the Cactus Ferruginous Pygmy-Owl, on the Gila River Indian Reservation would remain unrecorded. His obtaining of information by searching through old manuscripts combined with field studies and interviews with the few remaining Pimas who remembered a free-flowing Gila River is invaluable. It provides a very specific, well-documented example of what can happen when humans heedlessly disregard the potential consequences of their actions on natural ecosystems and the species that inhabit them. His observations on the recolonization of human-created riparian habitats by previously extirpated plant and animal species (such as the pygmy-owl) point to the potential for recovering those species by restoring riparian habitats. Some movement in that direction is now occurring in Arizona (e.g., see Fabre and Cayla 2009, Megdal 2005, Shafroth et al. 1999). Not the least of Amadeo's contributions is his bringing to the attention of modern Americans a lost natural heritage and an awareness of a different way of relating to their physical and biological surroundings. Largely because of such naturalist writers as Amadeo Rea, Rachel Carson, and Aldo Leopold, an increasingly larger proportion of the American public has come to view the natural world in much the same way the indigenous Pima did—with respect and reverence and a fear of the consequences if humans live out of balance with nature.

Notes

1. Another pygmy-owl, the Northern Pygmy-Owl (*Glaucidium gnoma*) also occurs in Arizona; however, in this paper we use the term "pygmy-owl" to refer exclusively to the Cactus Ferruginous Pygmy-Owl.
2. It is interesting to note that this landmark legislation occurred during the Richard M. Nixon Administration and received bipartisan support.

References Cited

Abbate, Dennis J., Alexander Ditty, W. Scott Richardson, and Ron J. Olding. 1996   Cactus Ferruginous Pygmy Owl Surveys and Nest Monitoring in the Tucson Basin area, Arizona - 1996. Urban Wildlife Enhancement Final Report # U95503. Arizona Game and Fish Department, Phoenix.

American Ornithologists' Union (AOU). 1998   *Check-list of North American Birds*, 7th ed. American Ornithologists' Union, Washington D.C.

Anderson, Anders H. 1972   *A Bibliography of Arizona Ornithology: Annotated*. University of Arizona Press, Tucson.

Bendire, Charles E. 1872 List of Birds Shot or Observed and Seen in the Vicinity of Tucson and Rillitto [sic] Creek Arizona in the Years 1871 and 1872. Hand-written notes: pp. 84–112. U.S. National Museum Archives (Copy Johnson Archives).

Bendire, Charles E. 1892 *Life Histories of North American Birds with Special Reference to their Breeding Habits and Eggs.* U.S. National Museum Special Bulletin No. 1. Smithsonian Institution, Washington, DC.

Bibles, Brent D., Richard L. Glinski, and R. Roy Johnson. 2002 Gray Hawk (*Asturina nitida*). In *The Birds of North America*, No. 652, eds. Alan Poole and Frank Gill. The Birds of North America, Inc., Philadelphia, Pennsylvania.

Boal, Clint W. 1997 *An Urban Environment as an Ecological Trap for Cooper's Hawks.* Ph.D. Dissertation (Department of Ecology and Evolutionary Biology). University of Arizona, Tucson.

Boal, Clint W., and Robert W. Mannan. 1998 Nest-site Selection by Cooper's Hawks in an Urban Environment. *Journal of Wildlife Management* 62:864–871.

Boal, Clint W., and Robert W. Mannan. 1999 Comparative Breeding Ecology of Cooper's Hawks in Urban and Exurban Areas of Southeastern Arizona. *Journal of Wildlife Management* 63:77–84.

Breninger, George F. 1898 The Ferruginous Pygmy-Owl. *Osprey* 2:128.

Breninger, George F. 1901 A List of Birds Observed on the Pima Indian Reservation, Arizona. *Condor* 3:44–46.

Brown, David. E., ed. 1982 Biotic Communities of the American Southwest: United States and Mexico. *Desert Plants* 4:1–342.

Burton, John A., ed. 1984 *Owls of the World.* Tanager Books, Dover, New Hampshire.

Center for Biological Diversity and Defenders of Wildlife. 2007 Petition to List the Cactus Ferruginous Pygmy Owl as a Threatened or Endangered Species under the Endangered Species Act. Available at http://www.biologicaldiversity.org/species/birds/cactus_ferruginous_pygmy_owl/pdfs/petition-to-list-cactus-ferruginous-pygmy-owl-03-2007.pdf (verified 4 December 2011).

Coues, Elliot. 1872 A New Bird to the United States. *American Naturalist* 6:370.

DeSemple, Daniel. 2006 Rio Salado Environmental Restoration Project. CH2M Hill for the Water Environment Foundation, Alexandria, Virginia.

Dobyns, Henry F. 1981 *From Fire to Flood: Historic Human Destruction of Sonoran Desert Riverine Oases.* Ballena Press Anthropology Paper No. 20, San Jose, California.

Elkins, Ron. 2011 Tres Rios – Water for the Desert. *Lakeline* Spring 2011:20–23.

Fred Phillips Consulting. 2008 Gila River Indian Community Restoration. Available at: http://www.fredphillipsconsulting.com/projects_gila_river.htm (verified January 2012).

Fisher, Anthony K. 1893 *The Hawks and Owls of the United States in their Relation to Agriculture.* U.S. Government Printing Office, Washington DC.

Flesch, Aaron D., and Robert J. Steidl. 2006   Population Trends and Implications for Monitoring Cactus Ferruginous Pygmy-Owls in Northern Mexico. *Journal of Wildlife Management* 70:867–871.

Gilman, M. French. 1909   Some Owls Along the Gila River in Arizona. *Condor* 11:145–150.

Glinski, Richard L. 1988   Gray Hawk. In *Proceedings of the Southwest Raptor Management Symposium and Workshop*, eds. Richard L. Glinski, Beth G. Pendleton, Mary Beth Moss, Maurice N. LeFranc, Jr., Brian A. Millsap, and Steven W. Hoffman, pp. 83–86. National Wildlife Federation, Washington, D.C.

Glinski, Richard L. 1998   Gray Hawk. In *The Raptors of Arizona*, ed. Richard L. Glinski, pp. 82–85. University of Arizona Press, Tucson, and Arizona Game and Fish Department, Phoenix.

Haury, Emil W. 1976   *The Hohokam: Desert Farmers and Craftsman; Snaketown, 1964–1965.* University of Arizona Press, Tucson.

Jacobs, Sky. 2007   Cactus Ferruginous Pygmy-Owl. *Wikimedia Commons.* Available at: http://commons.wikimedia.org/wiki/File:Cactus_Ferruginous_Pygmy-owl.jpg (verified 18 May 2012)

Johnson, R. Roy, and Steven W. Carothers. 2003   A History of the Occurrence and Distribution of the Cactus Ferruginous Pygmy-Owl (*Glaucidium brasilianum cactorum*) in Southern and Central Arizona: A Scientific Analysis of a Species at the Edge of its Range. Report to Southern Arizona Home Builders, Tucson.

Johnson, R. Roy, and James M. Simpson. 1971   Important Birds from Blue Point Cottonwoods, Maricopa County, Arizona. *Condor* 73:379–380.

Johnson, R. Roy, and James M. Simpson. 1988   Desertification of Wet Riparian Ecosystems in Arid Regions of the North American Southwest. In *Arid Lands: Today and Tomorrow*, eds. Emily E. Whitehead, Charles F. Hutchinson, Barbara N. Timmermann, and Robert G. Varady, pp. 1383–1393. Westview Press, Boulder, Colorado.

Johnson, R. Roy, Jean-Luc E. Cartron, Lois T. Haight, Russell B. Duncan, and Kenneth J. Kingsley. 2000   A Historical Perspective on the Population Decline of the Cactus Ferruginous Pygmy-Owl in Arizona. In *Ecology and Conservation of the Cactus Ferruginous Pygmy-Owl in Arizona*, eds. Jean-Luc E. Cartron and Deborah M. Finch, pp. 17–26. Forest Service General Technical Report RMRS-GTR-43, Rocky Mountain Research Station, Ogden, Utah.

Johnson, R. Roy, Jean-Luc E. Cartron, Lois T. Haight, Russell B. Duncan, and Kenneth J. Kingsley. 2003   Cactus Ferruginous Pygmy-Owl in Arizona, 1872–1971. *Southwestern Naturalist* 48:389–401.

Johnson, R. Roy, Richard L. Glinski, Steven W. Carothers, and Kenneth J. Kingsley. 2004   Urban Environments and the Cactus Ferruginous Pygmy-Owl (*Glaucidium brasilianum cactorum*): a Profile of Endangerment of a Species. In *Proceedings of the Fourth International Symposium on Urban Wildlife Conservation, May 1–5, 1999*, eds. William W.

Shaw, Lisa K. Harris, and Larry VanDruff, pp. 135–145. School of Renewable Natural Resources, University of Arizona, Tucson.

LaFreniere, Gilbert F. 2007   *The Decline of Nature: Environmental History and the Western Worldview.* Academica Press, Bethesda, Maryland.

Mannan, Robert W., Clint W. Boal, Wendy J. Burroughs, James W. Dawson, Tracy S. Estabrook, and W. Scott Richardson. 2000   Nest Sites of Five Raptor Species along an Urban Gradient. In *Raptors at Risk*, eds. Robin D. Chancellor and Bernd U. Meyburg, pp. 447–453. WWBGP/Hancock House, Blaine, Washington.

Megdal, Sharon B. 2005   Environmental Restoration Projects in Arizona: the U.S. Army Corps of Engineers' Approach. Final Report, Water Resources Research Center, University of Arizona, Tucson.

Miksicek, Charles H. 1984   Historic Desertification, Prehistoric Vegetation Change, and Hohokam Subsistence in the Salt-Gila Basin. In *Hohokam Archaeology along the Salt-Gila Aqueduct, Central Arizona Project, Environment and Subsistence*, eds. Lynn S. Teague and Patricia L. Crown, pp. 53–80. *Arizona State Museum Archaeological Series* 150(7).

Millsap, Brian A., and R. Roy Johnson. 1988   Ferruginous Pygmy-Owl. In *Proceedings of the Southwest Raptor Management Symposium and Workshop*, eds. Richard L. Glinski, Beth G. Pendleton, Mary Beth Moss, Maurice N. LeFranc, Jr., Brian A. Millsap, and Stephen W. Hoffman, pp. 137–139. National Wildlife Federation, Washington, D.C.

Monson, Gale. 1998   Ferruginous Pygmy-Owl. In *The Raptors of Arizona*, ed. Richard L. Glinski, pp. 159–161. University of Arizona Press, Tucson, and Arizona Game and Fish Department, Phoenix.

Monson, Gale, and Allan Phillips. 1981   *Annotated Checklist of the Birds of Arizona*, 2nd ed. University of Arizona Press, Tucson.

Periman, Richard D., and Jeffery F. Kelley. 2000   The Dynamic Environmental History of Southwest Willow Flycatcher Habitat: a Survey of Changing Riparian Conditions through Time. In *Status, Ecology, and Conservation of the Southwestern Willow Flycatcher*, eds. Deborah M. Finch and Scott H. Stoleson, pp. 25–42. USDA Forest Service General Technical Report RMRS-GTR-60. U.S. Department of Agriculture, Forest Service, Rocky Mountain Research Station, Ogden Utah.

Phillips, Allan, Joe Marshall, Jr., and Gale Monson. 1964   *The Birds of Arizona*. University of Arizona Press, Tucson.

Pima-Maricopa Irrigation Project. 2012   Education. Available at: http://www.gilariver.com/education.htm (verified 13 January 2012).

Proudfoot, Glenn A., and R. Roy Johnson. 2000   Ferruginous Pygmy-Owl (*Glaucidium brasilianum*). In *The Birds of North America, No. 498*, eds. Alan Poole and Frank Gill. The Birds of North America, Inc., Philadelphia, Pennsylvania.

Rea, Amadeo M. 1983   *Once a River: Bird Life and Habitat Changes on the Middle Gila.* University of Arizona Press, Tucson.

Rea, Amadeo M. 1988   Habitat Restoration and Avian Recolonization from Wastewater on the Middle Gila River, Arizona. In *Arid Lands: Today and Tomorrow*, eds. Emily E. Whitehead, Charles F. Hutchinson, Barbara N. Timmermann, and Robert G. Varady, pp. 1395–1405. Westview Press, Boulder, Colorado.

Rea, Amadeo M. 1997   *At the Desert's Green Edge: An Ethnobotany of the Gila River Pima.* University of Arizona Press, Tucson.

Rea, Amadeo M. 1998   *Folk Mammalogy of the Northern Pimans.* University of Arizona Press, Tucson.

Rea, Amadeo M. 2007   *Wings in the Desert: A Folk Ornithology of the Northern Pimans.* University of Arizona Press, Tucson.

RECON Environmental, Inc. 2007   Final Work Plan for Rillito River Ecosystem Restoration Project Areas 2 and 3, Tucson, Arizona. Prepared for Macro-Z Technology, prepared by RECON Environmental, Inc., Tucson, Arizona.

Redman, Charles L., and Ann P. Kinzig. 2008   Water can Flow Uphill: A Narrative of Central Arizona. In *Agrarian Landscapes in Transition: Comparisons of Long-term Ecological and Cultural Change*, eds. Charles L. Redman & David R. Foster, pp. 238–271. Oxford University Press, New York.

Richardson, W. Scott, Jean-Luc E. Cartron, David J. Krueper, Lauren Turner, and Thomas H. Skinner. 2000   The Status of the Cactus Ferruginous Pygmy-Owl in Arizona: Population Surveys and Habitat Assessment. In *Ecology and Conservation of the Cactus Ferruginous Pygmy-Owl in Arizona*, eds. Jean-Luc E. Cartron and Deborah M. Finch, pp. 27–46. USDA Forest Service General Technical Report RMRS-GTR-43. U.S. Department of Agriculture, Forest Service, Rocky Mountain Research Station, Ogden, Utah.

Robinson, William H. 1930   *Our Friendly Birds.* Chandler Arizonan, Chandler, Arizona.

Rosenberg, Kenneth V., Robert D. Ohmart, William C. Hunter, and Bertin W. Anderson. 1991   *Birds of the Lower Colorado River Valley.* University of Arizona Press, Tucson.

Russell, Stephen M., and Gale Monson. 1998   *The Birds of Sonora.* University of Arizona Press, Tucson.

Shafroth, Patrick B., Barbara Tellman, and Mark Kendig Briggs. 1999   *Riparian Ecosystem Restoration in the Gila River Basin: Opportunities and Constraints.* Water Resources Research Center Issue Paper No. 21. Water Resources Research Center, College of Agriculture, University of Arizona, Tucson.

Swarth, Harry S. 1914   A Distributional List of the Birds of Arizona. *Pacific Coast Avifauna* 10:1–133.

Swarth, Harry S. 1920   *Birds of the Papago Saguaro National Monument and the Neighboring Regions, Arizona.* U.S. National Park Service, Washington, D.C.

U.S. Fish and Wildlife Service (USFWS). 1997   Endangered and Threatened Wildlife and Plants; Determination of Endangered Status for the Cactus Ferruginous Pygmy-Owl; Final Rule. *Federal Register* 62:10730–10747.

U.S. Fish and Wildlife Service (USFWS). 2002   Endangered and Threatened Wildlife and Plants; Designation of Critical Habitat for the Arizona Distinct Population Segment of the Cactus Ferruginous Pygmy-Owl (*Glaucidium brasilianum cactorum*); Proposed Rule. *Federal Register* 67:71032–7164.

U.S. Fish and Wildlife Service (USFWS). 2006   Endangered and Threatened Wildlife and Plants; Final rule to Remove the Arizona Distinct Population Segment of the Cactus Ferruginous Pygmy-Owl (*Glaucidium brasilianum cactorum*) from the Federal List of Endangered and Threatened Wildlife; Withdrawal of the Proposed Rule to Designate Critical Habitat; Removal of Federally Designated Critical Habitat; Final Rule. *Federal Register* 71:19452–19458.

U.S. Fish and Wildlife Service (USFWS). 2011   News Release [October 4, 2011]. Cactus Ferruginous Pygmy-Owl does not Warrant Endangered Species Act Protection. U.S. Fish and Wildlife Service, Arizona Ecological Services Field Office, Phoenix, Arizona.

White, Lynn., Jr. 1967   The Historical Roots of our Ecologic Crisis. *Science* 155:1203–1207.

Wilcox, Renee L., W. Scott Richardson, and Dennis Abbate. 1999   Habitat Characteristics of Occupied Cactus Ferruginous Pygmy-Owl (*Glaucidium brasilianum cactorum*) Sites at the Suburban/Rural Interface of North Tucson, Arizona. Arizona Game and Fish Department, Phoenix.

Witzeman, Janet L., Salome R. Demaree, and Eleanor L. Radke. 1997   *Birds of Phoenix and Maricopa County, Arizona*, 2nd ed. Maricopa Audubon Society, Phoenix, Arizona.

"To Feed all the People": Lucille Clifton's Fall Feasts for the Gitga'at Community of Hartley Bay, British Columbia

Nancy Turner[†], Colleen Robinson[‡], Gideon Robinson[§], and Belle Eaton[‡]

With thanks to all her family and friends who remember her generosity and teachings, we dedicate this paper to the memory of Lucille Clifton, her husband Heber Clifton, and to all the children, youth, and Elders of the Gitga'at Nation.

Abstract

Lucille Clifton, Eagle Matriarch of the Gitga'at (Tsimshian) community of Hartley Bay on the north coast of British Columbia, passed away in 1962 at the age of 86. She and her husband, Heber Clifton, were important and respected leaders of the Gitga'at Nation. Through her knowledge of traditional foods, her dedication to her community, and her teachings to her grandchildren and other Gitga'at children, Lucille had a tremendous and enduring influence on the Gitga'at's present status as a people who still rely on and celebrate their traditional foods. Lucille's grandchildren (including two co-authors of this paper), themselves now respected elders, recall that Lucille and the other Eagle women regularly hosted a feast around Thanksgiving every year from the 1920s to the 1950s, in which they served an array of traditional foods, including cambium of Western Hemlock (*Tsuga heterophylla*) and Amabilis Fir (*Abies amabilis*), edible seaweed (*Porphyra abbottiae*), Pacific Crabapples (*Malus fusca*) and Highbush Cranberries (*Viburnum edule*) in whipped oulachen grease, many different fish and shellfish dishes, and a variety of other dishes from the marine and terrestrial environments of Gitga'at territory. Today, as traditional food is increasingly recognized as vital for Indigenous Peoples' health and well-being, Lucille's teachings are as important as ever, helping her descendants to maintain their resilience, self sufficiency, and cultural identity in the face of immense global change.

† School of Environmental Studies, PO Box 3060 STN CSC, University of Victoria, Victoria, BC V8W 3R4; [nturner@uvic.ca]
‡ Colleen Robinson and Belle Eaton, G.D., Hartley Bay, BC V0V 1A0
§ Gideon Robinson passed away in 2006.

Introduction

In every community there are people who stand out as leaders, teachers, and mentors (Garibaldi 2003; Welch et al. 2011). Through their strong personalities, their deeds, their skills and their wisdom, they serve as examples for others to follow, and they set standards by which the entire community measures itself. Long after they have gone, they continue to serve in this special role, and their name evokes many memories, stories, and images for all who knew them. Lucille Clifton (**Wilh Puun** "big whale"[1]) of the Gitga'at (Tsimshian) community of Hartley Bay on the north coast of British Columbia was one of these people. She died half a century ago, yet she is still well remembered by everyone in the village who is old enough to have known her.[2] In this paper, we focus on one particular aspect of Lucille's contributions: her knowledge of traditional food and its preparation, and how she continuously reinforced the importance of this food for her community by preparing it and serving it to the whole Gitga'at community at an annual fall feast. The feasts that she organized and hosted are still well remembered today, despite the regular occurrence of feasts at Hartley Bay (Tirone et al. 2007). Notably, Lucille's feasts are part of a long tradition of Gitga'at feasting (see Anderson 1984, 2004; Campbell 1984; Miller 1984). Here we suggest that, through her hard work, interest, and leadership, she actually helped reinforce the feasting tradition and encouraged its continuation to the present day. Lucille's exceptional influence in supporting and maintaining the Gitga'at indigenous food system is obvious, even to visitors to the community. The combination of her training and background, the force of her personality, her position as a community leader, and her intense knowledge and interest in food and in the health and well-being of her people, reflects the remarkable contribution a single individual can make in retaining cultural knowledge and practice even during times of intense change.

Lucille's example bears close scrutiny, because it enables us to better understand a key pathway of cultural knowledge transmission and because it shows at a very personal level how food plays such an integral role in mediating an Indigenous people's relationship with the lands and waters of their territory. The story of Lucille's life and influence has many counterparts throughout the world, in communities facing rapid and unrelenting change from external forces, communities at risk of losing their unique cultures, including their traditional foods, because of the tides of environmental, social, and economic change that threaten to overwhelm them (Kuhnlein et al. 2009; Singh 2004; Singh and Sureja 2006; Turner and Turner 2008; Turner et al. 2008).

Lucille Clifton was known as **No'o** ("Mother") to virtually everyone in Hartley Bay. Both she and her husband Heber Clifton (**Hadi'ix**) were important and respected leaders of the Gitga'at Nation (Figure 1). Lucille was the Eagle Clan matriarch of Hartley Bay for over half a century. She was born in 1876 and died on September 6th, 1962 at the age of 86.[3] Lucille's grandchildren, themselves now mature adults and elders, have especially vivid recollections of her, and her special qualities, values, and knowledge. The feasts that Lucille organized,

Figure 1. Lucille Clifton (*No'o*), centre, with other Gitga'at matriarchs, ca. 1950s. Lucille's friend Annie Robinson (married to Heber Clifton's cousin) is on the left, and her sister-in-law Myria Wilson (Heber's sister) on the right, 1987. Courtesy of Helen Clifton and Teri Clifton Robinson; Gitga'at First Nation.

directed and provided for the community are only one aspect of her legacy in the Gitga'at community. All of the elders in Hartley Bay today remember her stories, songs and teachings that she shared with them when they were young.

Elizabeth Dundas (pers. comm. December 2003), whose mother was a good friend of Lucille's, clearly recalled her travels with Lucille by boat as a child. Lucille used to take Elizabeth and her brother Archie Dundas with her to Gil Island, Fin Island, and all over Gitga'at territory. Everywhere they went, Lucille would be telling stories and singing songs to the children. Often the stories referred to specific places and special landmarks they passed on their travels. Elizabeth said she would never forget the picnics she had with Lucille. There would always be cooked potatoes and dried salmon or halibut *wooks,* with eulachon grease. There might be dried berries as well and other treats that still make Elizabeth's mouth water many years later.

Belle Eaton had similar memories. When nobody was around to take them to Old Town, they would paddle up in a canoe, or use a rowboat both going and coming. Lucille had a large sail made out of sugar bags sewn together, and as they rowed, paddled, or sailed along, she would tell stories or sing to them. Some of the stories were about the places they passed by in the boat. Belle also remembered that every night, right after dinner, around 6 or 7 o'clock, Lucille would take all the children into the dining-room, where they would sit in a circle while she told them stories of *Txemsm* and other legendary characters. Others remember her tucking them into their beds and telling them stories or singing songs until they fell asleep. Some of Lucille's songs were in *Sm'algyax* [Tsimshian] and some, particularly hymns, were in Chinook Jargon, the old trade language, which she spoke fluently.

Lucille, as leader and Eagle matriarch, was also a mediator in the community. If any of the women in the village had had an argument and were quarrelling for some reason, Lucille would call them together for a cup of tea, talk to them, and then tell them to stand up, shake hands, forgive and forget. Her work in dispute resolution could still be a model for many communities today.

The feasts that Lucille Clifton and the other women of her Eagle Clan hosted in the fall for the entire village are outstanding in the memories of all today's elders. These feasts are remarkable for many reasons, but especially for the food that was served, which included largely traditional products of the land and sea from within Gitga'at territory. Feasting is a major cultural activity for Northwest Coast Indigenous Peoples in general, and Lucille's feasts serve as an example of the importance of traditional food and food gathering more generally as a mechanism for cultural interaction and identity, both reflecting and serving to perpetuate Traditional Ecological Knowledge and Wisdom (Jonaitis 1991; Tirone et al. 2007; Watts and Watts 2007). In recalling these feasts, people are remembering more than just the food that was served; they are bringing forward to the present time a whole constellation of associated knowledge and social relationships that can inform and strengthen people's ability to sustain their lifeways and culture into the future.

Much of the food served at these feasts was prepared by Lucille's own hands. This was the old-time food, some of it seldom harvested or eaten today, and in some cases unknown to the current younger members of the community. Yet, the elders of today had the privilege not only of sampling, but also acquiring a taste for, Gitga'at traditional food. This is important because research has shown that people like to eat foods they are familiar with and often do not enjoy foods that are new or different to them (Kuhnlein 1992; Parrish et al. 2007). As use of traditional food declines and marketed food, often less healthy, takes its place, food preferences change, which results in less traditional food being used, and so on, in a downward spiral of nutritional and cultural loss. As people stop seeking their traditional food out on the lands and waters, the cultural knowledge about these foods and environments also diminishes, and, one might argue, so do people's relationships with their home places (Devereaux and Kittredge 2008; Gitga'at Nation et al. 2003; Kuhnlein 1989, 1992, 1995; Turner and Turner 2008; Turner et al. in press). This gives even deeper meaning to the legacy of Lucille Clifton.

In this paper, we describe Lucille's feasts among the Gitga'at. Following a brief discussion of research methods and context, we begin our paper by describing Gitga'at food harvesting traditions to contextualize the descriptions of Lucille's feasts. We then provide a typical menu for one of Lucille's feasts, noting how the food for the feast was harvested and prepared. We end with a discussion of the importance of Lucille's feasts in a contemporary context, as a venue for teaching and strengthening cultural values and critical knowledge about the land and environment, and as an opportunity for reinforcing the use of nutritious foods that have sustained the Gitga'at and other coastal peoples for many generations. Individuals like Lucille Clifton were, and are, through the legacy of their knowledge and teachings, critically important in helping communities to retain their customs, maintain their resilience, and to withstand major changes and restructuring of their economies.

Methods and Context

The information we present here was documented during the course of ethnobotanical investigations with the Gitga'at Nation, under the broader interdisciplinary research program, *Coasts Under Stress* (Ommer et al. 2007). During this research, open-ended interviews were conducted with elders and other knowledgeable community members under protocols established between the *Coasts Under Stress* Research team and the Gitga'at Nation, as well as through the University of Victoria Research Ethics Review Board. One of the goals of *Coasts Under Stress* was to document social and environmental change, and assist local communities of both Pacific and Atlantic coasts of Canada in documenting and perpetuating traditional knowledge of the environment, and to demonstrate its importance to younger members of the communities. Participant observation and interviews were undertaken in the homes of elders, in the Gitga'at Cultural Centre, and out in various locations in Gitga'at territory, including the places described in this paper. Several publications have resulted from this work (cf. Kealey et al. 2006; Ommer et al. 2006, 2007; Parrish et al. 2007; Thompson 2004; Tirone et al. 2007; Turner and Clifton 2006, 2009; Turner and Thompson 2006; Turner et al. 2008). During interviews and discussions, memories of Lucille Clifton and her contributions to the community were reinforced many times—in particular her dedication to teaching her grandchildren and other children, and her perseverance in traditional food production and maintaining the Gitga'at way of life as exemplified by the annual feasts she organized. This recognition ultimately led us to develop this paper.

Traditional Gitga'at Food Harvesting Traditions

Lucille's work in food harvesting and preparation for her feasts—as well as for her family's year-round food supply, and for gifting and trade—followed a time-honored routine of seasonal harvesting at different key sites within Gitga'at territory (Figure 2). All the Gitga'at families of her day, in the early to mid 1900s, followed a traditional seasonal round in order to obtain and process the wide range of provisions that sustained them through the year. In

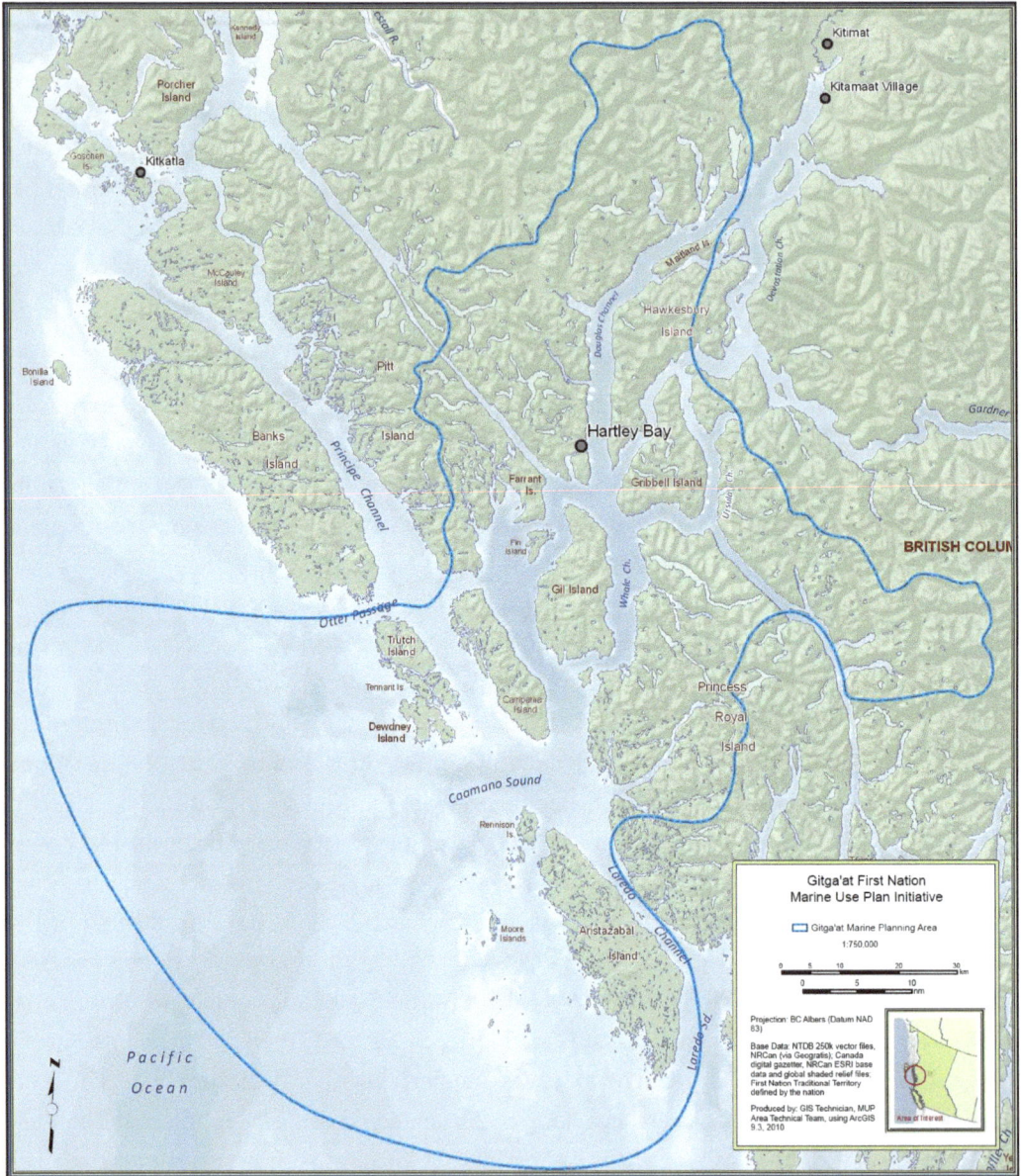

Figure 2. Map of Gitga'at territory (Gitga'at Nation, 2011).

these food production endeavors, Lucille was outstanding, by all accounts. Her feasts represented an integration of all of the food harvests through the entire growing season and were the focus of great anticipation and activity at the end of the harvest season.

Around the beginning of May, people traveled to Kiel, the Gitga'at spring camp on Princess Royal Island (where Lucille's youngest son Johnny Clifton was born in 1918). At Kiel, the women harvested and dried their year's supply of edible seaweed (*Porphyra abbottiae*) (Turner 2003; Turner and Clifton 2006), along with their other springtime foods (Table 1;

Table 1. Key seasonal foods of the Gitga'at Nation (cf. Turner and Thompson 2006)*

Spring Foods (especially from Kiel and Vicinity)	Gitga'at (Sm'algyax) name	Notes
Red Laver seaweed (*Porphyra abbottiae* Krishnamurthy)	*lhaask*	Harvested in May, mainly from Kiel: Princess Royal Island and nearby islands; dried and traded; sprinkled on soup, potatoes, fried and eaten as a snack (Turner and Clifton 2006; see discussion in text).
Halibut (*Hippoglossus stenolepsis*)	*txaw*	Harvested in fall, winter and spring, especially during the Kiel spring harvest camp; cut into thin strips (*wooks*) and dried; heads and backbones smoked and cooked into soup.
Spring Salmon (*Oncorhynchus tshawytscha*)	*yeeh*	Fished at Kiel and other places in the territory in spring; dried as *wooks*; red and white varieties, both enjoyed.
Sockeye Salmon (*Oncorhynchus nerka*)	*müsoo*	Fished at Kiel and other places in the territory in spring and summer.
Red snapper (*Sebastes ruberrimus*)	*ts'mhoon*	Fished at Kiel and other places in the territory in spring; hung to cure, then filleted and fried.
"Chinese slippers" (Gumshoe Chitons) (*Cryptochiton stelleri*)	*ts'ak*	Harvested around Kiel, baked, then sliced; nowadays frozen.
Smaller chitons (*Katharina tunicata* and other spp.)	*'yaanst*	Harvested around Kiel, especially by children and youth; boiled and eaten.
Northern Abalone (*Haliotis kamschatkana*)	*bilaa*	Formerly a great delicacy, harvested with care at the lowest tides; abalone now protected from harvesting because of impacts of commercial harvesting.
Harbour Seal (*Phoca vitulina*)	*üüla*	Hunted occasionally in spring, fall and winter; used for meat and oil; flippers cooked separately; see discussion in text.
Thimbleberry shoots (*Rubus parviflorus* Nutt.)	*ooylh*	Young shoots peeled and eaten raw in spring, sometimes dipped in grease and sugar.
Salmonberry shoots (*Rubus spectabilis* Pursh)	*ooylh*	Young shoots peeled and eaten raw or cooked in spring, sometimes dipped in grease and sugar.
"Wild rhubarb" (western dock) (*Rumex aquaticus* L. var. *fenestratus* (Greene) Dorn)	*lak'oots*	Leaves and leafstalks cooked and eaten with oulachen grease and riceroot.
Cow-parsnip (*Heracleum maximum* Bartram)	*p'iins, layoon*	Young budstalks and leafstalks peeled and eaten fresh in April and May.
Spring Foods (especially from Kiel and Vicinity)	**Gitga'at (Sm'algyax) name**	**Notes**
Northern Riceroot (*Fritillaria camschatcensis* (L.) Ker Gawl.)	*miyumbmgyet*	White starchy bulbs dug in spring and fall, steamed and eaten with grease and sugar, and sometimes with "wild rhubarb."
Eggs of seagulls (*Chroicocephalus philadelphia*, *Larus* spp.) and Black Oystercatcher (*Haematopus bachmani*)	*lgumet* (eggs); *gaguum* and *gyedmxł*	Harvested carefully, only one or two from each nest, and at the beginning of the season, allowing time for the birds to lay and hatch more eggs; cooked and eaten as a delicacy.

Table 1 continued.

Oulachen grease and smoked oulachens (*Thaleichthys pacificus*)	*ḵawtsi* (grease); *'wah*	Oulachen grease and smoked oulachens traded from Haisla people at Kitamaat and from the Nisga'a at the mouth of the Nass River.
Summertime Foods (from various places around Hartley Bay)	**Gitga'at (Sm'algyax) name**	**Notes**
Edible cambium of Amabilis Fir (*Abies amabilis* Dougl. ex Loud.)	*ksiiw*	Harvested in June and July when the bark is easily removed in pieces from the trunk; cambium is fried or cooked and served with grease and salmon egg "cheese"; see discussion in text.
Edible cambium of Western Hemlock (*Tsuga heterophylla* (Raf.) Sarg.)	*ksiiw*	Harvested in June and July when the bark is easily removed in pieces from the trunk; cambium is fried or cooked and served with grease and salmon egg "cheese"; see discussion in text.
Salmonberries (*Rubus spectabilis* Pursh)	*maḵooxs*	Berries picked in early summer and eaten fresh; nowadays made into jam or frozen; golden, ruby and dark colour forms.
Thimbleberries (*Rubus parviflorus* Nutt.)	*ḵoo*	Berries picked in early summer and eaten fresh or dried; nowadays made into jam or frozen.
Red Huckleberries (*Vaccinium parvifolium* Sm.)	*wüleéxs*	Berries picked in early summer and eaten fresh or cooked and dried into cakes; nowadays made into jam or frozen.
Salal berries (*Gaultheria shallon* Pursh)	*dzawes*	Berries picked in early summer and eaten fresh or cooked and dried into cakes; nowadays made into jam or frozen.
Gray Currants (*Ribes bracteosum* Dougl. ex Hook.)	*waakyil*	Berries picked in early summer and eaten fresh or cooked and dried into cakes; nowadays made into jam or frozen; sometimes mixed with other berries.
Alaska Blueberries (*Vaccinium alaskaense* Howell)	*smmay, wo'oksil*	Berries picked in early summer and eaten fresh or cooked and dried into cakes; nowadays made into jam or frozen.
Oval-leaved Blueberries (*Vaccinium ovalifolium* Sm.)	*smmay, wo'oksil*	Berries picked in early summer and eaten fresh or cooked and dried into cakes; nowadays made into jam or frozen.
Labrador Tea (*Rhododendron groenlandicum* (Oeder) K.A. Kron & W.S. Judd)	*ḵwila'maxs*	Leaves picked from peat bog areas in summer and fall, after flowering, dried then boiled to make tea.
Late Summer and Fall Foods, especially from "Old Town," Kitkiata Inlet	**Gitga'at (Sm'algyax) name**	**Notes**
Potatoes (*Solanum tuberosum* L.)	*sgusiit*	Grown in gardens; sometimes purchased from Nuxalk and others; boiled and served with grease, seaweed, or cooked in soup.
Turnips (*Brassica rapa* L.)	*'yaanahuu*	Grown in gardens; sometimes purchased from Nuxalk and others; boiled until soft, or cooked in soups.
Carrots (*Daucus carota* L.)	*'kawts, galots*	Grown in gardens; sometimes purchased from Nuxalk and others; boiled until soft, or cooked in soups.

Humps, or "humpies" (Pink salmon) (*Oncorhynchus gorbuscha*)	*stmoon*	Caught in fall, especially at Old Town; partially smoked; eggs made into "caviar" and salmon egg cheese.
Coho Salmon (*Oncorhynchus kisutch*)	*wiiix*	Caught in fall, especially at Old Town; dried; eggs made into "caviar" and salmon egg cheese.
Chum salmon (*Oncorhynchus keta*)	*gayniis*	Caught in fall, especially at Old Town; boiled in soup; eggs made into "caviar" and salmon egg cheese.
Crabs (*Cancer magister* and other spp.)	*k'almoos*	Caught in fall, winter and spring in waters around Hartley Bay and at Old Town.
Canada Geese (*Branta canadensis*)	*ha'ax*	Hunted at Old Town in the fall; roasted or made into soup.
Snow Geese (*Chen caerulescens*)	*lhii'wn*	Hunted at Old Town in the fall; roasted.
Mallard ducks (*Anas platyrhynchos*)	*nanaat, nana, an'ana*	Hunted at Old Town in the fall; roasted or made into soup.
Grouse (*Bonasa umbellus* and other spp.)	*maxmeex*	Hunted at Old Town and elsewhere in the fall; roasted.
Black-tailed Deer (*Odocoileus hemionus*)	*wan*	Hunted at Old Town and elsewhere in the fall; different cuts prepared into steaks, stews, ribs; deer fat used in medicine.
Pacific Crabapples (*Malus fusca* (Raf.) C.K. Schneid.)	*moolks*	Picked from around lakes and estuaries in late summer and fall, especially at Old Town; at least five varieties named; cooked and stored in grease; see text discussion.
Highbush Cranberries (*Viburnum edule* (Michx.) Raf.)	*lhaaya*	Picked from around lakes and creeks in late summer and fall; cooked and stored in grease; see text discussion.
Blueberries and other late ripening fruits (*Vaccinium* spp.)	*smmay* and others	Picked, especially at Old Town, served fresh or made into jam.
Pacific Silverweed (*Argentina egedii* (Wormsk.) Rydb.)	*yeen*	Dug in fall and spring, steamed and served with grease and sugar.

Winter and Early Spring Foods	Gitga'at (Sm'algyax) name	Notes
Woodfern rootstocks (*Dryopteris expansa* (K.B. Presl) Fraser-Jenkins & Jermy)	*aa*	Rootstocks dug in fall, winter and early spring, cooked in underground pits and served with grease.
Clams (*Saxidomus giganteus* and other spp.)	*tsa'ax*	Dug at low winter and spring tides from beaches around Hartley Bay, Clamstown and *K'dis koos* (*Kish kosh*).
Cockles (*Clinocardium nuttallii*)	*gaboox*	Dug at low winter and spring tides from beaches around Hartley Bay, Clamstown and *K'dis koos*.
Herring eggs (*Clupea pallasi*)	*ksaloow* (eggs: *xs'waanx*)	Eggs harvested in spring from giant kelp fronds and from hemlock branches submerged in quiet bays and inlets like Cornwall Inlet. Cooked and eaten with potatoes and grease; sometimes dried; nowadays frozen for storage.

* This list is by no means exhaustive; it covers only the more common traditional foods of the Gitga'at.

Figures 3, 4, 5) (Gitga'at Nation et al. 2003). Sometimes they took their first harvest of sea-weed, once dried, up Douglas Channel to Kitamaat (where Lucille Clifton and others had relatives) to trade for oulachen grease and various products from the inland regions. They then returned to Kiel to harvest seaweed for their own use.

Most people moved back from Kiel to Hartley Bay for a short time in June to store their preserved spring foods. Then, over the summer, many people went fishing or moved to the nearby canneries to work in the wage economy. Colleen's and Belle's mother and father, Ma-bel and Herbert Ridley, often went to work in the canneries, and their children would stay with *No'o* ("Mother", i.e., their grandmother Lucille). During the summer, the women picked berries of many types (Table 1). They also went to places around Hartley Bay, such as Turtle Point on Gil Island to harvest edible inner bark of hemlock and Amabilis Fir, and to tend their gardens of potatoes and turnips, harvesting this produce at the end of the summer.

In the late summer and fall, around September, the families travelled to "Old Town," or Kitkiata, at the juncture of the Quaal and Kitkiata rivers on the north side of Douglas Chan-nel, towards Kitamaat from Hartley Bay. Old Town is the original home of the Gitga' at, before the entire community moved to Hartley Bay over a century ago. When they went back to Old Town, they would take a few stores—sugar, flour, coffee—and eat mostly the foods they harvested from that area. The people fished for salmon, usually humps, or "humpies" (Pink Salmon) first and then Coho, hunted deer, Canada Geese and other gamebirds, and picked their winter's supply of late-ripening blueberries, crabapples (Figure 6), and Highbush

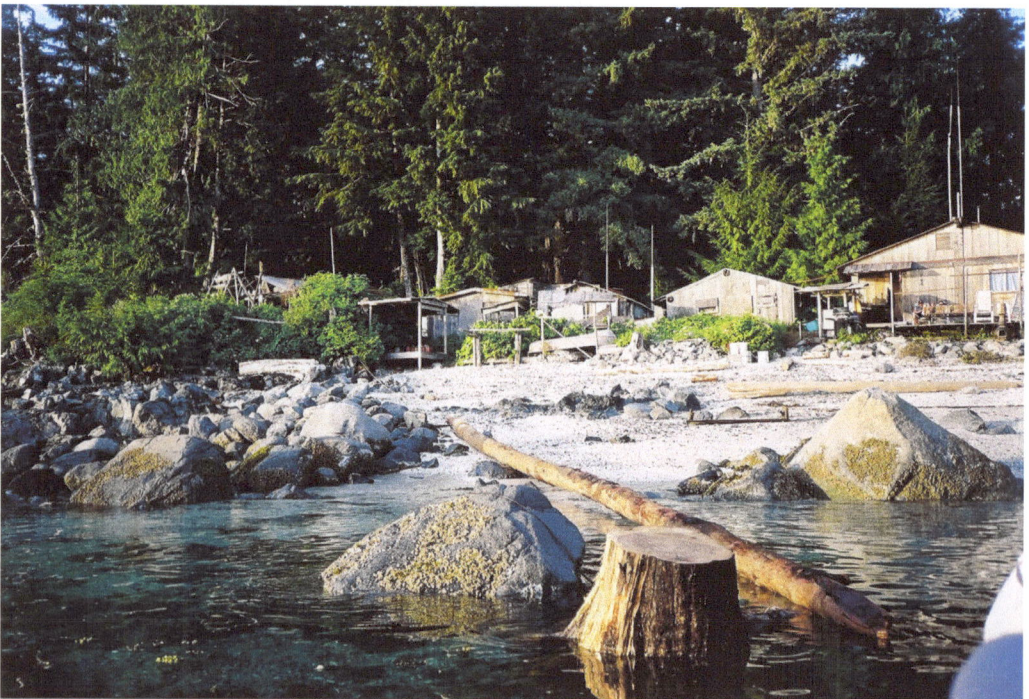

Figure 3. Kiel, Gitga'at spring harvest camp, May 2003.

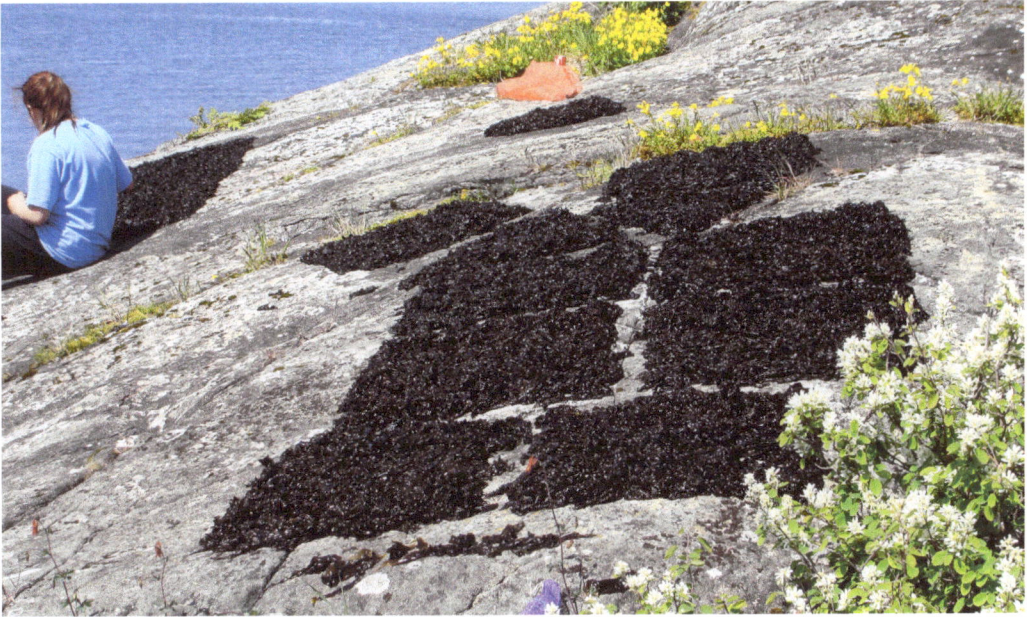

Above: Figure 4. Drying seaweed (**lha'ask**) on the rock at Kiel, May 2004.

Figure 5. Belle Eaton preparing Gumshoe Chitons, Kiel, May 2007.

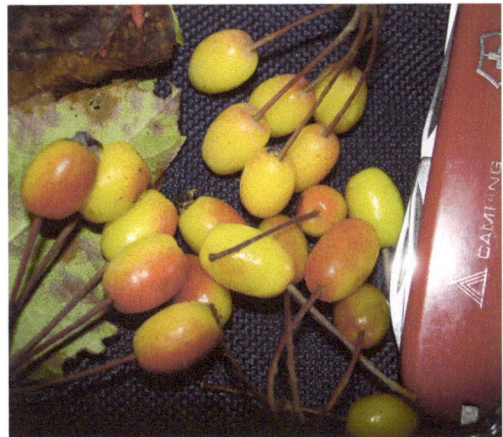

Figure 6. Pacific Crabapples (**moolks**), Hartley Bay, September 2005.

Cranberries (Figure 7). Then, in mid-October, they returned to Hartley Bay for the winter, although the harvesting round continued, as people went to certain locations like **K'dis koos** (**Kish kosh**) and Clamstown to get clams and cockles in the winter months, to quiet bays and inlets for herring eggs in the early spring, and then ventured up to the Nass River around March to participate in the oulachen harvest and trade for oulachen grease (Figure 8). The exact times of travel to and from these places depended upon the weather conditions, tides, and other factors.

Lucille's Fall Feasts

In this section, we provide details of Lucille's annual feast, highlighting the diversity of foods she and her grandchildren, together with other Eagle Clan women, harvested and prepared. This account is largely based on the recollections of Belle Eaton and Colleen Robinson, who, as children and young adults helped their grandmother with all aspects of the feast's preparations. The memories of Lucille's youngest son, Hereditary Chief Johnny Clifton (**Wamood-mx**), and his wife Helen Clifton, and of Colleen's husband Gideon Robinson, and other relatives and community members, are also included (Figures 9, 10).

Figure 7. Highbush Cranberries (**lhaaya**) at Teboyget Lake, **K'dis koos** (**Kish kosh**) Inlet, August 2007.

Figure 8. Oulachen grease (**k'awtsi**) from the Nass River, and rockfish curing, Kiel, 2003.

Left: Figure 9. Helen and Chief Johnny Clifton at Kiel, 2002.

Below: Figure 10. Colleen and Gideon Robinson, June 2003.

Preparing for the Feast

Every year, shortly after returning to Hartley Bay from the fall camp at Kitkiata, Lucille started to plan her fall feast, together with all the members of the Eagle Clan (Clan membership is matrilineal, inherited through the mother's lineage.). The Eagle Clan feast was not the only such feast to be held. Lucille's husband Heber and his Blackfish (Killerwhale) Clan also hosted feasts for the community, as did the Raven Clan (Mildred Wilson, pers. comm. 2003). Lucille herself hosted another Eagle feast in the spring, before all the people dispersed for their fishing and other harvesting activities (Margaret Anderson, pers. comm. 2003). However, Lucille's fall feast was the most memorable, and probably the most sumptuous, of all. It featured many of the favorite customary, nutritious foods that had been harvested and processed in traditional ways from Kiel, Kitkiata, and other places around Gitga'at territory. The timing of the feast varied from year to year, but usually it was around Thanksgiving time in late October or early November, and it was generally considered as a "thanksgiving" event and it tended to coincide with that holiday.

Right after her return from Old Town, Lucille would call the Eagle women together. They would discuss the best date for the feast, the types and quantities of food required, who would provide and cook it, how the invitations would be made, protocols for seating, babysitting arrangements, and other such details. Johnny Clifton (pers. comm. 2003) recalled that, before the days of radios, messengers were sent around the village to call the people to the feast; "You would send someone to tell everyone that the food is ready." At a recent feast (2005), this practice of personally delivered, verbal invitations to each household to attend was resumed. The women of the clan—including Lucille's daughters and their daughters, in the case of her feasts—prepared the food, providing dishes, preserves, condiments, cooking pots, and anything else needed from their own households. The tables were set, each under the charge of one woman who, with her helpers, set out all the food for her table in a particular order, for the guests to help themselves.

The Guests

At the time, as today, feasts included the entire community; members of the other clans, who were not involved in preparing the feast, were the invited guests, along with representative leaders of other communities. In the earlier years, when a smaller, older hall was used for the feast, there wasn't enough room to allow children to attend, but all the adults of the village were invited. Johnny Clifton recalled that there were generally 120 to 150 people in attendance at his mother Lucille's feasts. Then, when a larger new hall was built, gradually they let children come, and a small force of women was assigned to help look after all of them. Helen Clifton recalled that their oldest son, Albert (now Hereditary Blackfish Clan Chief), even as a toddler, would come and sit at the head table with his grandmother Lucille. He would have to stay there for the entire time, and couldn't leave; once the feast had started, it was considered bad manners to leave the hall (Helen Clifton, pers. comm. 2003).

In Lucille's time, the members for each clan—Eagle, Raven, and Blackfish (Killerwhale) —sat together in their own sections of the hall. There were also a few people in the Wolf Clan, who usually joined with the Blackfish. At Lucille's feast, the Ravens sat on one side, the Blackfish on the other, with the Eagles hosting and serving. The subchiefs, speakers and those holding special positions were seated at the head table, just as they are today. The chiefs and special guests were well looked after; the hosts always made especially sure that the chiefs and their wives were comfortable.

Protocols

The fall feast was a celebration for the entire community. It was a solemn and respectful occasion. The guests were addressed by the groups they represented: Chiefs, Matriarchs (highborn women), highborn people (their children), people and children ("little ones"). When children first started to attend the feasts, they were kept very quiet. Elders recalled that there were no babies crying when the chief was speaking, or when visiting chiefs were talking. Any children who cried or made noise were taken out of the hall right away. It was considered highly disrespectful to interrupt a speaker.

Although the Eagle Clan provided most of the food at Lucille's feasts, others also contributed. For example, a hunter from another clan—a grandson or someone else—might provide a seal or some other food for the feast. Sometimes this contribution was requested from the Clan. On one occasion, Helen Clifton (who is in the Blackfish Clan) recalled, Lucille (her mother-in-law) had been unable to get enough Coho to serve at her feast. That fall, Helen's son Dennis had caught many "humpies." They were plentiful and he got a whole net-load of them, about 60 fish. Helen and her family cleaned the fish, cut the fins off the backs, and prepared them to hang up to smoke (Figure 11). They arranged them over the rafters in the attic of Lucille's house to complete the drying. Her mother-in-law Lucille sent a messenger to Helen to ask her to come over to where the Eagle women were holding the planning meeting for the feast. This was after the meeting had been concluded, since it would be inappropriate for anyone outside the clan to actually participate in such a meeting, Helen said. Lucille then formally asked her whether she would be willing to have them use these dried humpbacks for their Eagle feast. Of course Helen agreed, and they took and used all the fish. Lucille did not say very much at the time, but that Christmas, Helen received a very special gift from her. Similarly, a person contributing a seal or some other food who was not of the host clan would also receive a gift of a blanket or some other valued item.

The Menu

The menu for Lucille's feasts varied each year, depending on availability of the different kinds of food. However, there were standard dishes, remembered by all as typical of her feasts

Figure 11. Helen Clifton in her smokehouse, 2005.

(Figure 12). Most of these foods were served at other feasts as well, but the particular combination and diversity of the foods at Lucille's feasts was by all accounts exceptional.

Half-smoked Coho [*ts'aal üüx*]
When she was at Old Town in the fall, Lucille would try to get and preserve about 500 Coho each year. Coho is a fish rich in oil when it is still in the ocean, but it loses its oil when it starts up the river to spawn. Because of this oil, ocean-caught Coho turns rancid easily, but when caught from the river, then dried and thoroughly smoked, it preserves well. This processing was critical in the days of Lucille's feasts, before there were freezers. Nowadays, people simply freeze their Coho and don't need to worry about it turning rancid (Johnny Clifton, pers. comm. June 2003). Before the dried Coho was served at the feast, it had to be soaked in water for several days. When it was properly prepared, both the bones and the skin could be eaten. In Lucille's day, the river at Hartley Bay was cleaner than it is today, and the women preparing the dried Coho for the feast would put the fish into gunnysacks, which were hung off the bridge into the river, letting the fresh water run through them. They were then heated and served.

Scorched, Soaked, Dried Humpback (pink) Salmon [*'wiiyuu st*m*oon*]
In some years, humpback salmon were (and still are) plentiful at Old Town, and Lucille liked to get about 1000 "humps" each year. Unlike Coho, they do not have strong tasting oil, and

Figure 12. Menu for Lucille Clifton's Eagle Clan Fall Feasts for the Gitga'at Community of Hartley Bay (with special thanks to Helen Clifton, Elizabeth Dundas, and Mildred Wilson; Elizabeth's mother Cecelia, often stayed at Old Town with Lucille and the children).

Menu Eagle Clan Fall Feast

Starters
ts'aal üüx (half-smoked Coho) and
'wiiyuu stmoon (dried, soaked humpback)
with
k'awtsi (oulachen grease) and/or
kbaüüla (seal oil)

Next Course
ksiiw (inner bark of hemlock and/or Amabilis Fir), preserved
with
üüskm laan (salmon egg "caviar", fermented) and/or
luayaa (salmon egg "cheese," cured and smoked)
and
k'awtsi or *kbaüüla*

Main Course
Cooked garden vegetables
sgusiit (fresh garden potatoes, boiled and drained)
'yanahuu (turnips, boiled)
'kawts, galots (carrots, lightly steamed)
with
saxoolk'a (toasted, crumbled seaweed – *lha'ask*)
and
lhiyoon and *eétsam anaay* (breads) with jams of
moolks (crabapples), *smmay* (Alaska Blueberries), and/or *dzawes* (Salal)
xslaxs (strips of seal flipper, singed, cooked)
üüla (seal meat)
samimwan (venison stew)
and/or
ha'ax (Canada Goose) soup

Dessert
moolks (crabapples) and *lhaaya* (Highbush Cranberries), parboiled, mixed with
whipped *k'awtsi* (oulachen grease)

dayks ("Indian ice cream") with
wo'oksil (Oval-leaved Blueberries), *smmay* (Alaska Blueberries),
dzawes (Salal), and/or *waakyil* (Gray Currants)
sweetened with sugar

oranges, apples

Beverages
tii (Salada tea, clear and unsweetened) and/or
k'wila'maxs (Labrador Tea)

they are still silver when they enter the river. They are prepared and dried, and the tail sections smoked. For serving at the feast, they were soaked, scorched over a fire, then eaten dipped in oulachen grease or seal oil.

Oulachen Grease [k̲'awtsi]
This was obtained through trade from Nisga'a and Haisla friends and relatives, at the mouth of the Nass River and at Kitamaat, respectively. Usually, it was exchanged for dried edible seaweed, as described previously.

Seal Oil [kbaüüla]
Oil rendered from the Harbor Seal (*Phoca vitulinus*) was sometimes used as a condiment at the feasts, alongside, or as a replacement for, oulachen grease. If oulachen grease was in short supply, one of the men in the Eagle clan might hunt a seal just to obtain enough oil for Lucille's feast (see also under Seal, below).

Edible Tree Cambium [ksiiw]
Another favorite food that many of the elders today remember, but few have tasted recently, is *ksiiw*, the cambium and secondary phloem ("inner bark") of Western Hemlock [*gyiik*] and Amabilis ("balsam") Fir [*hooks*]. Harvest time was usually in June, when "the sap is rich" (i.e., the cambium is thickest and juiciest) and the bark is most easily removed from the tree. Men usually were the ones to harvest the bark. After cutting off large rectangular sections of the bark, they carried the pieces down to the beach or some other nearby open area, where the women scraped off the edible tissue into a bucket with a special hand-held blade (Figures 13, 14, 15), taking care not to let the cambium get dirty because it is sticky and difficult to clean. People used to harvest this food at Turtle Point on Gil Island, where the prime trees grew (Johnny Clifton and Helen Clifton pers. comm. 2003; Elizabeth Dundas pers. comm. 2005, 2006). Helen Clifton explained that the inner bark was harvested in the same way as cedar bark for basketry (which was done around the same time of year). That is, a piece of bark about one third of the circumference of the trunk (~20 cm wide and 60 cm high) was harvested from each tree.

Once harvested, the cambium tissue was processed in one of several ways. Sometimes it was simply spread out to dry in the sun and then put into jars for storage. Alternatively, it was cooked with sugar in large steel pots on the stovetop or in a Dutch oven for about half an hour, depending on the quantity. It could also be fried together with oulachen grease. Elizabeth Dundas cautioned that when cooking the cambium, it must be continuously stirred so it wouldn't burn. The cooked product was cooled, put in jars, and then stored in a cool place.

At feasts, the women added oulachen grease and sugar to the *ksiiw* just before it was served. Several people noted that *ksiiw* helps to counteract any potential poisonous sub-

Above left: Figure 13. Archie Dundas harvesting *ksiiw,* June 2004.

Above right: Figure 14. CMT (Culturally Modified Tree) from *ksiiw* harvest above Hartley Bay by Archie Dundas, ca. 1945; the tree is still living today, 2011.

Right: Figure 15. Elizabeth Dundas scraping off *ksiiw* (Amabilis Fir), June 2004.

stances in salmon eggs (see next entry), and therefore it was generally eaten with salmon egg "caviar" (*üüskm laan*).

Salmon Egg Caviar, or "Stink Eggs" (*üüskm laan*)
This fermented dish is considered a delicacy, but is very exacting to make, and can cause food poisoning or botulism if not made properly or with the right type of eggs. Lucille and the other women made this delicacy while at Old Town. Because of the dangers, few people make it today. Coho salmon were preferred for making this dish, but Tina Robinson noted that humpback salmon eggs could also be used. Especially with Coho, the eggs should always be from fish that have left the ocean and returned to the freshwater rivers in the fall (Helen Clifton pers. comm. 2003).

The eggs are removed from the salmon and laid in criss-crossed layers in a large container, located in a cool, dry place, out of any direct sunlight. The best and safest container for making *üüskm laan* is a wooden barrel or a porcelain crock; originally bentwood cedar boxes would be used. Belle and Colleen cautioned that the salmon eggs should never be processed in containers made of aluminum, or any iron enamelware that is chipped or rusted because this could render the eggs toxic. Furthermore, plastic bags should not be used, because they could get punctured and the contents could become contaminated with botulism.

The barrel or crock is lined with a clean, unbleached cotton flour or sugar sack, and the eggs, placed inside the sacking, are covered in fresh rainwater (collected from wooden rain barrels, not metal drums or from the tap). Once filled, the container is covered with a lid, so that no additional rainwater can get in. Every day, the water in the barrel is drained off and new water added. This process is continued until the water is clear, with no traces of blood, and the eggs are completely soft, whitish and opaque, as if they had been cooked.

Once the "cooked" stage is reached, after about a week to ten days, the salmon eggs are ready for the next stage of processing. A hole is dug in the ground in a cool place and lined with Skunk-cabbage leaves (*Lysichiton americanus* Hultén & H. St. John) and Thimbleberry leaves (*Rubus parviflorus*). The eggs, wrapped in cotton sacking, are placed in the pit and covered with additional Skunk-cabbage leaves. Occasionally they are tested to see if they are at the right consistency. After a couple of weeks the "caviar" is ready to eat. Sometimes these strong-smelling fermented eggs are called "stink eggs," but for those who have acquired a taste for them, they are delicious. The fresh caviar should be eaten within two weeks to two months after it is made. More recently, the eggs have been stored in jars for their final processing rather than buried in a pit.

Salmon egg caviar is an excellent accompaniment to potatoes, fish, seaweed, grease and *ksiiw*, or edible tree cambium. Helen Clifton commented that you cook potatoes, and serve *üüskm laan, ksiiw,* and a side of fish, and you have "a meal by itself." At Lucille's feasts, as noted above, the caviar was usually served together with processed *ksiiw* and oulachen grease or seal oil.

Salmon Egg Cheese [*luayaa*]

For her feasts, Lucille also served *luayaa* or "salmon egg cheese," made with fresh *üüskm laan* caviar (see previous description) and smoked Coho eggs. The smoked eggs were prepared over the same time period as the *üüskm laan*. Some of the Coho eggs, still encased in the egg sacks, were laid across cedar *wooxs* (long split sticks used for smoking and drying food) in the smokehouse and turned frequently until they were dried and cured. The smoke helped to preserve them and after this, they were tied in bags, ready for use in making *luayaa* or for winter storage as smoked eggs.

To make *luayaa*, the smoked eggs and *üüskm laan* are layered. The fresh eggs form the top layer, and their juice soaks into the smoked eggs. Over time, this combination thickens to the consistency of peanut butter. It is like a thick, rich jam, and is dark brown—the color of fall, as noted by Helen Clifton. She commented that you have to acquire a taste for this dish. The *luayaa* could be fried in grease and eaten with potatoes for an everyday meal. Tina Robinson (pers. comm. 2005) remembered it fondly in another recipe: "Oh, that smells good when my mother does it, and she jars it! You boil it and put it in layers [like a casserole]: seaweed, grease, eggs; it's so good." At Lucille's feasts, *luayaa* was almost always eaten with *ksiiw* (edible tree cambium), served with oulachen grease and sugar.

Garden Vegetables: *sgusiit* (potatoes), *'yanahuu* (turnips), *'kawts, galots* (carrots)

Heber and Lucille Clifton maintained a garden at Turtle Point at the north end of Gil Island (where the community cemetery is at present). They grew mainly potatoes (*Solanum tuberosum* L.), but also other vegetables. Sometimes, too, a boatload of potatoes, carrots (*Daucus carota* L.) and turnips (*Brassica rapa* L.) would come to Hartley Bay from Bella Coola. If the Gitga'at people hadn't been able to grow enough in their own gardens, they would buy their winter supply of these vegetables from the Nuxalk. Bowls of boiled potatoes, with the skins on, were served with bowls of cooked turnips and carrots with the main course at Lucille's feasts. In earlier times, feasts might have included cooked Pacific silverweed roots (*yeen*) and other native root vegetables.

Toasted, Crumbled *lhạạsk* Seaweed [*saxoolk'a*]

Dried, chopped seaweed (*Porphyra abbottiae*) was presented in dishes at the centre of the table as a delicious accompaniment and condiment for the salmon eggs, potatoes, grease and other food at the feast. As noted previously, this seaweed was harvested in the spring in the vicinity of Kiel and dried on the rocks there. After the seaweed was brought back to Hartley Bay it was further processed, being re-moistened with salt water, then compressed and cured in bent-wood cedar boxes in layers interspersed with Salal leaves (*Gaultheria shallon* Pursh) or Western Redcedar (*Thuja plicata* Donn ex D. Don) boughs. After about three days it was taken out, chopped on wooden blocks, then redried and stored in airtight containers, to give it the very best flavor. A full description of the knowledge and use of this highly important and nutritious food, and of the changes in harvesting and processing practices that have oc-curred is found in Turner and Clifton (2006) and Turner and Thompson (2006).[4]

Breads [anaay]: lhiyoon and eétsam anaay

The Eagle women would have bread of some kind at every table. This was usually a special kind of elongated bread, or bannock, called **liyoon** or fried bread (**eétsam anaay**), both of which are still made and served at feasts today. The breads were served with dishes of jam or jelly of crabapples, or thick blueberry, or Salal berry jam.

Seal Meat (iüüla)

Harbor Seal was a good source of both meat and fat. As noted previously, people render seal fat into oil, which can be used as a condiment, sometimes as a substitute for oulachen grease. For Lucille's feasts, especially if oulachen grease were in short supply, an Eagle man might go out and hunt a seal for the oil, as well as for the meat. The person skinning the seal would leave a lot of fat on the carcass, and this would then be cut off and processed separately. The seal meat was cut into pieces and boiled until soft, then served at the feast as a sort of stew. The flippers (**xslaxs**) were considered a great delicacy and a high-class food. Only a few women knew how to prepare seal flippers properly. The fur was singed off the flippers, which were then boiled until soft. They were then cut into strips and served, especially to the chiefs and matriarchs at the head table.

Venison [wan] and other Game

Lucille's feasts—like the feasts of today—usually featured stew or soup of venison (deer meat), Canada Goose, or some other type of game: whatever the Eagle men were able to get around the time of the feast. The stews were cooked up in large pots and ladled out into bowls for the guests.

Crabapples (moolks) and Highbush Cranberries (lhaaya) Served in Whipped Oulachen Grease (k̲awtsi)

This dish was an important component of the feast's menu. The women and children of the Eagle Clan, including Colleen and Belle, helped Lucille pick **moolks** (crabapples) and **lhaaya** (Highbush Cranberries), as well as **waakyil** (wild Gray Currants), and the "big black fall blueberries" (**sm maay**) (Johnny and Helen Clifton, pers. comm. June 2003). The **moolks** were picked in bunches, as they grew, with their stems still attached. There were big stands of crabapple trees along the river in Old Town, which allowed them to pick large quantities of this fruit. The **lhaaya** were usually picked around the lakes and along the creeks in the vicinity of Hartley Bay.

Lucille's granddaughter Marjorie Hill demonstrated how the crabapples would have been prepared for Lucille's feasts. She filled an enamel pot with the ripe crabapples, their clusters still intact. She just barely covered them with water, then placed the pot on the stove to cook. She stirred the crabapples with a large spoon, from the bottom to the top of the pot. The fruits are cooked to the right stage when the stem comes off the fruit easily when twisted. The crabapples are then cooled quickly by soaking them in cold water, to prevent the fruit from becoming over-cooked and mushy. They are then air-dried, to prevent them from molding, before being mixed into oulachen grease for long-term storage.

Lucille obtained oulachen grease for her feasts and for general consumption during the rest of the year by trade from the Nisga'a of Nass Valley. According to Marjorie Hill, the Nass grease is preferred because it is more strongly-flavored than Kitamaat grease and it whips better. The grease is whipped by hand with a little fresh water, or even snow, until it was white and frothy like whipped cream. One cannot have warm hands to do this, or the grease will not whip. Ernie Hill Jr. said that you have to turn your fingers upwards as you whip with your hands in order to get the best results. Lucille used to have big crocks for the grease, and for the crabapples mixed in grease, which they would store on the ground in the smokehouse. When properly prepared, the **moolks** in grease could just be left all winter in the crock, or in a wooden barrel, with people taking out as much as they needed for the feasts or other occasions.

The **lhaaya** (Highbush Cranberries) are prepared similarly to the **moolks.** They are often picked while still greenish and hard. Then the stems are removed, and berries soaked in water until they become bright red. Because of their acidity, they keep well submerged in water, or can be drained, dried, and mixed with grease, with or without **moolks**. Just before the serving, for Lucille's feasts and others, sugar would be mixed with the **moolks** and **lhaaya** to taste. Belle recalled that if the feast was early enough in the fall season and the harvest was good, Lucille would mix fresh late-ripening blueberries together with the **moolks** and **lhaaya**, with grease, water, and sugar.

In the olden days, the elders recalled, all the women had big wooden barrels to store their crabapples and Highbush Cranberries in, and all of them would set some by to contribute to the feasts, as well as serving them on a regular basis to their families. Clyde Ridley recalled that Lucille (his grandmother) used to put by about four or five 5-gallon barrels packed with crabapples and Highbush Cranberries every winter. She kept some separate, and some mixed together, for her feasts.

"Indian Ice Cream" (*dayks*): Berries with Whipped Grease, Snow or Water, and Sugar

Dayks is a similar dish, also often served at Lucille's feasts, comprised of oulachen grease whipped with snow or water, together with blueberries (*wo'oksil*), Gray Currants (**waakyil**), Salalberries (*dzawes*) or any other kinds of berries, and sweetened with sugar. Belle recalled that they used to serve this dish as a treat, not only at feasts, but at any time when there was a family gathering.

Lucille's grandson Clyde Ridley and the other young people used to pick berries for her. Clyde recalled that they used to get blue all around their mouths, from eating the berries while they picked. Originally, the berries were stored by cooking them in large pots to a jam-like consistency, then spreading them out onto Skunk-cabbage leaves to dry. Clyde remembered that they had cedarwood trays (similar to trays used for seaweed-drying), for drying berry cakes, to about an inch (2.5 cm) thick. He said the dried berry cakes looked like chewing tobacco. Once dried, the berry cakes (with Skunk-cabbage leaves if these were used) were rolled up, tied and put into cedar bentwood boxes, which were placed into holes in the ground lined with sand. The boxes could be dug up whenever the berries were needed. When they wanted some berries to eat, they would just cut or break off a chunk and soak it in water. For feasts, whole cakes would be taken out and soaked. (Nowadays, few people have time to pick such quantities of wild berries, and when they do, they just put them in the freezer to preserve them, or they make them into preserves, jams, and jellies.)

Apples and Oranges
These fruits, imported by the case, were placed on the tables at Lucille's feasts and other similar feasts, for the guests to help themselves or to take home after the feasts. It was expected that people would take home any leftovers from the feast as well.

Beverages
Johnny Clifton recalled that there was always "quite a bit of strong tea [*tii*]" served at Lucille's feasts, but generally no juice or water, at least in the earlier days. The tea was Salada brand, placed loose (not in tea bags) in teapots for each table, and no sugar or milk provided. Later, Johnny recalled, "they served tea, coffee, or whatever you wanted." "Indian tea," or Labrador Tea (*Rhododendron groenlandicum*), called **k'wil̲a'm̲axs** ('ever-green'), was also often served. The leaves were collected from boggy places around Hartley Bay or elsewhere in the territory, then dried. To make the tea, a few handfuls of the leaves were placed in a pot of water and boiled for about half an hour until the tea is a brownish color.

Feasting Today

Feasting is still an important tradition for the Gitga'at and other First Nations communities. Planning and hosting a feast is a major social activity and responsibility. Guests from other communities up and down the coast—from Kitkatla and Kitamaat, for example, are still invited as they were in Lucille's day. On June 21st, 2003 the entire community held a feast to celebrate the opening of **Waaps Wahmoodmx,** the new Gitga'at Cultural Center at Hartley Bay. This feast was a modern version of those hosted so many years ago by Lucille Clifton. There were honored chiefs and matriarchs from several neighboring communities (Kitkatla, Klemtu, Kitamaat), as well as representatives from the organizations that supported the building of the center: David Suzuki and Tara Cullis from the David Suzuki Foundation, Michael Uehara of King Pacific Lodge, and a representative of the Lodge company from California, who were seated at the head table. Many family members came home especially for the feast. Women from each of the clans served. Colleen's daughter Mona Danes organized who had responsibility for each table. There were beautiful dishes, provided by each woman from her own household, and specially made linen napkins to commemorate the occasion. As at the time of Lucille's feasts, the invitations were personally delivered to each household by young men who were designated for this purpose.

Since this was an "all clans" feast, the food was provided by many community members. For example, Ernie Hill Jr., the head Eagle Chief, and his son Cam, caught, cooked and cleaned two enormous pots full of crabs. They and a couple of other fishermen had caught a huge halibut, about 54 kg (120 pounds) and two meters long, the Saturday before, just for the feast. Many families fried the halibut or prepared kippered salmon (red and white springs). There were many kinds of salads: potato salads, pasta salads, and tossed green salads. Several kinds of bread were served, with butter and jam, just as with Lucille's feasts. There were plates of cantaloupe, honeydew melon, and watermelon, and slices of cake. Towards the end, apples, bananas, and oranges were handed out to all the guests. Coffee and juice were served to anyone who wanted them. There were sugar bowls and cream pitchers of crystal and fine porcelain. Dishes of mints and saltwater taffy were set out on the tables. Before the feast, the children and youth of each clan performed many dances. Following this the House was formally opened with a prayer from Reverend Ernie Hill Sr. and a song sung by Graham Clifton. The guests were each announced as they entered, and were seated.

The spirit of Lucille's feasts and the knowledge system that they represent are still alive and represented in today's feasts. Some of the foods served are different now: salads instead of *ksiiw* and *üüskm laan*, imported fruit for dessert instead of *moolks* and *laaya* with whipped oulachen grease. Handing out oranges and apples is a practice that goes back for many generations, however, probably as long as these fruits have been available in any quantity (At some feasts, Japanese oranges have been passed out.). As well, there are still many local, traditional foods that are served, including smoked salmon, halibut, crabs, herring eggs, cockles, and seaweed. The people at the *Waaps Wahmoodmx* feast were seated together around the tables, not with their clans. This makes it more difficult to remember what clan someone belongs to. Nevertheless, the dances featuring each clan, and other festivities such as the Aboriginal Day parade, in which the clans prepare their own floats and each provides a portion of the entertainment, help to keep the clan relationships and identities strong.

The role of the feast in promoting community pride and cohesion is as strong as ever. Showing appreciation for and recognizing all those who contributed is still an essential responsibility of the chiefs and their families. The changes in feasting are reflective of broader changes in peoples' lifestyles, in the foods consumed, and in technologies for preparing them.

In the early days, for example, people picked and ate many more wild berries and wild plant foods, and consequently, they were served more at feasts.

Discussion

It is no coincidence that many people still remember Lucille Clifton's fall feasts. They were a part of the fabric that held the entire community together. Even today, although the circumstances are different in many ways, memories of Lucille's feasts and the other feasts of the past help to guide the protocols and practices for contemporary feasts and celebrations at Hartley Bay and for the way of life of the Gitga'at. By the mid 20th century, many Gitga'at families had adopted eating marketed foods for most of their nutrition. Because of Lucille's feasts, members of acculturated families could taste, savor, and reacquaint themselves with the valuable traditional foods of their ancestors, and carry that knowledge forward to today. The children and young adults who tasted the foods, and who learned the skills and values associated with traditional foods and community feasts from Lucille Clifton and others like her, are now the teachers and role models for the children and youth of today. In this way, Lucille's wisdom and knowledge is perpetuated and she continues as a leader in spirit even though her life ended decades ago.

The feast that Lucille and the Eagle women hosted every year was critically important, not just for the food that was provided, but because of its promotion of group cohesion, of the essential need for sharing and helping each other in order for all to be able to survive. Symbolically and in reality, the thanksgiving feast was a true reflection of such values. The different foods that were served at Lucille's feasts, each part of the bounty of the land and the sea that has provided for the Gitga'at for countless generations, are embodiments of a rich system of knowledge. This knowledge system, commonly known as Traditional Ecological Knowledge, is generally recognized as a knowledge-practice-belief complex relating to peoples' use of and relationship to their environment. It incorporates four interrelated levels: local environmental knowledge and skills, resource management systems, social institutions that help facilitate sustainable use of the environment, and worldview, or peoples' attitudes about the environment and the resources they rely upon (Berkes 2012; Turner et al. 2000). Each of these components is reflected in Lucille Clifton's feasts.

Detailed, practical local knowledge of the foods and other resources that sustain the people, and in particular, how to harvest, process, prepare and serve them, is perhaps the most obvious component of Traditional Knowledge underlying Lucille's feasts. There is a great deal of traditional ecological knowledge about berries and other plant foods that is represented in the feasts. People had to know the best time to harvest the foods, and the best places to get them. A food like the wild crabapples was immensely important: Marjorie Hill said that when you go to pick the crabapples you don't just pick a few; you pick lots and lots—"you pick them by the sack" (Figure 16). Crabapples (***moolks***) were one of the most significant types of plant foods for the Gitga'at and this is reflected in the fact that several major varieties of these are named and recognized in their language.

At a broader level, Lucille and the other community members had to know how to care for the resources, how to regulate their harvest and monitor the habitats so that they would continue to yield their bounty of food and materials. Selective harvesting, knowing how many fish to leave for spawning in the river, for example, and following the time-tested methods for hunting and fishing, as well as having proprietorship over specific harvesting localities, were some of the ways in which this was done. Within Gitga'at territory, some places and resource gathering sites, like the crabapple orchard noted previously, were owned by Chiefs and other individuals within a specific clan. It was their responsibility to look after these sites, and to oversee how they were used by and shared with the people. Highbush Cranberry patches are another example of such resource ownership. This level of knowledge and cultural practice is also embodied in Lucille's feasts and in her teachings.

Social institutions, including the family and the matrilineal clans, serve as a culturally prescribed means of ensuring that everyone in the group is valued and provided for. These institutions permeate every stage and aspect of the feasts and their preparation, including the very hosting of the feasts by the clan members, and the protocols for recognizing the clans and the leaders in the seating and other protocols. The very role Lucille played in caring for and teaching her grandchildren while their parents were occupied with their work is an aspect of the institution of the family in Gitga'at life, and it carries on to this day (Figure 17).

Finally, the worldview or philosophy underlying the feasts is critical to their understanding and their role in helping to support and sustain the people. These were truly feasts of thanks. According to Helen and Johnny Clifton (pers. comm. 2003), giving this feast each year was Lucille's way of say-

Figure 16. Marjorie Hill and crabapples, 2005.

Figure 17. Nelson Robinson, Lucille's great great grandson, examines (and tastes) the seaweed his grandmother Helen Clifton is drying in Hartley Bay, 2010.

ing, "I'm glad nobody got hurt this summer. I'm glad you've looked after yourselves; I'm glad we're all back together; I'm glad about all the good food the Creator has given me." Looking upon the food as a gift of the Creator, and treating the food and all who partook of it with appreciation and respect, never wasting it, and sharing it with the entire community: these are values that Lucille herself held, and that she passed along to her children and grandchildren.

The role of individuals like Lucille Clifton is as important and critical as ever, in every community. These people, wise and knowledgeable and willing to share with and teach others, have a special function in a community. They are focal points for knowledge, experience, and teachings for survival and sustenance, individuals who can maintain a vast storehouse of important information and pass it on to others to benefit from at a later time.

The community and personal values Lucille taught and modeled in her own life, as well as her skills and knowledge of survival and environmental management, have helped those who have succeeded her to maintain their lives in the face of major social and economic restructuring. Her descendants and the others at Hartley Bay have faced loss of their livelihoods and major changes to the fisheries industry in the past few decades, causing hardships for many families. At one time, there were 30 fishing boats operated by Gitga'at fishers, and now there are only a couple. The use of traditional food has declined significantly, partly in response to changing food preferences and lifestyles, and partly due to a loss and deterioration of available resources. It has been demonstrated (cf. Kuhnlein 1989, 1992) that taste and appreciation of a given food declines once people stop using it. As Ernie Hill Jr. stated (pers. comm. 2001), "The more you eat the [traditional] foods, the more you like it."

Many of the older people today still remember foods like *ksiiw* and *üüskm laan,* and enjoy reminiscing about the times when they used to harvest and prepare such foods routinely. Belle Eaton used to make salmon egg caviar until very recently, following the methods she was taught by Lucille. Elizabeth Dundas prepared *ksiiw* a few years ago, and shared it with her friends. Unfortunately, though, people say that the quality of some of the foods has declined. Colleen and Gideon said that the salmon eggs today are different than before: They don't change color the way they used to, and they don't taste right. They aren't very good for making "caviar." They attribute this to the scarcity of "really wild salmon"; most of the salmon now are hatchery fish, and they have a different taste. Elders like Elizabeth Dundas suggest that even the berries are not as plentiful nor of as high quality as previously. Annetta Robinson and Archie Dundas prepared crabapples whipped with oulachen grease in the old way at Old Town, but whereas formerly, the water for this dish would come straight from the creek, now the creek is too polluted from logging to be used in cooking. Now, the Gitga'at are facing what is perhaps the most challenging threats to the integrity of their territory and food production systems: a proposal by Enbridge called the "Northern Gateway" project for a major oil tanker route along Douglas Channel, past Hartley Bay and the islands and waters of their territory, bringing oil from the Alberta oil sands via pipeline to Kitimat, and from there to oil markets in China and elsewhere in the world (Anon 2009; Coastal First Nations Great Bear Initiative 2010b; Haisla First Nation 2010; Swanson 2010). Surely, the legacy of Lucille Clifton, the knowledge she helped perpetuate and continued importance of seafood to the Gitga'at resulting in part to her teachings and example, will help to combat this looming threat.

Conclusions

Feasting was and continues to be a central cultural institution; far more than simply providing nutrition, feasts bring community members together and reinforce the importance of sharing, supporting, and helping one another. These values are stressed by today's leaders, and are reflected in the teachings and examples still demonstrated and enacted during community feasts.

At a time when the use of traditional food is increasingly recognized as important for maintaining peoples' health and well-being, Lucille Clifton's teachings and knowledge are more significant than ever. The community and personal values Lucille taught and modeled in her own life, as well as her skills and knowledge of survival and environmental management, have helped those who have succeeded her to maintain their lives in the face of major social and economic restructuring.

Aboriginal people in particular are susceptible to so-called lifestyle diseases like heart disease and diabetes, and this is due at least in part to changes in their traditional diet. Remembering and celebrating Lucille Clifton and all that she stood for is not just a nostalgia for some past utopia, it is one key to maintaining a community's resilience in the face of change. The lessons she provided, and continues to provide, for flexibility, innovation, strength, and resourcefulness, for leadership, teamwork, and accepting responsibility, for self reliance, respect, appreciation, humor, and generosity: all these are keys to continued well-being for the Gitga'at and other coastal communities.

Notes

1. Her Gitga'at name, which has been inherited by her granddaughter Marjorie Hill.
2. Two of the authors of this paper, Colleen Robinson and Belle Eaton, sisters, are Lucille's matrilineal granddaughters. They and their siblings are among those who knew their grandmother well and spent time with her when they were growing up. Belle Eaton, who spent every summer with her until she was 14 years old, remarked, "She was quite a grandma and great grandma for everybody here."
3. Heber Clifton, born in the 1870s, passed away on January 1st, 1964. Lucille and Heber Clifton had nine children: Louis (the eldest), Ed, Bob, Violet (Marjorie Hill's mother), Edith (Alan Robinson's mother), Emily, Mabel, George, and Johnny. Johnny Clifton, chosen to be hereditary Gitga'at chief *Wahmoodmx* after the death of his brother, Ed, was born on May 15, 1918. He married Helen Clifton, who remembers Lucille well. Chief Johnny Clifton passed away in 2004, and was succeeded by their son Albert, who formally assumed his father's Chief name *Wahmoodmx*. Mabel and her husband Herbert (who was originally from Kitkatla) had nine children, including Colleen and Belle, who are coauthors of this paper, and Clyde, whose recollections are included here.
4. See also Nuxalk Food and Nutrition Program (1984); Turner et al. (2009).

Acknowledgements

Amadeo Rea epitomizes all that is good in the field of ethnobiology. His work is exemplary and his contributions to the documentation of Indigenous Peoples' food systems, and to the fields of conservation, historical geography and ethnoecology have been immense. It is such a pleasure to dedicate this chapter to Amadeo and his work.

We would like to thank the many Gitga'at community members for sharing their memories of Lucille Clifton and her fall feasts and stories with us. We are especially grateful to Chief Johnny Clifton and Helen Clifton, Chief Albert Clifton, Teri Clifton Robinson, Kyle Clifton, Archie Dundas, Elizabeth Dundas, Reverend Ernie Hill Sr. and Marjorie Hill, Chief Ernie Hill Jr., Lynne Hill, Cam Hill, Clyde Ridley, Alan Robinson, Annetta Robinson, Bobby Robinson, Tina Robinson, and Dick Wilson and Mildred Wilson. We also thank Pat Sterritt, former Chief Councilor, and the Gitga'at Nation Chief and Council for permission for Nancy Turner and her colleagues to participate in research with the Gitga'at Nation. We are grateful to Ellen M. Torng, CEO of the Hartley Bay Band Council, and to Dan Cardinall and Chris Picard, for help and advice, and to Craig Outhet for the map. Thank you, also to Dr. Margaret Anderson for her contributions, and to Judith Thompson (Edosdi), Victoria Wyllie de Echeverria, Dr. John Lutz, and Dr. Anne Marshall of the University of Victoria, and to Coasts Under Stress MCRI research project (Rosemary Ommer, PI), and SSHRC research grant (# 410-94-1555) to N. Turner for supporting this research. Many thanks to Dr. Dana Lepofsky and Dr. Marsha Quinlan and to an anonymous reviewer for their editorial genius and advice. We are grateful to Cheryl Takahashi, our Society of Ethnobiology's Webmaster and computer technologist, for creating the final page layouts so effectively.

References Cited

Anderson, Margaret Seguin (ed.). 1984   *The Tsimshian: Images of the Past, Views for the Present*. UBC Press, Vancouver, BC.

Anderson, Margaret Seguin. 2004   Understanding Tsimshian Potlatch. In *Native Peoples: The Canadian Experience* (Third Edition), eds. R. Bruce Morrison and C. Roderick Wilson, pp. 408–430. Oxford University Press, Toronto, ON.

Anon. 2009   Summit Galvanizes Opposition to Enbridge Northern Gateway Pipeline. *Summary Report, All Nations Energy Summit*, June 5–6, 2009. Moricetown, BC.

Berkes, Fikret. 2012   *Sacred Ecology: Traditional Ecological Knowledge and Resource Management* (Third Edition). Taylor & Francis, Philadelphia, PA.

Campbell, Ken. 1984   Hartley Bay, British Columbia: A History. In *The Tsimshian: Images of the Past, Views for the Present*, ed. Margaret S. Anderson, pp. 3–26. UBC Press, Vancouver.

Coastal First Nations, Great Bear Initiative. 2010   Enbridge Northern Gateway Pipeline: Coastal First Nation Concerns. Information Bulletin – March 2010. Available at: coastalfirstnations.ca

Devereaux, Fiona, and Kate Kittredge. 2008   Feasting for Change: Reconnecting to Food, Land and Culture. Office of the Community Nutritionist for Aboriginal Health, Victoria, BC.

Garibaldi, Ann. 2003   Bridging Ethnobotany, Autecology and Restoration: The Study of Wapato (*Sagittaria latifolia Willd; Alismataceae*) in Interior British Columbia. M.Sc. Thesis. University of Victoria, Victoria, BC.

Gitga'at First Nation. 1987   *Hartley Bay: 100 years* (100th Anniversary album, 1887–1987). Compiled by Eva Ann Bolton (now Hill), Terri-Jo Clifton and Jodi Hill, under Helen Clifton and Ernie Hill Jr. Project funded through Challenge '85. Hartley Bay, BC.

Gitga'at Nation, with Robin J. Hood and Ben Fox (directors). 2003   *Gitga'ata Spring Harvest*. A Co-production by the Gitga'at Nation and Coasts Under Stress Major Collaborative Research Initiative (R. Ommer, P.I.), University of Victoria. Victoria, BC.

Haisla First Nation (Gerald Amos). 2010   Hundreds Gather in Northern B.C. Against Enbridge Oil Tanker Plan. Press Release. Marketwire - May 29, 2010. Kitamaat Village, British Columbia. Available at: http://www.marketwire.com/press-release/Hundreds-Gather-in-Northern-BC-Against-Enbridge-Oil-Tanker-Plan-1268318.htm (verified 7 June 2010).

Jonaitis, Aldona (ed.). 1991   *Chiefly Feasts: The Enduring Kwakiutl Potlatch*. University of Washington Press, Seattle.

Kealey, Linda, Heidi Coombs, Nancy J. Turner, and Sheila Yeomans. 2006   Knowledge, Power and Health. In *Knowledge and Power, CUS book*, ed. Peter Sinclair, pp. 107–128. ISER Books, St. John's, NL.

Kuhnlein, Harriet V. 1989   Factors Influencing Use of Traditional Foods among the Nuxalk People. *Journal of the Canadian Dietetics Association* 50(2):102–108.

Kuhnlein, Harriet V. 1992   Change in the Use of Traditional Food by the Nuxalk Native People of British Columbia. *Ecology of Food and Nutrition* 27 (3–4): 259–282.

Kuhnlein, Harriet V. 1995   Changing Patterns of Food Use by Canadian Indigenous Peoples. Paper presented at the Third International Conference on Diabetes and Indigenous Peoples, Winnipeg.

Kuhnlein, Harriet V., Bill Erasmus, and Dina Spigelski (eds.). 2009   *Indigenous Peoples' Food Systems: The Many Dimensions of Culture, Diversity and Environment for Nutrition and Health*. Centre for Indigenous Peoples' Nutrition and Environment, McGill University, Montreal, QC, and Food and Agriculture Organization of the United Nations (FAO), Rome.

Miller, Jay. 1984   Feasting with the Southern Tsimshian. In *The Tsimshian: Images of the Past, Views for the Present*, ed. Margaret S. Anderson, pp. 27–39. UBC Press, Vancouver.

Nuxalk Food and Nutrition Program. 1984 *Nuxalk Food and Nutrition Handbook*. Nuxalk Nation, Bella Coola, BC.

Ommer, Rosemary E., Carrie Holcapek, Robin J. Hood, and Coasts Under Stress Research Team. 2006   *Voices on the Edge*. University of Victoria, Victoria, BC, and Memorial University of Newfoundland, St. John's, NL.

Ommer, Rosemary, and the Coasts Under Stress Research Team. 2007 *St. John's Coasts Under Stress. Restructuring and Social-Ecological Health.* McGill-Queen's University Press, Montreal, QC, and Kingston, ON.

Parrish, Chris C., Nancy J. Turner, and Shirley Solberg. (eds.). 2007 *Resetting the Kitchen Table: Food Security, Culture, Health and Resilience in Coastal Communities.* Nova Science Publishers, New York.

Singh, Ranjay K. 2004 Conserving Diversity and Culture – Pem Doma. *Honey Bee* 15(3):12–13.

Singh, Ranjay K., and Amish K. Sureja. 2006 Centurion Women and Diverse Knowledge Systems. *Indian Journal of Traditional Knowledge* 5(3):413–429.

Swanson, Eric. 2010 Dogwood goes to Enbridge 2010 AGM. Available at: http://dogwoodinitiative.org/blog/enbridge-agm-2010.1 (verified 6 June 2010).

Thompson, Judith C. (Edosdi) 2004 Gitga'at Plant Project: The Intergenerational Transmission of Traditional Ecological Knowledge Using School Science Curricula. MA Thesis. School of Environmental Studies and Department of Educational Psychology and Leadership Studies, University of Victoria, Victoria, BC.

Tirone, Susan, Blythe Sheppard, Nancy J. Turner, Lois Jackson, Anne Marshall, and Catherine Donovan. 2007 Celebrating with Food. Food and Cultural Identity: Feasts, Ceremonies and Celebrations. In *Resetting the Kitchen Table: Food Security, Culture, Health and Resilience in Coastal Communities*, eds. Christopher C. Parrish, Nancy J. Turner, and Shirley M. Solberg, pp. 145–160. Nova Science Publishers, New York.

Turner, Nancy J. 2003 The Ethnobotany of "Edible Seaweed" *(Porphyra abbottiae* Krishnamurthy and Related Species; Rhodophyta: Bangiales) and Its Use by First Nations on the Pacific Coast of Canada. *Canadian Journal of Botany* 81(2):283–293.

Turner, Nancy J., Marianne B. Ignace, and Ronald Ignace. 2000 Traditional Ecological Knowledge and Wisdom of Aboriginal Peoples in British Columbia. *Ecological Applications* 10 (5):1275–1287.

Turner, Nancy J., and Helen Clifton. 2006 "The Forest and the Seaweed": Gitga'at Seaweed, Traditional Ecological Knowledge and Community Survival. (chapter published in two books). In *Eating and Healing: Traditional Food as Medicine*, eds. Andrea Pieroni and Lisa L. Price, pp. 153–178. Haworth Press (USA). See also: *Traditional Ecological Knowledge and Natural Resource Management*, ed. Charles Menzies, pp. 65–86. University of Nebraska, Lincoln.

Turner, Nancy J., and Helen Clifton. 2009 "It's so Different Today": Climate Change and Indigenous Lifeways in British Columbia, Canada. *Global Environmental Change*, 19(Special Issue, eds. J. Salick and Nanci Ross):180–190.

Turner, Nancy J., Robin Gregory, Cheryl Brooks, Lee Failing, and Terre Satterfield. 2008 From Invisibility to Transparency: Identifying the Implications (of Invisible

Losses to First Nations Communities). *Ecology and Society*, 13 (2):7. Available at: http://www.ecologyandsociety.org/vol13/iss2/art7/ (verified 8 December 2011).

Turner, Nancy J., Thelma Harvey, Harriet V. Kuhnlein, and Sandra Moody. 2009   The Nuxalk Food and Nutrition Program, Coastal British Columbia, Canada: 1981–2006. In *Indigenous Peoples' Food Systems: The Many Dimensions of Culture, Diversity and Environment for Nutrition and Health*, eds. Harriet V. Kuhnlein, Bill Erasmus, and Dina Spigelski, pp. 23–44. FAO. Food and Agriculture Organization of the United Nations, Rome, Italy and Centre for Indigenous Peoples' Nutrition and Environment, Ste. Anne de Bellevue, QC.

Turner, Nancy J., Anne Marshall, Judith C. Thompson (Edosdi), Robin J. Hood, Cameron Hill, and Eva-Ann Hill. 2008   "Ebb and Flow": Transmitting Environmental Knowledge in a Contemporary Aboriginal Community. In *Making and Moving Knowledge: Interdisciplinary and Community-Based Research in a World on the Edge*, eds. John S. Lutz and Barbara Neis, pp. 45–63. McGill-Queen's University Press, Montreal, QC, and Kingston, ON.

Turner, Nancy J., Mark Plotkin, and Harriet Kuhnlein. In press.   Integrity of Indigenous Food Systems: Global Environmental Challenges. In *Indigenous Peoples' Food Systems for Health: Interventions for Health Promotion and Policy*, ed. Harriet V. Kuhnlein et al., FAO Book 3. UN Food and Agricultural Organization, Rome, Italy.

Turner, Nancy J., and Judith C. Thompson (eds.). 2006   *Plants of the Gitga'at People. 'Nwana'a lax Yuup*. Gitga'at Nation, Hartley Bay, BC, Coasts Under Stress Research Project (R. Ommer, P.I.), and Cortex Consulting, Victoria, BC.

Turner, Nancy J., and Katherine L. Turner. 2008   "Where our Women used to get the Food": Cumulative Effects and Loss of Ethnobotanical Knowledge and Practice. *Botany* 86 (1):103–115.

Watts, Annie, and Dolly Watts. 2007   *Where People Feast: An Indigenous People's Cookbook*. Arsenal Pulp Press, Vancouver, BC.

Welch, John R., Dana Lepofsky, Megan Caldwell, Georgia Combes, and Craig Rust. 2011   Treasure Bearers: Personal Foundations for Effective Leadership in Northern Coast Salish Heritage Stewardship. *Heritage and Society* 4 (1):83–114.

Contributors

E.N. Anderson is Professor of Anthropology, Emeritus, at the University of California, Riverside. He received his Ph.D. in anthropology from the University of California, Berkeley, in 1967. He has done research and published widely on ethnobiology, cultural ecology, political ecology, and medical anthropology, in several areas, especially Hong Kong, British Columbia, California, and the Yucatan Peninsula of Mexico. He is a past President of the Society of Ethnobiology.

Cecil H. Brown is a Distinguished Research Professor Emeritus at Northern Illinois University and a Faculty Associate at the University of West Florida. His interests include linguistic anthropology, ethnobiology, and New World prehistory. He is a past President of the Society of Ethnobiology.

Steven W. Carothers is an ecologist and the founder of SWCA Environmental Consultants. He received his Bachelor and Master of Science degrees in Biology from Northern Arizona University and his PhD in Zoology from the University of Illinois. He has many natural history interests and has studied the effects of Glen Canyon Dam on Grand Canyon riverine and terrestrial ecosystems for over 35 years. He currently spends his time between Austin, Texas and his home in Flagstaff, Arizona.

Belle Eaton and **Colleen Robinson** are sisters, both elders of the Gitga'at Nation, of Hartley Bay, British Columbia. They grew up in Hartley Bay, and spent long periods of time with their grandmother, Lucille Clifton, especially when their parents were working in the canneries and fishing industry along the coast. They, and Colleen's late husband **Gideon Robinson**, each experienced Lucille's teachings, and learned about traditional food—including harvesting and preparation from Lucille and the other elders of the day.

Patience Epps is an Associate Professor in the Department of Linguistics at the University of Texas at Austin. Her research interests involve descriptive and documentary work on indigenous Amazonian languages, typology, language contact and language change, and Amazonian prehistory.

Kevin Feeney received his law degree from the University of Oregon in 2005, and is currently working towards a Ph.D. in cultural anthropology at Washington State University. His interests include ethnobotany, shamanism, and the religious use of psychoactive plants.

Catherine "Kay" S. Fowler is Professor Emerita in the Department of Anthropology, University of Nevada, Reno. Her research interests include ethnobiology, cultures and languages, and Great Basin indigenous peoples. Kay was elected to the American Academy of Arts and Sciences and the National Academy of Sciences in 2011 and named Distinguished Ethnobiologist for the Society of Ethnobiology in 2012. She is a past President of the Society of Ethnobiology.

Wendy C. Hodgson is Herbarium Curator and Research Botanist at the Desert Botanical Garden, Phoenix, Arizona, where she has worked for nearly 40 years. Her interests are the flora of the Southwest, all plants spiny and succulent, the role of plants in past cultures, and sharing with others the world of plants.

Eugene S. Hunn is Professor Emeritus in the Department of Anthropology at the University of Washington. His ethnobiological researches span more than 40 years, primarily in southern Mexico and with Native American communities in the Pacific Northwest. He has authored and edited many publications, including the books Tzeltal Folk Zoology, Nch'i-Wana 'The Big River', and A Zapotec Natural History. He is a past president of the Society of Ethnobiology and is also an avid birder.

Dorothy House is an environmental consultant, working with SWCA Environmental Consultants in Flagstaff, Arizona. Prior to that she was a member of the professional staff at the Museum of Northern Arizona's Harold S. Colton Research Center in Flagstaff. She completed her undergraduate work at SUNY Binghamton and graduate work at Denver University. Her interests and areas of expertise are interdisciplinary, dealing with several aspects of the natural and cultural history of the American Southwest.

John R. Johnson, Ph.D., has served as Curator of Anthropology at the Santa Barbara Museum of Natural History since 1986. He holds a position as Adjunct Professor of Anthropology at the University of California, Santa Barbara where he has taught an annual course on California Indians since 2004. Johnson specializes in the archaeology and ethnohistory of Native Americans in central and southern California.

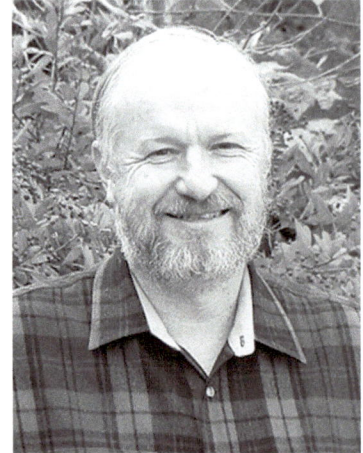

R. Roy Johnson has conducted scientific studies in the American Southwest for 60 years. Having advanced degrees in both ornithology and botany, he is the author of more than 200 scientific papers with his major research focused on riparian ecosystems in arid regions. Since retirement in 1992, he is living with his wife and co-researcher, Lois T. Haight, on a desert tract on the outskirts of Tucson, Arizona.

Kenneth J. Kingsley earned his B.A. at Prescott College in 1972, when he was one of the bird nerds that hung out with Amadeo Rea. He earned a M.S. at the University of Nevada, Las Vegas, and a Ph.D. at the University of Arizona. He worked his entire professional career as a consultant in ecological research and management, most of it as a senior scientist with SWCA Environmental Consultants. Now semi-retired, he volunteers at Zion, Great Basin, and Saguaro National Parks and the Tucson Botanical Gardens.

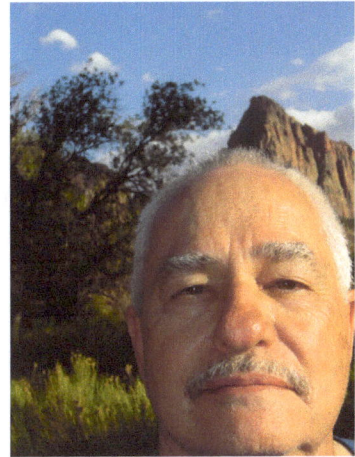

Dana Lepofsky is a Professor in the Department of Archaeology at Simon Fraser University. Her research focuses on the NE Pacific and the Society Islands, French Polynesia. She is interested in past human-landscape interactions and draws on archaeology, traditional knowledge, and paleoecology to understand these relationships and to apply this ancient knowledge to the management of resources today. She is a past President of the Society of Ethnobiology.

Eike Luedeling, Ph.D., works as a Climate Change Scientist at the World Agroforestry Centre (ICRAF) in Nairobi, Kenya. His primary research interests are the responses of natural and human systems to climate change and the development of robust climate change adaptation strategies.

Charmion McKusick came to the University of Arizona in 1949 intending to study physical anthropology, but changed to ethnozoology at Point of Pines Archaeological Field School in 1952. She has identified fauna from archaeological sites located throughout the southwestern US and Mexico. She focuses specifically on Indian domestic turkeys, Mexican macaws, birds of sacrifice, and the Salados of the Arizona Uplands.

Gary Paul Nabhan is the Endowed Chair in Sustainable Food Systems at the University of Arizona, and frequently writes the Ethnobiology for a Diverse World column for Journal of Ethnobiology. A former student and co-author of Amadeo Rea, he credits his fondness for eating road-kills to decades of field work with his mentor, the Turkey Vulture.

Marsha Bogar Quinlan is an Assistant Professor in the Department of Anthropology at Washington State University. Her research examines usage, taxonomy and local ecological knowledge of plants and animals, with particular attention to health, ethnomedicine, and medical ethnobotany. Her fieldwork has been in North America, the Northeast Amazon, and the Caribbean.

Amadeo M. Rea, ornithologist, went to Arizona in 1963 to do field work among the Pima and has been recording their ethnobiology ever since. He did his master's degree at Arizona State University and his doctoral work at the University of Arizona. He has published four books on Pimans. When not writing, he is designing and building straw bale houses. He is a past President of the Society of Ethnobiology.

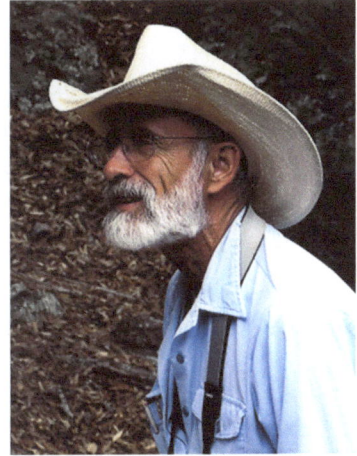

Jan Timbrook, Ph.D., is Curator of Ethnography at the Santa Barbara Museum of Natural History, where she has worked since 1974. Her research on the Chumash and other native Californian peoples focuses on ethnobotany, ethnozoology, material culture, and environmental management. She is a past President of the Society of Ethnobiology.

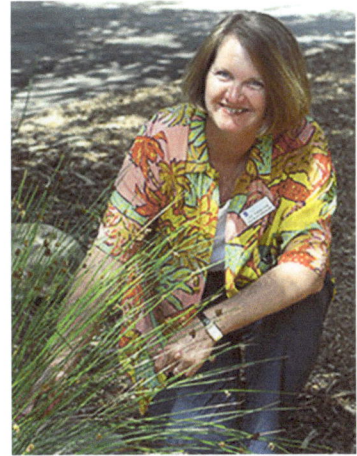

Nancy Turner is an ethnobotanist who has been working with and learning from First Nations elders in British Columbia for over forty years. She has authored and coauthored many books and papers on ethnobotany and ethnoecology of northwestern North America. She is a past President of the Society of Ethnobiology.

Søren Wichmann is a linguist who has held positions at University of Copenhagen, Universidad de Hermosillo, Leiden University, and, since 2003, at Max Planck Institute for Evolutionary Anthropology. Originally specializing in Mesoamerican languages and writing systems he has published widely on these topics, but in recent years his interests have widened to language and prehistory on a world-wide scale.

www.ingramcontent.com/pod-product-compliance
Lightning Source LLC
Chambersburg PA
CBHW061134030426
42334CB00003B/32